AF361383

AN INDWELLING VOICE

Sincerities and Authenticities in Russian Poetry

STUART H. GOLDBERG

An Indwelling Voice

Sincerities and Authenticities in Russian Poetry

UNIVERSITY OF TORONTO PRESS
Toronto Buffalo London

© University of Toronto Press 2023
Toronto Buffalo London
utorontopress.com

ISBN 978-1-4875-4455-3 (cloth)   ISBN 978-1-4875-4456-0 (EPUB)
                                  ISBN 978-1-4875-4457-7 (PDF)

Library and Archives Canada Cataloguing in Publication

Title: An indwelling voice : sincerities and authenticities in Russian
   poetry / Stuart H. Goldberg.
Names: Goldberg, Stuart, 1971– author.
Description: Includes bibliographical references and index.
Identifiers: Canadiana (print) 20230182488 | Canadiana (ebook) 20230182593 |
   ISBN 9781487544553 (cloth) | ISBN 9781487544577 (PDF) |
   ISBN 9781487544560 (EPUB)
Subjects: LCSH: Russian poetry – 19th century – History and criticism. |
   LCSH: Sincerity in literature. | LCSH: Authenticity (Philosophy) in
   literature. | LCSH: Romanticism – Russia.
Classification: LCC PG3051 .G65 2023 | DDC 891.71/309384–dc23

Cover design: Val Cooke
Cover image: Ansal Ünsal, "Whisper" (2020)

We wish to acknowledge the land on which the University of Toronto Press
operates. This land is the traditional territory of the Wendat, the Anishnaabeg,
the Haudenosaunee, the Métis, and the Mississaugas of the Credit First
Nation.

University of Toronto Press acknowledges the financial support of the
Government of Canada, the Canada Council for the Arts, and the Ontario Arts
Council, an agency of the Government of Ontario, for its publishing activities.

For my parents, Barton and Joan

Contents

Acknowledgments

From the first discussion of the potential of the project in a café near the Pushkin House in Saint Petersburg to his comments on individual parts of the manuscript and invaluable encouragement in difficult moments, David Bethea has always been there for me.

Luba Golburt, Alexander Zholkovsky, Lada Panova, and Martin Daughtry read long sections of the manuscript, and not only offered judicious advice but buoyed me with their friendship. Michael Wachtel, Irene Delic, Harsha Ram, Kirill Ospovat, Oleg Lekmanov, Joachim Klein, Alexander Levitsky, Sarah Pratt, Edward Waysband, Igor Pilshchikov, Joe Peschio, and Alyssa Gillespie gave helpful comments and suggestions on various parts of my argument at various stages. My thanks go out to all of them. I appreciate the thought-provoking questions posed at my lectures by the faculty at the Atlanta Slavic Studies Seminar, Princeton University, the University of California, Berkeley, and the University of North Carolina, Chapel Hill. I thank the readers at the University of Toronto Press for their extensive and valuable commentary. All shortcomings are of course my own.

Anna Stenport, then Chair of the Georgia Tech School of Modern Languages, gave excellent advice on my proposals. The staff of the Manuscripts Divisions of the Russian National Library and the Institute of Russian Literature (Pushkin House) graciously assisted me with my research. The staff of Emory University Library were highly accommodating, particularly during a year of research leave which I spent in the Woodruff Library. I thank them, and I thank Juliette Stapanian, the Chair of Emory Russian and East Asian Languages and Cultures, who invited me as a visiting scholar and arranged for my library access.

This project could not have been completed in its current scope without the generous support of an American Council of Learned Societies fellowship. I am grateful and honoured that *An Indwelling Voice* was chosen.

I thank Stephen Shapiro of the University of Toronto Press, who quickly believed in this book and has been wise and efficacious in shepherding it to completion.

Several portions of the book have appeared previously in other form. Chapter 1 is revised from "The Poetic Device and the Problem of Sincerity in Gavrila Derzhavin's Verse," *Slavonic and East European Review* 95, no. 2 (2017); and the first half of chapter 2 is an extension of "Creating the Sincere Voice: One Poetic Device in Pushkin's Lyrics of the 1830s" in *A/Z: Essays in Honor of Alexander Zholkovsky*, edited by Dennis Ioffe, Marcus Levitt, Joe Peschio, and Igor Pilshchikov (Academic Studies Press, 2017). Chapter 4 grew out of a kernel of several pages that appeared in the conclusion to my first book, *Mandelstam, Blok and the Boundaries of Mythopoetic Symbolism* (Ohio State University Press, 2011) and upon which I first attempted to expand in "Sootnoshenie podlinnosti-iskrennosti v poetike Mandel'shtama i Bloka" in *Miry Osipa Mandel'shtama. IV Mandel'shtamovskie chteniia* (Izd. PGPU, 2009). An early version of parts of chapter 6 appeared as "Original Sincerity: Some Thoughts on the Poetry of Boris Ryžij," *Russian Literature* 67, no. 1 (February 2010). My thanks goes out to the editors of these publications. I thank the Manuscripts Division of the Russian National Library for sharing the image of the autograph of Dmitry Venevitinov's "<On the New Year (1827)>," which appears as an illustration to chapter 2.

I would also like to thank here two teachers at Williams College without whose influence I would not have set out down the path that led me to this book. I fell hard for the Russian language under the spell of Donald Singleton, who remains for me an unparalleled model as a language teacher. And Darra Goldstein gave me my first schooling in how it is possible to read poetry.

Finally, I thank my wife, Dina, my partner and sounding board, whose encouragement and love have sustained me.

Abbreviations

IRLI   Institutut russkoi literatury (Pushkinskii Dom), Saint Petersburg
L.   Leningrad
M.   Moscow
OED   *Oxford English Dictionary*
PSS   *Polnoe sobranie sochinenii* (except in relation to Lermontov and Mandelstam, in which case – *Polnoe sobranie stikhotvorenii*)
PSSP   *Polnoe sobranie sochinenii i pisem*
RNB   Rossiiskaia Natsional'naia Biblioteka, Saint Petersburg
SPb.   Saint Petersburg
SS   *Sobranie sochinenii*
SS8   *Sobranie sochinenii* in eight volumes, etc.

A Note on Transliteration

In citations, I have used the modified Library of Congress transliteration without diacritics. In most cases, in the text and discursive portion of footnotes, I have used forms easing recognition and pronunciation for English speakers (e.g., Lydia Ginzburg, rather than Lidiia; Mayakovsky, rather than Maiakovskii; Grigoryev, rather than Grigor'ev; Solovyov, and not Solov'ev). Some names have been left in the Library of Congress style, though this may be at odds with pronunciation, when these are the more prevalent forms in English (e.g., Potemkin, Ogarev).

AN INDWELLING VOICE

Introduction: The Sincere Voice, or How Sincerity Is Written and Read in Russian, and Not Only Russian, Poetry

With no lyric "I," there is no voice.

– Boris Eikhenbaum

… the most precious question of the current moment, the question about the *truth* which we demand from art.

– Apollon Grigoryev

In order to reach the goal, one has to accept and account for the wind blowing in a somewhat different direction.

– Osip Mandelstam

What if many disagreements of literary taste are actually, in no small part, disagreements about sincerity – about what constitutes sincerity, how sincerity sounds, and how demonstrably one ought to evoke it? How would this change our approach to the study of sincerity, or poetry? What might we gain through the attempt to differentiate these contrasting and overlapping sincerities, to explore their cultural constructedness and analyse their modes of implementation?

This study is founded on the conviction that we can, in fact, gain a great deal, including insights into literary history, poetics, and the semiotics of production and reception of the *sincere voice* (or sincere voices). In the pages that follow, I attempt to trace how, over the course of more than two centuries, conceptualizations of sincerity and the ways in which poets have inscribed sincerity in their poetry have changed. This exploration is organized as a series of case studies, historically contextualized close readings teasing out the pragmatic framings and poetic devices that have supported diverse embodiments of the sincere voice. I focus here on the Russian context, but the trends examined also resonate with the development of Western literature, a trajectory which Russian literature since the mid-eighteenth century has roughly, though not precisely, paralleled.

The diachronic approach I take is dictated by the unstable nature of sincere expression. Ernst van Alphen and Mieke Bal begin their introduction to an influential compilation of articles on the rhetoric of sincerity from an acknowledgment of sincerity's "bodily, linguistic and social performances." Sincerity, they argue, is "culturally specific" and dependent not only on words, but on gesture, tone, mimicry, and other often subtle cues.[1] What these conceptions foreground is the fact that sincerity, in semiotic terms, implies not only a speaking subject, but also an anticipated listener and the necessity of adequate communicative strategies and overlapping cultural codes in order for the message – in this case, the truthfulness, or authenticity, of the utterance – to be heard.[2] Sincerity is thus, in its performative embodiments, not immutable, but culturally embedded and ever-evolving.

In poetry, a sense of the work's sincerity is inevitably dependent on the cumulative reading experience and expectations of the audience, and this goes also for the primary reader, the poet.[3] At the same time, words, particularly poetic words, carry the memory of past poets' usages and past poets' emotions, and words and stylistic modes can become eviscerated with use.[4] How does one, after this, endeavour to write in a sincere voice, meaning not a voice that expresses one's "true" emotions in an unadulterated and unmediated fashion (if such a thing were indeed possible), but a voice that others *and oneself* will perceive as resonantly sincere?

I posit that there is a link between the necessity to continually reinvent sincerity (or at least its formal embodiments) and the evolution of poetry (in the broadest sense). A comment by contemporary Russian poet Olga Sedakova testifies to this ongoing need to renew sincerity. Asked at a lecture how her "religious" poetry differs from "devotional" poetry, Sedakova spoke of the former maintaining a consciousness of "how this would look alive and unfeigned *after everything that we know*."[5] In other words, tangible sincerity in poetry depends on a consciousness of tradition (intellectual, poetic, religious) in historical development. As a result, it is constantly necessary to reinvent sincerity as poetic "device" – something of a paradox: immediacy must be actively achieved, with the effect not of undermining, but of elevating that rare, tangible sense of immediacy.[6]

This resourcefulness and malleability of the sincere voice complicates any definition we might bestow upon it. Nonetheless, there are some persistent qualities to be observed. The sincere voice in poetry is firstly a *human* voice, a voice which somehow manages by its inflections to imply a thinking and speaking subject constituted outside the frame of literature. A sincere voice is also a voice that has the qualities necessary to convince its interlocutor that it speaks in good faith, conveying – though not necessarily directly – that which it believes to be a truth, or truths, about self or world. Moreover, it expresses these truths not as a function of their being universally accessible or accepted, but in a manner that demonstrates their being personally experienced, interrogated, lived.[7]

Preliminaries

This working definition is intentionally cast broadly enough to encompass a range of "sincere" voices. These include voices insinuating not so much a "congruence of avowal and [...] feeling" (Trilling's much-quoted definition of sincerity) as truth to a self that is not, or at least not overly or overtly, conventional (which is to say, those intimating authenticity). Nor does the above definition exclude voices availing themselves of indirect modes of expression, including irony.[8] Below, I employ the terms "sincerity" and "sincere voice" in contexts where there is no explicit need to differentiate between sincerity and authenticity. I do this for a couple of reasons. First, while there are periods and phenomena for which one term or the other seems intuitively a better fit, the concepts in truth overlap.[9] That segment of the "Venn diagram" which encompasses the sincere but not authentic – the earnest but shallow and commonplace – is not engaged here and stands outside the limits of what this researcher would call "poetic" sincerity. By the same token, it is difficult to imagine an "authentic" (i.e., true to self) voice that is not *at some level* "sincere," if only in the principled rejection – however expressed – of others' inadequate values systems. Second, a broadening of the term "sincerity" is supported by Russian historical usage. The authors of two of the most ambitious statements on sincerity in Russian literature, Apollon Grigoryev (nineteenth century) and Vladimir Pomerantsev (twentieth century) both use "sincerity" (iskrennost') in an expansive sense.[10] In part, this usage is linked to linguistic realities, since *podlinnost'* (the native Russian term for authenticity) does not traditionally carry the same connotations of truth "to one's own personality, spirit, or character" that its equivalent has come to in twentieth- and twenty-first-century English.[11]

Clearly not every form of ironic expression has equal potential to simultaneously resonate as sincere. Irony that does, however, is not uniquely characteristic of our recent post-postmodern culture.[12] Rather, it is the character of the irony deployed that regulates its *availability* to the sincere voice. Unconducive are forms of irony directed at a perpetual, radical destabilization of meaning[13] and forms that actively seek to divide their audience, to establish a community of insiders and a community of "dupes," who are intended to perceive themselves as the irony's target.[14] Particularly conducive to amalgams with sincerity are those species of irony that leave in their wake not negation, but the renewed *possibility* of affirmation. This is an irony that creates space, in the face of doubt, for *belief* built upon a recognition of human limitations (epistemological and otherwise) and an implicit acknowledgment of "what we know now."[15] (And we have all been living in an age of doubt and critical scepticism about the world and its ordering at least since the eighteenth century.) As we will see, in the early twentieth century, poet Nikolai Gumilev dubbed one such phenomenon "luminous irony, not undercutting the roots of our faith" (svetlaia ironiia, ne podryvaiushchaia kornei nashei very). We can observe a playful ironic voice that renews the possibility of seriously taken odic praise in Gavrila Derzhavin's poetry as early as the 1780s.[16] Of course, sincerity constructed on a substrate of irony has become widespread and widely recognized in our own times.

The "discursive communities" that enable irony (Linda Hutcheon) have an important role to play likewise in the reception of sincerity.[17] These communities coalesce around common or overlapping cultural codes and reader experience. For no two readers does this cultural and experiential framework precisely coincide. However, areas of commonality are great enough to allow for mutual agreement as much as contention.[18] Crucially, when we encounter conflicting reader impressions concerning the sincerity or sincere sound of a text, this should not be seen as a hindrance to the study of resonant sincerity or a repudiation of the possibility of sincerity's meaningful inscription. Considered differences of taste and opinion regarding sincerity, far from being a liability, provide insight into the diverging conceptualizations of sincerity they represent.[19] Indeed, it was a perception of the potent impact of such differences on literary production, reception, and evolution that set me working on sincerity as a problem and larger project.

Two Poles in the Conceptualization of Sincerity

In the body of this study, I hope to show that these "tastes" in sincerity are not chaotic, but rather gravitate to one of two idealized poles in sincerity's conceptualization. One of these poles is much more familiar to most readers, so much so, in fact, that one or another of its components is often presumed an invariable component on the basis of which sincerity's presence or absence can be tested. This is that understanding of poetic sincerity which emerged most fully and prominently in the Romantic period. To generalize greatly, glossing over for now the variability and divergent emphases that mark individual conceptualizations, sincerity thus understood is typically linked to seriousness, intensity of feeling, immediacy of expression, openness, and confessionality.[20] This type of sincerity tends to be antagonistic to (or at least suspicious of) irony and jest, seeing the ironic as destructive of the seriousness and earnestness demanded by sincerity. It often finds a correlate of strong feeling in fervent expression and can be suspicious of form, ornament, and polish (i.e., art), in that these can throw immediacy of expression into suspicion. It tends to reward, or even demand, personal confession. When it engages political and social contexts and can be seen as an example of Foucault's "fearless speech," it tends to be forthright, unambiguous, direct.

There is, however, another radically different pole of poetic – and perhaps also interpersonal – sincerity. It tends to name itself less often, likely because the banner of "sincerity" has been grasped so firmly by the other side, and certainly also because its adepts, while no less concerned with truth and no less serious about the import of their words, tend not to elevate sincerity as a central *value* of literature or to demand it from others.[21]

This sincerity is the unacknowledged forefather of the ironic modalities of earnestness practised by our contemporaries. Its practitioners tend to see evidence of sincerity (which tends towards "humanity" rather than "seriousness") in modulation of voice and diversity of experience and mood, including humour. They tend to eschew direct confession and treat the personal with caution. And they often use irony – especially self-deprecating irony – as a building block of the sincere, ensconcing and transcending in this way some degree of scepticism in relation to world and self, but, at the same time, not parting with a fundamental belief in the potential of language – and especially poetic language – to express personal and transpersonal truths. They tend to be suspicious of *perpetual* intensity of speech and feeling, unbroken seriousness, and others' excessive focus on the self. And they tend to recognize, and be unfazed by, the fact that poetic expression is not factually immediate, that a *medium* intercedes between self and page.[22]

Examples of this type of sincerity can be observed over the entire chronological sweep of this book and seem to come to the fore in loose alternation with the competing outlook. In the eighteenth century, Derzhavin supplants, at least at the outset of his career, the high-pitched

Lomonosovan ode, Alexander Pushkin swallows up Sentimentalism, Mandelstam upends, in this sense, the mythopoetic Symbolists (in important ways, late Romantics), and the ambivalently ironic "new sentimentality" of Timur Kibirov revises not only the more radical post-modern irony of early Conceptualism, but also the self-seriousness of Soviet mid-century poetry.

A particularly potent and explicit statement of this approach to sincerity is given by Pushkin:

> For those who love Catullus, Gresset and Voltaire, for those who love poetry not only in its lyric transports and in the doleful inspiration of the elegy, not only in the expansive creations of drama and epic, but also in the playfulness of jest [shutka] and in cerebral amusements inspired by lucid gaiety – sincerity is precious in the poet. It is pleasant for us to see the poet in all states, [all] transformations of his mercurial and creative soul: in sorrow and in joy, in the soaring of ecstasy and in the respite of feelings – in Juvenalian outrage and in petty annoyance at a tiresome neighbour … I am awed by the creation of *Faust*, but I love epigrams etc. ("V[asily] L[vovich] P[ushkin]'s Trip" ["Puteshestvie V.L.P." 1836])[23]

We will examine this passage in more detail in chapter 2. For now, suffice it to say that there are good reasons we should take Pushkin at his word here in this roundabout and seemingly idiosyncratic definition of sincerity. First, the embedding of this commentary within a "review" of Ivan Dmitriev's light-hearted poetic joke at the expense of Pushkin's poet-uncle – fewer than one hundred lines "published" in fifty copies handed out to friends twenty-eight years earlier – in fact, makes the statement more consistent. Pushkin is true to the ethos he describes, linking, rather than distinguishing, jest and seriousness. Second, we may surmise that Pushkin decided to write his "review" *because* it offered an opportunity to express his thoughts on sincerity, and on its abuses in his contemporaries' "lyric transports" and the "doleful inspiration of the elegy." After all, there was no pressing need to review the mostly forgotten Dmitriev's unavailable "book."

When writers, and readers, encounter the works of those drawn to the opposite pole, "misunderstandings" arise regarding sincerity. For the latter group, the emotional excesses and, often, the unbending seriousness of the former can sound histrionic or staged. To the former, the relative artistic distance practised by the latter can sound aristocratic or aloof, mocking or, alternatively, "small." As a shorthand, I will sometimes call these two conceptual nexuses "expressive" (first-pole) and "modulated" (second-pole) sincerity.

It is not hard to see that the second mode, which is usually less "doctrinaire" regarding the quality of sincerity and incorporates some of the same forms of scepticism that have driven sincerity's critics and self-critics, is less vulnerable to some of the traditional critiques and more able to reconcile within itself seeming contradictions without breaking down. The idealistic, and often maximalizing, *demands* placed on the poet by the first pole can make it particularly problematic, and the tendency of these problems to draw the active attention of sincerity's own most zealous practitioners paradoxically makes the more direct mode of sincerity the more engaged with the sort of analytical self-reflection (which is to say, divided consciousness) that persistently challenges sincerity claims.[24] Still, within the confines of one version as much as the other, the successful inscription of *resonant* sincerity in poetry, the projection of a palpably sincere voice, requires a certain excess, an "above-and-beyond" in relation to collective and individual poetic norms as well as conventionalized, culturally coded verbal "gesture." A "resonantly" sincere voice in my parlance is one that goes beyond a lack of evidence to the contrary or simple historical, situational, or genre-based assumptions to impress upon the reader, not through avowals, but through its framings and devices, its sincerity.

Take the refrain "Rage, rage, until the dying of the light!" from Dylan Thomas's villanelle, "Do Not Go Gentle into That Good Night" (1951).[25] Despite the elder Thomas's illness, biography thwarts attempts to read the *projected* situation of the poem – bedside with a fading father – literally.[26] There are no outright avowals of sincerity, and the intricately wrought and demanding villanelle form would seem inherently unconducive to attempts, particularly in the mid-twentieth century, to express oneself with a palpable immediacy. And yet, the poem challenges any impulse to deny the speaker the full force of the feeling expressed. Seamus Heaney, having commented on his disappointment in rereading many of Thomas's poems years after first acquaintance in youth, writes that *this* poem "fulfills its promise precisely because its craft has not lost touch with the suffered world," making its "verbal elaborateness" "neither otiose nor merely ornamental."[27] How this happens at the juncture of semantics, pragmatic framing, and poetic device is visible, for instance, in that second refrain. Within the highly charged pragmatic situation *projected* – in a productively deceptive way[28] – the potentially cloying alternating refrains of the villanelle come to function as incantatory remonstrations, and, in this function, their outwardly irregular, but, in truth, entirely formalized, return feels, each time, on cue. There is no pretence to the use of everyday, idiomatic English – even "until the dying of the light" is surely a "poetic" phrase (if also biographically underwritten, given the elder Thomas's profound vision loss). However, the long syllables of this line's opening spondee ("Rage, rage …") allow these initial words to gather a passionate intensity.[29] Their phonetic stretching (liquid followed by long vowel and affricate), levelled stress, and syntactically and prosodically mandated intonational pause impede the progress of the poem's highly traditional iambic pentameter, creating a sonic conduit for the emotion-laden command to "rage."[30] These factors add up to a subtle excess to pure semantics and to the demands of poetic tradition.[31]

To understand why this excess to semantics is so important to resonant sincerity, it will be helpful to take a look at what it means to project a voice and how sincerity appears to be decoded by readers. First, however, since sincerity's notorious inadequacies have begun to swing into view, it is worth reviewing some of the issues that underlie its chequered history in discussions of lyric poetry. Critics have suggested sincerity's faultiness and one-sidedness as a world view; its tendency towards manneredness and hypocrisy; its susceptibility to commerce and commodification; its purportedly inevitable "failure" as literary method due to conflicting demands of spontaneity and literary impact, performativity and disavowal of performance, as well as sincerity's circular logic – the fact that sincerity depends on language or other external signs to express inner feeling, while "the only evidence for the writer's feeling is the external signs or words." New Criticism and structuralism challenged sincerity through – correctly – rejecting the idea of an unconstructed lyric persona, while deconstructionism and postmodernism denied outright the possibility of a stable self that does not dissolve in language. Rehabilitation of sincerity as a critical concept has occurred primarily as a corrective to the impersonalizing of the poem in New Criticism and post-structuralism and to postmodernism's pervasive, decentring irony.[32] I strive to circumvent these debates, as should be clear from the above, by focusing attention not on sincerity per se but on the sincere voice and the poetic ecosystems and devices developed to support it.[33]

In spite of these "flaws," the sincere voice – perhaps a plural would be better given its diversity – has remained an elusive but valued quality through many different periods, and the issue of how it emerged in Russian poetry and how it is produced and renewed is a vital one for poetics. This book will attempt to demonstrate that, despite the philosophical and linguistic barriers, poets have achieved meaningful successes in the embodying of sincerity and that it is possible to analyse and tentatively reconstruct the factors underlying this achievement.

Voice

So, what is a voice? From the growing interdisciplinary literature on the subject, we can draw two key conclusions relevant to the present study. First, while a voice does not have to be original, or reflexive, it is by nature individual, and – taken in a non-metaphorical sense – is grounded in the physical.[34] In the compelling words of Italo Calvino:

> A voice means this: there is a living person, throat, chest, feelings, who sends into the air this voice, different from all other voices. A voice involves the throat, saliva, infancy, the patina of experienced life, the mind's intentions, the pleasure of giving a personal form to sound waves. ("A King Listens")[35]

Particularly interesting here is the connection between the physical preconditions of voice and the "patina of experienced life." It is the physicality and materiality of voice which suggest to the listener the presence of an individual, with all the experiential and emotional baggage this implies. And it can be the emotional and physical "fallout" of a lived existence which lends the individual voice its characteristic sound.

Second, the individual voice, as we perceive it, is precisely an excess to the linguistic code. What we hear as individual is the audible surplus beyond those characteristics of the utterance that have parsable meaning. According to Mladen Dolar, a voice is "the material element recalcitrant to meaning."[36] It is doubtful whether this excess to the Saussurean "alterity" of phonetics can be seen as a countervailing pure presence.[37] We apply mental categories to voices – squeaky, gruff, booming, breathy, low, high – and these qualities can have their own culturally defined auras and can participate in higher-level semiotic codes.[38] However, individual voices' materiality and resistance to analytical probing lend them an aspect of presence in a way that differs from the auditory signals usually processed by the competent listener *automatically* as phonemes, or such higher-level signifiers as intonation.

How then can we apply the concept of voice to poetry – metaphorically, as it must be with regard to written language, but more rigorously than in the typical primarily narratological or descriptive senses?

> *A sincere voice in poetry, in order to be a voice, has to be an individuality growing out of an excess beyond semantics.*

This postulate helps explain the enduring connection between the sincere voice and the lyric, which, when successful, always implies an excess irreducible to parsable semantics: "where a commensurability [...] with paraphrase is discovered, the sheets are not rumpled, there poetry, so to speak, has not lain."[39] It also explains a potential vulnerability of maximally prosaic embodiments of the "New Sincerity" in contemporary poetry. By stripping poetry to bare semantics, one can remove the obstacles erected by artifice but simultaneously undermine the presence of voice.[40]

A sounding voice is, moreover, experienced as interior, and simultaneously exterior, to the speaker and physically penetrates the hearer's body. When an individual voice is powerfully inscribed in a written text, when the illusion of preservation of the author's individuality and interiority is so strong that it is experienced as metaphorically penetrating by the reader, it can seem that the voice has attained an ongoing, living presence within the written record.[41] This voice becomes "an indwelling voice."

A Partial Paradigm for the Semiotics of Decoding Sincerity

In this book, I have adopted throughout an "agnostic" attitude towards sincerity per se, which is not necessarily fictive, but is firmly inaccessible. In literature, outside of ungrounded assumptions, sincerity gains a relatively stable phenomenological reality as a sincere voice. As such it must be performed, whatever the level, or lack, of consciousness or intentionality attached to that performance.[42] Sincere voices in poetry are, however, culturally specific and demand renewal, so their concrete embodiments are ever-changing. How then can sincerity be *read*?

The broad definition of the sincere voice in poetry above noted that such a voice "somehow manages *by its inflections* to imply a thinking and speaking subject" and "has *the qualities necessary* to convince its interlocutor that it speaks in good faith." The vagueness of these categories was intentional. As we have seen, sincerity can mean radically different things in different contexts. Moreover, because of the wearing of poetic language, the continuing viability of the sincere voice in poetry is linked to its ability to discover new inflections, new pathways to insinuate good faith. However, we can also conclude that the landscape cannot be entirely chaotic if readers are to recognize the sincere voice in fresh guises.

Likely, in decoding sincerity, there is some reader check as to what is believable as a potential world view to which the poet might honestly subscribe, given the reader's knowledge of and presumptions about the poet and the world.[43] Suppose I say I would love to live in a house in which all of the walls, furniture, and fixtures are fuchsia. Likely, I will not be believed. If I say this in such a way that no stray gesture or inflection betrays a disconnect between "avowal" and "feeling," we call this deadpan, and those who do believe me will be regarded as gullible. But passing such a believability test is a low bar for resonant, poetic sincerity and tells us, therefore, little about the poetry or its reception. A variation of this same test might consider psychological verisimilitude. How believable is it that such a speaker would exhibit a given psychology? However, psychological verisimilitude is both highly subjective and, also, ambiguous in its implications. After all, psychologically believable portraits often form the basis of fictions. To the extent that such a factor might be operative within the poems, it will be considered below primarily through the category of demonstrably "earned" truth. Reliability of the "speaker," which is to say the broader context of the reader's previous judgments regarding this particular speaker's (or author's) sincerity, may also play a role, and a particularly strong one for certain readers. As a corollary, the overarching cohesiveness of a given poet's oeuvre, as presented to readers, can contribute to a sense of the sincerity of individual works. However, in this study, we will focus primarily on the functioning of the sincere voice within smaller contexts and without the crutch of a pre-existing trust or suspicion.

On what other planes, then, can a poet's "sincerity" potentially be evaluated by the reader, and how? One may have noted that, in the description of two idealized poles in the conceptualization of sincerity above, *none* of the traits described can actually serve as a guarantor of sincerity. They are all secondary, associated characteristics.[44] However, the fastness with which these notions, especially the confessional traits, attach themselves to sincerity in individual world views indicates that they serve as a basis for evaluating the "circumstantial evidence" through which we inevitably, and usually less than consciously, judge sincerity's presence – or in literature, the presence of a "sincere voice."[45]

In this light, we can hypothesize that the decoding of the sincerity of individual utterances by *potentially sympathetic, but also critical* readers or interlocutors often proceeds in something like the following (generalized, abstracted, and artificially sequential) manner.[46] The primary characteristic of sincerity – *truth value of the expressed in relation to an inner world* – is not verifiable, which is also to say, not readable.[47] Rather, the reader or interlocutor has a certain, likely unformulated, and to an extent fluid, conception of sincerity, which invokes a constellation of *secondary* traits, some of which are attributive and some discrediting. (Again, in the most familiar, loosely "Romantic," expressive species of poetic sincerity, the attributive traits can include seriousness, immediacy, intensity of feeling, openness, and confessionality.) These traits (or their absence) can be inferred by the reader in a given context in part through potential markers, some fairly stable, some ad hoc (i.e., functional specifically in a given context) or iconic, some indicated by presence, some by absence.

One can also *testify* to the presence of such traits, or sincerity itself, but indirect indications, because of their more "subliminal" quality, are more convincing than outright avowals, which inevitably suggest to the reader the possibility of disingenuousness or self-deception. Sincerity, writes Jane Taylor only a shade too categorically, "is something of an intangible precisely in that its affects and its effects must remain beyond calculation, must exceed rational description and instrumental reason. [...] Whenever 'sincerity' names itself, it ceases to exist."[48]

At the same time, markers must be activated and supported by pragmatic framings,[49] which project discursive and ontological situations, the text's relationship to and function in regard to speaker, audience, and world. Such framings can be generated through text-immanent elements or extratextual literary "facts," particularly when the latter are engaged by the text or actively shaped by the author.[50] In addition to pragmatic framings, *compositional* framing often plays a role in supporting the sincere voice by creating a backdrop in relation to which relevant elements gain salience.

Pragmatic framings are ineffectual without felicitous devices or markers supporting the sincere voice. Devices are, in turn, mute as regards sincerity in the absence of pragmatic framings, though some devices may themselves imply a tentative pragmatic framing for the text. In general, the degree of salience of any given feature (marker or framing) of a text in regard to its sincere, neutral, or insincere resonance will be dependent on the individual reader code (i.e., conception of sincerity). What is more, convincing pragmatic contextualizations can, given a receptive reader code, frame the poem-speech act as a "deed." The latter effect is exacerbated when a political or social stance is implied, as in Lermontov's "Farewell, unwashed Russia" ("Proshchai, nemytaia Rossiia," 1841) or Allen Ginsberg's "Howl" (1956).[51] In the Soviet period, given that the entire work of a poet could be illicit (as with Mandelstam, for instance, in the 1930s), even the slightest or most abstract of poems can serve as "stolen air" (vorovannyi vozdukh), which is also to say, a verbal "deed."

Let us take, as a brief example of the hypothetical functioning of this paradigm, the opening two lines of one of Romantic poet Fedor Tiutchev's poems following the death of his long-time lover and muse Elena Denisyeva. The symbolist author Dmitry Merezhkovsky said of Tiutchev, partially in respect of these poems, that "No one has ever expressed the most terrifying and pathetic truth about himself more mercilessly, more fearlessly than Tiutchev."[52] The poem begins:

Есть и в моем страдальческом застое
Часы и дни ужаснее других ...[53]

(There are, even in my anguished stagnation,
Hours and days more awful than the rest ...)

Tiutchev's (and his reader Merezhkovsky's) implicit conception of sincerity hews to our first pole – "expressive" sincerity. In these lines, *intensity* of feeling is registered through a two-leveled comparison ("i v moem" [*even in my* (as compared to others', your experience)], and "uzhasnee drugikh" [(hours and days) *more awful* than the rest]). This double comparison establishes a grand scale for the speaker's feelings, while simultaneously generating a common frame of reference with the reader. Intensity is also conveyed in the phonetically "heavy" and semantically weighted word "stradal'cheskom" (anguished, from *stradalets*, one who suffers much, especially as a martyr). This word, with its 13 phonemes, slows the reader, iconically embodying "anguished stagnation."[54] Finally, the ellipsis implies a realm of experience surpassing description. (Simultaneously, the eliding of an attempt at such "impossible" description implies a productive reticence, a desire not to falsify in the midst of confession.) *Immediacy* is conveyed in the neutral word order, with only "Est'" (There are) shifted quite naturally for emphasis, as well as in the simplicity of the prevailing colloquial diction, which complements and sets off the singular phrase "stradal'cheskii zastoi" (anguished stagnation). *Openness* is underscored semantically (but also in a way that engages pragmatics) in the baring of a private sphere of the speaker's emotional life, his admission of his "anguished stagnation" of feeling. The intense suffering of the speaker is the result of what seems to him objectionably *inadequate* emotion, as will become even clearer later in the poem.

The function of these many-levelled markers is reinforced and foregrounded through pragmatic and biographical framings. These include higher-order qualities like Tiutchev's well-known and mostly consistent stance of the poet-dilettante, little concerned with the fate of his creations,[55] which, together with his apparent failure to circulate this poem, reinforces the sense that it answers an inner impulse; the fraught context of the memorial poem, which raises the stakes – and potential resonance – of adequate commemoration;[56] the biographical context, known to Russian high society from the time of the poem's composition and to readers from its first full publication in 1903,[57] and which strongly reinforces the identity of despairing speaker and poet; as well as the implicit gesture at a reader by way of the comparison "i v moem" (lit., in my too), collapsing the social distance between poet and audience and generating a subtle intimacy.

These features – pragmatic and textual – conspire to establish a nexus within which the poet's "sincerity," as a quality attaching to his utterance, is articulated for the culturally proximate reader. What is more, we might surmise that a certain "redundancy," a mutual rein-forcement of "similarly directed" features in this passage, helps more potently inscribe this quality. If one had to try to pinpoint the "above-and-beyond," that singular, though simple, "discovery" that trans-forms these lines' potential sincerity into a resonant sincerity in the original Russian, I think it would be the subtle "i" (too/even), which simultaneously generates scale and reaches out to the reader's realm of experience.

The following two lines of the poem are, however, far more bound up in cultural paradigms and poetic diction:

Их тяжкий гнет, их бремя роковое,
Не выскажет, не выдержит мой стих.

(Their weighty oppressiveness, their fateful burden
My line cannot express, cannot withstand.)

The two parallel formulas – "tiazhkii gnet" (weighty oppressiveness) and "bremia rokovoe" (fateful burden) – are not yet quite clichés in Tiutchev's time, though particularly the first was already well on its way to becoming one. The speaker immediately recognizes these for-mulas as linguistically inadequate to his experience – otherwise, they would have precluded the following "cannot express." If the first half of line 4 strongly evokes the postulates of the poet's earlier, philosoph-ically inclined "Silentium!" (1830), his aphoristic call for and resonant betrayal of silence, in "ne vyderzhit" (cannot withstand), he adds a new note. The power and burden of his suffering is so great it threatens not simply a failure of words, but the smashing of its poetic vessel. This shipwreck will emerge more evocatively further on in the poem, but here, not ineffable suffering seems to win out, but structure – with these lines' double rhetorical doubling and even the classical caesura after the second foot of Tiutchev's iambic pentameter holding steady. Impossi-bility of expression here becomes a trope underscoring the ineffability of the poet's suffering.[58] Still, in these first four lines, we see a stark illustration of *the distinction between writing in a sincere voice and writing about sincerity.*

To the disappointment of some and the relief, surely, of others, the readings in this book, while based upon an awareness of the above theoretical model, will not insist upon explicitly defining the phenomena examined in the poems as pragmatic framings or structural or semantic markers of the secondary traits of sincerity. Nor will this book be an attempt to produce even to the extent it is possible a catalogue of such features. Rather, it will be dedicated to the maximally flexible examination of the functioning of the sincere voice in individual contexts.

Because of sincerity's shifting and almost antithetical conceptualizations and culture-specific development, there can be no universal, rhetorical classification of markers of sincerity. Let us consider, for a moment, the quality of intensity of voice, which can be seen as a potential verbal indicator of "the spontaneous overflow of powerful feelings."[59] Tentative markers for this trait might include everything from an exclamation point and the intonation it conveys, or Marina Tsvetaeva's ubiquitous dashes and the energetically elliptical syntax they facilitate, to lexicon and idiom laced with extreme semantics, morphological features (in Russian, superlatives and augmentatives; prefixes of excess and transcendence like v[o]z-, iz-, za-, pre-; forms of *perfectiva tantum* conveying forceful actions – *khlynut'*, *rinut'sia*, *rezanut'*; etc.), anaphora and other forms of repetition, stylistic markers (different, of course, in differing cultural contexts).[60] We can find clusters of the above features, for instance, in the final two stanzas of Andrey Bely's full-throated "Russia" ("Rossiia," 1908) or lines 8–14 of Mikhail Lomonosov's "Ode on the Day of Ascension to the Throne … 1746," which also foreground the resounding of the "gromk[ii] glas[]" (loud voice) of the hills and trees – to the very stars (a compound superlative). Or consider Marina Tsvetaeva's "Poem of the Mountain" ("Poema gory"), a long poem about the end of a passionate adulterous relationship written in 1926. Tsvetaeva was a modern master of the intense voice: "Chernoi, ni dnes', ni vpred' / Ne zatknu dyry" (lit., neither today, nor ever will I plug the black hole).[61] To fully appreciate these lines we need to experience the unique articulational energy bound up in *ch'órnai, ni dn'és', ni vpr'éd'* (note especially the dense, palatalized and progressively augmented consonant clusters of *dnes'* and *vpred'*) as well as the gaping quality of the double middle vowel *y* (ы), surrounding the liquid *r*, in the word "hole/pit" in the genitive case. (Mandelstam wrote of the nineteenth-century Italian singer Angiolina Bosio having her mouth torn apart "to the ears" by the "ungodly, impossible sound 'y'" [nebyvalyi, nevozmozhnyi zvuk 'y']).[62] The first stanza of the next part reads:

Та гора была, как грудь
Рекрута, снарядом сваленного.
Та гора хотела губ
Девственных, обряда свадебного[63]

(That ridge was like the chest
Of a recruit felled by a shell.
That ridge craved *virgin* lips,
[Demanded] a wedding rite)[64]

We can note the web of dense, inventive sound play, the extravagance and forcefulness (cemented through semantics) of the very deep hyperdactylic rhyme (snar'ádəm sválinnəvə – abr'ádə svádibnəvə [knocked on his back by a shell – a marriage rite]) in the equirhythmic second and fourth lines. In general, the rhythmic pattern establishes perfectly equirhythmic – but for one word break – odd lines and even lines while powerfully contrasting these to each other (quasi-anapaestic onset with masculine clausula [rising intonations] to hyperdactylic opening with hyperdactylic clausula [falling intonations]).[65] Together, this rhythm and rhyme as well as twinned enjambements and anaphora all contribute to a powerful intensification along the poem's "paradigmatic" (Lotman), vertical axis – which is to say, an accentuating of the juxtaposition between the vehicle of the simile in lines 1–2 and the hybrid metaphor/metonym of lines 3–4, which fill analogous spaces in the text.[66] And it is in these spaces that extreme language is concentrated. There is the violent simile, "kak grud' / Rekruta, snariadom svalennogo" (like the chest / Of a recruit felled by a shell), the illogical (in context) and graphically underscored "*virgin* lips," which forces us to seek deeper meanings (perhaps a sacrifice?), the "wedding rite," which underscores the grand solemnity, and possibly fatedness, of the anticipated coupling, but also, through a subtle irony, its physicality and its illicit quality. The pursuit just of the source of these lines' "intensity" thus leads us to a web of ad hoc devices, operating on various intertwined levels of the text, from phonetic and rhythmic to semantic and rhetorical (tropes).[67]

But this is just the beginning of our woes. Tsvetaeva also leaves us an epigraph, from Hölderlin: "[…] All parting lovers speak as if drunk and love affect [torzhestvennost'] …"[68] The question is thus begged by the poet herself: is Tsvetaeva's intense speech here bloated with affect, or is this the affectation that tries, but fails, to hide an abyss of real emotion?

Joseph Brodsky said about Tsvetaeva that she is

the most sincere Russian poet, but this sincerity, first and foremost, is the sincerity of sound – like when someone cries out from pain. Pain is biographical, the cry impersonal […] In literature, as in music, [biographical] experience is something secondary. The material available to this or that form of art has its own linear, unstoppable [bezotkaznaia] dynamic. […] Experience is more or less the same for everyone. One can even suppose there were people with experience graver than Tsvetaeva's. But there weren't people with such a command of – with such a submission [podchinennost'] to the material. Experience, life, the body, biography – in the best case can absorb the recoil. The charge is sent into the distance by the dynamics of the material.[69]

Brodsky's approach to sincerity here is deeply influenced by modernism. The poetry is sincere through its truth to an ideal form dictated from without by the (verbal) material. However, this sincerity also emerges as the expression of pain that is real – pain which, in Tsvetaeva's case, moulds itself into the form of virtuosic verbal intensity.[70]

But intensity can – as is well known – also be put on, whipped up, ritualized, a debt to fashion, exhibitionist. In other words, without a sense of measure, propriety, social and literary context, it is impossible to even begin to evaluate its relationship to sincerity.[71] A yet bigger problem is that the quality of intensity itself switches its loyalties as concerns sincerity and insincerity within specific cultural and poetic contexts and from one reader community to another.[72] In certain periods, and for certain poets and reader groups, intensity of expression can be a powerful collateral indicator of sincerity (as Brodsky above). For other readers, however, unabated intensity comes off as vocal strain and thus functions as a *contraindication* of sincerity. (Such was the case regarding Lomonosov and his followers for the writers around the *Companion of the Enthusiasts of the Russian Word* [Sobesednik liubitelei rossiiskago slova] in the 1780s and regarding Bely for Mandelstam in the 1910s and 1920s.) Thomas Love Peacock wrote of Wordsworth and the Lake Poets: "'The highest inspirations of poetry are resolvable into three ingredients: the rant of unregulated passion, the whine of exaggerated feeling, and cant of factitious sentiment …'"[73]

Conversely, in the material that follows, we will often see *reserve* employed as a sincerity device. The poet leaves the dearest thoughts unspoken and, in this way, guards him- or herself against their falsification or profanation.[74] But restraint can also read as insufficient candour or aristocratic aloofness.

Colloquialisms, prosaicisms, slang, dialect, and idiom can be used in certain circumstances to evoke a non-literariness and human immediacy.[75] However, the same stylistic devices can be used neutrally or in a plainly ironic or postmodern sense. What is more, expressly poetic, elevated language can also be effectively renewed and deployed in the service of the sincere voice, given the proper context. (Compare the archaic, Slavonic "dnes'" [today] above. This word would have sounded a bit stilted or "archaizing" in a poem from the 1820s, but, in Tsvetaeva's usage a century later, it becomes effectively assimilated to the context through its semantic and articulational parallelism with "vpred'" [in the future], lending rather an air of significance to the otherwise coarse imagery ["ne zatknu dyry" (I'll not plug the hole)].)

In some cultural contexts, unfinishedness, rough edges, imperfections read as sincere or authentic.[76] At the same time, some of the most stunning effects of resonant sincerity are created through masterful manipulations of poetic language, which can in no way read as unfinished. For one poet or cultural context, excessive quotation may imply an inability to speak as an independent self. For another, dense allusion may lie at the heart of his or her idiolect, constituting a richly developed poetic *language* that in no way impugns sincerity.[77]

The upshot of all this is that analysis of the functioning of the sincere voice in poetry can, and must, rely on formal markers and pragmatic contextualization, but only when these are put in the service of an analytical framework wary of the differing ways in which sincerity is conceptualized and thus encoded, embodied, and read in different cultural contexts. This also means that the researcher's subjectivity, in a matter as elusive as sincerity, cannot be entirely surmounted. To mitigate this subjectivity, I have made an effort to ground my attestations, whenever possible, in contemporary and historical evaluative statements and to thoroughly anchor the understandings of the text presented here in the literary, social, and historical dynamics of their time.[78] I have also been guided by the definition proffered at the beginning of this introduction, which lends an overarching coherence to the diverse manifestations of the sincere voice considered below.[79]

Ultimately, a claim that audible or "resonant" sincerity emerges in these poems must involve a judgment similar to a claim that a certain passage reads in the literary and linguistic context of its time (or another time) as palpably ironic. Such a judgment may be based not simply on individual predilection, but on textual and contextual analysis of readable signs.[80] Of course, even then, any such claim remains open to question, and the ultimate test, as in any not solely empirical work of literary scholarship, will be whether others find the attribution compelling. Despite these methodological difficulties, I believe that the case studies which make up this book have much to tell us about sincerity, how it is encoded and decoded and how it has evolved. Perhaps, they even have something to say about sincerity outside the literary framework.

The Structure of This Study

In choosing the specific phenomena that are subjected to analysis below, I have striven for breadth but also have remained cognizant that this study can be most impactful if it presents a counterpoint to the main body of writing on poetic sincerity, which has focused heavily on works in the confessional mode. While I often put the phenomena I look at into comparative perspective (sometimes in passing, sometimes in greater detail), the focus in the readings is on Russian poetry. Russian literature, over the last two centuries, has paralleled the development of Western literature, traversing the same major movements and periods, a similarity which gives the new story I tell about the evolution of the lyric direct relevance to a broader cultural history. At the same time, a quasi-religious concept of the "poetic Word" that first emerged in the eighteenth and early nineteenth centuries and literature's long-standing pre-eminence as a venue for free expression of ideas in a nation where freedom of expression and press were regularly stymied have often placed unusual demands on the poet's sincerity, even when the poetry itself is not socially engaged. And the fates of Russian poets have helped equate poetic speech with a deed and ratify the idea that the right to speak as Poet is bought at a high, and real, price. While not all poets or readers have bought into this tradition, many have. Additionally, for linguistic and cultural reasons, formal aspects like metre and rhyme have been retained in Russian poetry to a greater degree than, for instance, in the Anglo-American tradition. A study of Russian poetry, therefore, can help demonstrate that abandonment of formal strictures is only one path to the renewal of poetic language and that freer verse is no more inherently capable of conveying sincerity, thereby eroding a widespread cultural myth.[81]

The book's case studies begin in the Russian 1780s, a distinctly pre-Romantic, even pre-Sentimentalist, context.[82] Chapter 1 examines the ways in which, through experiments with modulation of voice and irony that go far beyond the introduction of his "amusing style" (zabavnyi slog), Derzhavin was able to produce, in the most unlikely of places, the panegyric ode "Felitsa" (1782), a voice that sounded resonantly sincere to a broad group of his contemporaries, including, particularly, fellow writers. It goes on to analyse why Derzhavin failed to repeat this feat elsewhere and how, at times, he achieved it anew and with different means – for instance, through his invention of a new "destabilizing" odic strophe and even more radical experiments with irony and lyric subjectivity in "On Fortune" ("Na Schast'e," 1789). En route, a comparison is drawn between Derzhavin's late-eighteenth-century and modernist sincerities.

The next two chapters examine four poets' "idiosincerities" in the Romantic era. Their ambitious scope is connected to the increased attention to and heightened desirability of sincerity during this long period. The first section of chapter 2 considers Pushkin's conceptualization of sincerity, which hews to our second pole, before analysing a signature compositional-stylistic device appearing in two poems of radically contrasting genre in the 1830s. This device draws upon the wornness of poetic language and tropes to establish a backdrop against which a potently individual voice suddenly achieves a resonant, localized presence.

The second section demonstrates the sources in Western European Romanticism for the conceptualization of sincerity implied in Dmitry Venevitinov's writings and poetry. This is an early Romantic (in conceptual, rather than strictly chronological, terms) version of "expressive," first-pole sincerity. An exceptional scholar-reader, Lydia Ginzburg, however, finds little of the Romantic in Venevitinov's poetry. Was, then, the popular image of Venevitinov, who died at age twenty-one, as prototypical Romantic poet largely a useful "marketing" ploy constructed by and for his circle (as Ginzburg argues)? By examining the assumptions about Romantic sincerity built into the thinking of Venevitinov and his friends and then analysing in this light material traces of such a Romantic sincerity preserved in one of Venevitinov's drafts, I attempt to show why Venevitinov's friends, who had privileged access to the poet's creative process, indeed experienced him as a Romantic, and Romantically sincere, poet par excellence.

Chapter 3 pairs two Late Romantic sincerities. The opening section looks at Mikhail Lermontov, an acknowledged problematic master of sincere affect. After considering questions raised by the often indignant, "rhetorical" sincere voice that brought him initially notoriety, it looks at how he innovates to achieve deeper and more broadly accessible sincere resonances in the poetry written not long before his early death in 1841. Particular attention is given to three strategies: "disarming" of the Byronic speaker in ways that mutually disarm the reader; inscription of a more versatile voice (representing a potential shift in the direction of "modulated" sincerity, perhaps under the influence of Pushkin after the latter's death); and the dismantling of cultural matrices to demonstrate truths independently experienced and interrogated.

In the second section of chapter 3, I explore the poetic devices and compositional and pragmatic framings through which "Gypsy" abandon, as a specific subspecies of Romantic sincerity or authenticity, is encoded in Apollon Grigoryev's poetry. I also delineate some justifications from Grigoryev's own writings for an authorial understanding of this "mask" as a potentially sincere voice. It can be argued that the Gypsy modality allowed Grigoryev, who was both given to excessive passions and sceptical of strained voices, to co-opt the vocal overstrain which mars some of his other poems.

In chapter 4, I take an extended look at how an exemplary Russian modernist, Osip Mandelstam, delineates his own poetic sincerity, drawing distinctions on the backdrop of sincerity's conceptualization by the leading lyric poet of the preceding generation, the Symbolist Alexander Blok. After teasing out Mandelstam's implicit understanding of sincerity/authenticity, I briefly examine the writings of the Anglo-American modernists, which, in their more explicit argumentation, shed additional light on the internal logic of Mandelstam's modernist structuring of sincerity. The chapter then moves on to readings of poems by Blok and Mandelstam. It is my argument that differences in poetics linked to the poets' divergent conceptualizations of sincerity were a primary factor conditioning these two exceptional poets' mutual stinginess in recognition of each other's work, and that the nature of their dissatisfactions can tell us much about the construction of the competing conceptualizations of sincerity they represent. In other words, in this chapter, it is the poets who stand as readers.

Chapter 5 considers the problem of mid-century sincerities in a totalitarian context. Analysis of three key essays related to the problem of sincerity in literature and poetry and published before or immediately after Stalin's death helps to tease out specificities of a characteristic individual, but universalizing, "ethically oriented" mid-century approach to sincerity, one which of necessity interacts with the strongly politicized public sincerity practices of the Stalinist and post-Stalinist period. In the body of the chapter, I examine Anna Akhmatova's long poem *Requiem* (1935–62), which presents rich material to problematize the functioning of this mid-century sincerity. In its construction, *Requiem* navigates between mid-century expectations and context and Akhmatova's modernist roots, while in terms of reader reception, it has charted a dividing line between mid-century and more recent reader attitudes. In the final pages of chapter 5, we turn to an unusual, irony-dependent mid-century sincerity in a 1946 poem by Second World War veteran Konstantin Levin.

Chapter 6 takes us to the near present with an analysis of two turn-of-the-millennium voices. First, we consider Boris Ryzhy, who finds ways to continue to project a sincere voice of a traditional cast and leaning towards our first, "expressive" pole. Then, we look at the later poetry of Timur Kibirov, a one-time "fellow traveller" of Russian Conceptualism (postmodernism) and long-time proponent of a "new sentimentalism" who strongly embodies our second, "modulated" pole and frequently grounds sincerity in and on an ironic tone and sensibility. Each takes on the challenge of producing a late-coming sincere voice in different ways, but without a rejection of verse form.

It is to these case studies that we now turn. In doing so, I hope to demonstrate the persistence of the "sincere voice," as well as the historical situatedness and individuality of each instantiation of it.

1 The Problem of Sincerity and the Poetic Device in Gavrila Derzhavin's Odes

Researchers studying sincerity have tended to focus on its pitfalls. Jürgen Habermas, appealing to the cultural norms that undergird mutual understanding and acceptance of speech acts, notes that the claim to sincerity, like other validity claims, can be supported with "reasons" and that expressive self-presentations, "like constative speech acts [...] can also go wrong."[1] They can also, however, go unexpectedly right, and it is possible to tease out, through historically contextualized close readings, the rhetorical structures, pragmatic framings, and poetic devices that allow this to happen.

In the Russia of Gavrila Derzhavin's day, the burden of a poetic past was not a key factor inhibiting poetic sincerity. Rather, a lack of a model for a modern, resonantly sincere voice (with some exceptions and intimations, especially in spiritual odes and satire) confronted a growing sense of the need to forge one. And still, in this period, which predates the full-fledged Romantic cult of individuality and originality, we can talk no less than in the Romantic era about the need to invent and reinvent, in each individual poetic context, a sincere voice.

Moreover, if the formal, philosophical, and pragmatic obstacles to sincerity are manifold in our day, they were surely no less so in eighteenth-century Russia. At that time, "corporate" authorship – odes presented by and as the speech of formally constituted groups – competed with individual authorship, genre and canonical models strongly determined content, and literary life gravitated towards the imperial court.[2] Derzhavin's generation was the first in Russia to synthesize Enlightenment resistance to flattery with the first flowerings of European Romanticism, especially in religious poetry, forming an expectation of and demand for truth and, ultimately, sincerity in verse.[3] That the moment of emergence of this latent demand within Russian literature coincided with the publication in 1783 of Derzhavin's ode

"Felitsa" (1782) is nicely documented by Joachim Klein, and is not in hindsight unexpected.[4] For, in this poem, I would argue, Derzhavin's contemporaries *heard* what, for many of them, could be recognized as a conspicuously sincere voice in poetry.[5]

Klein's article contextualizes the demand for sincerity in panegyric poetry in the 1780s in light of the binary of *lest'* ("flattery"), on the one hand, and *istina/natura* ("truth/nature"), on the other, looking at "Felitsa" in its social and literary context. Derzhavin found himself in a thorny situation as both civil servant and panegyric poet – his praise suspect due to the obvious potential for gain, his writing suspect in drawing him away from the competing demands of service. As Elena Pogosian has shown, his difficulties in this regard were only exacerbated by concurrent petitions regarding his financial situation.[6] Notably, there was a core of writers united around Princess Ekaterina Dashkova's *Companion of the Enthusiasts of the Russian Word* (Sobesednik liubitelei rossiiskago slova) who noted in "Felitsa" an entirely new and desirable truthfulness introduced to the panegyric ode, and it enjoyed wild success among readers.[7] However, "Felitsa" did not enjoy the same success among the courtiers, who rained on Derzhavin accusations of "indecent flattery," or, unequivocally anyway, with Catherine herself. After the empress's initial gift of a diamond-encrusted snuffbox filled with five hundred gold *chervontsy* (ten-rouble coins) was followed by Derzhavin's brazen and ill-considered request, passed on through Alexander Bezborodko, for a 30,000 rouble loan, Catherine ridiculed Derzhavin publicly on the pages of the *Companion*, calling his bluff.[8]

Klein and Pogosian's studies document a desire for sincerity, cultural matrices into which it would have to be written, and pragmatic obstacles Derzhavin as author faced. However, they leave open the key question that I wish to raise in this chapter. How is Derzhavin able *poetically* to inscribe a sincere voice in his verse despite the inherent obstacles? According to Derzhavin in a 1786 letter to Dashkova, the disparity between Elizabeth's deeds and her praises undermined the resonance of Mikhail Lomonosov's odes, while Catherine's commensurateness to her odic image underpinned the resonance of his own.[9] However, this purported commensurateness is insufficient to explain either the success of "Felitsa" in embodying the poet's "sincerity" for the reading and writing public or the weakness of the later "Felitsa's Portrait" ("Izobrazhenie Felitsy," 1789). Derzhavin himself felt the need, in regard to the latter, for post factum apologetics and effectively placed these poems in different classes.[10] The first part of this chapter will be devoted to the question of why "Felitsa" and "Felitsa's Portrait" have precipitated such different reactions.

Before I do this, however, I will briefly note the curious typological similarity, despite the chronological distance, between the approaches to sincerity taken *implicitly* by Derzhavin and the twentieth-century Acmeist (modernist) poet Osip Mandelstam – a similarity which helps highlight some of the issues surrounding Derzhavin's own sincerity.[11] For one thing, personal candour and confession are not central to sincerity for these two authors. For another, both poets practise a sincerity that is interwoven with and underpinned by irony, and, particularly, self-deprecating irony. I would argue that the analogies between these poets' second-pole ("modulated") approaches to sincerity are conditioned in part by a typological similarity in the reigning first-pole ("expressive") literary modes they confronted as young poets.[12]

Mandelstam's distrust in the authenticity of Symbolist art was linked to the Symbolists' histrionics. As he wrote in "A Letter about Russian Poetry" ("Pis'mo o russkoi poezii," 1921), "They immediately took the highest, most tensile note, deafened themselves and did not use the voice in its organic potential for development."[13] The poetry of the Symbolists generally – Mandelstam separates Alexander Blok from the rest – seemed to be spoken at an unbendingly high pitch, engendering a "hypertrophy" of the lyric "I" and a departure from the range of expression of the human voice.

The Acmeists challenged this paradigm through what Mandelstam would describe as a change of taste.[14] And that new taste included what Nikolai Gumilev called "luminous [svetlaia] irony, not undermining the roots of our belief" – that is, irony which does not undermine, but undergirds sincerity.[15] For Mandelstam, this was often a subtle, self-deprecating irony, which worked paradoxically not to diminish the lyric "I," but to shore up his claims to those elements of the Symbolist project (prophetism, insight) that the Symbolists had allegedly fumbled through their overreaching and hence unconvincing claims.

Derzhavin confronted a similar problem and with similar tools. The mid-century panegyric ode of Mikhail Lomonosov and his followers – despite formalist critic Yury Tynianov's claims for the intonational richness demanded by its rhetorical bent[16] – was extremely limited in its emotional and intonational range. Lexicon, syntax, and manner of declamation all contributed to elevation of the subject matter. The most impassioned, fervent tone was taken from the outset ("Vostorg vnezapnyi um plenil" [sudden rapture has enthralled [my] mind]) and maintained, as much as possible, through elaborate and multifarious variations, to the conclusion.[17] The literal volume of this output was attested to constantly by the poets themselves: *shum, grom, rev, plesk* (noise, thunder, roaring, clapping) are constant attributes. Even when an odist like Vasily Petrov purports to depart from this tradition, as in the opening lines of his well-known "Ode to the Magnificent Carousel" ("Oda na velikolepnyi karusel'," 1766) – "Molchite, shumny pleskov gromy, / Chto slyshny v Pindara ustakh" (Be still, loud thunders of sprays, which sound in Pindar's lips) – he ends up sounding flashy, hyperbolic, pompous and just plain loud:

Я странной слышу рев музыки!

(I hear the roar of strange music!)

Не столь сияют в небе звезды,
Не столь красен денницы всход,
Не столь торжественные въезды
Верх римских в древности высот
Блистательны и пышны были

(Not so do the stars in heaven shine,
Not so pulchritudinous the rising of the sun,
Not so were the regal chariot entrances
Above the Roman heights in antiquity
Resplendent and luxurious.)[18]

By the early 1780s, the panegyric ode was mired in repetition, practised by numerous epigones – with up to fifty odes per year appearing during the second Turkish War[19] – and often used by poets of lower class for commercial gain. After "Felitsa" was published in the *Companion*, contemporaries like Maria Sushkova, Osip Kozodavlev, and V.M. Zhukov, sensing its rare resonance, praised the poem for its "istina" ("truth") and implicitly sincerity.[20] The reply of Ermil Kostrov, in its choice of tropes, happens to sound uncannily like an Acmeist manifesto:

Наш слух почти оглох от громких лирных тонов,
И полно, кажется, за облаки летать,
Чтоб, равновесия не соблюдя законов,
Летя с высот, и рук и ног не изломать:
        Хоть сколь ни будем мы стараться
        В своем полете возвышаться,
Фелицыны дела явятся выше нас,
        Ей простота приятна в слоге,
        Так лучше нам, по сей дороге
Идя со скромностью, к ней возносить свой глас.[21]

(We have been all but deafened by the loud tones of lyres,
And enough, it seems, of flying past the clouds,
So as, not obeying the laws of equilibrium,
Plummeting from the heights, to break both arms and legs.
        However we might try
        To rise up in our flight,
Felitsa's deeds will show above us,
        Simplicity of phrase is pleasing to her,
        So better for us walking this road
With modesty to lift up to her our voice.)[22]

In the face of the "loud tones of lyres," the gesticulative rhetoric and histrionics of his time, Derzhavin introduces a subtlety of voice.

Derzhavin himself perceived his success in "Felitsa" in terms that underscore the achievement of a distinctly elusive sincere *voice*. Pressed by the empress, he struggled and ultimately failed to repeat his performance. As he reports: "Everything came out cold, forced,and ordinary, as in the verse of other run-of-the-mill producers of poetry [kak u prochikh tsekhovykh stikhotvortsev], where one hears only words, and not thoughts and feelings."[23]

There are a number of higher order strategies, previously described, that contribute to the novelty of "Felitsa" and combine organically to make it a masterpiece.[24] Firstly, the well-motivated Eastern and fairy-tale colouring, through ambiguously distancing the addressee, "Felitsa," from Catherine, allowed for a familiarity of address and stylistic playfulness that were indeed revolutionary in the Russian ode.[25] Second, Derzhavin's choice to make the poem's "I" dissolute and a mirror of the recognizable vices of Catherine's courtiers facilitated the introduction of humour.[26] Third was the choice to write an ode unlinked to any occasion and implying, therefore, an inner imperative. Fourth, play between wishfulness and reality in the poet's description of Catherine, though present earlier, for instance, in the odes of Lomonosov, conceived of as a mode of moral instruction,[27] here was far more organic and effective because of the potential distinction between "Felitsa" and her ideal realm and the Russia of Catherine, her prototype and creator. This device allows each sufficiently good-willed reader to assume that where the portrait, for him or her, exceeds the sitter, we are talking about Felitsa; where it fits, we are talking about the empress. Finally, and most famously, there is Derzhavin's *zabavnyi slog* (amusing style), which mixes low-style lexicon into the high-style odic context.[28]

These innovations collaborate to establish a framework within which a sincere voice can emerge but remain insufficient in and of themselves to generate sincerity's presence. What feels real in "Felitsa" is not the mask of the *murza* (Tatar nobleman) with his grittier language, but the voice of the man who dons it, a voice which is recognizably human in a world of figures so visibly distorted and deformed by social and literary etiquette. What makes this voice feel real is 1) its seeming resistance to cultural, social, and literary norms (largely encompassed in the elements described above), but also 2) its range of modulation, the subtlety of tone and tonal shifts, which can only be made evident through the closest analysis, but which we cannot help but feel.[29] This appearance of a human voice, in all of its intonational complexity, including irony and, most importantly, *dynamics*, is like the appearance on the scene of the fortepiano after the harpsichord (or perhaps the kettledrums).

Take the second stanza:

Подай, Фелица, наставленье,
Как честно и правдиво жить,
Как укрощать страстей волненье
И счастливым на свете быть.
Меня твой голос возбуждает,
Меня твой сын препровождает;
Но им последовать я слаб:
Мятясь житейской суетою,
Сегодня властвую собою,
А завтра прихотям я раб.

(Give, Felitsa, [wise] instruction
How honestly and true to live,
To tame the turbulence of passions
And be happy in the world.
I am aroused by your voice,
I am guided by your son,
But I am weak to follow them:
Tossed by life's vanit[ies],
Today I am master of my will,
But tomorrow fancy's slave.)

In the first four lines we have a crescendo, built through anaphora (in lines 2 and 3), inversion in specifically the high-flown "strastei volnen'e" (turbulence of passions) of line 3, and rhythmic acceleration, as the lines' pyrrhics move back from third to second to the first foot – with motion coming to a stop in "I schastlivym … na svete byt'" (And be happy … in the world) – a decided decrescendo in relation to the preceding lines. This pattern is then repeated. Anaphora and crescendo:

"Menia tvoi golos *vozbuzhdaet*, / Menia tvoi syn *preprovozhdaet*" (note the deep rhyme and the accumulation of an extra syllable in the rhyme word, which makes this sixth line sound heavier than the preceding one). "No im posledovat' ia slab" (But I am weak to follow them) – again, decrescendo. Then, again, louder, starting from the muscular "miatias'" (tossed): "Miatias' zhiteiskoi suetoiu / Segodnia vlastvuiu soboiu" (Tossed by life's vanit[ies], / Today I am master of my will). And inversion and deflation: "A zavtra prikhotiam ia rab" (But tomorrow fancy's slave; sounding perhaps more flip in the original Russian). These decrescendos are particularly emphasized given that they are precisely at the strong points of the stanza – the fourth as well as the seventh and tenth lines, which Derzhavin himself, as Tynianov points out, would adapt to the expression of maxims and aphorisms.[30]

Derzhavin's 1808 revision of the strophe's second line – "Kak *pyshno* I pravdivo zhit'" (How to live *luxuriously* and truthfully) – nicely reinforces the sense of a sincere voice in this strophe. While outwardly the phrase fulfils Lomonosov's call for the "juxtaposition of somewhat distant ideas," one can easily envision the complex, weak-willed hero who wants to combine honesty (truth to self) with *pyshnost'* (luxury) – a lesser vice that tickles the self-image.[31] This usage also places Derzhavin's hero outside normative ethical patterns and narratives (Christian; Graeco-Roman; Anacreontic as an allowable variation) that underlie so much eighteenth-century poetry, with its tendency towards moralization, and which depersonalize so much mid-century elegy, epistle, and love poetry.

Stylistic play in "Felitsa" harmonizes with the slightest shifts in sense. A far cry from "high – Felitsa, low – *murza*" or "high – moral, low – amoral," the *murza* can talk about "himself" (or rather, the parodied courtiers) in high style as long as the context motivates it:

То плен от персов *похищаю,*

То стрелы к туркам *обращаю;*

То, *возмечтав,* что я султан,

Вселенну устрашаю взглядом;

То вдруг, прельщаяся *нарядом,*

Скачу к *портному* **по** *кафтан.* (emphasis mine)

(Either I take the Persians captive,

Or incline to the Turks my bows;

Or, fancying myself a Sultan,

I awe the cosmos with a glare;

Or, suddenly, enticed by an outfit,

I race for a caftan to the tailor.)

Here high style is valenced negatively, embodying empty and self-indulgent daydreaming; low (at the end) represents the even more vapidly self-indulgent; the shift is "sudden" and impactful.

In semantic/ideological terms also, the poet is remarkably subtle. He ends a mostly straightforward and seriously intoned strophe:

Еще же говорят не ложно,
Что будто завсегда возможно,
Тебе и правду говорить.

(What's more, they say without falsehood
That supposedly at any time,
One can even speak truth to you.)

Even as this passage expresses one of the poet's central appreciations of Catherine and her reign, its playful manner undermines its conclusiveness. In the first place, "govoriat *ne lozhno*" (they say *without falsehood*) is not an entirely categorical way to attest to the truth of this statement about Catherine. In the next line, the seemingly extraneous "budto" (supposedly) functions to underscore for a second time that this is reported speech but also unnecessarily distances the poet from the claim. And, in the final line, the only proximately translatable "i" in "i pravdu" hints again at a subtle distancing, a tinge of surprise or doubt. When the lines are taken at face value, this is the put-on surprise or doubt of the *murza*, the foreigner who finds it hard, given his world of experience, to believe the extent of Felitsa's virtue.[32] But in the same set of lines the poet hints at his more direct knowledge through the phrase "ne lozhno" (without falsehood), forcing us to question his distance (and his mask). The ambiguities call out for Catherine herself to claim and affirm this quality. The same is true to an even greater degree when the poet describes an ideal realm of justice in the final stanzas of the ode and, through the phrase "U trona razve tvoego!" (If anywhere, at your throne! [or, with disbelief: Can it be at your throne!]) asks and even dares Catherine to claim it.[33]

A focus on stylistics has led at least one researcher to see in the final stanza of "Felitsa" "excessive zeal," noting that it "could almost have been written by Lomonosov, as it replicates a uniformly high panegyric style."[34] In truth, however, this stanza too is full of subtle gradations and play:

Прошу великого пророка,
Да праха ног твоих коснусь,

Да слов твоих сладчайша тока
И лицезренья наслаждусь.

(I beg the great prophet
That I might graze the dust of your feet.
That I might savour the sweetest stream of your words
And the vision of your countenance.)

The high style here does not tell the whole story. The "straight" third
and fourth lines, expressing Derzhavin's no doubt sincere desire for an
audience with Catherine, are set off by the initial two. We cannot ignore,
of course, the fact that this strophe's prophet is not a Judaeo-Christian
one, but Muhammed. The image arising is thus quite shifted, the poet's
mask retained, then intensified by the orientalist image of servile gen-
uflection in the second line. These two lines are spoken with a distinct
accent. In addition, Derzhavin's play with the image of the Eastern flat-
terer signals his awareness of the shaky ground he occupies and of the
nature of his own balancing act.[35]

Derzhavin's closing continues in traditional and rather predictable
images until the third to last line:

Небесныя прошу я силы,
Да, их простря сафирны крылы,
Невидимо тебя хранят
От всех болезней, зол и скуки;
Да дел твоих в потомстве звуки,
Как в небе звезды, возблестят!

(I ask the heavenly powers
That, spreading out their sapphire wings,
They guard you invisibly
From all maladies, ills, and boredom;
That the sounds of your acts will come to glitter
In posterity like stars in the heavens.)

The lightly intoned – and middle/low style – "skuki" (boredom) (ad-
ditionally emphasized through the breaking of the grammatical par-
allelism that existed between the plural forms "boleznei" [maladies]
and "zol" [ills]) is remarkable for the familiarity of address to the odic
subject that it implies, because it is entirely out of place in the formulaic
series of well wishes the poet is conveying, and because it once more
reinforces a sense of the poet's intimate knowledge of the Tsarina's

character. And is it anything less than playful that in the final two lines Derzhavin displaces the appropriate desire for Catherine's deeds to shine with a desire for his own words in her honour to sparkle from the firmament like stars? As Anna Lisa Crone asserts, Derzhavin will eventually come to place his words in a status of equality with the monarch's deeds.[36] Already here, he slyly does.

It is this poetic virtuosity of instrumentation, tastefully employed, this playfulness, infused with irony, knowing winks, and *a broad range of vocal intonation and dynamics*, that makes the poem feel like it is being spoken by a human interlocutor, despite its august addressee and highly formalized strophic structure. But how does one achieve this again? One can't simply write a "Felitsa II" as the same constellation of devices, framing, and content will not *sound* the same a second time.

In 1789, Derzhavin wrote another ode to Catherine. While he strongly emphasized the sincerity of "Felitsa," in regard to "Felitsa's Portrait," he felt compelled in his explanatory notes to admit that he was fishing for a new appointment after his dismissal from the governorship of Tambov, trial for abuse of power and insubordination, and then exoneration. Unable as he was to get an audience with the new favourite, Platon Zubov, "there remained no other means but to turn to [his] talent."[37]

There is little doubt that the reception of "Felitsa's Portrait," starting with friend and confidant Vasily Kapnist's "Report to the Court Author from the Chimneysweep of the Catherinepraise [translating literally the city's name] Muses" ("Raport leib-avtoru ot Ekaterinoslavskikh muz trubochista," 1789), has underscored its lesser sincerity. Lappo-Danilevsky takes Kapnist far too much at his word in pinpointing his objection to Derzhavin's poem in the practical impossibility of composing a single portrait reflecting such a wide range of sublime activity and in the baroque/Lomonosovian poetics of the work.[38] He ignores the irony and power differential apparent in Kapnist's title, which places Derzhavin in the compromised role of "court author" vis-à-vis Kapnist's outsider "chimneysweep" as well as the irony conveyed in repetitions and even exaggerations of Derzhavin's hyperbolic praise by Kapnist, author of the rather more acerbic "Ode to Slavery" ("Oda na rabstvo," 1783).[39]

Later readers, though more solicitous than Kapnist, have continued to underscore the poem's ambivalent status. In the early twentieth century, the poetically conservative Vladislav Khodasevich felt obliged to briefly defend the sincerity (per se) of "Felitsa's Portrait," clearly sensing the aura of lingering doubt that attached to it.[40] Klein mentions, in connection with the poem, "a contradiction of the principle of panegyric disinterestedness (but not necessarily of the principle of poetic sincerity)."[41]

I would argue that Derzhavin intended a work that would convey sincerity but fell short of the mark. The issue is not the poet's potentially lesser belief in Catherine six years later but his failure to generate a compelling poetic mode to express – and, particularly, to temper – his purported belief. "Felitsa's Portrait" is built around several inventive and playful "escape hatches" that potentially should have allowed Derzhavin to flatter Catherine without parting with his integrity. First, and most successfully, his requests to the artist Raphael regarding how to depict Catherine, couched as they are in a vast array of inventive conditional forms, give him the possibility to speak ambiguously: "predstav', chtoby [...] besstrashno b [...] svobodoi b [...] rekla b [...] sodelai, chtob [...] pripomni, chtob [...] iavi iskusstvom chudotvornym" (present that […] would fearlessly […] would through freedom […] she would say […] make that […] recall that […] reveal in wonder-working art).[42] Is what he asks Raphael to depict accomplished reality or the desires of the poet? Second, the fairy-tale trappings should provide, as in "Felitsa," an added level of distance, incomplete identity between the ideal Felitsa and Catherine, the too-human addressee. Third, the high praise that Derzhavin extends to Catherine is, if we are to lend credence to his explanatory notes, based on real events and has its roots in them.[43]

So, what went wrong? For one, fairy-tale colour was in disharmony with the poem's overarching Anacreontic subtext and trope – the request to the artist to produce a likeness of the beloved, whom the poet describes. Unsurprisingly, in the fifty-eight stanzas of this, Derzhavin's longest poem, one can count on fingers the instances of fairy-tale or oriental colour. What examples there are function more as an allusion to the previous "Felitsa" ode than a dynamic component of the present one's poetics. However, without this colour, the productive dualism inherent in Felitsa-Catherine in the earlier poem dissipates. And this impacts the lyric subject as well: paradoxically, he is, without his mask, more conventional and thus seemingly less real.

In addition, cognitive dissonance emerges in the space between the desired and the real. In the eleven strophes that expand upon the line "Izobrazi mne mir sei novyi" (Depict for me this new world), the conditional mode does its double duty as the poet sets out a pointedly idyllic vision of an ideal realm, with bureaucrats who keep sacred the laws and guard the public interest, a watchful ruler who actively keeps them in line, and fair and impartial courts. The lack of these things was of course Derzhavin's own pet peeve and the source of his travails as governor of Olonets and Tambov and on trial in the Senate. However, in "Felitsa" there were playful cues that the ideal is *not necessarily* the real (not to mention a plane of satire of contemporary mores). Here, no tonal or other cues are given to differentiate the poet's ideal from the real achievements of Catherine's rule, which, in most places, are described in starkly hyperbolic terms:

> Представь мне, в мысли восхищенной,
> Сходила бы с небес она;
> Как солнце грудь, в ткани зеленой,
> Рукой метала семена;
> Как искры огненны, дождились
> Златыя б зерна в снедь птенцам:
> Орлы младые разбудились
> И воскрылялись бы к лучам.
>
> Яви искусством чудотворным,
> Чтоб льды прияли вид лилей;
> Весна дыханьем теплотворным
> Звала бы с моря лебедей,
> Летели б с криком вереницы,
> Звучали б трубы с облаков:
> Так в царство бы текли Фелицы
> Народы из чужих краев.
>
> (Present to me, in thought ecstatic,
> How she descends from the heavens;
> Her breast like the sun, in verdant cloth,
> She would cast seeds;
> Like fiery sparks rain
> Golden grains to feed the fledglings:
> The young eagles would awaken
> And take wing, soaring to the rays.
>
> Make visible with wonder-working art,
> That ice take the form of lilies;
> That Spring with its warming breath
> Call from the sea the swans,
> The strings [of birds] would fly with a cry,
> Trumpets would sound from the clouds:
> So to the kingdom of Felitsa
> Would flow peoples from foreign lands.)

These strophes, as per Derzhavin, relate to sowing the seeds of enlightenment, the education of military youth, and the German colonists, things which do not seem commensurate with the strophes' language.[44]

Towards the end of the ode, the poet protests his sincerity and the truthfulness of the emergent portrait (Raphael being revealed as his alter ego in the final lines): "Черты одной красот ей ложно / Блюдися приписать в твой век" (Be wary not to add in all your life / A single false brushstroke to her charms). However, Derzhavin could not have been unaware that immediately after this, in the poem's finale, he casually swaps the narrow, rocky mountain road to virtue – "the rose without thorns" of Catherine's fairy tale and the "Felitsa" ode – for a diamond mountain of glory with a godlike Felitsa astride the summit in place of a temple.

Ultimately, I believe, Derzhavin's praise in "Felitsa's Portrait," though virtuosic in its inventive variation, was too hyperbolic, too extended, too monotonal, too straightforward and at the same time too contrived not to leave the impression of an opulent construct. Despite formal and conceptual innovations, the resonant odic sincere achieved in the earlier masterpiece does not materialize. This is not to judge the quality of the poem more broadly. It is under no obligation to fulfil anyone's abstract demands regarding sincerity and, at the least, met Catherine's expectations for an offering.[45] Still, Derzhavin seems to have lost here the finessed sense of balance and contemporary taste that was his "safe passage" in "Felitsa."

Earlier in the same year, during his trial, Derzhavin wrote his ode "On Fortune" ("Na Schast'e," 1789). Derzhavin himself called his style in "On Fortune" "ironic,"[46] and here is strong evidence for any doubters that, in poetry, irony and an impression of candour, irony and the sincere voice, can go hand in hand. The impact of the poem is supported, though not of course determined, by a simple but potently productive revision of the odic strophe. This formal innovation tacitly undergirds what seems to be a purely pragmatic candour and freedom, which Derzhavin himself excused by noting that the poem was purportedly "Pisannaia v Moskve na Maslinitse 1789 goda, kogda i sam avtor byl pod khmel'kom" (Written in Moscow during Maslenitsa [Carnival], 1789, when the author too was carousing).[47] The impression of candour is also aided by Derzhavin's formulation within the ode of a lyric subject yet more evocatively personal than that in "Felitsa," though, at the same time, one remarkably reticent.

The canonical ten-line odic strophe had consisted of a quatrain with alternating rhyme and two tercets: AbAbCCdEEd.[48] Poets of Lomonosov's school, as Tynianov notes, used this as backdrop to create a variety of rhetorical intonations by varying the breaks between syntactic units.[49] However, the rhyme scheme itself had an inertia that tended towards rounded stability. In "On Fortune," Derzhavin replaces this traditional strophe with one that begins with a couplet, followed by a quatrain with alternating rhyme, but with the masculine endings falling on odd, rather than even, lines, and then a quatrain of enclosing rhyme: AAbCbCdEEd. This arrangement wreaks havoc with expectations and with the interaction between rhyme and syntax in the poem. As Derzhavin never uses the opening couplet to express some completed, sententious thought, the opening syntagmas for the most part occupy the first three or four lines of the stanza.[50] This introduces a lilting, off-balance feel very much in concert with the drunken gait implied in the poet's description of his own condition when writing the poem and with the off-balance, topsy-turvy state of the world he describes – a world in which the fate of humankind is governed by fickle and irrational Fortune:

> […] все везде в разгулье,
> Политика и правосудье,
> Ум, совесть и закон святой,
> И логика пиры пирует,
> На карты ставят век златой,
> ....
> Вселенну в трантелево гнут;
> Как полюсы, меридианы,
> Науки, музы, боги пьяны,
> ....
> Весь мир стал полосатой шут […][51]

> ([…] everything everywhere is in a [drunken] revel,
> Politics and justice,
> Intelligence, conscience, and divine law,
> And logic is off feasting,
> The golden age is bet at cards,
> ....
> They raise the bet on the universe thirty-fold;
> Like poles, meridians,
> The sciences, the muses, the gods are drunk,
> ....
> The whole world has become a striped fool […])

The greatest inertia throughout the poem is for a three-line opening: AAb (a pattern familiar through its prominent role in the conclusion of traditional rounded odic strophes). The effect of this composition is often to mute the masculine rhyme in line 5. The first seven lines end up *feeling* like an unrhymed tercet (AAb) followed by an unrhymed quatrain (CbCd). An example is strophe 4, which has a three-line introduction, four-line exposition, and three-line ironic closure.

Consider the effect in one of the poem's most conceptually important stanzas establishing the relationship between Fortune, Catherine, and Derzhavin's "boyar" oppressors. Here, the first syntactic/semantic structure of the strophe is effectively four lines long:

В те дни, ни с кем как несравненна,
Она, с тобою сопряженна, –
Ни в сказках складно рассказать,
Ни написать пером красиво, –
Изволит милость проливать,
Изволит царствовать правдиво,
Не жжот, не рубит без суда;

(In these days, she, so highly incomparable,
She, conjoined with you –
In fairy tales one couldn't tell it smoothly,
Or write it neatly with a plume –
Deigns to shower her benevolence,
Deigns to reign righteously;
Doesn't burn or lop [heads] without trial;)

Our progress through the strophe is effectively paused by the highly ironic interjection, which is a prosaicization of the widespread fairy-tale formula "ni v skazke skazat', ni perom napisat'" (one couldn't tell it in a tale, nor write it with a plume). The unexpectedly and unnecessarily plural "skazkakh" (fairy tales) – the singular "skazke" scans identically – and especially the superfluous "skladno" (smoothly) and "krasivo" (neatly, prettily) underscore the irony with which, at this moment, the poet approaches Catherine's "incomparability."[52] In lines 5–7, the infelicitously formal/polite "Izvolit" (deigns, consents) again signals the poet's irony. Compare the more natural, straightforward, and "odic" *milost' prolivaet* (showers [her] benevolence), or the even stronger "l'esh' na nas shchedroty" (you rain on us generosity; Lomonosov), "L'et radost', trepet vkrug sebia" (Rains joy, trembling about itself; Radishchev describing "Law" in his ode "Freedom" ["Vol'nost'," 1783?]).[53] This taut tercet is held together by semantic unity, lexical and syntactic repetition (Izvolit – Izvolit; Ne zhzhot – ne rubit) and delicate sound play (*prolivat' – pravdiva*; prav*diva* – bez s*uda*; cf. also m*ilost'* pro*livat'* – ru*bit bez* suda) – i.e., by everything but its rhyme: bCd. The stanza famously concludes:

> А разве кое-как вельможи
> И так и сяк, нахмуря рожи,
> Тузят инова иногда.

> (Just (not that it's significant) some which way [her] potentates
> First in one fashion, then another, scowling their pusses,
> Thrash someone now and again.)

"Inova" (one or another, someone) clearly refers to the poet himself.[54] The productive new rhyme scheme, combined with the inertia of four- and three-line odic syntagmas, leads to destabilization, harmonizing with the strophe's irony: AAbC bCd EEd.

Even after allowing for the genre, Derzhavin's rejection of courtly etiquette and the exigencies of established social roles is striking. Compare this passage to a March 1789 letter that the poet, confined to Moscow by will of the Senate and subject to trial as per Catherine's own ukase, sent to the empress through Arkady Tersky begging for an audience to present his case. Derzhavin comes close to expressing the key accusation of strophe 10, but without its ironic bite: "And as, at the same time, I am removed from my office and another is appointed in my place, I have, during Your Imperial Majesty's enlightened and compassionate reign, not only without trial, but without the examination of my responses, been punished." He ends his letter: "My only hope is God and thou, Tsarina, may thy will be done with me!"[55] Both strophe and letter appeal to truth. If in the letter, however, the "I" ultimately affirms his abject dependence on "God and [contiguous and stylistically deified] thou," "On Fortune" ends in a markedly different manner.

Destabilization through Derzhavin's revision of the odic strophe is the case in one way or another through much of "On Fortune." There are, however, two places in the poem that demanded a different feel. The first is the opening: to be a successful anti-ode, the poem has to preserve the sense that it is an ode.[56] Here, the poet achieves the necessary elevated cadence by breaking his strophe down into more stable and rounded halves (5 + 5; AAbCb CdEEd). This structure is also clearly present in stanza 3, where it camouflages the off-rhyme *kletku-izdevku* (as these words fall within different five-line "stanzas"). Overall, this gives, despite the "shifty" second stanza, a relatively ceremonious, stable, and perhaps serious coloration to the poet's odic address to and initial sketch of Fortune.

The second place, in which the poet even more radically shifts the poem's feel, is the final stanza. After torrents of outwardly directed and self-deprecating irony, Derzhavin suddenly switches to a "rounded" strophe in the traditional rhyme scheme:

Увы! еще ты не внимаешь,
О счастие! моей мольбе,
Мои обеты презираешь;
Знать, неугоден я тебе.
Но на софах ли ты пуховых,
В тенях ли миртовых, лавровых,
Иль в золотой живешь стране, –
Внемли! – шепни твоим любимцам,
Вельможам, королям и принцам:
Спокойствие мое во мне!

(Alas! still you don't hearken,
O Fortune! to my plea,
You disdain my pledges;
'Twould seem I do not please.
But be you on plush couches,
In the shade of myrtles, laurels,
Or living in a golden land,
Hear me! – and to your favourites whisper,
To potentates and kings and princes:
My serenity – is in my hand!)

In this assertion of independence, inner strength, and calm, whatever lurching fate – and ongoing trial – may bring, sense, syntax, and rhyme converge; stability re-emerges. Indeed, this final switch in rhyme scheme can be seen as tacit confirmation of the poet's recognition of the nature of his now-abandoned "ironic" strophe.

The flexibility and adroitness with which Derzhavin chooses and fills these strophic forms is reminiscent of the agility of movement that animates "Felitsa." The effect is understated, certainly flying under the radar of a casual reading, and I would argue that it is precisely this subtle felicity that abets the reader's sense of the adequacy of the words to their situational impulse. Moreover, if this formal device supports, on a subliminal plane, the sense that the poet speaks without cognitive dissonance, the poem's pragmatic framing, which engages public knowledge of the poet's situation, helps satisfy a demand for the imprimatur of lived experience.

Recent research has diverged on the ode's tone, both asserting the independence of the piece and its pervasive, unflattering irony and insisting that it ought to be seen as an example of persiflage– gallant and ambiguous ridicule of the cultured other.[57] For our purposes, however, it is more productive to consider not how the poem might have sounded to Catherine, but how it must have sounded to Derzhavin's elite readership in the early 1790s as it circulated "secretly" in manuscript.[58] Recall the "subtitle" from Derzhavin's "Manuscript of the 1790s": "Written in Moscow during Maslenitsa, 1789, when the author too was carousing." It is a reasonable presumption, if not the only possible one, that the poem as initially recorded in that manuscript, prior to any changes made in preparation for the calligraphic volume for Catherine, quite adequately reflects its form as it was spread in the period immediately preceding. And, here, Derzhavin plays a double game. Outwardly, he "softens" the poem's impact, excusing its unusual outspokenness in the criticizing of his age by noting that it is part of the carnival spirit of Maslenitsa and that he was drunk when he penned it. However, this is done with a wink, because, at the same time, he indicates the place and time of its writing (Moscow, late winter 1789), which, to his reading audience – that relatively narrow circle that might have circulated the poem in these first few years after its writing – would clearly have resonated, in the context of such lines as "Бояря понадули пузы / И я у всех стал виноват" (The boyars have puffed up their bellies, / And I'm at fault before all) as a specific reference to the poet's corrupt trial in the Senate.[59] At the same time, transparent and personal references to Derzhavin's persecutors, either through sound play (*"Gudok gudit na ton skripitsy"* – Ivan Vasilyevich Gudovich) or expansive and telling description (the stanza and attached notes ["Rukopis' 90-kh," 1. 83 ob.] devoted to Petr Vasilyevich Zavadovsky), reinforce the presence of "Derzhavin" and his trial in the text.

Having thus established this fundamental identification of the lyric "I" and his situation, Derzhavin uses the backdrop of his oppression to give a powerfully personal emotional resonance to such potent, but nondescript, statements as "V glaza patriotizma pliuesh'" (You spit in the eyes of patriotism), "sud'bami smertnykh puntiruiut" (The fates of mortals are bet on cards), and "Tuziat inova inogda" ([They] thrash someone now and again).[60]

For, in reality, the reticent Derzhavin maintains barriers that guard his personal space at the same time he generates an inwardly directed, "candid" voice, which is capable of expressing indignation, distress, desire, and personal freedom. While references to Derzhavin's persecutors are quite specific, nothing relating to the poet is. We know, for instance, that our hero was often visited by the muses, wrote poetry, and felt "vostorg" (rapture, transport, strophe 16) – but this is nothing unexpected given the centrality of rapture to the aesthetics of the Russian ode.[61] Though details like the colloquial "vcheras'" (yesterday) help generate a tone of personal immediacy in this strophe, there is not a single specific reference to Derzhavin or his works.[62] This can be contrasted to the rich evocation of Catherine and her works in strophe 9, which is devoted to *her* writing.

This distance is maintained, in one way or another, in all of the self-directed strophes. The two others that depict the hero's happy and fortunate past (14–15) are also nondescript and perhaps represent, as much as self-portraiture, camouflaged satire somewhat in the vein of the *murza* stanzas of "Felitsa."[63] In the stanzas that precede the final strophe, Derzhavin again employs this device, but more pointedly. Strophe 20 proceeds in a tone of unusually emotional entreaty which makes it resonantly personal. However, starting from 1791, the stanza does double duty, as, in it, Derzhavin appears to don the mask of Grigory Potemkin, Fortune's jilted lover, in his final attempts to return Catherine's favour.[64] (We can, in fact, wonder whether the stanza was added to the text after 1789, given that we possess no textual evidence of the poem's initial form.)

Слети ко мне, мое драгое,
Серебряное, золотое
Сокровище и божество!
Слети, причти к твоим любимцам!
Я храм тебе и торжество
Устрою, и везде по крыльцам
Твоим рассыплю я цветы;
Возжгу куреньи благовонны
И буду ездить на поклоны,
Где только обитаешь ты.

(Fly down to me, my dearest,
Silver, golden
Treasure and divinity!
Fly down, count me among your favourites!
A temple for you and a festivity
I will arrange, and everywhere along your porches
I will sprinkle flowers;
I will burn sweet-smelling incense,
And I will ride to pay my respects
Wherever you may dwell.

When Catherine had taken Zubov as her new favourite, Potemkin, holding on to the hope that he could return her favours, travelled back from the Turkish war to Petersburg, to his fabulously luxurious Tauride Palace in an attempt to woo the Empress at a pageant-spectacle ("torzhestvo") of unheard-of extravagance. In the gardens, according to Derzhavin's description of the event, one was greeted by a shrine to the empress, an "open-sided Altar" with jasper chalices, icon-lamps, flowery chains and garlands, and among its eight columns "on a porphyry pedestal with a golden inscription ["Materi otechestva i mne premiloserdoi" ("To the Mother of the fatherland, she, who is to me most compassionately loving," Derzhavin's note)] [...] the image, carved from pure marble, of the divinity [*bozhestvo*] by whose generosity this house was raised."[65]

Potemkin was a tragic figure with whom Derzhavin clearly sympathized on some level, and here the irony is so subtle that the stanza can also read as the heartfelt plea of the lyric persona. In the following stanza, the tone shifts to burlesque as the poet impersonates his tormentor, Zavadovsky, recognizably, but through the mask of the lyric "I," as a crass, hypocritical buffoon and Philistine.

Even in the strophe that is the emotional peak of Derzhavin's self-description and self-deprecating irony and which contains the most direct reference to his biography, a notable distance is maintained:

А ныне пятьдесят мне било,
Полет свой счастье пременило,
Без лат я Горе-богатырь;
Прекрасной пол меня лишь бесит,
Амур без перьев нетопырь,
Едва вспорхнет и нос повесит.
Сокрылся и в игре мой клад;
Не страстны мной, как прежде, Музы;
Бояря понадули пузы,
И я у всех стал виноват.

(But now I've hit fifty,
Fortune has changed its flight,
I'm the Sad-sack Warrior without mail;
The lovely sex just makes me fume,
Cupid without feathers is a bat,
Barely flits up and hangs its nose.
My prize has hidden in the game too;
The Muses are enamoured of me no more;

The boyars have all puffed up their bellies,
And I'm at fault before all.)

Derzhavin here likens himself to the king of Sweden, lampooned by Catherine in her potentially scandalous "Tale of the Sad-Sack Warrior Kosometovich [literally, Crooked Shot]" ("Skazka o Gore-bogatyre Kosometoviche," 1788). Presumably, we should read "I'm the Sad-sack Warrior *without mail*" as implying that, relieved of his position as governor, Derzhavin continues a futile struggle against the corrupt bureaucratic establishment. However, such a reading is dependent on quite active speculation on the part of the reader. The ribald Anacreontic lines about sexual impotence seem powerful in their immediacy, probably due to the "muscularity" of their language and sound patterning (amur bis peryif nitapyr'). At the same time, they are just that – Anacreontic. The insinuation that inspiration has left Derzhavin is clearly undermined by the text itself. Finally, in the opening line, the number "fifty" is valuable for its rounded resonance, not biographical accuracy. As several authors have noted, Derzhavin was forty-six in 1789. And yet, even as the biographical Derzhavin recedes, a voice emerges that we can easily associate with a man in his state of tribulation, a voice which is all the more real for its self-deprecating irony.[66]

Through this play with resonant biography, I believe that Derzhavin comes close to formulating in this poem a new and ultimately very productive type of lyric hero – for the first time in Russian literature. The great diversity of tone, and particularly the mask of the buffoon in the penultimate stanza, hardly equatable to Derzhavin, prevents this from coming to full fruition. Still, the poem implies to the reader a speaking hero with a salient biographical myth, a myth that has a public, real-life dimension beyond his interaction with Catherine as poet. Derzhavin, in effect, uses his real biography as an amplifier to raise the poem's satire and social criticism to a new level of resonance and authority. In doing so, he takes a stance that will be much employed in the Russian poetic tradition.[67] This hero becomes the conduit for what can be construed as the not literal, but potently honest self-expression of a man in Derzhavin's position. Of course, to the extent that a lyric hero emerges, Derzhavin's is distinctly pre-Romantic, particularly in his values, which are entirely in congruence with the Enlightenment.

This tonally complex poem, which mobilizes multifarious, distinct modalities of irony (compare also particularly strophes 13, 18, 19) and plays with distance and immediacy in its fashioning of a proto-lyric hero, becomes an expression of the poet's most radical candour and of his transgression of bounds of propriety delimited through his participation in the tradition of panegyric poetry and the civil service. For these reasons, and also in no small part due to Derzhavin's potent revision of the odic strophe, which sets the reader slightly off-balance, mirroring the vagaries of the universe it depicts, "On Fortune" likely rang sincere to many in its time, as it still does to some readers in our own. One may surmise that an impression of potentially dangerous "candour" was a part of that appeal which assured the poem's success in the early 1790s as an underground phenomenon.

We see that sincerity in poetry is neither literal, nor, having been once intimated, secure. Even during the pre-Romantic stage, in which individuality of experience and perception is only a nascent and transient value, it is in the nature of the sincere voice that it must be actively generated, and generated anew in successive poems. We can observe this through both success and failure in Derzhavin's poetry, and this process itself should be seen as inextricable from the development of the language of poetry – its inner musculature, and its ephemeral and idiosyncratic devices. Without this ongoing poetic "labour," that special aura of palpable sincerity, which has been highly desirable in lyric poetry but is actually quite rare, is impossible.

2 Romantic Sincerities I

1 FROM GENRE TO THE SINCERE VOICE (ALEXANDER PUSHKIN)

The middle of the second decade of the nineteenth century saw the emergence in Russia of nascent Romantic-expressive notions of the relation between poet and lyric subject.[1] In "A Note about the Poet and Poetry" ("Nechto o poete i poezii," 1815), Konstantin Batiushkov, the leading elegist of the day, wrote:

> I wish [...] that a science was made of the life of the poet. [...]. The first rule [...] ought to be: live as you write and write as you live. Talis hominibus fuit oratio, qualis vita [such as people's speech was, so was their life; Seneca, Epistles 19.114]. Otherwise all the resonances of your lyre will be false [or, off-pitch; fal'shivy].[2]

Vasily Zhukovsky, Russia's other leading poet of this period, expressed consonant sentiments in 1814 in the "letter-diaries" he wrote for Masha Protasova: "This is my *codex*. *Write* (and in this, a rule – live as you write, so that [your] compositions will be not a mask, but a mirror of [your] soul and deeds)." And in another place: "*For me*: [...] Live as you write. Sincerity in regard to the [morally] unsightly (durnoe)."[3] These ideas also began to seep into poetic practice. Lazar Fleishman notes an "orientation toward the author's 'candour' and 'sincerity'" evident already in Batiushkov's elegies of the mid-teens.[4] Readers, less aware of the complexities of literary subjectivity than writers as readers, had even earlier begun to equate author and "author." As Lotman writes: "Almost all of [Nikolai] Karamzin's [1766–1826] works were perceived by readers as the immediate autobiographical disclosures of the writer."[5]

As we look at these notions, several caveats apply. First, the idea that one lives as one writes and writes as one lives has a classical pedigree (hence Batiushkov's Latin maxim from Seneca, who, in turn, identifies it as a Greek proverb). Moreover, this concept had been propagated in relation to the elegy already by the seventeenth-century classicist poet Boileau ("C'est peu d'estre Poëte, il faut estre amoureux [...] Il faut que le coeur seul parle dans l'élégie" [It is too little to be a poet, one must be in love [...] The heart alone must speak in the elegy]).[6] Second, we can note in these statements the general emphasis on living as one would write. A coherent image of the writing precedes the ordering of the life, not the other way around.[7] This, in fact, makes much sense in the Romantic (or proto-Romantic) context, in which, to generalize, life was to reflect artistic ideals, rather than art life's quotidian realities.[8] However, still in the Sentimentalist vein, the moulding of life (and with it writing) is bound up with what are seen as universally desirable positive qualities – virtue, wholesomeness, sensitivity, a good heart.[9] We thus remain at a notable remove from Romantic individuality. Moreover, there was some doubt within the poets' circle whether the self-image prescribed and projected in their writings indeed fit the reality of the poet's inner world.[10]

At the same time, this nascent expressive subjectivity was strongly mediated by the system of genres, with its correlation of genre and mood. It was only through the totality of the poet's work in several genres that that the writer's soul could be adequately expressed.[11] This milieu was the birthing ground of Alexander Pushkin's talent, and we will see that particularly this latter aspect impacted his own understanding of the poet's sincerity.[12]

From Pushkin's ability to convincingly inhabit different perspectives and subjectivities (his proverbial "Proteanism"),[13] to his simultaneous, radically opposing projections of the same object or theme,[14] from the ("conservative") continuing pull on him of eighteenth-century literary modalities and genre-consciousness,[15] to his ("progressive") literary-biographical myth building,[16] a bounty of evidence militates against attempts to read a direct, or unconstructed, sincerity into Alexander Pushkin's poems.[17] At the same time, Pushkin could be a highly effective purveyor of the sincere voice, as, among other things, a plethora of naïve and non-naïve biographically inflected readings of his poetry attest.[18] Boris Gasparov remarks that "Paradoxically, it is precisely Pushkin's 'literariness,' his total immersion in the verbal, intonational, stylistic, and image-driven movements from which the poetic work arises, that makes possible the authenticity and personal concreteness with which his social and emotional experience, individuality and life circumstances find expression in his poetry."[19] In part, what follows will be an attempt to demonstrate how this paradox operates.

The extent to which a freedom from any convention of literal sincerity continued to operate in Pushkin's circle as late as the 1830s is attested with particular eloquence in a text by Prince Pyotr Viazemsky. Viazemsky ends the poem "Predestination" ("Predopredelenie"), published with Pushkin's implicit imprimatur, if not necessarily agreement, in the memorial 1832 issue of *Northern Flowers* (*Severnye tsvety*), with what sounds like a veritable anti-sincerity manifesto. Poetry is immediate, but discoupled from any self that exists prior to or outside of the creative process, any "authenticity" of emotion that would be guaranteed through its relation to such a self:

Над ним [поэтом] минутного влиянья
Всесилен роковой закон:
Без думы, скорби иль вниманья
Поет, страдает, любит он.[20]

(Over him [the poet] the fateful law
Of ephemeral influence is all-powerful:
Without thought, mourning, or attention
He sings, suffers, and loves.)

At the same time, Pushkin himself hardly saw his art as detached from his world view. His writings were indeed a playground of multiplicitous and stereoscopic perspectives, but not of infinitely varied and arbitrary values. He wrote to Viazemsky,

Why do you bemoan the loss of Byron's notes? To hell with them! Thank god they're lost. He confessed himself in his verse, unwittingly, taken with the ecstasy of poetry. In cold-blooded prose he would have lied and schemed, here trying to impress with sincerity, there sullying his enemies [...] Leave curiosity to the crowd and be with genius.[21]

The great poet's human essence, then, is expressed unwittingly and inexorably in the collectivity of his works, despite a multiplicity of masks (a prominent feature of Byron's poetry). Pushkin's works, we can infer, are also, collectively, an expression of his self, just not a direct one.[22]

The mature Pushkin seems to locate the artist's sincerity in contradistinction to the demands of Sentimentalism and Romanticism and in the totality of the artist's character, interests, moods, and modes:

> For those who love Catullus, Gresset, and Voltaire, for those who love poetry not only in its lyric transports and in the doleful inspiration of the elegy, not only in the expansive creations of drama and epic, but also in the playfulness of jest [shutka] and in cerebral amusements inspired by lucid gaiety – sincerity is precious in the poet. It is pleasant for us to see the poet in all states, [all] transformations of his mercurial and creative soul: in sorrow and in joy, in the soaring of ecstasy and in the respite of feelings – in Juvenalian outrage and in petty annoyance at a tiresome neighbour …
> I am awed by the creation of *Faust*, but I love epigrams etc. ("V[asily] L[vovich] P[ushkin]'s Trip," 1836)[23]

Pushkin is, at first glance, provocatively idiosyncratic here, but he is not inconsistent. Beyond an expected dismissal of sincerity in drama and epic (cf., however, on Byron above), he reserves his greatest scepticism regarding sincerity for "lyric transports [poryvy]" (i.e., a central modality of Romantic poetry) and the "doleful inspiration of the elegy." The target is unsurprising, given that these were the forms of literary expression most popular, and most abused, in his own poetic heyday and, at the same time, those with the greatest pretence to the immediate expression of personal emotion and experience.[24] At the same time, he forcefully underscores that wit and humour (along with, presumably, a generous dose of irony) are components for him of sincere expression.[25] He names as exemplars of sincerity Voltaire, with his elegantly playful and subversive burlesque *The Maid of Orleans* (*La Pucelle d'Orléans*, 1730–62?) and Jean-Baptiste-Louis Gresset, author of the witty and ribald *Ver-Vert, or The Voyages of the Parrot of Nevers: A Heroic Poem* (*Ver-Vert, ou, Les voyages du perroquet de Nevers: poème heroïque*; publ. 1734), and "The Cloister" ("La Chartreuse," 1734), which influenced the Arzamasian friendly epistle.[26] The inclusion of Catullus shows us that Pushkin reads and understands him independently of Romantic fashion (as innovator of genuine love poems), reads him entire, with his unflinchingly coarse epigrams, elegant mythological poems, compositional sophistication, inside jokes, and banter.[27]

This approach, this taste, one might say, as regards sincerity, puts Pushkin distinctly on one side of what I have described above as two ideal poles in the conceptualization of sincerity.[28] On the one side are those who tie sincerity (or authenticity) to earnestness, candour, unfettered emotion, in some periods, particularly the laying bare of the darkest corners of the soul – i.e., to the poetic confession. On the other are those who feel that poetic sincerity demands and is implied in the full range of expression of the human voice as well as its subtlest modulations. For the former, irony is a destructive force that challenges sincerity. For the latter, irony can become an undercurrent of the sincere voice. For the latter, the emotional excesses and, often, the unbending seriousness of former can sound histrionic or staged, to the former, the artistic distance practised by the latter can at times sound aristocratic, aloof.

In what follows, I will examine in Pushkin's works not biographical sincerity (the pursuit of which is futile) or avowals of sincerity (and their potential ideological and rhetorical inconsistencies), but rather the sincere voice, which is the "audible" result of a purportedly successful encoding, or "performance," of sincerity by the poet, whether intentional or not, and irrespective of whether or not it is in fact biographically sincere. To this end, I will explore the functioning of one complex (multidimensional) compositional/stylistic device, to which Pushkin appears to have turned, consciously or unconsciously, in order to engender a sincere voice in his lyrics of the 1830s.

A resonantly sincere voice, I will argue, emerges in strangely similar ways in two poems by Pushkin from the 1830s, which grow out of radically different genre traditions.[29] Both betray a certain pattern – a sudden flash of sincerity or immediacy, in other words, of what feels to the reader like a momentary revealing of a "true" Pushkin from behind masks of artistic perfection and protean elusiveness, and which is constructed as a counterpressure or release from a preceding accumulation of traditional imagery and phraseology.

The first example is Pushkin's late elegy, "For the shores of a distant homeland" ("Dlia beregov otchizny dal'noi," 1830). Note that the elegy as a genre is pulled between an imperative to express strong feeling (i.e., to be at least *outwardly* sincere) and a strong inertia, despite a breadth of theme and quite meaningful artistic evolution over the first quarter of the nineteenth century in terms of plot, emotional register, and phraseology.[30] The second example comes from Pushkin's "I have erected myself a monument not made by human hands" ("Ia pamiatnik sebe vozdvig nerukotvornyi," hereafter, "Monument," 1836). A monument or "capstone" poem broadly speaking is first and foremost a poem of self-positioning, and hence does not easily lend itself to immediacy. The fact that these poems represent contrasting poetic modes – elegy and Horatian ode – makes the compositional and technical similarity to be demonstrated particularly curious.

¹ Для берегов отчизны дальной   For the shores of a distant homeland
² Ты покидала край чужой;   You abandoned a foreign realm;
³ В час незабвенный, в час печальный   In an indelible hour, an hour of sorrow
⁴ Я долго плакал пред тобой.   Long before you did I cry.
⁵ Мои хладеющие руки   My numbing hands
⁶ Тебя старались удержать;   Tried to hold you back;
⁷ Томленье страшное разлуки   The terrible langour of parting
⁸ Мой стон молил не прерывать.   My moan implored you not cut short.

⁹ Но ты от горького лобзанья   But from the bitter embrace
¹⁰ Свои уста оторвала;   You wrested your lips;
¹¹ Из края мрачного изгнанья   From a land of dreary exile
¹² Ты в край иной меня звала.   You called me to another land.
¹³ Ты говорила: «В день свиданья   You said: "On the day of [our] meeting
¹⁴ Под небом вечно голубым,   Beneath an eternally blue sky
¹⁵ В тени олив, любви лобзанья   In the olives' shade, kisses of love
¹⁶ Мы вновь, мой друг, соединим».   We'll again, my friend, conjoin."

¹⁷ Но там, увы, где неба своды   But there, alas, where the firmament
¹⁸ Сияют в блеске голубом,   Glistens with sky-blue sheen,
¹⁹ Где [тень олив легла] на воды,   Where [the shade of olives has fallen] on waters,
²⁰ Заснула ты последним сном.   You fell into your final repose.
²¹ Твоя краса, твои страданья   Your beauty, your suffering
²² Исчезли в урне гробовой –   Vanished in the burial urn –
²³ А с <ними> поцалуй свиданья …   And with <them> the kiss of meeting …
²⁴ Но жду его; он за тобой …[31]   But I wait for it; you owe it still …

As is well known, the first two lines of this poem had initially read: "*Для берегов чужбины дальной / Ты покидала край родной*" (For the shores of distant *foreign region* / You abandoned a *native* land). Pushkin's biographer Pavel Annenkov called the reversal "much harder to explain" than a revision to the opening of "Under the blue sky of her native land" ("Pod nebom golubym strany svoei rodnoi," 1826),[32] while Pavel Shchegolev, in a questionable biographical reading, contested the traditionally posited addressation of the poem to Pushkin's Odessa flame, the Austrian-Italian Amalia Riznich, arguing that the change was made to camouflage a secret, true addressee, a conclusion also reached by Georgy Makogonenko.[33] Modest Gofman, followed by Mikhail Bakhtin, in an unfinished early essay, and Samson Broitman, have seen here, instead, a shift in perspective (from *his* to *hers*).[34] All these reactions are impacted, I will suggest, by a common, at times perhaps not wholly conscious desire not to see in this strikingly penetrating poem a questionable change of addressee.[35] That the latter set of authors is stretching to justify the "shift in perspective" is indicated 1) because it is quite unnatural to say in Russian "Ty pokidala krai rodnoi" (You abandoned [your?] native land) about a woman who is returning to her homeland, 2) because Pushkin had already, in 1826, conceived this geography from *Riznich*'s more effectual perspective, and 3) because Odessa, where Pushkin and Riznich parted, though the most pleasant and urbane of Pushkin's places of exile, was "krai rodnoi" (native land) to neither. Skirting this argument entirely, we can note that even before these changes the poem functioned as a renewal of a particular prototypical elegiac plot.

Consider what appears to be Pushkin's initial conception. In the earliest extant version of the poem, we already find the lovely architectonic structure highlighted by Bakhtin. It can be paraphrased as: parting (ersatz death) → [leading to] the promise of a kiss (thwarted); [then] death → [leading to] an ersatz kiss (to be paradoxically realized).[36] At the same time, we find a partial regendering of that archetypal situation most concretely rendered in the parting scene from Konstantin Batiushkov's 1811 "Elegy from Tibullus. A Free Translation" ("Elegiia iz Tibulla. Vol'nyi perevod").[37] There Tibullus, the male poet, is departing:

[...] Час гибельный настал,

И снова Делия, печальна и уныла,

Слезами полный взор невольно обратила

На дальный путь. Я сам, лишенный скорбью сил,

«Утешься», – Делии сквозь слезы говорил;

«Утешься!» – и еще с невольным трепетаньем

Печальную лобзал последним лобызаньем.[38]

([…] The mortal hour arrived,

And once more Delia, sorrowful and downcast,

Reflexively turned her tearful gaze

To the long road (ahead). I myself, robbed of strength by grief,

"Be consoled" – said to Delia through tears,

"Be consoled!" – and then with uncontrolled trembling

Kissed my sorrowful one with a final kiss.)

Batiushkov-cum-Tibullus's poem, which, like Pushkin's elegy, contains an embedded idyll, also ends with a scene of *imagined* reuniting, next to which Pushkin, in his copy of *Essays in Verse and Prose* (*Opyty v stikhakh i proze*, 1817), wrote "Prelest'" (Delightful).[39]

In Pushkin, however, it is the heroine who departs, rather than the hero, and it is the heroine, not the hero, who offers consolation, though, at the same time, the hero's tears, his fading (cf. "lishennyi skorb'iu sil" [robbed of strength by grief; Batiushkov] and "moi khladeiush-chie ruki" [my numbing hands; Pushkin]) and his final "lobyzan'e" (kiss) are retained. Even in this initial version of Pushkin's poem, the architectonic structure and regendering represent a significant poetic *zamysel*, a concept worthy of development.[40] However, it was Pushkin's sparse but subtle changes to the draft that allowed the unchanged final words to sound with the ring of tangible sincerity they now enjoy.

Two potentially contradictory impressions hold sway as we read the final version – acceptance of the poem as a fully formed and highly potent lyric statement and, when we look closely, a recognition of its remarkable concatenation of elegiac (and idyllic) formulas. How does the poem retain its resonance for non-naïve readers despite these elegiac clichés, and what purpose do they serve? I will posit that, here, they do more than just provide a system of ready semantic/emotional resonance.[41]

The opening change, which turns a gender reversal within a prototypical elegiac situation into a truly new emotional-situational framing (the bewailing of the *woman's* departure, and not of her exile, but her *return home*) is, I would assert, enough to set the reader feeling that we have here something new, specific, personal, allowing the reader to enjoy the artistic beauty with which the elegiac situation is developed without particularly questioning its relevance in regard to an actual life.[42]

After this, the force of literary cliché in the poem traces an arc of traditionality that first intensifies and then abates – from the innovative opening lines (1–2) through the moderate cliché used by the lyric persona in lines 3–12, to the beautiful, but static and traditional, idyllic formulas of the heroine's direct speech (lines 13–16),[43] and then back to the hero's animated transformation of the same images in elegiac, rather than idyllic, mode in lines 17–19,[44] and, after a redux of elegiac formulas in lines 20–2, to escape from elegiac cliché in lines 23–4,[45] and finally, a leap into a whole new element in the final half line.

The poem's posthumous 1841 publication in the almanac *Dawn* (*Utrenniaia zaria*) with the typically elegiac one-word title "Parting" ("Razluka") underscores the extent to which Pushkin's contemporaries sensed its identity as elegy. Note the following elegiac topoi, which are reproduced: memory and sorrow (l. 3); appellation to an addressee with free-flowing, sincere, and potent feeling (ll. 4, 8); [death]/fading/illness of the hero (l. 5); pained parting and a bitter or bittersweet kiss (ll. 7, 9); an inversion of the "pathetic fallacy" (ll. 17–20);[46] the all-swallowing grave (ll. 21–2).

The heroine's words in lines 13–16 (together with some elements contributed in their transformation below – the shine of the heavens, the waters) can be compared to a number of idyllic and quasi-idyllic passages from Batiushkov's elegies. Consonant images occur in several contexts, including a general one ("Ni krotkii blesk lazuri neba" [Not the meek shine of the azure of the sky] from "Awakening" ["Probuzhdenie," 1815?]);[47] the Russian South ("Pod nebom sladostnym poludennoi strany" [Under the sweet sky of a Southern land] from "Tauris" ["Tavrida," 1815]);[48] Italy ("Лазурь и пурпуры безоблачных небес, / Вы, тополы, вы, древние оливы" [Azure and crimson of the cloudless heavens, / You, poplars, you, ancient olive trees]; "Pod nebom sladostnym Italii moei" [Under the sweet sky of my Italy] both from "The Dying Tasso" ["Umiraiushchii Tass," 1817]);[49] and Elysium. The latter is represented in passages from "Elegy from Tibullus" ("vechnyi mai mezh roshchei i polei" [eternal May among the groves and fields]; "shum biiushchikh vod" [the sound of beating waters])[50] and "Elysium" ("Elizii," 1810) ("Долу, к тихим берегам […] Там, под тенью миртов зыбкой, / Нам любовь сплетет венцы" [Down, to the quiet banks/shore […] There, in the dappled shade of myrtles, / Love will braid us crowns]).[51]

One may also fruitfully compare the heroine's promise, particularly in its aspect of eternity/stasis ("Pod nebom *vechno* golubym") to Friedrich Schiller's "Elysium," with its "Ewiger Mai" (eternal May; cf. Batiushkov), reuniting of true lovers after death, and their ensuing "ewig Hochzeitfest" (eternal wedding feast).[52]

The heroine's words thus, even allowing for Mediterranean olive trees in the place of myrtle, do not simply represent idyllic cliché, or even a clichéd vision of Riznich's Italy, but contaminate this latter topos with an allusion to the Elysian idyllic topos of the elegy.[53] This layer of allusion functions as more than just a harbinger of the heroine's death and foreshadowing of the true nature of the meeting. It also serves to underscore the figmental, static, and conventional nature of her imagining of the meeting.

For, both emotionally and stylistically, the words in quotation marks can hardly represent a living woman's speech – even, it seems, the speech of one who has read far too many elegies and idylls.[54] Any true voice the heroine may have had is clearly lost to the pursuit of poetic perfection. (The evocative power of these sparse images and the musicality of the phrasing is indeed extraordinary.) At the same time, it is the *emotional paucity* of the heroine's beautiful promise that sets off as a foil the unexpectedly meaningful hope for repayment in the final lines.

Broitman senses a transcending of elegiac cliché in these final lines. He locates this in well-noted rhythmic irregularities, but also in the stylistic change from "lobzan'e" to "potsalui" (both, kiss).[55] "Potsalui," however, while stylistically neutral rather than marked, was used by the elegiac poets,[56] and Pushkin himself uses these words as synonyms in contiguous lines.[57] "Potsalui svidan'ia" (the kiss of meeting) is, moreover, a subtle poetic trope, a form of metonymy. So this would not seem to be the source underlying Broitman's entirely valid impression.

The seemingly minor changes Pushkin made to these lines on the draft assure that no hint of awkwardness or hesitation will distract from the final three words.[58] In the original version, the line "No sladkii potsalui svidan'ia ..." (But the sweet kiss of meeting ...) had been too corporeal[59] and, together with the ensuing "Ego ia zhdu; on za toboi ..." (It I await; you owe it still ...) lacked the syntactic cohesion and flow of the final version. In addition, the inversion in this latter line was slightly infelicitous (*ego* [*it*] as opposed to what?).

The final version – "А с <ними> поцалуй свиданья ... / Но жду его; он за тобой ..."[60] – corrects these inadequacies. Moreover, the easing of the syntactic break between the lines has the effect of accentuating the syntactic break before the final three words. A reversed foot sets these words apart, almost like a line break. (Such a foot is far more common in Russian iambs in line initial position, as in lines 3 and 13 above.)[61] Stylistically, this final three-word phrase is particularly "non-poetic." The concept of a debt upon which this usage is based is, after all, an unpoetic concept. Dictionaries give almost exclusively prosaic instances. What can be *za kem-nibud'*? Examples include *rubl'*, *nedoimok, delo, mazurka, otvet* (a rouble, arrears, [next steps in a] matter, a dance, a reply), in a satirically prosaic moment in Griboedov's *Woe from Wit* (*Gore ot uma*, completed 1824) – a card debt; in Pushkin's prose, famously – *vystrel* (a gunshot).[62] Here, it is particularly the concreteness of the debt (the kiss she promised and had almost violently broken off) that is underscored and which plays off the not-this-worldly context in which it is to be paid.

Beyond stylistics, however, the poem's success is strongly bound up in the "pragmatics" of this phrase within the world of the poem. In deep contrast to the consolatory, but coolly detached words of the "heroine," this slightly playful but poignant intonation is appropriate between lovers. It gathers a particular freshness and emotional intensity in that it is directed not only to the departed, but to the deceased. Moreover, lines 17–22, though written in the second person, are made up of narrative exposition that can be directed towards the heroine (who is presumably aware of the circumstances of her death) only as tribute. In contrast, lines 23–4 seem spoken to and for the heroine. Unlike the preceding lines, they communicate new information, a new "take" on events and the promise. Because of this contrast, the reader has a sense, here, of sudden access to the hero and heroine's private interaction.

Finally, the belief in an afterlife projected here is anything but doctrinal or conventionalized. (Cf., in our definition of the sincere voice, "truths ... personally ... interrogated or lived.") The last thing we imagine, despite the Edenic images of the heroine's invitation, is an embodied meeting in a Dantean Christian paradise or sentimentally imagined Elysium.[63] In any case, we are not asked by the poem to envision a material paradise or, in fact, to believe in the reality of the kiss ourselves. Rather, the lyric persona's belief is a priori personal, an expression of his inimitable individual feeling, and in the subtle logic of the final line, it is the fact of the heroine's debt that inspires his belief: "*No* zhdu ego; on za toboi ..." (*But* I wait for it; you owe it still ...).

In the poem's three final words, the "otherworldly" (the concept) combines organically and unexpectedly with the casually intimate (the style) to draw us from the stable dichotomies of the elegiac world view upon which Pushkin has so far played in his various rearrangements and inversions, and bring us, instead, into a realm of experiential transcendence. The extent of the lift that we experience together with the hero is dependent both on the depth of the resonantly and unexpectedly personal emotion of the final words and the ballast of elegiac clichés which is instantly heaved off.

Like "For the shores," which recasts elements of the elegiac tradition, "Monument" begins with significant revisions to the Horatian/ Derzhavinian model – primarily, ode 3.30 ("Exegi monumentum ...") and "Monument" ("Pamiatnik," 1796) – made from within that model's plot structure. Feinberg and Proskurin's analyses, for instance, demonstrate the extent to which Pushkin is able in the first stanza to compact a monstrously complex network of meaningfully intersecting cultural references into a very few words, boldly contrasting his legacy with that of Tsar Alexander and, in general, worldly power and glory, and inscribing into the cultural paradigm of the poetic "monument" a personal and contemporary context.[64] We may add that, if Derzhavin's monument, like Horace's, is ersatz architectural – imagined as a physical structure though it is immaterial – Pushkin's is an ersatz monument with a human face. This human face emerges implicitly as a contrast (in one possible reading) to the face of Tsar Alexander, according to legend sacrilegiously sculpted on the angel atop the pillar on Palace Square; through the "glavoiu nepokornoi" (insubmissive head) by which Pushkin's monument exceeds the pillar in stature – a *head*, which naturally ought to carry a face, and a character trait – *nepokornyi* – which puts a "face" onto it; and finally, through the epithet attaching to the monument itself – *nerukotvornyi* (not made by human hands), which carries with it as an echo the indelible image of Spas Nerukotvor[en]nyi (Saviour Not Made by Human Hands), that striking form of icon that is precisely a disembodied face.[65] Derzhavin's opening stanza, in comparison, is almost entirely impersonal and differs quite insignificantly from that of Horace.

The middle stanzas, however, contrast with this bravura opening. Formally beautiful, they can seem surprisingly untelling in terms of Pushkin's legacy. Here, despite a number of revisions accommodating to his needs the Horatian/Derzhavinian ur-text ("доколь в подлунном мире / *Жив будет хоть один пиит*" [while in the sublunar world / *A single poet lives*], the adapted – though functionally analogous – accomplishments of the fourth stanza), Pushkin follows particularly closely the conventions of the "microgenre" to which the poem belongs.[66] As Lev Pumpiansky notes, no other literature was able to generate a monument poem that would stand at the centre of a modern cultural tradition.[67] This in and of itself speaks to Pushkin's remarkable creative achievement. At the same time, the wide-ranging readings that attempt to make sense of the middle stanzas, and particularly stanza 4, speak to their problematic status as the heart of Pushkin's legacy poem.

Lines 5–6 and 9–12 hew particularly closely in their topoi to Derzhavin's "Monument" and "Swan" ("Lebed'," 1804) and their Horatian sources (Odes 3.30 and 2.20), while the arguments surrounding stanza 4 betray a range of bewildered reactions to Pushkin's choices:

И долго буду тем любезен я народу,
Что чувства добрые я лирой пробуждал,
Что в мой жестокой век восславил я Свободу
    И милость к падшим призывал.[68]

(And long will I be loved by the people,
That I aroused with my lyre meritorious/good feelings,
That in my cruel age I glorified Freedom
    And called for mercy on the fallen.)

To wit: Is this vision of Pushkin's legacy the semi-ignorant opinion of the "people," which Pushkin rejects (as Mikhail Gershenzon argues), or, again, the opinion of the people, who have their own measure of what is important in poetry and with whom Pushkin on some level agrees (as Vladimir Solovyov contends)? Is this a shift to a future perspective, as Pumpiansky finds, in which "no one will care about 'new sounds'" (from the draft version)? Why did Pushkin's long-standing and frequently expressed resistance to demands for social utility in poetry change here (Solovyov and Gershenzon)? And why did Pushkin switch to the utilitarian "chuvstva dobrye" after having ("firmly and without the usual [thick] corrections," according to Semyon Vengerov) written "zvuki novye" (new sounds)? Isn't this a "rejection of self" (samootritsanie), even artistic "suicide" (Alexander Evlakhov)? Might Pushkin even be ironic here? Could the whole poem be a parody of Derzhavin's text (Vikenty Veresaev)?[69]

Or perhaps we should simply decide (along with Mikhail Alekseev and others) that Pushkin is being perfectly – and uncharacteristically – straightforward here.[70] Sergei Bondi gives the finest apology for the fourth stanza. He unsurprisingly ties "vosslavil ia Svobodu" (I glorified Freedom) to the importance for the Decembrists of Pushkin's revolutionary poetry and writes of "chuvstva dobrye" (meritorious/good feelings): "It would take an analysis of all of Pushkin's poetry to confirm the impression from Pushkin's poetry as a whole, clear, it seems to me, for every serious and sensitive reader, of a feeling of a special profundity, truth and grace [svetlost']."[71] Most impressive is his analysis of the topos of mercy for the fallen in Pushkin's works from 1826 to 1836, which is as thorough and compelling as Gershenzon's and Solovyov's elucidations of Pushkin's rejection of demands for the utility of art.[72] At the same time, however, Bondi's great receptivity to the Pushkin of stanza 4 leaves him indisposed to the final stanza, which he finds superfluous: "Everything is already said [...]" [sic!].[73]

Whatever we feel about these arguments, it is hard to argue against the fact that stanza 4, on its own, provides a foreshortened image of Pushkin's legacy. Granted, there were good reasons, poetic and pragmatic, for the changes in the manuscript. In comparison even to Horace's "Aeolian song," not to mention Derzhavin's "zabavnyi slog" (amusing style), which is so precise and capacious in regard to his stylistic innovation that it is used today as shorthand in literary scholarship, the draft version, "zvuki novye" (new sounds), is strikingly nondescript. Also, in the line "Chto zvuki novye dlia pesen ia obrel" (That I found new sounds for songs), the rhyme-mandated Slavonic, high-style pronunciation of *obrel* harmonizes with archaic elements of the poem's odic style but could introduce a hint of incongruousness.[74] "I milost' k padshim prizyval" (And called for mercy on the fallen) was also far more precise and evocative (particularly of "Stanzas" ["Stansy," 1826]) than "Miloserdie vospel" (Sang mercy), which can sound like the memorializing of a ruler's past act, rather than a calling of the ruler to conscience. In addition, David Bethea's framework for looking at Pushkin, which incorporates a potential anxiety before Derzhavin as a man of deeds and poet of deeds, may help explain why he chose to highlight these socially oriented aspects of his legacy here.[75] And yet, in total, these central three stanzas can seem awkwardly suggestive of the Soviet Pushkin, the sanitized Pushkin of the jubilees.

The final stanza is quite different, departing even more radically than the first from Horace and Derzhavin:

> Веленью Божию, о Муза, будь послушна,
> Обиды не страшась, не требуя венца,
> Хвалу и клевету приемли равнодушно,
>   И не оспоривай глупца.

> (Be obedient, o Muse, to God's instruction,
> Not fearing insult, nor demanding [laurel] crown,
> Accept praise and slander with indifference,
>   And don't dispute a fool.)

The kernel of Pushkin's development is present in the end of Horace's poem: "[…] sume *superbiam* / quaesitam meritis" (lit., assume the pride [haughtiness? aloofness?] by merit procured).[76] In Mikhail Lomonsov's translation, this was already "vzgordisia" (be proud); in Derzhavin – "возгордись […] И презрит кто тебя, сама тех презирай" (be proud […] And whoever shall disdain you, disdain them yourself).[77] This aloofness, conveyed in a single word's secondary connotations by Horace, becomes the heart of Pushkin's stanza. But Pushkin's aloofness relates not only to his critics, but also to those who laud him. In his most radical departure from the ur-plot, he tells his muse to neglect entirely the laurels that are the heart of Horace and Derzhavin's closings (and of which he is already certain): "ne trebuia ventsa."[78] "Pushkin 'undoes' Derzhavin by turning his proud sentiments inside out," writes Bethea, also underscoring the "hint of pride" that goes along with these "three imperatives of acceptance" and the way that this pride is, in the end, "miraculously, indistinguishable from Christian humility."[79] All this represents a radical departure from and complication of Derzhavin/Horace.

The poem follows a pattern now familiar from "For the shores." After a potent and quite original opening and then a series of formally perfect, but perhaps insufficiently personal statements, a personal voice begins to break through (the final stanza). Then, in the poem's final words, we experience a leap into a new element, a new degree of *personal*, which at the same time only gestures at a more authentic, more unmediated inner life. For, at the same time, in harmony with the aloofness Pushkin claims here for his muse, he shuts down any confessionality in this very moment of sudden self-revelation: "I ne osporivai gluptsa" (And don't dispute a fool).

In addition to its intonation, which is built upon aphoristic brevity, mild rudeness, and emotionality, all characteristics distinguishing it from the preceding three lines, as in "For the shores," there are formal elements that set this final line apart. Like the fourth line of each preceding stanza, it is a short iambic tetrameter line.[80] In addition, a mild rhythmic dissociation is experienced when we set the final rhyme in the context of the preceding syllables (ne trebuia ventsa-ne osporivai gluptsa).[81]

The personalizing effect also relates to this line's semantics. The terseness, self-assurance, but also boldness implied in Pushkin's decision to forgo a more positive, directly self-flattering ending,[82] the centredness this implies, particularly on the backdrop of consonant elements, for instance, in "To the Poet" ("Poetu," 1830) and "From Pindemonti" ("Iz Pindemonti," 1836), are palpably evocative of Pushkin, at the least the Pushkin we think we know, the "Pushkin" that Pushkin has created and left for us.

Alexander Zholkovsky's analysis of Pushkin's invariants, and particularly the highly characteristic invariant structure he calls "prevoskhoditel'nyi pokoi" (roughly, aloof calm, the calm of [achieved] superiority), can help us better understand why the impression of "Pushkin's" presence is so powerful in this final stanza, despite the traditionality of the topos.[83] The invariant situation "prevoskhoditel'nyi pokoi" implies a victorious elevation (stasis) over the fray, over the passions, conflicts, and contradictions (motion) that seek to embroil (and in the past embroiled) the lyric subject (or other figures/objects to which this condition is imputed). Both the opening and closing stanzas of "Monument" present clear examples of different facets of "prevoskhoditel'nyi pokoi."[84] Because this situation runs as a leit-motif, developing organically and in manifold variations throughout Pushkin's works, readers of "Monument" who are familiar with these works cannot help but sense that the relation to the world implied in these stanzas was part of Pushkin's personal truth, a truth deeply interrogated through art. For those familiar with the poet's biography, which Pushkin himself sets into complex play with the literary record,[85] this appears also to be a truth interrogated through life – in the crucible of literary polemics and in the face of social indignity, personal smears, and the injustice of Pushkin's reduced status as a writer in the public opinion not only of enemies, but of associates, in the 1830s.

Could one then conclude, perhaps, that what I call the sincere voice is really an illusion, a misapprehension of what is better characterized as the aura attaching to invariant elements of Pushkin's "Poetic World," i.e., his creative identity? It seems not. Embodiments of the poet's invariants emerge in every manner of genre and context, and, of course, not every realization betrays a pointedly sincere intonation. And still, particularly for a poet like Pushkin (or Derzhavin, or Mandelstam, or Khodasevich), one who falls on that side of the sincerity divide where integrity of vision outweighs confessionality, harmony with the author's invariants can be an important component of the emergent aura of the sincere voice.

Lydia Ginzburg, in her article "Pushkin and [Vladimir] Benediktov," notes Pushkin's simultaneous, differing public and private (i.e., within his circle) stances on that poet's work.[86] Here, in one poem, we have the impression of Pushkin working in two modes, public and private – not in the sense that the last stanza contains private information, but in the sense that it seems crafted for and addressed to self, that the implied audiences differ, even if the real ones do not.[87] In addressing himself – and not just formally, through the stand-in of his "genius," the muse – Pushkin reveals himself, despite his much-remarked protectiveness in regard to his private sphere, or at least gives us the sense that he does.

As we have seen, in both "For the shores" and "Monument," the final phrase

1) represents a personal truth, the persuasiveness of which is linked not to its being universally accessible or accepted, but to the sense that it is interrogated or lived by the poet;
2) is set off and accentuated syntactically, stylistically, and through other formal means, and can thus be seen as a single "verbal gesture";
3) is marked by an unconventional (given the literary/genre context) and, at the same time, unexpectedly apropos and intimate intonation; and
4) because of a shift in implicit audience, can be experienced, together with its immediate context, as a moment of sudden access on the part of the reader, following more traditionally oriented ("public") passages.

In addition, the composition of the two poems, despite their radical divergence in terms of genre and the stylistics thus implicated, follows a common arc from the individual to the traditional and genre-dependent, back to the individual and finally into a new quality of voice. This creates initial "buy-in" on the part of the reader in terms of the poem's relevance to an individual life as well as cultural resonance and, at the same time, importantly, a store of traditionality, on the backdrop of which the radical departure of the final lines and then the final phrase can be adequately perceived.

We may argue about whether the voice that emerges in these closing phrases is an example of resonant sincerity, and for whom. Sincerity is, after all, mutable and code-dependent. However, there is little question that the phrases *resonate* and that what underlies their potency is an isomorphic complex of poetic devices. I believe it possible to call this isomorphic complex of devices a method and the resulting intonation an example of Pushkin's highly successful inscribing in his poetry of a sincere voice.

In "Monument," however, Pushkin achieves not simply a sincere voice, but the simultaneous projection of sincere *voices* seemingly at odds with one another and speaking to divergent reader groups. To illustrate above the workings of that sincerity device in my own opinion most central to the poem's functioning, it was necessary to maintain a single, coherent "reader code." This I have done, to the best of my ability, with one exception – the paragraph where the floor was given to Bondi. Bondi and Alekseev (both highly competent readers) see the fourth stanza in a teleological context powerful enough to represent a differing cultural code. This is a context in which the poet's open shift from a professed rejection of utility to an evaluation of poetry based on its positive impact in the world would be seen as a moment of triumphant personal growth revealed.

One might surmise that readers likely to align most closely with our main reading would be less prone to express themselves in ways that implicate the sincerity of the poem, confirming a perception of a sincere voice.[88] Still, it is telling that, while Alekseev and Bondi see the poem's culmination occurring in stanza 4, other historical readers (whom I am not identifying with my own specific reading) find precisely that stanza problematic, or "public," in tone and apprehend the author's personal perspective rather in stanza 5. The circumspect and thorough Pumpiansky, in a text never prepared for print, while setting this latter stanza in the context of Pushkin's agonizing social and literary position in the 1830s, suddenly exclaims – "O heartfelt beloved, o best of men, who can relate your suffering!" [O serdechnoliubimyi, o luchshii iz liudei, kto skazhet tvoi stradaniia!].[89]

It is, moreover, possible to anticipate, if not confirm, yet another reader code relevant to and engaged in "Monument." This is a code specific to Pushkin's circle. Analysis of key subtexts relevant to these readers leads us off in another direction, implying a different, but complementary, potential locus of the poem's personal voice and, hence, sincerity. A brief analysis of the poem from this perspective can be found in the appendix – "Another Vista on Pushkin's 'Monument.'"

2 ROMANTIC CHARISMA AND THE MATERIAL TRACE (DMITRY VENEVITINOV)

With this [letter] you will find [some of] Dmitry's poems. You know that he often felt the necessity to express himself in verse, or rather – to turn every minute of life into poetry. This is why there is such an abundance of his small poems. The poems I am including no one has but me. He wrote one of them while greeting the New Year at my place [...]

V.F. Odoevsky, letter to M.P. Pogodin[90]

In Dmitry Venevitinov (1805–27), readers in posterity have a curious example – not the only one of course – of traces of what might be called a Romantic charisma without the body of poetic masterpieces it portended. Venevitinov died exceedingly young, before reaching his twenty-second birthday, and after his death contemporaries commonly saw him as a poet who had not yet realized his potential for greatness, but who certainly would have. We find this view expressed more or less explicitly, for instance, in the foreword his friends wrote for the first, poetical, volume of his *Works* (1829; foreword dated 1827) as well as Nikolai Polevoi's review in *Moskovskii Telegraf* (1829) and Nikolai Nadezhdin's review of the second volume in *Teleskop* (1831).[91]

Lydia Ginzburg sees Venevitinov's posthumous reputation as a Romantic poet par excellence largely as the not disinterested work of friends and colleagues. She points out a deep debt in his poetry to the elegiac tradition of the eighteen-teens and twenties; he writes, she notes, in a language of worn, monovalent "poeticisms." According to Ginzburg, those close to Venevitinov came to his poetry with a particular "literary mindset" and were thus able to read a German philosophical Romanticism out of hints that laced his poetry. The broader readership, however, recognized him instead as an elegiac or meditative poet of the Pushkin-Baratynsky school.[92]

If Venevitinov failed to overcome the phraseological burden of the elegiac tradition, he nonetheless made an uncommonly powerful impression on those with whom he came into contact. He was the intellectual and creative nucleus of the Moscow circle of Liubomudry (Lovers of Wisdom), enthusiasts of German Romantic philosophy. Pushkin, while polemicizing with Venevitinov's aesthetic positions in "There is a wondrous rose" ("Est' roza divnaia: ona," 1827) and "Poet" (1827),[93] clearly esteemed him and agreed to actively collaborate with Mikhail Pogodin and the former Liubomudry, who disbanded after the Decembrist uprising, on a journal that Venevitinov championed, the *Moscow Herald* (*Moskovskii vestnik*).[94] "He is a wonder, not a person; I am in awe of him [blagogoveiu]," wrote Fedor Khomiakov, soon after becoming Venevitinov's housemate.[95] Petr Pletnev recalled that "throughout the winter Venevitinov spent in Petersburg, he was the most intriguing novelty, the gem, the dear guest in every company where intelligence, talent or social success are valued."[96] Venevitinov's death, by all accounts, was acutely mourned.[97]

I hope to find a material trace of the Romantic charisma that attached to Venevinitov in the draft of the poem Odoevsky mentions in his letter. First, however, it will be necessary to unravel Venevitinov's *conception* of sincerity, as overtly and implicitly expressed in his poems. I will argue that it was a meaningful overlap (though not of course equivalence) of Venevitinov's personal identity with the ideal image he expounds that makes it possible for his close friends to recognize in good faith his authenticity as "Romantic" poet, with all the implications for sincerity this entails.

The concept of sincerity presented in Venevitinov's poems and reinforced in his image as Romantic poet posthumously projected by his friends is quite starkly opposed to Pushkin's and gravitates to the opposing, "expressive" pole of sincerity. This concept represents a given "taste" in sincerity and also implies a certain "code" for identifying it, for reading it out of situations and poetic works. For Venevitinov, in contrast to Pushkin, sincerity is built around intensity and high seriousness, as well as an ideal of immediacy and unconstructedness.

Thus, where Pushkin values vocal range and modulation, Venevitinov inclines to intensity and force of emotion and expression. (As we will recall, this latter quality was a key element of the ode of Lomonosov and his followers against which Derzhavin had productively rebelled in the 1780s.)[98] Where Pushkin values humour and playfulness, the multiplicity of tone reflective of the multifaceted individual, Venevitinov champions seriousness. Where Pushkin sees the author's identity mediated through multifarious genres and poetic contexts, visible only "willy-nilly,"[99] and appears to have meticulously crafted the moments of palpable sincerity discussed in the previous section, Venevitinov sees the true poet's creativity as a direct and immediate expression of inner experience. The unsubtle way in which these attitudes are at times conveyed in his poetry makes him a particularly excellent exemplar of certain stereotypically Romantic ideas about sincerity that were circulating at the time.

Thus, Madame de Staël, a key popularizer of German Romantic aesthetics, asserts poetry's perpetual lofty seriousness: "The enigma of human destiny is nothing to the generality of men; the poet has it always present to his imagination"; "In order to conceive the true grandeur of lyric poetry, we must wander in thought into the ethereal regions"; "[…] to jest is to descend."[100] In his 1800 Preface to the *Lyrical Ballads*, William Wordsworth, who is not likely to have directly influenced the Germanically inclined Venevitinov, famously and pithily refers to the poet's "spontaneous overflow of powerful feelings."[101] But similar sentiments were expressed already by a precursor of the German Romantics, J.G. Sulzer:

> When the poet is in a state of enthusiasm, his "thoughts and feelings irresistibly stream out in speech," and he "turns all his attention to that which goes on in his soul; forgets the outer circumstances which surround him …"[102]

These qualities – an elevated seriousness (in contrast to society), disinterestedness regarding audience and the afterlife of the poet's verse, immediacy of expression – are clearly modelled in Venevitinov's aptly titled "Poet" (1826). The poet is "son of the gods," in whose eyes shines the "limpid ray of lofty thoughts." He looks with calm upon the "miasma of [material] pleasures," the "fickle youth, / The raving cry, immodest laughter, and unbridled happiness" that swirl around him in society. Only very rarely does he let slip a "fleeting smile." "The quiet genius of contemplation / Has set from birth / The seal of silence on his lips." However,

> Когда ж внезапно что-нибудь
> Взволнует огненную грудь, –
> Душа *без страха, без искусства,*
> Готова *вылиться* в речах
> И блещет в пламенных очах.[103]

> (When suddenly something
> Stirs [his] fiery breast –
> [His] soul is ready *without fear, without art,*
> To *pour itself out* in speech
> And flashes in [his] ardent eyes.)[104]

The poet does not, in the moment of creativity, fear the judgment of others or the potential inadequacy of his own speech. He is unconcerned with artistic perfection.[105] Rather than actively form his experience into an aesthetically polished work, he values the immediate expression of his emotional "transports" (poryvy).[106]

"Poet" presents an idealized figure.[107] The biographical Venevitinov hardly sat in company – at least the company of friends – with the "seal of silence on his lips," though he did have some distaste for high society, its values and its entertainments, and he would often become, according to contemporaries' impressions, reticent, with a "sad smile."[108] Indeed, he writes in a letter to his brother Aleksei from late 1826 or early 1827 that he has clammed up since leaving Moscow.[109] According to housemate Fedor Khomiakov, he was occupied exclusively with poetry and work late that fall.[110] He was also, however, a relentless and effective organizer for the *Moscow Herald* that winter, using social visits to bring many Petersburg writers into the fold. And at least at one point during his five months in Petersburg, Venevitinov got into "the full swing" of Saint Petersburg social life, "paid visits, went to soirees and balls."[111] During this last year of his life, Venevitinov tried his hand at a few epigrams (perhaps under the influence of Pushkin), and, before leaving Moscow in 1826, he composed no less than a vaudeville skit for the name day of a woman of whom he was deeply and hopelessly enamoured – the talented, older, married, and involved with another princess Zinaida Volkonskaya. Even so, Venevitinov felt the need to write a sanguine, but serious, even primly intoned poem to friend Fedor Skariatin excusing his foray into such a lowly genre.[112] "Poet" is written in the third person and doesn't insist on an equality between the ideal "poet" and the poem's humanly fallible author – not that the dots would not have been connected by readers, who were bound to see it as a statement of Venevitinov's own principles.

The importance of sincerity within Venevitinov's system of aesthetic conceptions is conveyed in his insistence on the truth value of poetry and on poetry's ability to infectiously communicate feelings, the content of the poet's inner world. The success of poetry, attested in "Poet and Friend" ("Poet i drug," 1827), lies in the ability to agitate the mind of a fervent youth in dream[s] and show the old man in "unfalse works" (trudy nelzhivye) the "imprint of the soul" (dushi pechat'). At the same time, however, we should note that the "something" that stirs in the poet's "fiery breast" in "Poet," while true to his soul, is not yet representative of what will become in other Romantics a forceful personal "authenticity," an identity of self at all moments with an immutable inner core.[113] This "something" stirring is not "invented," it has objective

value, and it must be linked to feelings rooted in the poet's nature.[114]
However, in consonance with the Romantic precept of "unconscious"
creation, the receptive poet, like "a nightingale," lets his creativity fol-
low transitory and externally influenced moods and stimuli:[115]

И струны верные мои
С тех пор душе не изменяли.
[…] И беглым мыслям простодушно
Вверяюсь в пламени стихов.

(From thence my faithful strings
Have not been untrue to my soul.
[…] And I simpleheartedly entrust myself
To transitory thoughts in the flame of verse.)[116]

This conciliation of momentary impulse and personal core is well en-
capsulated by Fedor Khomiakov, who calls the series of poems Venevi-
tinov wrote in November and early December 1826 "as if his journal,
expressing always his *true* [istinnye], *passing* [minutnye] feelings."[117] A
kindred ethos is elegantly expressed by Percy Bysshe Shelley: "Man
is an instrument over which a series of external and internal impres-
sions are driven, like the alternations of an ever-changing wind over an
Aeolian lyre, which move it by their motion to ever-changing melody.
But there is a principle within the human being and perhaps within all
sentient beings, which acts otherwise than in the lyre, and produces not
melody, alone, but harmony […]."[118]

Similarly, the difficulties of composition have not crystalized
for Venevitinov into what may be called the Romantic language
conundrum – a belief in the inadequacy of words to the expression of
the inner life.[119] A version of this dilemma had been conveyed quite
forcefully in the West by Byron, in *Childe Harold's Pilgrimage*, Canto III,
XCVII (publ. 1816), and in Russia, in Zhukovsky's programmatic poem
"The Inexpressible" ["Nevyrazimoe," 1819], the latter, however, only
published in an almanac in 1827, the year of Venevitinov's death.[120]
Venevitinov, rather than experience the inadequacy of language to ex-
press the inner life as an immutable, unavoidable impasse, believes in
the power of inspiration and genius to overcome the difficulty, as we
see in his "Solace" ("Uteshenie," 1826). It is clear from this poem both
that Venevitinov believes in the power of the *inspired* word to ad-
equately communicate feeling and that he does not place himself in
the category of those "Promethean" geniuses who can actively seize
and pass the flame, for whom such expression is a regular occurrence.

Rather, he has an expectation, or better, a belief, taken entirely on faith, that he has been given at least a modicum of the gift and that he too will one day pronounce the potent, fiery word which can ignite his reader's breast in co-experience.

To these components of Venevitinov's optimistic Romantic version of poetic sincerity, seriousness of purpose and intensity of experience are an implicit corollary. Outside of them, the Romantic does not experience the transport required to adequately and infectiously express his feelings. For this, genius/inspiration is required. However, genius is absent in the composition of lower, humorous forms. As Venevitinov remarked about his vaudeville: "[…] ne genii / Moei dushoiu obladal" (not genius / Possessed my soul).[121]

Venevitinov's unbending seriousness of purpose and commitment to the lofty world of poetic fancy, implied already in "Poet," is perhaps most clearly stated in "Sacrifice" ("Zhertvoprinoshenie," 1826 or 1827). In the face of the "insidious siren" of life, which threatens health, happiness, and contentment, the poet insists:

> Но не отымешь ты, поверь,
> Любви, надежды, вдохновений!
> Нет! их спасет мой добрый гений,
> И не мои они теперь.
> Я посвящаю их отныне
> Навек поэзии святой
> И с страшной клятвой и мольбой
> Кладу на жертвенник богине.

> (But, believe [me], you won't take away
> [My] love, hopes, inspirations!
> No! My beneficent genius [spirit of personal inspiration] will save them,
> Nor are they mine now.
> I dedicate them henceforth
> Forevermore to sacred poesie
> And with terrible oath and with pleading
> Lay them on the altar of the goddess.)

The intended meaning is clearly that Venevitinov will sacrifice the love, hopes, and inspirations that ought to fill his still very young life to the "goddess" of poetry, rather than bringing them to fruition within the world – a terrible oath. His "plea" must be that the poetry he creates is worthy of the "goddess" and that his hope in his personal, "beneficent genius" is not misplaced. Otherwise, the Romantic's experience will find no refuge in the eternity of poetry; the sacrifice of *life* will have been for naught.

Mikhail Lunin wrote about the politically engaged oppositional aristocrats of his day, the Decembrists: "They renounce life and *through this attest to* the veracity of their charge [pravdivost' svoego poslaniia], the truth of their convictions [nachal] and the legitimacy of their authority [vlasti]."[122] Venevitinov purports to perform a similar operation. Renunciation of life becomes the high road to authority, in poetry as in politics – a trump card in the pursuit of sincerity and authenticity.

M.H. Abrams finds the Romantic taste for "intensity" deriving ultimately from Longinus's concept of the sublime, with its component of "vehement and inspired passion."[123] Thus, for Coleridge, "'Passion must be [the] Soul of Poetry," while Keats wrote that "'The excellence of every art is in its *intensity*'" and that "Poetry should surprise by a fine excess [...]."[124] Venevitinov had clearly, very early on, reached a similar conclusion. In an 1825 article devoted in part to a defence of the new Romantic mode ("A Critique of Mr. Merzliakov's Essay" ["Razbor rassuzhdeniia g. Merzliakova"]), he wrote:

> Our poetry [i.e., contemporary Romantic poetry] may be compared with a powerful voice, which, crying out from on high to the heavens, awakens echoes on all sides and is strengthened in its surge [poryv].
> [...] [The poetry of Goethe, Byron], as if a torrent, rushes to the infinite [...][125]

In Venevitinov's poetry, this intensity and volume can be observed nowhere better than in the sonnet "To you, o pure Spirit" ("K tebe, o chistyi Dukh," 1824 or 1825):

> *Греми надеждою, греми любовью, лира!*
> В преддверьи вечности *греми его хвалой!*
> И если б рухнул мир, затмился свет эфира
> И хаос задавил природу пустотой, –
> *Греми! Пусть сетуют* среди развалин мира
> *Любовь с надеждою и верою святой!*[126]

> (*Thunder with hope, thunder with love*, [my] lyre!
> On the threshold of eternity *thunder with his praise*!
> And if the world should fall, the ether be eclipsed
> And chaos strangle nature with [its] void –
> *Thunder*! [Then] from the wreck of the world
> *May love and hope and sacred faith voice their complaint*!)

Even allowing for youthful exuberance, it is quite remarkable that Venevitinov finds it possible to combine the verb "gremet'" ([lit.] thunder, clatter, resound) with love and hope.[127]

"To you, o pure Spirit," together with another sonnet of 1824 or 1825 ("Calmly my days flowered in life's vale" ["Spokoino dni moi tsveli v doline zhizni"]) and Venevitinov's 1825 "Epistle to R<ozhali>n" ("Poslanie k R<ozhali>nu"), represent the height of the poet's idealist Romantic verse. In these latter two poems, elegiac cliché is employed, but to describe crises transpiring, it seems, wholly in the landscape of the mind.[128] In the next stage of his poetic development, which will take place primarily in Saint Petersburg, events and crises will presume a locus in the real world, and, together with this shift, Venevitinov will turn to a "quieter," if still intense, "lyre" for self-expression.[129]

In their beatifying "Foreword," Venevitinov's friends echo him in emphasizing his unabating seriousness, intensity, and the free expression of deep feelings:

> "[…] his very life […] was none other than a succession of poetical feelings and impressions"; "[…] despite the gaiety, even abandon with which he often gave himself up to a fleeting disposition of spirit, his character was entirely melancholic"; "[…] everywhere [in his verse] is visible the outpouring of free feeling"; "But this feeling was deep: he tried to retain forever within himself all momentary transports of the soul and in himself alone sought the answer to all riddles of existence"; he has "an ardent heart, flaming only for the beautiful."[130]

Given that, for Venevitinov's circle, these are qualities which underlie sincerity, it is unsurprising that they go on to assert that

> Readers will find in his works the *imprint* of a beautiful, elevated soul. The faithful mark of a true talent is that *sincerity*, that *lack of pretense* with which he *gives himself up to his persuasions* [svoim vnusheniiam] and *pronounces these*. This sincerity is not subject to doubt in the works of Venevitinov […][131]

However one-sided, however exaggerated his friends' portrait, however circular (drawing upon Venevitinov's self-presentation) and however simultaneously traditional it may have been (shadowing the iconography of other familiar young, unrealized geniuses like Alexander Petrov and Andrei Turgenev),[132] however, in addition, useful this image may have been in the late 1820s to their literary and journalistic polemics, it is impossible to conceive the cult of Venevitinov – friends gathered on the day of his death for twenty-five years – as well as contemporaries' reactions to the poet, without positing at least some kernel of truth.[133]

Somehow, Venevitinov, without being a Keats or a Shelley or a Mickiewicz, which is to say, without producing poetry of genius, had to meaningfully evoke for them an *authentic* Romantic inspiration, which entailed and was indivisible from truth, and sincerity.[134] Clearly the spark of intelligence and talent that marked everything Venevitinov undertook – philosophy and its popular exegesis, translation, criticism, poetry, pictorial art, and music – was important to his contemporary reception.[135] Perhaps also the portents in his poetry of his, as it turned out, imminent death made a deep impression on contemporaries.[136] But I will argue that there was something more – a charisma growing out of an authenticity in the role of Romantic poet – and that, moreover, we can locate the material trace of this charisma.

As elsewhere in this study, I am most concerned with the successful *performance* of sincerity. In regard to Venevitinov, however, this performance does not so much rest on the success of a lasting inscription of the sincere voice in the poet's chosen words. These words are indeed unsatisfying in the sense noted by Ginzburg, and, in fact, roughly diagnosed by Venevitinov himself not long before his death.[137]

We can still, however, attempt to recover the physical trace or artefact of that charismatic presence which validated for Venevitinov's companions the authenticity of his poetry as a whole as a work of Romantic creation. The site for our "excavation" will be the poet's draft of "<On the New Year (1827)>," the text of which Vladimir Odoevsky sent in his letter to Pogodin (see figure on p. 73). The draft is housed in Odoevsky's archive at the Russian National (Public) Library in Saint Petersburg and would appear to have been left with Odoevsky, or at any rate, in his apartments, at the end of the New Year's celebration in question.[138] The details of the physical appearance of the draft aid its words in conveying qualities that harmonize with Venevitinov's description of the ideal (Romantic) poet and his friends' posthumous description of Venevitinov himself. These qualities include the fluency and unredacted nature of the artistic process (intimating the presence of inspiration); the embeddedness of the Romantic poet within, but separate from, the life that surrounds him as well as the seriousness of the "poet's" thoughts and preoccupations and the intensity of his experience.[139]

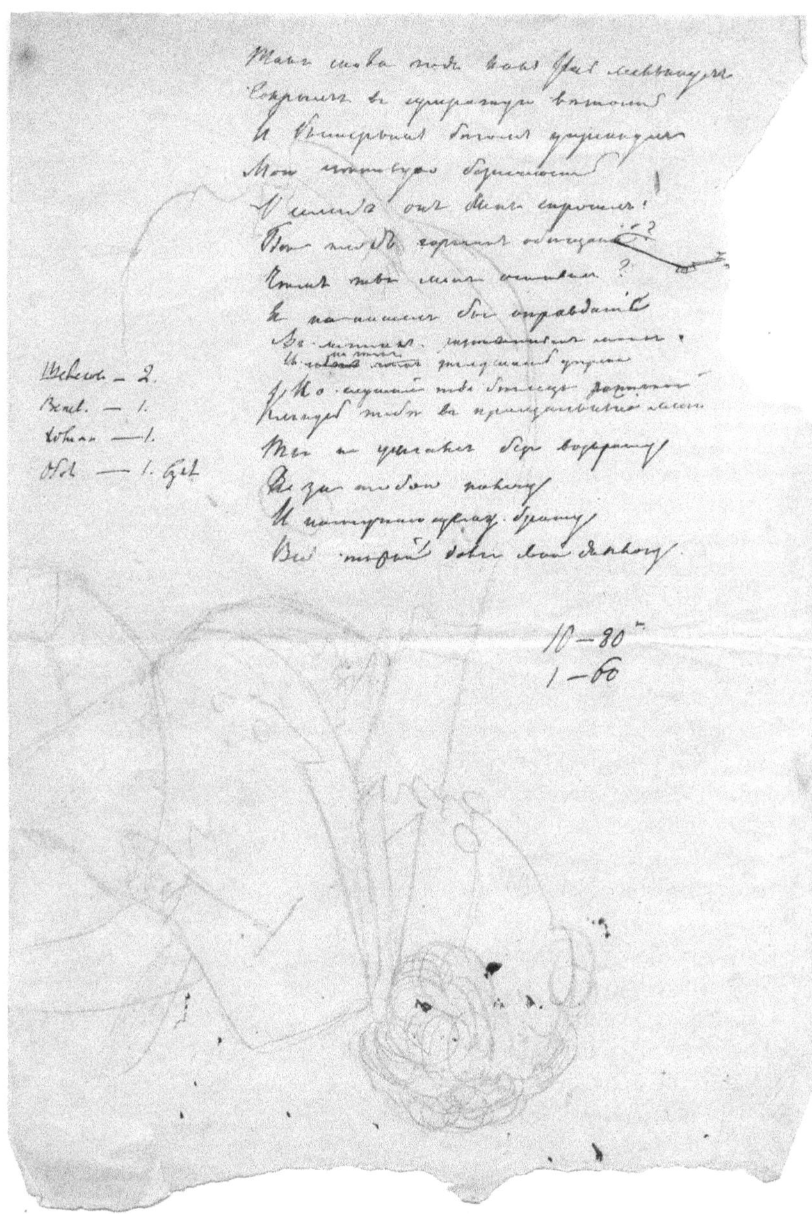

Autograph of Dmitry Venevitinov, "<On the New Year (1827)>" ("So another year<,> like a shade<,> has flitted past"). Manuscripts Division, Russian National Library (Saint Petersburg). Archive of V. F. Odoevsky, f. 539, ed. kh. 1484.

Here is the text of the poem:

<На Новый (1827) год>[140]
Так снова год<,> как тень<,> мелькнул<,>
Сокрылся в сумрачную вечность<,>
И быстрым бегом упрекнул
Мою ленивую беспечность<.>
О<,> еслиб он меня спросил:
Где плод горячих обещаний?
Чем ты меня остановил?
Я не нашел бы оправданья
В мечтах рассеянных моих<!>
И не чем заглушить упрека<!>
Но слушай ты<,> беглец жестокой<!>
Клянусь тебе в прощальный миг<:>
Ты не умчался без возврату<,>
Я за тобою полечу
И наступающему брату
Весь тяжкий долг свой доплачу.
          <Полночь на I-е Января>

(<On the New Year (1827)>)
So another year<,> like a shade<,> has flitted past<,>
Shrouded itself in gloomy eternity<,>
And with its swift stride rebuked
My lazy blitheness<.>
O<,> if it were to ask of me:
Where is the fruit of your hotheaded promises?
What did you do to halt me?
I would find no vindication
In my scattered dreams<!>
I have nothing to mute the rebuke<!>
But listen you<,> cruel fugitive<!>
I swear to you in the instant of parting<:>
You have not dashed off without return<,>
I will fly after you
And to [your] advancing brother
Pay to the last my whole grave debt.
          <Midnight of the 1st of January>)

It has been an unspoken axiom within this book that the manner
in which a poet's words approach their final form is not significant

to their sound.[141] There is, however, a context where the manner in which the poem is formed is of relevance. This is when the pragmatics of the work is linked to the situation of its becoming. "<On the New Year (1827)>" is such a poem. In its themes, it is unremarkable, a typical elegiac pondering of the frustration of a year too quickly passed. However, the date provided in the initial, posthumous publication – "Polnoch' na 1-e Ianvaria" (Midnight of the 1st of January) introduces a radical claim. It is as if the poet's thought process occurs precisely at midnight, even as if the poem is formed during the striking of the clock. This identification is reinforced in the poem's text as Venevitinov makes his oath "v proshchal'nyi mig" (at the parting instant) and calls 1827 the passing year's "nastupaiushchii brat" (looming/advancing brother), a designation impossible once the hour has fully struck. These phrases force us, if we are to take the date seriously, to read the poem as completed at midnight in a feat of "sympathetic magic." Moreover, the text of the poem repeatedly references speed ("god [...] mel'knul" [a year flitted past]; "bystrym begom" [lit., quickly running]; "Chem ty menia ostanovil?" [What did you do to halt me?]; "beglets zhestokoi" [cruel fugitive; lit., one who has run away]; "ty ne umchalsia bez voz-vratu" [you have not sped off without return]; "Ia za toboiu polechu" [I will fly after you]).

This speed is echoed in the artefact of the poet's draft, in light of which the poem's precipitous formation, presumably shortly before midnight, seems not so unlikely. On a sheet of paper with two torn, uneven edges, situated above and at 90 degrees to a well-executed pencil caricature and covering an incomplete one, we see the poet's draft in ink. Judging by the handwriting, a relative calm with which the opening lines were penned gives way to greater speed, and, in some places, the words begin to look like a cardiogram. (Note esp. "остановилъ"; "разсѣянныхъ моихъ.") After lines 1–8, the poet apparently dropped down to create a new strophe, beginning from the forceful "Klianus'" (I swear). However, as he developed his thought further, this original ninth line, which, as expected, introduced a new rhyme, fell outside of the rhyme scheme. The finished second thought, which occupied five lines, ended up rhyming eFgFg. That this happened in the "heat of creation" is corroborated by the eF, which would have continued the less common MFMF alternating rhyme used in the opening stanzas. Lines 1–8 and 12–16 together form a complete thought and did not necessarily require any addition. All of this was put on paper with no corrections other than, possibly, that in the word "opravdan'ia" (vindication; changed from the plural incited by the rhyme scheme) and maybe a brief false start in line 14.[142]

At this point (or some later point, though this seems unlikely, given that the draft remained with Odoevsky), the poet ameliorated his rhyme scheme by interpolating three new lines following line 8. This is clearly a later insertion as the characters are smaller and the vertical spacing tighter in order to fit the three lines into the space between the two existing strophes. Venevitinov makes this completion in fine form. The new line 9 ("V mechtakh rasseiannykh moikh<!>" [In my scattered dreams<!>]) continues the thought of line 8 across the boundary between quatrains, both expanding it and making it more concrete. In any case, no tension at all is perceived with the preceding line. It also seems natural, though not predetermined, that this line rhymes with the old line 9 (ultimately, line 12) which had been calling out for a rhyme partner. The remaining space is then filled with a couplet, generating a central quatrain of encircling rhyme. Line 11 ("No slushai ty<,> beglets zhestokoi<!>" [But listen you<,> cruel fugitive<!>]) more forcefully introduces the final lines' apostrophe of the departing year (in lines 1–8 – "on" [he/it], not "ty" [you]) and ties in quite naturally to the following "Klianus'" (I swear). Line 10 is the only one in which a phrase is crossed out and rewritten above (though this change too is a very minor one, from "нет чѣмъ" to "не чѣмъ"). This emendation perhaps indicates a waning of the poet's inspired state.[143] The poem is further integrated into its physical context and time-space by the multiple stray ink marks with which the poet speckled the bottom of the page in his haste.

So far I have commented primarily on what appears to be the poem's fluidity of composition. The poet's intensity and seriousness are inscribed in the poem's text and pragmatics. Rather than give himself up to enjoyments typical of the New Year, the poet spends his final minutes on highly self-critical introspection. (A more practically minded person could, after all, have made the case that he had hardly spent the year in vain – working to birth a new, potentially influential journal with Pushkin's extensive participation, starting a job at the Ministry of Foreign Affairs in Petersburg, and writing, that fall, more and higher quality original poetry than ever previously.) Intensity is conveyed in the poem's augmenting comparisons and epithets: *kak ten'*, mel'knul; *sumrachnaia* vechnost', *bystrym* begom, *lenivaia* bespechnost'; *goriachie* obeshchaniia; mechty *rasseiannye*; beglets *zhestokoi* (flit by *like a shade*; *gloomy* eternity; *quickly* running; *lazy* blitheness; *hotheaded* promises; *scattered*, or *idle*, dreams; *cruel* fugitive). It is also conveyed in a series of forceful verbs (mel'knul; [the slightly archaic and thus elevated] sokrylsia; upreknul; zaglushit' [flashed past; shrouded itself/vanished; rebuked; muffle/drown out]) and particularly in the poet's remonstrations (*slushai ty* [...] / *Klianus' tebe* v proshal'nyi mig [*listen you* [...] / *I swear to you* in the instant of parting]). But more than anywhere, Venevitinov's seriousness and intensity combine in the final line: "Ves' tiazhkii dolg svoi doplachu" (Pay to the last my whole grave debt). This last line has been read too literally as a reference to the uncompleted work that Venevitinov undertakes to make good on in the coming year.[144] The tone, however, is so intensified by the three emphatic qualifiers (*ves'*, *tiazhkii*, *do*plachu) that it would bridge almost on the comical if we are to take the line as a typical New Year's resolution to be more productive. Particularly in light of the verb "doplachu" (pay *to the last*), "ves' tiazhkii dolg" (my whole grave debt) begins to sound like the life itself that has been lent the poet. We are not, in fact, remiss in reading it this way. A similar mood emerges in Venevitinov's final preserved letter, written a week before his death to Mikhail Pogodin:

> Lately, self-doubt has weighed upon me. It is difficult to live when you've done nothing to deserve your place in life. One has to do something good, lofty, and one can't live and do nothing.[145]

The context for this doubt can be inferred further along in the letter, where Venevitinov remarks:

> I heard Lensbern at the Stroganovs'. He played Beethoven's opus 31, no. 1.
> The adagio of this sonata seized me, subdued me, shook me with the strength of its vast persuasion [vozdeistviia]. [...]
> I find no words – this is power.
> I envision this genius as an immeasurable quantity [neob"iatnaia velichina]. It seems to me that this great wonderworker will present the world an example of the majesty of the singular individual [chelovecheskoi lichnosti].[146]

While Venevitinov does not explicitly compare himself to Beethoven, it is clear that his great receptivity and equal ambition have run aground of the luminaries of Romantic art. Rational or not, the debt Venevitinov feels he owes in his New Year's poem is a work of true genius or, if he does not have the means to pay, life itself.

From the depths of this internal drama it is an abrupt transition to the biographical and social context of Venevitinov's poem, which also emerges from and is symbiotic with the draft. The greeting of the New Year, in the poem, is allegorized in the concept of an implicit accounting and the explicit paying of debts. On the draft, below the poem on the right-hand side, we see the figures "10 – 80" and directly below them "1 – 60," which can perhaps be read as some sort of accounting or score (whether in money or in some other "currency"). To the left of the poem, also in pen, we see four scribbled abbreviated names, which can be deciphered as [D.P.] Shelekhov, Venev[itinov], [F.S.] Khomiak[ov] and [V.I.] Obol[enskii]. After the first appears a dash and then a numeral 2 and a period. After the others, dash, numeral 1, period. After the final period is written "vzial" (took [it]). These markings likely refer to promises Venevitinov exacted that evening from co-revellers to submit work for the *Moscow Herald*.[147] While these particular markings pragmatically reference the concept of a debt – Venevitinov records himself among the three whose promises remain IOUs – they also gesture at a broader, not fully recorded human collectivity that surrounds the poet.

The young poet finds himself on the eve of the new year in the company of friends. And these friends are potential witnesses to his feat of well-timed and hotly paced creativity, demonstrating an intensity and inner seriousness in counterpoint to the New Year's milieu.[148] In this context, the poem, together with its draft, becomes, for the poet's friends and advocates, supporting evidence in the mythologizing of Venevitinov as Romantic poet.

The draft, moreover, materially substantiates the poem's implicit pragmatics. It is crucial to the integrity of Venevitinov's oath ("Klianus'") that it is given at this particular moment. His first sacrifice, *the earnest of his oath's fulfilment,* is that he steps away from the camaraderie of the New Year's celebration to engage in serious and self-critical reflection, and to write poetry.

The draft itself is thus "performed" (whether consciously or not) by Venevitinov, collected and conceptualized by Odoevsky, the most likely author of poem's date. And we see that the date, "Midnight of the 1st of January" – added to the poem in publication – becomes a verbal stand-in for the physical artefact of the draft and the living witnesses that attach to it, none of which can be transferred simply or cleanly to the printed page.

So, while it is true that a Romantic mindset and an understanding of the philosophical context to which Venevitinov appeals aided those close to him in reading out of his poems a Romantic world view (Ginzburg), the closest readers also had access to a type of information only obliquely registered in the poet's works themselves. They had access to charismatic performances of poetic creation that, within the high-Romantic world view, become the guarantee of the poet's inspiration, and hence authenticity. Ironically, the fact of the poet's self-doubt, by raising the plank to which his vision aspires, could only make this identification more convincing.

The role of Romantic poet, as conceived by Venevitinov, brought with it a whole complex of concepts about creativity ultimately implicating the poet's sincerity. In order for his sincerity to be "decoded," Venevitinov needs to pull only on one end of a chain – authenticity as Romantic, underscored by inspiration, seriousness, and intensity. For those who know him and share his preconceptions as well as for those infected by their vision, this makes the other end, sincerity, shimmer.

3 Romantic Sincerities II: Late-Romantic Sincerities

1 DISARMING THE BYRONIC HERO (MIKHAIL LERMONTOV)

Among Russian poets of the first half of the nineteenth century, Mikhail Lermontov was perhaps uniquely fascinated with and sensitive to issues of sincerity and theatricality. His complex relation to the sincere is visible, among other places, in his 23 December 1834 letter to Maria Lopukhina, which presents a deeply tangled play of self-analysis, posing, irony, and confession, crowned by the phrase "Please write to me, dear friend […] as I think myself to have been sufficiently sincere [assez sincère], sufficiently submissive in this letter to make you forget my crime of injury to [our] friendship."[1] Lermontov thus playfully eviscerates the idea of sincerity as an absolute quality, underscoring his feel for its performativity and relativity.

In Ginzburg's reading, Lermontov was the first major poet in the Russian tradition to forge a comprehensive lyric and life persona.[2] He was also perhaps the first poet in the Russian tradition not simply to struggle at times with the challenges and pitfalls of sincerity, but to place the problem of sincerity at the centre of his world view, to make it an ethical issue that cannot be elided.[3] This is not to say that Lermontov struggled always to be or seem sincere; indeed, it was often quite the opposite, as any reader familiar with his works and life – his extra-literary persona and the personae of his literary doubles – is aware. It is hardly surprising, then, that Lermontov's poetic "sincerity" was polarizing, with conflicting views expressed or implied by readers about one and the same text.[4] And yet, one can trace within Lermontov's poetry a distinct trajectory towards more compelling artistic modes for expressing sincerity.

David Powelstock, in his extensive study *Becoming Mikhail Lermontov*, lays out signposts of a long march towards poetic "authenticity," including the following:

1 The need – of which the exceedingly young author of tritely Byronic lyrics and long poems was quite cognizant – for a biography that could support his works' nebulous but passionate claims and their vague prophecies of scandalous notoriety.[5]
2 Lermontov's not entirely successful attempts to create a platform for a public "authenticity" through transgressive behaviour in society in the mid-1830s.[6]
3 The emergence of a supportive biography with the scandalous success of the fiercely accusatory poem on the death of Pushkin in 1837 and Lermontov's subsequent imprisonment and exile,[7] his publication of rhetorical/oratorical poetry reinforcing this public image.
4 And finally, the need to reconcile the "public authenticity" that had arisen on the basis of these rhetorical poems and his public biography with a "private authenticity" satisfying to the author himself and the more discerning reader. Powelstock links Lermontov's reconciliation of these two "authenticities" particularly to the establishing of intimacy with this more discerning reader.[8]

Building upon this platform, I will highlight the following constellation of factors shoring up a sincere affect in Lermontov's mature lyric poetry:

1 A biographical "pedestal."[9] Lermontov built a biography that could be the envy of a Byronic poet. It included speaking truth to power, persecution by the State and a degree of ostracization by high society, imprisonment, exile, battle on the front lines, duels, and seductions. At the same time, the heatedly rhetorical "public" poems, which formed the initial basis for Lermontov's notoriety, established for Lermontov's reading audience, through their function as "poem-deeds," a biographical link between author and works. Yet, as Powelstock notes, biography could be a hindrance, tying the poet to a public image since outgrown and no longer suiting his private sense of authenticity.
2 Verbal charisma. This charisma was embodied both in the heated rhetoric of the "public" poems, composed primarily towards the beginning of Lermontov's mature period, and in a sensitive, intimate, and often exquisitely and subtly musical mode that is experienced as the flip side of this rhetorical stridency in poems like his 1839 "Molitva" (Prayer).[10]

3 Versatility. In contrast to the copious early works, written from 1828 to 1832, the poems published and written in the final five years before Lermontov died in a duel in 1841 show quite a broad range of tone, type, and voice. They present Lermontov's formerly "Byronic" hero[11] not claiming a sensitive side, but demonstrating it in seductively intimate and quiet verse as well as being playful with close associates, generating a new type of "ballad" embodying lower-class voices, etc. From the standpoint of sincerity, this diversity of tone potentially opens Lermontov's poetry up to new readers who fall further towards the "Pushkinian" side of our divide and find sincerity underscored in the expression of a broader range of emotion and mood.[12]

4 Disarming the self – disarming the reader. "Antisocial" Byronic individualism could be expected to "arm" many readers against the poet, while the trenchant "public" poems were spoken from the voice of, and left room for solidarity with, an exceptional group of the like-minded, a concurring "we."[13] The final poems, however, time and again "let down their guard" in a way that can mutually "disarm" the "broader" reader.[14]

5 Deep thought and the breaking of cultural matrices. This can be linked to our definition of the sincere voice as one that expresses truths about self and world not as a function of their being universally accessible or accepted, but in a manner that demonstrates their being personally experienced, interrogated, or lived.

This heterogeneous cluster of elements and strategies engages almost all levels of the sincerity paradigm developed in this book, from pragmatic ("disarming") and biographical framing (biographical pedestal) to poetic devices (underlying verbal charisma and "disarming"), semantic developments supporting our definition of the sincere voice ("earned" truth), and a shift in implied conceptualization of sincerity from thoroughly first-pole ("expressive") sincerity to a more moderate position incorporating some elements of second-pole ("modulated") sincerity. It is not surprising that the cocktail could be a potent one. My primary goal, in my own analysis below, will be to illustrate how Lermontov activates the final three of these strategies: disarming of the self as a means of disarming the reader; deployment of a more versatile voice; and the breaking of established cultural matrices in a demonstration of "earned" truth. First, however, I will turn to some issues raised by Lermontov's rhetorical voice.

Lermontov's rhetorical/oratorical style, which fully emerged in "The Poet's Death" ("Smert' poeta," 1837) and provided the foundation for the poet's initial notoriety in this poem and others, like "Meditation" ("Duma"), "Poet" ("Poet") and "Believe Not Yourself" ("Ne ver' sebe"), is characterized by a focus on the expressive potentialities of the word to colour the phrase, rather than precise semantics; the piling up of tropes, which could countermand one another, but again lent expressive force; and a shift, in general, away from the word as centre of gravity to the period, which drew the reader constantly forward by means of its complex syntax and delayed semantic completion.[15] We can observe this style in Lermontov's brazen "epilogue" to "The Poet's Death":

> А вы, надменные потомки
> Известной подлостью прославленных отцов,
> Пятою рабскою поправшие обломки
> Игрою счастия обиженных родов!
> […] напрасно вы прибегнете к злословью –
> Оно вам не поможет вновь,
> И вы не смоете всей вашей черной кровью
> Поэта праведную кровь![16]

> (And you, arrogant descendants
> Of fathers notorious for infamous baseness,
> Who with slavish heel trampled the wreckage
> Of families wronged by the play of fortune!
> […] in vain will you turn to slander –
> It will not help you anew,
> And you will not wash away with all your black blood
> The poet's righteous blood.)

We may surmise that this type of poetic statement (here, accusing certain elements of Russian high society of complicity in Pushkin's fatal duel against Georges d'Anthès) was highly compelling as a sincere voice for a certain subset of readers, both because of a return to emotional intensity as a key indicator of sincerity (never, it is true, wholly abandoned by the "archaists," aesthetic opponents of Pushkin's "circle," in the 1820s) and, particularly, because of the breaking of social and political taboos. Moreover, since such public and "frank" speech was potentially, and in Lermontov's case factually, accompanied by real-world consequences, such a poem becomes a verbal deed, inherently the act of the poet *as person*.[17] And such deeds have the effect of cementing an equality between poet and speaker that can then bleed into the reception of the poet's other lyrics. In these poems, Lermontov does not so much speak in a "human" voice as imply a human speaker using his or her voice in its rhetorical capacity.

In fact, this sense of sincerity is unexpectedly akin to that which, according to Pogosian, dominated the early eighteenth-century Russian ode. Emotional intensity and, somewhat paradoxically for the modern reader, "correct," which was to say state-sanctioned, political sentiment were the key outward indicators of this pre-modern "sincerity."[18] In Lermontov's poetry, as in earlier "oppositional" poetry like Radishchev's "Freedom. An Ode" ("Vol'nost'. Oda," 1781–3) and the young Pushkin's "To Chaadaev" ("K Chaadaevu," 1818), emotional intensity and "correct" political sentiment are once again paramount to the author's claim as representative of "truth."[19] However, "correct" political sentiment has now shifted from that corresponding with the state viewpoint to one defined by its opposition to power and the status quo. This sort of binary will continue to play a profound role in Russian conceptions of sincerity.[20]

Lermontov's rhetorical voice could be suspect, however, for others. The principled flouting of public opinion, while it brought with it dangers – ostracization, incarceration, exile – also afforded the opportunity for notoriety. As Baron Rozen noted in a review at times insipid, at times insightful enough to be cited sympathetically by formalist critic Boris Eikhenbaum:

> Marvel at these lines [the final lines of "First of January"] as much as you like, but we will say […] that such a societally inappropriate and even unnatural spite […] is empty affectation on the part of a poet who lived in high society and for high society and tried in every way through [his] talent, wittiness, and daring [molodchestvo] to keep his name always, as they say, *au haut de la conversation*.[21]

Rozen, who collaborated with Pushkin, was hardly among the most reactionary elements of society. And if Lermontov was never going to reach the reactionaries, and hardly wished to, he was always interested in the perceptions of a broader readership: "The vehemence of [Lermontov's] contempt for fashionable society was matched only by the ardency of his desire to be recognized by it."[22]

Poems in which Lermontov's criticisms concern his whole generation, and thus the poet too, could likewise trigger conflicting opinions. Poet and critic Apollon Grigoryev found "much more pride and self-seduction [samoobol'shchenie]" in the self-denigrating confessions of "Meditation" than in a similarly themed poem by Nikolai Ogarev.[23] Belinsky, in contrast, perceived in this poem a profound sincerity, founded not on a truth to the poet's individuality, but on his innate ability to express feelings and experience common to many, i.e., on a *universalism*, the impact of which is supported by the poet's "stormy animation, the colossal energy of his noble indignation and deep sadness" as well as his gift of potent speech (the "diamond-like hardness of his line" [almaznaia krepost' stikha]).[24]

Lermontov's own acute philosophical scepticism regarding language and the self was bound to clash with his personal predilection for emotive language and rhetoric. It did, quite spectacularly, in "Believe Not Yourself" ("Ne ver' sebe," 1839), an encyclopedia of pessimistic reasons not to write, many hinging on questions of authenticity. The would-be poet, along, potentially, with the author himself, is told to fear inspiration like a plague ("kak iazvu"). It is valueless as the product of a pathological subjectivity – "tiazhelyi bred dushi tvoei bol'noi" (torpid delirium of your sickly soul), or worse, just a phantom, purposely aroused – "plennoi mysli razdrazhen'e" (the agitation of captive thought). True, one may be lucky and discover within one's soul a rare untapped source of "sweet sounds." But even then

> Стихом размеренным и словом ледяным
>   Не передашь ты их значенья.

> (You won't convey their meaning
>   With measured verse and icy word.)

Lermontov goes on to advise the "young dreamer" not to bare sorrow and passion before the clamorous (i.e., uninterested) world but also not to trade in anger or *pliant* angst ("poslushnaia toska"). Finally, the writer is told his woes hold nothing to surprise the crowd, who mask their own suffering, and among whom "hardly is there one [...] who has arrived at premature wrinkles / Without *a crime or loss!..*" (emphasis mine) – much-paraded attributes of the supposedly exceptional Byronic hero. These broadsides evoke Lermontov's own early, Byronic poetry but are also general enough to refer to his mature poetry or to all contemporary lyric poetry.[25] The poem ends by attacking poetry's *histrionics* in a blaze of *rhetoric*:

> Поверь: для них смешон твой плач и твой укор,
>   С своим напевом заученным,
> Как разрумяненный трагический актер,
>   Махающий мечом картонным ...

> (Believe it: comical to them are your lament and your rebuke,
>   With its melody by rote,
> Like a rouged tragic actor
>   Brandishing a cardboard sword ...)

The overarching paradox of the poem is of course that it ignores its own advice to act, rather than write, and not to bare one's psychic wounds. (The seemingly fatal vulnerabilities of poetry are clearly wounding to the speaker.)[26] In addition, despite the links between organicity and authenticity in Romanticism, "the lyric subject constantly shifts the axiology" on which the poem's arguments are grounded, moving always on to yet another vantage point.[27] The poem's coherence, despite all these contradictions, depends to a high degree on an infectious verbal charisma linked to intensity of speech and implied emotion.

Verbal charisma perhaps reaches its apogee in the antithetical "There is speech – the meaning" ("Est' rechi – znachen'e," 1840), which derives an understated intensity from the compactness of its amphibrachic dimiter quatrains with all feminine rhyme.[28] This poem, initially about lovers' speech, became *primarily* an apotheosis of the poetic word, though a fissure is still perceptible between the second and third stanzas, when, after a number of versions, Lermontov worked in an allusion to Nikolai Iazykov's programmatic "To the Poet" ("Poetu," 1831): "Могучей мысли свет и жар / И огнедышащее слово" (The light and heat of potent thought / And the firebreathing word).[29] In Lermontov:

Не встретит ответа
Средь шума мирского
Из пламя и света
Рожденное слово;

(Unanswered will be
Among the world's tumult
The word born
Of flame and light)

Here, we learn of a word transcendent in its power and antithetical to the impotent "icy word" and "measured verse" above.[30] This true poetic word's self-sufficiency, its "radiance" even, is reinforced in the mild agrammaticality of the third line (a rare, particularly by the 1840s, but not unheard of in poetry, declension of a neuter noun in -*mia* according to the rules of regular neuter nouns in -*e*).[31] This agrammaticality is, here, fortuitous, lending a sublime character to the word, which strains to break the bounds of sanctioned usage. Though its "meaning" is "dark or insignificant," this word overflows with its emotional charge (stanza 2) and commands the attention of the worthy, and the poet will run from prayer or battle to greet it – his true idol. Lermontov, in an act of charismatic "disarmament," tactfully ascribes this potent word *to the other*, even as he most compellingly generates it. He thus, in this poem, affirms the possibility of *poetic* speech capable of transcending the impasse of language and meaningfully, if not by means of rational discourse, opening to another the inner world of a complexly human subject.[32]

The Versatile Voice: "From Goethe" and "Gratitude"

Because Lermontov's notoriety emerged from the platform of his rhetorical poems, which made up the bulk of his first publications, his versatility was initially underscored first and foremost in the "quiet" poems of his final years.[33] It is instructive to look closely at one of these, "From Goethe" ("Iz Gëte," 1840), a free translation of the second of the "Wanderer's Night Songs" ("Ein Gleiches/Über allen Gipfeln" ["Another/Over All the Peaks," 1780]). According to Ilya Serman, "Suffering as the obligatory lot of the thinking person was sensed by Lermontov's generation in all of his poems, even in such a seemingly calm and untroubled poem as 'The peaks of the mountains.'"[34] Indeed, this diminutive poem, which announces itself as a translation, intimates a profound sense of a personal, perhaps even tragic, fate.[35]

> Из Гёте
> Горные вершины
> Спят во тьме ночной;
> Тихие долины
> Полны свежей мглой;
> Не пылит дорога,
> Не дрожат листы ...
> Подожди немного,
> Отдохнешь и ты.[36]

My own English text cannot possibly convey the simple allure of the original, though it does aim to reproduce its haiku-like texture and vividness:

> (From Goethe
> The peaks of the mountains
> Sleep in the night darkness;
> The quiet valleys
> Are full of fresh haze;
> No dust rises from the road,
> The leaves do not quiver ...

Wait a bit,
You too will rest.)

The poem, though still evocative of seriousness, openness, and im-
mediacy (the latter, above all, through its illusory simplicity and the
colloquial and natural diction of the final lines) is clearly also a mod-
ulated voice, one which lays down the mantle of intensity. The short
trochaic trimeter (six- and five-syllable) lines introduce a subtle, but
resolute rhythmic pulse. Goethe's rhythm is a variable *dol'nik*.[37] In con-
trast, Lermontov's trochaic trimeter embeds repeating rhythmic pat-
terns that split the poem into two sections. In the painterly first half,
twice, a line with pyrrhic second foot is followed by a line with all three
stresses realized: $\acute{\_}\_\_\_\_\acute{\_}\_$ / $\_\acute{\_}\_\acute{\_}\_\acute{\_}$ x2. In the second half (apophatic/
hortative), each line has a pyrrhic first foot: $\_\_\acute{\_}\_\acute{\_}\_$ / $\_\_\acute{\_}\_\_\acute{\_}$ x2. This
rhythmic homogeneity lends a hypnotic quality to the poem, as do the
semantic, syntactic, and phonic echos (Gornye vershiny … Tikhie doliny
… Ne pylit … Ne drozhat … *Ne dro*zhat … P*o*d*ozh*di *ne*mnogo). And this
hypnotic quality is in harmony with the calm but hyper-aware state that
comes in the night solitude, and within which the "poet's" reflection
arises.

Not only implicit suffering provides a connection to Lermontov's
persona, but also a sense of nature's harmony as well as the particular
mountainous topography, which, while deriving from Goethe's text,
accords with the central place of the Caucusus in Lermontov's works.
A yet stronger connection is to be found in the idea of that rest which
will emerge in death.[38] This sense, absent in Goethe's original, emerges
subtly, aided by Lermontov's eliding of Goethe's title, his subtle shifts
of imagery and tone, and the poem's context within his oeuvre.[39] The
final line harks back, in particular, to "Gratitude" ("Blagodarnost',"
1840), with its bitter, quasi-suicidal blasphemy, and forward to "I step
alone onto the road" ("Vykhozhu odin ia na dorogu," 1841), with its
transcendent image of a perpetual sleep, unceasingly full of life's vi-
tality, nature's harbouring presence, and the "sweet voice of song" –
which, the hero dreams, can supplant "the cold sleep of the grave."[40]

"From Goethe" immediately followed "Gratitude" in Lermontov's
1840 authorial collection, emphasizing the two works' radically con-
trasting tone. These two eight-line poems were clearly meant, in this
volume, to inscribe reciprocal and opposing mental states through
which the poet approaches his "world-weariness":

Благодарность
За всё, за всё тебя благодарю я:

За тайные мучения страстей,
За горечь слез, отраву поцелуя,
За месть врагов и клевету друзей;
За жар души, растраченный в пустыне,
За всё, чем я обманут в жизни был ...
Устрой лишь так, чтобы тебя отныне
Недолго я еще благодарил.

    (Gratitude
For everything, for everything do I thank you:
For the secret suffering[] of [my] passions,
For the bitterness of tears, the venom of a kiss,
For the vengeance of enemies and calumny of friends,
For the ardor of [my] soul – spent in the wilderness,
For all through which in life I've been deceived …
Just arrange it so that now
I won't thank you for much longer.)

The "you" in "Gratitude" ("masked" with lowercase for the sake of the censor) is transparently God.[41] Khodasevich called these final lines "the most blasphemous in all of Russian literature," their "brazenness of content" emphasized through "venomous prosaicism."[42]

"Gratitude" is the sort of text that is bound to evoke conflicting passions regarding its sincerity. On the one hand, the poem is written at the limits of emotional intensity, and, as in Venevitinov's "Sacrifice," the author's "staking" of his life, which becomes the ultimate trump card in his unequal dealings with God, makes for a powerful seal of intent. On the other, in its grand, acerbic confessionality, "Gratitude" cannot help but open itself up to suspicions of exhibitionism – such, after all, is the nature of *public* confession.[43] Despite the hardships Lermontov in fact endured or the appearance that he may indeed have "sought death," or at the least been indifferent to it, this poem's posture – it insists after the Byronic manner: I am more grand and tragic than any of you – has a tendency to raise the reader's defences. In essence, it asks one to choose: elevate the individualist-Byronic Lermontov or doubt his authenticity.

In contrast, the tone of "From Goethe" is notably disarming. Its sublime calm and intimations of suffering still elevate the lyric persona, who remains the *primary* addressee of the final lines, but it simultaneously leaves room for common ground with other sensitive individuals, other sufferers, other travellers. This was doubly underscored in the pragmatics of Goethe's original poem, which was inscribed on the wall of a hunting lodge on the Kickelhahn mountain and not published by the author for thirty-five years until 1815.[44] Just as Goethe's inscription was a graphic record of his *solitude*, but meant to be discovered by *fellow wanderers*, the reader of the published poem is made the intimate witness to Goethe and Lermontov's solitary reflection and simultaneously a potential addressee of its double-voiced consolation.

In addition, the poem's existence as a fragment makes it radically open. Goethe's poem, when he published it, followed a preceding "night song" with lines strongly evocative of Lermontov's lyric hero: "Ach! ich bin des Treibens müde! / Was soll all der Schmerz und Lust?" (O, I am tired of this business! / What's the point of all this pain and desire?).[45] Lermontov, however, omitted this first "song." He told an acquaintance he was unable to successfully translate it.[46] And by doing so, he refused to limit his musing to the experience of a specific cast of lyric subject.

The truth, however, is that Lermontov did, in a way, "translate" Goethe's first night song. "Gratitude," while taking its departure from the phraseology and maximalism of Vasily Krasov's positively intoned "Prayer" ("Molitva," 1839), also recasts through its unequivocally blasphemous, suicidal "prayer" the ambiguously suicidal *prayer* of the world-weary speaker of the first "Wandrers Nachtlied" (1776).[47] While Goethe's poem is not generally read this way (cf. esp. "mit Erquickung füllest" [lit., fills with pleasantness]), one can easily picture the act of "strong misprision" that would lead Lermontov in this direction. There is even perhaps a hint of such an intention in the original form of Goethe's second line: "Alle *Freud* und Schmerzen stillest" (Who stills all *joy* and pain).[48] Here is the full text in the 1815 version:

> Wandrers Nachtlied
> Der du von dem Himmel bist,
> Alles Leid und Schmerzen stillest,
> Den, der doppelt elend ist,
> Doppelt mit Erquickung füllest,
> Ach! ich bin des Treibens müde!
> Was soll all der Schmerz und Lust?
> Süßer Friede!
> Komm, ach komm in meine Brust!

> (Wanderer's Night Song
> You, who hails from heaven,
> Who stills all suffering and pain,
> Who doubly refreshes
> Him, who is doubly miserable,

O, I am tired of this business!
What's the point of all this pain and desire?
Sweet peace!
Come, o come into my breast!)[49]

The echo between the requests in "You who hails from heaven" and "Gratitude" strongly suggests an authorial intent behind Lermontov's printing of "Gratitude" and "From Goethe" contiguously in the edition of 1840. These poems do not just constitute a particularly striking versatility device, they configure Goethe's cycle into Lermontov's bifurcating personal idiom. Side by side, they produce an image of a poet unafraid to blaspheme, perhaps given to grandstanding, but also attuned to the natural world and with a living, sensitive inner core and charitable heart. This is, without abandoning Romantic biography, a rich amalgam and a far cry from the tritely Byronic hero who dominated the early verse and could show his head as late as "I look to the future with dread" ("Gliazhu na budushnost' s boiazn'iu," 1838).

Deep Thought and the Breaking of Cultural Matrices

If the emergence of a quiet voice, as in "From Goethe," was central to Lermontov's establishing of a "human" range of expression and emotion, another key factor in the structuring of the sincere voice in Lermontov's mature poetry was his emergence as a poet of deep and original thought. Two instances of a radical freeing of lyric subject and reader from the structuring cultural matrices of the day (implying the interrogation of received truths) may be found in "Motherland" ("Rodina," 1841) and "Valerik" (1840). In "Motherland," the poet begins by rejecting sets of competing ideological justifications for love of country, moved rather by what he *sees*, which is rugged, expansive, spare, but elevated by the poet's treatment to an undeniable dignity.[50] The final lines yet more radically demythologize the countryside:

И в праздник, вечером росистым,
Смотреть до полночи готов
На пляску с топаньем и свистом
Под говор пьяных мужичков.

(And on a holiday, by dewy evening,
I'm ready to watch until midnight
Dance with stomping and whistling
Beneath the chatter of drunken peasant men.)

These lines have been compared to Pushkin's "Teper' mila mne bala-laika / Da p'ianyi topot trepaka" (Now the balalaika is dear to me / And the drunken stomping of the *trepak*). However, Pushkin's images remain within the bounds of cultural stereotypes.[51] In Lermontov 1) the dance is described rather than presented as a known, digested entity (*trepak*); 2) the lines mention the drunkenness not of the dancers, an element of the topos, but of the local spectators among whom the "poet" stands; 3) "govor" (talk; dialect) is deflating; as is 4) the usually dismissive diminutive "muzhic*hk*ov."[52] It is the drunken chatter, not the ecstatic folk dance, which closes the poem, dominating the reader's perception, and consummating Lermontov's vision of Russia. His attesting of a personal, "strange love" for the imperfect motherland was to be exceedingly influential, modelling for future cultural figures from Alexander Blok to rock-poet Yuri Shevchuk how they might navigate their own complicated relationships to Russia.

The Challenge of "Valerik"

In "I am writing to you on a lark – in truth" ("Ia k vam pishu sluch-aino, – pravo," 1840), known widely as "Valerik,"[53] we would be wrong to focus too much attention on the lyric persona's "famous" short, elevated philosophical interlude: "[...] Pathetic man. / What does he want!.. The sky is clear, / Under the sky there is much space for all, / But continually and futilely / He alone contends – for what?" First, the lyric persona's thinking of this thought is interrupted, its pathos undermined by the conversation that immediately follows. Second, though this passage appears to have had an impact on Lev Tolstoy's prose and his pacifism, the thought is not altogether new, and I will argue that the poem's "earned" truth is palpable not simply in its indeed powerful demonstration that war is senseless, but in its re-evaluation of valour, of the *way* in which war provides meaning to those who fight. Through this shift, Lermontov thoroughly deconstructs, at least in poetry, his own prior values system, in which personal courage and heroism play an important role.[54]

For, while Lermontov was never quite at home in the guard units, and one would not attribute to him the ebullient hussar ethos of the early Denis Davydov, the "ideal of the heroic warrior [...] had occupied [Lermontov's] imagination since childhood. [...] 'If there is a war,' [Lermontov] wrote [in 1832], 'I swear to you in God's name that I will be ahead of them all.'"[55] As a young man, the beginning of a new Russo-Turkish war inspired him to write: "[...] polechu [...] Lovit' venok nebrennoi slavy!" ([...] I will fly [...] To seize the laurel of unfading glory!).[56]

"Valerik" has an unusual generic form, which welds a descriptive/narrative core (speaking, however, reams about the mindset of the observer) to an epistolary frame. Because the remorseless deconstruction of familiar personal and social mythologies of war was so far ahead of its time, the poem's ethos remained at least somewhat opaque to readers. Petr Kropotkin at the beginning of the twentieth century noted that "*Valerik* is considered by those who know what real warfare is as the most correct description of it in poetry. *And yet* Lermontoff disliked war [...]"[57]

The epistolary opening weaves idiom to generate a natural content, tonality, and phrasing, before later foundering in a circle of thoughts and diction imposed by the elegiac tradition. Then, in the fourth strophe, the poet executes a subtle transition from what has become a somewhat strident, self-directed discourse to novelistic observation. He gradually builds tension, using his sharp eye and ear, which catches snatches of disembodied dialogue, to arrive at one of the poem's intermediate climaxes, a clash between a Chechen and a Cossack horseman. Lermontov, however, immediately deflates the moment's pathos:

> Но в этих сшибках удалых
> Забавы много, толку мало.
> (But in these gallant clashes
> There's much entertainment, little sense.)

It was, however, precisely this sort of bravado (*molodechestvo*) that anchored the potent myth of the Russian cavalry officer. This myth pervaded the ethos of Hussar guard units like that to which Lermontov belonged prior to his first and second exiles and the Cossaks and other cavalry among whom he was stationed in the south.[58]

By framing this tautly narrated skirmish as a "tragic ballet," Lermontov demarcates a second transition, one to a discourse on war that stands explicitly outside the realm of culture:

> Зато видал я представленья,
> Каких у вас на сцене нет ...
>
> (But I've seen spectacles
> They don't put on your stages ...)

What follows is an attempt to systematically forgo the mythic and ideological drapery of war that perennially protects "cultured" writer and reader alike.

In the lines that describe the lead-up to the battle at the river "Valerik," what Lermontov elides is as important as what he includes. This is visible in relation to excised portions of the draft and in relation to a poem like "Chir-Iurt" (1831 or 1832), by Alexander Polezhaev, a university student exiled as a soldier. Polezhaev's Caucasian battle poem is often compared to "Valerik" in connection with its "soldier's-eye view" of the conflict and, presumably, its disturbingly violent imagery.[59]

First of all, Lermontov elides strategic context and narrative coherence, both well in evidence in Polezhaev's poem. In the draft, there had been at least a brief introduction giving more typical military/political contextualization ("Chechnya was rising up all around [us]; We weren't two thousand with a rifle ...") as well as still brief, but more conventional, descriptions of the action and surroundings that help the reader picture the battle more coherently.[60] In the final version, Lermontov instead plants us directly into the action – reducing details almost entirely to what is immediately visible and audible to an individual. Description and narration become fragmented, foregrounding direct personal experience and disorientation.

Secondly, throughout the main battle narrative, and, for the most part, the poem as a whole, Lermontov elides ideology, which is, in the words of Lionel Trilling, "not the product of thought; it is the habit or the ritual of showing respect for certain formulas to which, for various reasons having to do with emotional safety, we have very strong ties."[61] In Lermontov's poem, there is nothing to dignify the Russians above the Chechens or other local peoples. A daring Chechen horseman meets a daring Cossack horseman. "Zveri" (beasts) and "zveropodobnyi" (beastlike) were terms often used in official and artistic discourse about Chechens to designate fierceness, lack of conscience, predatorial instinct, and in general to dehumanize. In Lermontov's poem, however, Chechens and Russians are both reduced to "zveri." This presents a stark contrast to Polezhaev, in whose poem the Chechens are a "beastlike people" and whose text is pervaded with Imperial and Christian ideology privileging the Russians and, however ghastly war may be, justifying their use of overwhelming force.[62] (In Polezhaev's defence, the exiled poet was, somewhat miraculously, able to publish a graphic account of a massacre of Chechen civilians by Russian soldiers in book form in 1832 despite Nicholas's harsh censorship regime.)[63]

In "Valerik," Lermontov also avoids the language of *molodechestvo*. In a cheerfully sanguine letter to Aleksei Lopukhin (12 September 1840), he refers to the same battle using the phrase "gde byla *potekha*" (where the "fun" happened), a common idiom of hussar/Cossack speech (and reminiscent of this poem's "zabava" [entertainment] in which there is little "sense") and uses the word "ubylo" (lit., were subtracted) to recount Russian casualties. A *real* letter home demands that cultural norms of élan be maintained.

Nor, importantly, does Lermontov's poem elevate valour. (Polezhaev, in "Chir-Iurt," uses the word "slava," in the sense of military glory, without apparent irony five times.) Absent in both texts is a representation of the poet's own heroic conduct. In Lermontov's case, the commanding general's report read:

Lermontov [...] was tasked with observing the actions of the headmost assault column [...], which was connected with the greatest danger for him from the enemy, who was hiding in the woods behind trees and bushes. But this officer [...] performed the task given him with excellent bravery and self-possession and together with the first rows of the most courageous burst through the enemy barricades.[64]

In fact, Lermontov minimizes and deflates what may be an anonymized description of his own *molodechestvo*:

Все офицеры впереди …
Верхом помчался на завалы
Кто не успел спрыгну́ть с коня … (emphasis mine)

(*All* the officers are in the lead …
He [*or* they], on horseback, charged the barricades
Who didn't jump from horse in time …)

According to the testimony of an unsympathetic Baron Ludwig de Rossillon (Lev Rossil'on), "'Lermontov pranced about on a horse white as snow, on which, having dashingly cocked a cap of white linen, he rushed the Chechen barricades [zavaly]. Pure bravado [molodchestvo]! – for who rushes barricades on horseback?'"[65]

By forgoing political/historical context, ideology, narrative continuity, and individual bravery, the poet emphasizes a more universal, immediate, and humanistic meaning to what is happening:

[…] и пошла резня.
И два часа в струях потока
Бой длился. Резались жестоко,
Как звери, молча, с грудью грудь,
Ручей телами запрудили.
Хотел воды я зачерпнуть
(И зной и битва утомили
Меня) … но мутная волна
Была тепла, была красна.

> ([…] and the slaughter/slashing started.
> And two hours in the current of the river
> The battle went on. [Men] slashed cruelly,
> Like animals, silently, chest to chest,
> The stream was dammed up with bodies.
> I wanted to scoop some water
> (The heat and battle had tired
> Me) … but the cloudy water
> Was warm, was red.)

There is no division into us and them. All hack cruelly, like animals – in silence (an unexpected detail). Mixed blood befouls the water, the unnatural warmth of which is particularly expressive, engaging yet another sense: touch.

The myth-annihilating nature of this narrative part of the poem is cemented through the ironic reactions of a friendly Chechen, which emphasize how Russians construct a self-consoling story of the battle. The lyric speaker's brief, elevated philosophical discourse ("Pathetic man […] Under the sky there is much space for all […]") is *interrupted* by his Chechen "kunak" (pal).[66] A conversation ensues in which the speaker asks:

> – «А много горцы потеряли?»
> – «Как знать? – зачем вы не считали!»
> – «Да! будет, – кто-то тут сказал, –
> Им в память этот день кровавый!»
> Чеченец посмотрел лукаво
> И головою покачал.
>
> (– "And did the highlanders [i.e., Chechens] lose many?"
> – "Who knows? – why didn't you count!"
> – "Yes! This bloody day – someone said at this point –
> Will remain in their memory!"
> The Chechen glanced archly
> And shook his head.)

The Chechen, and with him Lermontov, clearly doubts that this day will be remembered by the Chechens as particularly tragic or a testament to worthy opponents' valour, in fact, that it will be marked within any local historical or cultural memory.[67] In contrast, Lermontov's own letter to Lopukhin takes a self-protecting stance similar to that debunked by the Chechen: "We lost [u nas ubylo] 30 officers and up to 300 infantry, but 600 of their bodies remained there – not bad, don't you think! [a ikh 600 tel ostalos' na meste – kazhetsia khorosho!] […]."[68] Lermontov's letter also triples the duration of the battle.

On this myth-deflating note, Lermontov ends the narrative portion of the poem and shifts back to his "letter's" audience, which clearly includes, over the shoulder of his love interest, the broader aristocratic readership in the capitals:

> Но я боюся вам наскучить,
> В забавах света вам смешны
> Тревоги дикие войны.
> Свой ум вы не привыкли мучить
> Тяжелой думой о конце.
> […] и вы едва ли
> Вблизи когда-нибудь видали,
> Как умирают. Дай вам бог
> И не видать: иных тревог
> Довольно есть. […]

> (But I fear I will bore you;
> [Occupied with] the amusements of high society, you find droll
> War's savage trepidations.
> You're not used to tormenting your mind
> With burdensome thought[s] of the end.
> [...] And I truly doubt that
> You have ever seen up close
> How someone dies. God grant
> You not see it: there are enough
> Other troubles. […])

While irony is present here, it is, for the reader-addressee, perhaps excused by the trauma of what the lyric subject has seen and described. Moreover, in Lermontov's only partly ironic "God grant," there is a humanity and empathy. In this way, while the lyric subject distances himself from his reader, he does not yet here "arm" the reader against him.

However, in the final lines, the lyric subject slips back into his usual relationship with his high society readers:

> Теперь прощайте: если вас
> Мой безыскусственный рассказ

Развеселит, займет хоть малость,
Я буду счастлив. А не так?
Простите мне его как шалость
И тихо молвите: чудак!..

(Now, farewell: if my
Artless tale will
Cheer you up, interest you even a tad,
I will be happy. And if not?
Forgive me it as an antic
And quietly say: strange bird!..)

If the thoughtful reader could say after the prior passage that, yes, indeed, we are preoccupied with trifles and yes, indeed, we do not know what war is really like, the reader of these final lines is forced to defend her- or himself from the cruelty of Lermontov's "razveselit" (lit., put you in a jolly mood), the bitter irony of his "khot' malost'" (even a tad).

In this way, the ending alienates the well-meaning and sensitive reader, that reader in whom, precisely, Lermontov takes an interest.[69] We register this as the raising of a defensive shield. Lermontov's lack of belief in the possibility of comprehension is thus "arming," if also understandable. Knowing both contexts, he knows he can only explain so much. Having lowered his defences to describe things that appear to be of deep meaning to him, in the final section, he again walls himself off through an irony which is *outwardly* self-deprecating. As self-deprecating irony, it is by nature "self-protective," but because it is so clearly only a *hollowly* self-deprecating irony, it is, at the same time, aggressive, or "assailing" (in Linda Hutcheon's terms).[70]

Still, the middle portion of the poem is quite successful in conveying the lyric subject's sincerity, which is here experienced primarily as a good faith attempt at a radically truthful relating of experience, undistorted by pre-existing cultural biases and frameworks. In the absence of ideology, the poem's simplicity of diction and extremely low density of tropes, most of which serve the purpose of vivid description ("Shtyki *goriat* pod solntsem iuga" [The bayonets *are aflame* under the southern sun]), combine with the use of precise military terminology and, particularly, the abundance of fragmentary novelistic detail to lend the work a sense of undoctored *reportage*.[71]

Most important, however, to the potential depth of the sincere resonance of this work is the rejection of the prevailing *ethos* of war. While the conclusion of Lermontov's contemporaneous "There is speech," in effect, places the poetic word above duty and valour ("I broshus' iz bitvy emu ia navstrechu" [And I will rush from a battle towards it]), "Valerik" was a more radical rejection. Here we see not a reordering of priorities, but a forgoing of the possibility of even personal value derived in war. In this, Lermontov anticipates the pacifism of Tolstoy, but also the post-Victorian, post–First World War writers of the "lost generation." Such a "truth" can only have seemed purchased through personal experience to any contemporary open-minded enough to hear it when the poem was published in 1843. And it is noteworthy that this "unprotected" stance could be taken, seemingly, only within the space of poetry.

In Lermontov's "Valerik," then, we hear two voices: one obtrusively posturing and self-defensive, the other challengingly earnest. In the outer frame, a psychologically wounded speaker cannot bring himself to offer respect or trust to the presumably casual peruser of his poem. At the same time, however, the deceptively "unstructured" centre portion extends just this trust and respect to the reader, who, it is implicit, needs only unobtrusive markers to follow the poet's subtly but powerfully made point – the ultimate senselessness not only of war, but of valour. And here, too, Lermontov is "disarming." He lays down the distinguishing mantle and protective guise of heroism, both positive and negative (Byronic), to speak to the reader as nothing more than an open-eyed and well-spoken witness. The reader is left with little reason to deny him that status.

2 A POETICS OF ABANDON (APOLLON GRIGORYEV)

Sincerity is a tricky thing [Iskrennost' – delo mudrenoe]; it doesn't always correspond to an effort to be sincere and is often even ruined by this sort of effort. Grigoryev himself loved to repeat this observation.

– Nikolai Strakhov[72]

[…] печаль же неистовая не есть поэзия, а бешенство.
([…] violent sorrow is not poetry, but frenzy.)

– Wilhelm Küchelbecker
(Кюхельбекер)

Our next poet, Apollon Grigoryev (1822–64), is not only preternaturally aware of and interested in sincerity, like Lermontov, but already, in the Victorian fashion, attaches to sincerity the highest value in art. At the same time, as we see in the first epigraph above, such enthusiasm does not mean that sincerity is to be construed as naïvely literal or unconstructed.

One particular modality for potentially sincere expression that Grigoryev developed, perhaps his most successful and certainly both the most original and influential, was a profound projection into Russian culture of "Gypsy" *abandon*.[73] The concept of abandon ("Complete freedom from constraint or convention; lack of inhibition or restraint" [*OED*]) provides a correlate to sincerity, or authenticity, in that it implies a divestiture from the cultural and social norms that prevent emotions and impulses from freely expressing themselves. Thus, abandon is a form of immediacy, an unmasking of internality. However, the self thus bared can be understood as one-sided, a potent but negative expression of self, which in this state is not a whole or not a best self, but is still quite a *real* self, a self which the ego in ordinary circumstances takes pains to hide from society's gaze. Abandon thus overlaps with Trilling's concept of "authenticity" as a mode of being critical of cultural mores but threatens to diverge from authenticity in channelling the experience of a certain *aspect* of the self to the detriment of the whole. In Russian, the closest equivalent is perhaps *bezuderzhnost'*; in Grigoryev's personal idiolect, the closest term is *besnovanie* (frenzying).[74]

Abandon for Grigor'ev functions as a solution to that particular sincerity puzzle he sets for himself. The first hurdle is an unambiguous, sanguine commitment to sincerity in literature. (In this, he is influenced particularly by Thomas Carlyle.)[75] Grigoryev, in his long essay "On Truth and Sincerity in Art" ("O pravde i iskrennosti v iskusstve," 1856), asks "1) does the artist have a right as a given person, with a given mentality, with feelings of a given sort, to enter into states of mind foreign to him, modes of sentiment more intense or less intense than those characteristic of his own mental cast, and 2) does the artist have a right as the son of a given age, a member of a given church and a given people to enter into a worldview and mode of feeling foreign to him as such?"[76] Emphatically no, Grigoryev answers. However, this maximalism is softened by his belief in the capacity for "objectivity," which allows artists to experience and convincingly convey imagined states, though not states not mentally inhabited or states the kernel of which does not exist within the poet's own being. Grigoryev values and finds sincere the creativity of Shakespeare, Dante, and Goethe, while demoting Byron's great subjective gift. Still, for Grigoryev, these remain questions of the "*truth* that we demand from art, of the sincerity of the artist's attitudes to life and of the sincerity of his gift [iskrennost' ego talanta]."[77] Though Grigoryev, in other places, uses sincerity to refer colloquially to confession, the acknowledging of personal faults, his judgment here that a particular artist's "gift" can be sincere, as opposed to his or her specific utterances, lends his concept of artistic sincerity an indivisible, metaphysical quality. Sincerity can thus indicate an underlying truth (or truth to self) of an entire oeuvre, or, rather, all within that oeuvre which is to be judged worthy.

The second hurdle is a scepticism before both the pose and the avoidance of the pose:

> If the pose, taken on by me, *the poser*, after comparison, seems to me, *the judge,* a pose which does not belong to me, but is borrowed or even (which should be differentiated) created in myself artificially [...], then an attitude forms in relation to this pose which is negative or outright mocking. [...] This defensive state is often even overly aggressive [...] and, avoiding by any means exposure as imitators, we are ready to reduce ourselves to a zero state, a pure *tabula rasa*, to *efface* ourselves [...]. In essence, this is nothing but a defensive position, i.e., a new, if not striking, then at least durable pose [...]. This process is so commonplace that it occurs even in the inner world of people who don't at all occupy themselves with mining their own psyches.[78]

Neither Romantic posture, nor its avoidance, which Grigoryev sees as equally artificial, leads to truth. And the "mining of the psyche" (dushevnoe rudokopstvo) evokes irony, even as Grigoryev himself engages in it. In this latter concern, he is both influenced by and reacting against the emergent passion for "reflection" (refleksiia), or critical self-analysis, in the 1840s and 1850s in Russia.[79]

Depending on one's point of view, "reflection" can either represent an uncompromisingly critical, and hence authentic, attitude to the self or self-absorbed navel-gazing. It can be seen as a sincere attempt to trace the self to its source, to obvert preconceptions and psychological defence mechanisms. However, it can also be seen as symptomatic of the divided self, which is never able simply to be itself, but is always observing itself from the side, and hence as an impediment to sincerity erected by "civilization."[80]

In practice, "reflection," when practised with verve and taken to its logical conclusion, is like an attempt to find the final bottom of a trick cabinet that has none (as exemplified in the serpentine discourse of Dostoevsky's "underground man"). The very shape of a discourse of reflection, consisting inevitably of dialectical twists and turns on the path to self-awareness, implies that there will always be yet another pivot, another ingenious manner to find flaws in the (self-)analysis. This perhaps explains why so much scholarship on sincerity, which has traditionally been attracted to poets who work in a confessional or self-analytical mode, is so bounteously critical of attempts on the part of authors to reach a stable sincerity. When sincerity is constructed, or when it is read out, in this manner, there is always yet another logical twist that can be added, another incongruity to which one can point.

Scepticism before both the pose and avoidance of the pose forces Grigoryev to navigate a straits between artificial passion and exaggerated, overcautious reserve: "We came to be suspicious in ourselves and, presumably, in our [literary] characters, of the elements [nachala] of alarm and passion, we began to accuse them of insincerity, of "elevation" [pripodniatost'] and "whipping up" [podogretost'] of feelings, not suspecting that we ourselves are about to fall into another type of insincerity, into a certain monomania of sincerity," in other words, into an avoidance of suspect emotion.[81] The Gypsy modality allows Grigoryev, who was both given to excessive passions and emotions and sceptical of strained voices, to overcome the straining that mars many of his poems, and to express, with a fresh voice, extremes of emotion. Grigoryev himself wrote that "Gypsies [...] possess an immediacy of impressionability and throw some light on the very question of immediacy of impressionability," and he challenged those who "suspect something artificial in their bursts [of emotion] and frenzying [besnovanie]."[82]

One testimony to the poet's success in navigating these straights in "O, you at least, speak with me" ("O, govori khot' ty so mnoi," 1857) and "Gypsy Vengerka" ("Tsyganskaia vengerka," 1857; below – "Vengerka [Hungarian (Dance/Melody)]" as it is titled in the autograph)[83] is offered by Alexander Blok, who was instrumental in reviving Grigoryev's poetic legacy at the beginning of the twentieth century. He called these poems "singular pearls, in their class, of Russian lyric poetry" that "even approach, in some manner, folk creativity: in their unbroken melody, the absence of earlier irritating ('psychological') stumblings and disruptions."[84] Given that Grigoryev's "Vengerka" is composed of a string of expressions betraying the lyric subject's psychological overwroughtness and constantly tacking in conflicting discursive directions, it seems safe to assume that what Blok is referring to is an overarching psychological and expressive unity. Blok, it should be noted, is a reader open to the tragic world view and emotional maximalism.[85]

Grigoryev, an unapologetic, if late, Romantic who proposed a new mode of criticism he called "organic," seeks, ideally, to express the self in ways that are simultaneously impassioned and natural.[86] And Gypsies could be seen by Romantic Europe as a conspicuous survival of the "natural man."[87] Still, organic does not mean uncomplicated or undivided. As Lotman and Mints note, "Grigoryev considers human nature contradictory, by origin tragically riven."[88]

A number of factors underscore how Grigoryev could have seen his creations in the Gypsy mode as sincere and "native" expressions of his own emotional experience, and hence, though part of a fictionalizing cycle, in accord with his definition of literary sincerity. First, Grigoryev was, according to the testimony of his good friend, the poet Afanasy Fet, a "passionate Gypsophile" (strastnyi tsyganist), who carried his guitar everywhere and was at home (one might say in Russian, *svoi chelovek*) among the Gypsies of the best Moscow chorus, led by Ivan Vasilyev, who would let down their guard in his presence and join him in song.[89] Second, Grigoryev's personality – given to strong passions, wild outbursts, and asocial behaviours – finds obvious correlates in the stereotype of Gypsy abandon. Third, in the poem which will be at the centre of our attention, his "Vengerka," Grigoryev grafts "Gypsy abandon" onto elements of Russian folk and urban lower-class as well as his own educated speech. The son of a déclassé aristocrat and a coachman's daughter, Grigoryev spent much time in childhood with lower-class children; in adulthood, in taverns and restaurants. He was a connoisseur of Russian folk song and a broadly cultured university-educated pedagogue. Hence, he drew from a personal, or at least highly familiar, vocabulary in all these registers.[90] Grigoryev does not thus attempt to impersonate a Gypsy or urban transient. Rather, he finds the correlative for his own emotional experience in "Gypsy" *emotion*, which did not, before his experiments, have an adequate vessel within Russian poetic culture.[91] At the same time, "Gypsy abandon," as a mode of being, appeals to stereotypical *Russian* self-conceptions like *shirokaia dusha* (an expansive soul), *dusha naraspashku* (a soul wide open, like an unbuttoned coat or shirt), *udal'* (dash, impetuousity), etc.[92] Such felicities surely facilitated Grigoryev's self-recognition as an organic and sincere voice in "Vengerka," but alone they can only lay the ground for a compelling voice to emerge.

The key question I hope to answer in the remainder of this section is how abandon is inscribed in the poetic text of "Vengerka." Sincerity is not homogeneous but is culturally embedded and mutable. It must be encoded by a speaker and decoded by a listener, who must share overlapping codes – in this case, conceptualizations of sincerity. Moreover, since fidelity to an inner world is not readable, it is only the *secondary traits* that adhere to individual conceptualizations of sincerity that can and must be evoked for successful *communication* of this quality to occur. One pole in the conceptualization of sincerity, overlapping the Romantic, valorizes qualities like seriousness, intensity of emotion, openness, and immediacy as the visible stand-ins for sincerity. Abandon is a distant cousin of this conception (one that, among other things, brackets seriousness). I will argue that abandon's correlatives in "Vengerka" are

1 intensity of unbridled emotion, conveyed primarily through extreme statement;
2 unapologetic egoism – which contrasts with Grigoryev's posture elsewhere in the "Struggle" ("Bor'ba") cycle, where he repeatedly sacrifices and hides his feelings to spare the heroine's emotions, even when he judges her;[93]
3 rejection of norms of "cultured" behaviour and expression, visible linguistically in the poem's substandard language and situationally in the wild and embittered drinking posited; and
4 formal and stylistic aspects which telegraph the lack of a "filter," i.e., immediacy of expression.

At the same time, abandon can only be experienced as *a release from constraint* – internal and external, and a backdrop of reserve or constraint is crucial to supporting the potent sense of abandon that will emerge in "Vengerka." This reserve exists both internally, within the poem itself, in which, in accordance with the musical structure of the *vengerka*, stretches of restraint and abandon alternate, and also externally, as part of the broader framework of the "Struggle" cycle, which establishes struggle for self-control as a central theme.[94] This forced, but psychologically untenable, self-restraint, indicated both thematically and formally, precedes and prepares the climax of the cycle in the two Gypsy-themed poems.

Here, feeling is externalized through music, represented or gestured at within the poems themselves. Grigoryev himself saw in Gypsy music a particular "motion, which can be compared to a clearly audible pulse, *now restrained, now feverishly troubled*, but always surprisingly true in its disquiet."[95] In the first of the two poems, passion and reserve are interwoven, forming a powerful emotional texture. In the second, moments of reserve and passion alternate. At the same time, the pregnant reserve of the first serves to prepare and set off as a foil the passionate abandon of that which follows.

The immediate backdrop for "Vengerka" thus becomes the *interwoven* intensity and reserve of "O, you at least, speak with me." The latter poem develops a topos that goes back to Schiller's "To Emma" ("An Emma,"publ. 1797), with its experience of the beloved as a distant and silent star, and Princess Zinaida Volkonskaya's fascinating "To My Star" ("Moei zvezde," 1831; published in the memorial issue of Delvig's almanac *Severnye tsvety na 1832 g.*).[96] Even when we do not consider the hauntingly intense, but simultaneously restrained Gypsy melody that has become indelibly tied to the poem's words, and which quite possibly formed their backdrop for Grigoryev as well, the regular metre and stanzas, in which a self-contained syntax is reinforced through repeatedly closing with a "heavy" dactylic, and usually longer, word (*semistrunnaia, prikovana, iadovitoe, nedopetuiu*), continually curb the forward momentum, retarding and keeping in check the speaker's striving towards his star. In addition, the rhythmic diversity of the odd-numbered lines contrasts with the rhythmic homogeneity of the even-numbered lines (which tend very strongly to a second peon: _ ′ _ _ _ ′ _ _). An impulse to freedom is thus repeatedly and demonstrably pulled into check.[97]

In "Vengerka," "abandon" is structured as a radical verbal immediacy and a stripping of cultural superstructures. This is a projection of "Gypsy culture" as Grigoryev perceives it, but one conducted, as far as the speaker is concerned, from a place of such proximity that it is experienced as an expression of qualities inherent to him and his native culture, though perhaps not fully expressible in his native idiom.

A look at the poet's technique from early on in "Vengerka," when the music the lyric subject hears and his emotion, developing in parallel, are just beginning to heat up, is sufficient to demonstrate the poem's quality of extreme statement:

> Квинты резко дребезжат,
>> Сыплют дробью звуки ...
> Звуки ноют и визжат,
>> Словно стоны муки.
>
> Что за горе? Плюнь, да пей!
> Ты завей его, завей
>> Веревочкой горе!
>> Топи тоску в море!

> (The fifths quaver harshly,
>> Sounds rain like scattershot ...
> Sounds nag and shriek,
>> As if moans of torment.
>
> What grief is that? Send it to hell [lit., spit], and drink!
> Braid it, braid

> Your woe into a rope!
> Drown your sorrow* under the sea!)

The first stanza here unites a precise musicological term, "kvinty" (fifths), immediately betraying the speaker's education, with highly expressive and impressionistic language. After a series of onomatopoeias – *drebez-zhat*, *drob'*, *sypliut* – the sounds become personified, evoking for the lyric subject vocalizations of the tormented: whimpering, shrieking, moaning.

This personification is all the motivation we will get for the sudden discursive shift in the next stanza. It opens with a self-directed rhetorical question: what's your calamity to you? And then the answer – spit on it and drink! But this is clearly a brave face, as the command to drink (pei) calls forth the internal rhyme *zavei* (braid), leading the poet into a paradoxically expansive, suicidal discourse: braid it, braid your woe into a rope! The final line, in which the poem's rhythm (shifting patterns of trochaic tetrameter and trimeter, masculine and feminine rhyme) first definitively breaks down, or, alternatively, shifts to the exaggeratedly folkloric (see below), combines the suicide motif with a hyperbolic image of an ocean of drink.

A certain simple directness and emotional intensity is also conveyed in the dense, though pointedly simplistic, sound play, with two triple rhymes (gore, gore, more; da pei, zavei, zavei) and rash of alliteration (Pliun' da Pei; zaVei ... zaVei / VereVochkoi; Topi Tosku). Sound, imagery and, likely, rhythm, as well, speak to folk roots.

In this distorted rhythm and overzealous rhyme and alliteration an echo of the clowning fair barker (*raeshnyi stikh*) is perhaps audible; below, in the "Chibiriak" couplet there will be hints of the *skomorokh* (old Russian singing jester). As Fet writes, "In this *vengerka* [he refers to the song] through the comic-ecstatic dance form [skvoz' komicheski-pliasovuiu formu] bursts the anguished carousing of obliterated happiness."[98] Grigoryev himself referred, in masked autobiographical prose, to his "expansive and soul-grabbing, moaning, singing and bitterly humoristic 'Vengerka.'"[99] The "Poet," the "last Romantic," as Grigoryev called himself, debases himself with his street rhymes as much as his drink. And this leads one to wonder whether in the mix here there isn't yet another deeply Russian mode of behaviour – *iurodstvo*, or holy-foolishness, in which the self-debasing conduct and public suffering of the holy fool are imitative of Christ's passions. These lines, particularly when spoken

---

*Untranslatable "toska" is a feeling of nagging emptiness, usually conveyed as anguish, sorrow, angst, ennui.

by an *intelligent* aware of his "fifths," seem balanced at the paper-thin boundary between *nadryv* (emotional overstrain) and *iurodstvo*.

The lyric subject's suddenly unfettered egoism, contrasting to his previous protective attitude to the heroine, is clearest in the passage:

> Неужель я виноват
>   Тем, что из-за взгляда
> Твоего я был бы рад
>   Вынесть муки ада?
> Что тебя сгубил бы я,
>   И себя с тобою …
> Лишь бы ты была моя,
>   Навсегда со мною.

> (Can I really be blamed
>   That because of your gaze
> I would be happy
>   To suffer the torments of Hell?
> That I would ruin you,
>   And myself with you …
> If only you would be mine,
>   Always with me.)

We are perhaps reluctant to uncritically accept these dark claims on the backdrop of the earlier poems of the cycle and of later lines of this same poem – "Milyi drug, prosti-proshchai, / Proshchai – bud' zdorova!" (Dear friend, forgive-farewell, / Farewell – be well!). However, we can observe an egoism which appears less self-aware, and hence less histrionic, in the lines:

> К сердцу сердцем прижмись!
> На тебе греха не будет,
> А меня пусть люди судят,
>   Меня бог простит …

> (Press [your] heart to mine!
> You won't bear the sin,
> And [as for me] let people judge me,
>   God will forgive me …)

As we can see from Fyodor Tiutchev's contemporaneous Denis'eva cycle, or Lermontov's "Vindication" ("Opravdanie," 1841), which perhaps influenced it, Russian poets at this time were well aware of the destructive social and psychological cost of an illicit and ill-conceived affair for the woman involved. In the earlier poems of the cycle, Grigoryev, while his hero maintains decorum in their relationship, faults the heroine especially for allowing calculation to enter into her life choices (that is – biographically – for choosing a stable and well-to-do mediocrity over an older, talented, somewhat dissolute man who has never proposed and is legally still married). Here, his appeal to the heroine with the words "let people judge me" (the older, married man?) and "God will forgive me" sounds tone deaf. And this childish self-centredness, which is also a licking of wounds, is likewise a symptom of abandon.

Abandon is also visible in a rejection of cultural norms of behaviour and expression, linguistically, in the poem's substandard language and situationally in the wild, and embittered drinking evoked: "zagul likhoi"; "buin[oe] pokhmel'[e]"; "gor'k[oe] vesel'[e]" (roughly, a fiendish bender; raucous alcohol fog;[100] bitter merriment). Substandard folk and lower-class urban (or merchant-class?) morphology, accentuation, and phonetics are well-noted in the scholarship: "otchego b ne *godilós'*"; "*ochenno* uzh skverno"; "po *besonnyim* nocham";[101] "zhizn'" (pronounced *zhist'*, rhyming with prizhmis').[102] Grigoryev also employs evocatively déclassé idiom: "Plevoe uzh delo"; "Govoria primerno." (The homespun substandard quality of these phrases is not conveyable through transation.) It is notable that this language use emerges not at the outset, but towards the middle of the poem as emotion is progressively inflamed by the intensifying music.[103]

The absence of an affective filter is also insinuated through gradually intensifying disruptions of rhythm (like the substandard language, peaking towards the middle of the piece) and mercurial, ill-motivated shifts in discursive framing. Both intensity of emotion and what Liszt calls in his description of Gypsies "the rapid succession of contradictory movements" and "this perpetual to-and-fro of discordant emotions" (rapide succession de mouvements contradictoires; ce va-et-vient perpétuel d'émotions discordantes) is illustrated in the discursive twists and turns of the following lines:[104]

Бásaн, бásaн, басанá,
Басанáта, басанáта,
Ты другому отдана
Без возврата, без возврата …
Что за дело? ты моя!
Разве любит он, как я?
      Нет – уж это дудки!
Доля злая ты моя,
      Глупы эти шутки!

Нам с тобой, моя душа,
       Жизнью жить одною,
Жизнь вдвоем так хороша,
       Порознь – горе злое!
Эх ты, жизнь, моя жизнь …
К сердцу сердцем прижмись!
На тебе греха не будет,
А меня пусть люди судят,
       Меня бог простит …

Literally, and, where appropriate, idiomatically, this is:

(Básan, básan, basaná.
Basanáta, basanáta,
You are given to another
With no recourse, no recourse …
What's it matter? You are mine!
Does he really love like me?
       Fat chance he does!
You, pernicious lot of mine,
       These jokes are poor!
You and me, my soul,
       Are stuck in one life together,
Together life's so fine,
       Apart – grief unrelenting!
What a life, my life …
Press [your] heart to mine!
You won't bear the sin,
And [as for me] let people judge me,
       God will forgive me …)

After a Romani, or quasi-Romani, interlude that sounds like ecstatic gibberish to the Russian ear, we are confronted (in line 85 of the poem) with a bald-faced statement of the poem's central fact – she is given to another.[105] The next line, which appears to continue this denotative statement, is actually evaluative, conveying severity with its emphatic repetition of "without recourse." These lines are followed by a rhetorical question ("Chto za delo?" [What's it matter?]), then a counterfactual statement ("You are mine"), then another rhetorical question (this time addressed primarily to *her*, not to self) and, after this, a rude retort (to her) – "Net – uzh eto dudki!" (Fat chance he does!). Then, the speaker addresses his fate/lot, decrying life's mocking cosmic irony. (This is, after all, biographically, the second time a sophisticated *she* has rejected him for a mediocrity.) At the same time, we understand that the illocutionary force of this statement ("Glupy eti shutki!" [These jokes are poor!]) is implicitly an empty and ill-defined threat.[106] This is followed by a dictum ("You and me, my soul Are stuck in one life together"), now addressed ambiguously, either to the heroine, or (less likely) literally to his soul – bitterly true if the latter, stubbornly self-deceiving in the former case. These lines are followed by another, even more self-apparent maxim in folk idiom, now without a specified addressee. Then the speaker addresses his life, but can't find the words to express what he wants to say to and about it, other than the opening "Ekh, ty," which amounts approximately to "What a raw deal you are!" Then he addresses, apparently, *her* again, but now with an imperative, followed by an (irrational) justification. The strophe closes with a statement of faith – in his own forgiveness from future, imagined sin. Though not clear in the English translation, the Russian, where all these discursive vectors are bound together by tight rhythm and rhyme, is quite gripping. The whole passage seems to convey a profound mental agitation, correlating to the state into which we picture the speaker descending as his life, or at least dreams, slip away.

The poem's trochaic rhythm is first interrupted – or not, as we will see below – by "Verevochkoi gore […] topi tosku v more" – and then again, quite suddenly by "Chibiriák, chibiriák, chibiriáshechka / S golubými ty glazámi, moia dúshechka" (Chibiriak, chibiriak, chibiriashechka / You have blue eyes, my darling), with its anapaestic trimeter and then trochaic hexameter or, more precisely, three feet of third peon ($\_\_\acute{\,}\_$). In these two rhyming lines with identical two-syllable anacrusis, three beats and dactylic clausulae, but with an interval that grows from two to three unstressed syllables, burgeoning pathos[107] crosses over into an echo of the old Russian *skomorokh*. It is not implausible that "chibiriak" stands in for **chembariak*, hypothetically, a resident of Chëmbar, in Ryazan Province, where Mikhail Vladykin, Grigoryev's rival, had his estate. This would make the blue-eyed and slate-black haired Leonida Vizard a newly minted "chembariashka," or in the endearing diminutive, "chembariashechka."[108] In this reading, these clowning lines convey the bitterest irony.

The culmination of rhythmic distortion, however, occurs two-thirds of the way through the poem at the end of the "up-tempo" segment described above, which also features the greatest discursive instability, and immediately before a shift to the next "subdued" segment, introduced with the words "Vnov' unylyi perebor, / Zvuki plachut snova" (Again a melancholy [guitar] phrase, / The sounds sob again). That is, these words form the emotional climax of the central frenetic section of the poem:

> Эх-ма, ты завей
> Веревочкой горе ...
> Загуляй да запей,
> Топи тоску в море!

Literally, this is

> Ekh-ma [a powerfully expressive interjection], braid
> [Your] grief into a rope ...
> Have a drinking bender,
> Drown your sorrow under the sea!

The third line can mean both enter into a many-day, morning-to-night drinking binge (indicated twice in the line with two different verbs), in fact, the more common meaning, or mean drink to forgetfulness (of the specified grief).

To understand the rhythmic structure of the first line it is best to start with an analysis of the third: Загуляй да запей. It is constructed analogously to the 5 syllable + 5 syllable folk metre, with a main phrasal stress on the third syllable of each hemistich and an optional subsidiary word-stress on the first syllable, as well as a caesura between the hemistiches, but here a *masculine*, rather than dactylic clausula in each hemistich: (`) _ ΄ | (`) _ ΄ (Zaguliái | da zapéi).[109] The impression that this is a folk structure is strongly reinforced by the inclusion of a *semantically null* "da" (and) in the first syllable of the second hemistich, in this position highly characteristic of the 5+5 metre.[110] The phrase, after all, consists of an action and its appositive: *zaguliai-zapei*!

We can now return to the first line, which rhymes with and parallels that just considered. This is the most rhythmically distorted and perhaps the most ecstatic of the entire poem. The caesura falls after the opening "Ekh-ma," and the second hemistich takes the same form as the second half of line 3, but with a realized mild stress on *ty*. As regards the first hemistich, a drawing out and strong stress on each of the two syllables of this interjection, it seems, is indicated, with an eliding of the unstressed syllable that ought to separate them. In a sung performance, one can easily imagine the retarding which roughly equalizes the musical time elapsed in the two phrases: Ékh-má, | tý, zavéi.

Given that back-shift in diminutives (*lebedúshka, golovúshka, prigoródok*), is well attested in folk poetry,[111] it seems plausible that the second line should be pronounced with a radical, even cloying folk accentuation, retaining the trochaic pulse of the poem: not *verëvochkoi*, but *verevóchkoi gore*. This seems all the more possible in light of other clearly folk-intoned passages, like "Kak bolit to li bolit / Bolit serdtse, noet" (roughly, Oh, how my heart aches). Note the use here of "to li" as an (unstressed) two-syllable enclitic (compare, in real folk song, "Kak bolit to li bolit u muzha golovka" [oh, how my husband's head aches])[112] as well as the obvious call for contrastive artificial accentuation, a regular feature of folk songs, in "Bólit serdtse, noet" (my stress mark).[113]

If artificial stress in the folk manner was intended by Grigoryev for the second line, it seems possible he might also have intended it even for the fourth. However, there, to maintain the trochaic pulse, the performer would need to introduce *two* artificial stress shifts – "*tópi tósku v móre.*"[114] Without the shift we have a grating clash of two stressed syllables in multisyllabic words (excluded in conventional Russian versification); with it, the emergence of an extreme, even clowningly, folk-tinged voice. The incongruity would be additionally accentuated by the rhyme, uncharacteristic of the authentic Russian folk poetry where one might hear such a stress shift. Either way, the collective, forceful rhythmic irregularity of these four lines demonstrates the cycle's speaker breaking habitual bonds of decorum in concert with an exceptional emotional state.

To the extent that overstraining of emotions shades into irony here, this irony becomes potently self-debasing. But, again, self-debasement is a potential facet of abandon. Self-destructive irony thus becomes a component of Grigoryev's sincere affect.

In "Tsyganskaia vengerka," it is not ultimately the individual statements that bear a sincere resonance for a receptive reader, one who like Blok operates with a similar cultural code, nor is it a complex "face" that might emerge from the speaker's stylistic mash-up. Rather, the residue of sincerity is to be found in the emotional quality of self-debasement and abandon that pervades the whole. Its coherence is precisely an underlying incoherence of discursive strategies, thoughts, and rhythms, dictated by agitation and held together by a common emotional and musical thread … or, maybe, rope.

Each of the four Romantic-period authors we have looked at found unique paths, individual poetic alchemies, so to speak, to embody in poetry a sincere voice. When we consider how they conceptualized sincerity, however, a clearer trajectory emerges. Though incorporating many aspects of Romantic poetics in his work in a deeply meaningful way, Pushkin – born in 1799, six years before Venevitinov – was still weaned on the literature of the eighteenth century and Sentimental-ism. He understood Romantic conventions of authorship as just this – conventions, even as he strove for adequate self-expression, conducted through a variety of genres and voices. Venevitinov was an adept of German Romantic philosophy, particularly Schelling. He experienced both his poetic productivity and its inadequacies against the backdrop of the larger-than-life image of the poet propagated by Romanticism, and his ideas, or better ideals, regarding poetic sincerity are much in concert with Romantic thought. Lermontov belonged to a new generation growing up with Romanticism as a fait accompli. (Romanticism had arrived in Russia in the early 1820s, roughly the same time the movement reached France.) The simultaneous attraction and visible failing of Byronic Romanticism made him particularly sensitive to the disjuncture between image and essence in projected literary and life personae, raising sincerity as a problem and challenge.[115] The even younger Grigoryev styled himself as the "last Romantic" and pursued Romantic ideas with commensurate enthusiasm. He benefited not only from reading Schelling, but that ardent promoter of sincerity from the second generation of English Romantics, Carlyle. Even so, an awareness of sincerity's constructedness remained.

Only in the latter part of the nineteenth century did not only an ideal of sincerity, but a profound *trust in its availability*, begin to take hold. The most conspicuous product of this belief, in Russia, was the phenomenon of Semyon Nadson – unflinchingly earnest consumptive sufferer and prophet of freedom – and his readers. Nadson was idolized in his own day, abandoned as a byword for bad taste in later decades:

Don't laugh at Nadsonovshchina [...] we don't understand and don't hear as they heard and understood. [...] all the time a feverish literary work, candles, applause, burning faces [...]. Like summer insects under the intensely heated glass of a lamp, the whole generation was singed and burnt on the flame of literary fêtes with garlands of allegorical roses, and these gatherings had the character of a cult and sacrifice to atone for the generation. Here came those who wanted to share the fate of the generation to the very death – the snooty remained on the sidelines with Tiutchev and Fet.[116]

But we will skip ahead, leaving aside Nadson, along with some more durable phenomena of mid-nineteenth-century poetic sincerity, to talk about how the sincere voice fared in the quite distinct era of modernism.

4 A Fault Line in Modernism

Traces of poets' failure to recognize one another's purported sincerity provide some of the most potent tools available to us to pry apart competing conceptualizations of sincerity as they are realized in practice. It is something of a cliché that readers most strongly attracted to the poetry of Osip Mandelstam are left slightly cold by Alexander Blok and vice versa. Undeniably, a durable scepticism, or only grudging recognition, marked the mutual reception of the poets themselves. For Mandelstam this was, in significant part, a scepticism vis-à-vis the tragic stance of Blok's lyric hero, which to him seemed to border on tragic pose.[1] Blok's dissatisfaction appears to relate ultimately to an aversion to craft that displaces, or tries to stand in for, the artist's outsized persona, his or her *lichnost'*.[2] Both of these attitudes have dimensions linked to sincerity.

My goal in this chapter will be to flesh out the particular sincerity fault line that divides Blok's and Mandelstam's poetics both in conception and in praxis. While I believe that the radical shift implied in such a comparison is symptomatic of a broader generational turn, in that embarrassment of riches which was Mandelstam's generation of Russian modernist poets, each of his illustrious rivals overcame the Symbolist heritage and the gravitational pull of Blok's charismatic voice in a different way. Mandelstam's approach cannot be facilely extrapolated even to his Acmeist cohort.[3] And still, the contrast between Mandelstam and Blok remains a suggestive and significant one. At issue is a shift in taste exemplary of the transition from the late-Romantic modernism of Blok's mythopoetic Symbolism to more narrowly modernist, or high modernist, writing.[4] Moreover, Mandelstam's understanding of sincerity (expressed primarily implicitly) bears repeated comparison to the ruminations of the Anglo-American modernists, and these conjunctions, which I will point to in the second section of the chapter, strongly affirm – despite notable divergences in poetic practice – the structural and stable nature of this particular modernist sincerity, even perhaps the consistency of development of such a sincerity as a distinct phenomenon given the cultural forces converging at the time.

Lionel Trilling, from his vantage point in the early 1970s, saw Western modernism preparing the soil for a devaluation of sincerity that occurred in the twentieth century. Some of the most influential authors of the "classic literature of our century," i.e., modernism, "took the position that, in relation to their work and their audience, they were not persons or selves, they were artists, by which they meant that they were exactly not, in the phrase with which Wordsworth began his definition of the poet, men speaking to men."[5] However, when we look at the works of Mandelstam, a modernist par excellence, we have to acknowledge that the poem's thrust, while arising from divergent semantic vectors and "ambivalent antitheses," as well as subtle and antiphonal play among subtexts, is not a matter of indifference for the poet.[6] Nor, despite a notable reticence towards the personal, is Mandelstam's poetry on the whole *impersonal*.[7] And Mandelstam's "engagedness" – first and foremost, the extreme value and importance that the poet attaches to *words* – means that authenticity or distortion of the voice remain valid categories in discussing his poetry, something we see strongly confirmed in his own essays about the Symbolists.[8]

That sincerity and authenticity are, in fact, not so much devalued in modernism, as transformed, is yet clearer in the Imagist/Objectivist context of Anglo-American poetry, where poets are given to using the term "sincerity."[9] Below, I will dig deeply into how this modernist sincerity is constituted.[10] Such a vision of sincerity may seem, in its distance from lingering Romantic stereotypes, unfamiliar to many readers, but, as we have seen and will see, it also gravitates towards a much broader pole in the understanding of sincerity, both pre- and post-Romantic and both Western and Russian.

To reiterate: in contrast to that sense of sincerity which foregrounds in various combinations seriousness (earnestness), confessionality, candour, immediacy and intensity of expression, the second pole finds indications of sincerity in a diversity of mood and voice, including irony, which can speak to humanity; it is suspicious of unbroken seriousness, excessive focus on the self and vocal strain, and it recognizes and accepts that linguistic and artistic mediums intercede between speaker and audience. But how are these two poles realized in the modernist context?

Mandelstam vs. Blok

Mandelstam's attitude towards sincerity, or authenticity (the latter term feels intuitively the better fit for his poetry), must be teased out of his writings in hints, and Blok's counterexample will serve as an effective foil to foreground salient elements. To begin with, for Mandelstam, authenticity in the abstract is a constant ("poetry is the consciousness of one's rightness").[11] However, the realization of poetic authenticity in time is dependent upon constant change:

> Poetic speech is a crossbred process, and it is composed of two sounds: the first of these sounds is the, to us, audible and palpable transformation of the very instruments of poetic speech, arising in motion, in the impulse; the second sound is speech itself, that is, the intonational and phonetic work executed by the above-mentioned instruments. [...]
>
> Poetic speech or thought can be said to sound only with a great degree of conditionality, since we hear in it only the crossing of two lines, of which one, taken in and of itself, is absolutely mute; while the other, taken outside of instrumental metamorphosis, is bereft of any significance and any interest and can be paraphrased, which, in my opinion, is the surest sign of the absence of poetry [...].[12]

The first of these two crossing lines, that which in isolation is mute, is the metamorphosis over time of the implements, the musculature of poetry.[13] Without this, verse, no matter how talented the author, will not be poetry. Only the constant metamorphosis of the tools of poetry, its inner generators, can assure the uniquely multi-semantic charge of the poetic image.[14]

The versifier's lines do not sound because his or her speech and world view are constructed of clichés and associations already embedded in language and tradition and resurrected without interrogation. The 1880s poet Nadson is, for Mandelstam, "bad" (plokh), among other qualities, and despite the reality of his personal tragedy, because his "sincere" language and identity are bound by cliché.[15] Herein lies the source of Mandelstam's criticism of the Symbolist rhymes so beloved of his teacher of literature, the poet Vladimir Gippius: *kamen'-plamen'* (stone-flame), *plot'-Gospod'* (flesh-the Lord), *liubov'-krov'* (love-blood).[16] Mandelstam felt the strong compulsion to "work speech [like a craftsman works material, S.G.], not heeding, just the two of us" (rabotat' rech', ne slushaias', sam-drug).[17] Gippius's rhymes imply a laziness of creative will; patterns of thought suggested in the superficial realities of the language are perpetuated. Moreover, in the case of *liubov'-krov'* (love-blood) especially, these linguistic realities inscribe, in both civic and decadent poetry, a simplistic and questionable ethics.[18]

Blok, unlike Nadson, is a poet. While he is, for Mandelstam, a gatherer of the poetic formulas of the nineteenth century,[19] his ship has its own "build."[20] Blok's development as poet ("Letter on Russian Poetry") implies his own understanding of poetry as work and his active search for an authentic voice,[21] as do his discomfort with his own "mask" and the ossification of his image in the public eye.[22] Still, one senses that, for Blok, sincerity is conceptualized as a stable quality, and is in any case not dependent upon an abstract need to transform the implements of poetry. Poetic development, in Blok's verse, is, rather, driven primarily by changes in the poet's world view, which reflect his experience and the historical development of events and discourse.[23] Nor does cliché present a *problem* for Blok. As Tynianov wrote, "[Blok] prefers traditional, even trite images (commonplace truths), since in them is preserved old emotion; slightly updated it is stronger and deeper than the emotion of a new image."[24]

For Mandelstam and Blok, not only the constancy but also what constitutes the artwork's authenticity are differently understood. For Blok, as it should be for a neo-Romantic, a key locus of the artwork's authenticity is the person or persona of the artist. It is no accident that he conceives his life's production of lyric poetry as a "'trilogy of being embodied as a human being'" (trilogiia vochelovecheniia).[25] And Blok's vision of the "person-artiste" (chelovek-artist) ("The Wreck of Humanism" ["Krushenie gumanizma," 1919]) demonstrates in no uncertain terms the importance for him of the artist as extraordinary individual (lichnost').

The poet Ilya Selvinsky's maxim – "A talented poet is sincere; a major poet is candid"[26] – seems, when faced with Blok's poetry, quite apropos. Blok's poetry presents an image of extreme candour that hinges upon seeming violence towards the "interests" of the self, understood in conventional terms. This includes Blok's existential "heart pleads for death" (serdtse prosit gibeli),[27] his "betrayal" of his own social sphere, and his diary-like exposing of the poet's "falls" (padeniia). Unlike the "misdeeds" of a decadent like Valery Briusov, for whom flirtation with the devil was a form of pure exhibitionism, positively valenced by the poet, Blok's "falls" retain their tragedy. His vices, however ecstatic, never lose their coloration as sin.[28]

For Mandelstam, "candour" is not a relevant category. If anything, personal candour is perceived negatively, even if Mandelstam's assertion – "My memory is inimical to all that is personal" – must be taken as hyperbole.[29] Personal candour, however, must be understood as distinct from the charismatic and cathartic *directness* of "Fourth Prose" – which transgresses all bounds of social propriety – and of many poems especially of first half of the 1930s, which meld frank speech with self-deprecating irony.[30]

By the 1930s, the concept of "priamizna/priamota" (straightness/directness) comes to fulfil the role of the closest analogue for "sincerity" (iskrennost') in Mandelstam's idiolect. Unsurprisingly, however, this straightness is idiosyncratic and complex. He speaks with "brutal directness" words most unstraightforward in their tone: "Я скажу тебе с последней / Прямотой: / Всё лишь бредни, шерри-бренди, / Ангел мой" (I will say to you with brutal / Directness, / All's just prattle, sherry brandy, / Angel mine) and laments the poet Andrei Bely: "Где прямизна речей, // Запутанных, как честные зигзаги" (Where is the straightness of speech // Tangled like honest zigzags; "10 January 1934" ["10 ianvaria 1934"]). Straightness and propulsion – the comparison as it develops is to a speed skater – emerge for Mandelstam in a synthesis of seemingly antagonistic vectors.[31]

Formal perfection clearly had meaning for Blok. Evidence of this, if it is needed, can be found in his remarks on his unsuccessful attempts to fix the technically imperfect poems of the first book.[32] Mandelstam – as is powerfully evidenced by his scepticism towards the tragic stance of the older poet – sensed and thirsted for a grounding of art in life. And yet a simple juxtaposition of book reviews by the two poets illustrates well the depth of their differences.

In asking, in 1908 (towards the middle of his poetic path), why one is left cold by the often formally perfect poetry of Nikolai Minsky, Blok answers: "the *incomplete sincerity* of the poet. I think that we no longer have any right to doubt that great works of art are chosen by history only from the number of those of a *'confessional'* nature. [...] Only that creation where [the artist] *burned himself to ash* [...] can become great." He goes on to say that "if this [immolated] soul is vast it moves many generations, many peoples, many centuries." However, "Any truth, confession, be it paltry, ephemeral, parochial [...] we accept with open arms [...]."[33] In stark contrast, Mandelstam wrote, in reviewing Bely's prose in 1923, "The sincerity of Bely's book is a question lying beyond the bounds of literature [...]. A bad book is always a literary and social crime, always a lie."[34]

Thus, for the Blok of 1908, literary value is ultimately derived from sincerity. For Mandelstam, sincerity is only possible in combination with literary worth.

Another measure of the artwork's authenticity for Blok, inasmuch as he fits the mould of Ivanov's "Realistic" Symbolism, is its relation to the transcendent Other. (Ivanov takes his usage of the word "realistic" from the medieval philosophical movement, which, in contrast to nominalism, recognized words as linked to Neoplatonic essences.) The Eternal Feminine will fade, in Blok's poetry, as that anchor, that external truth against which the personal is weighed, and which must be intuited by the poet. However, the Other itself will remain in the form of the rumble of history (the poet's "ear to the ground") and the elemental "spirit of music." When this music ceases to be audible, the poet himself largely falls silent – a phenomenon sensed by both poet and readers during the final years of Blok's life.[35]

Mandelstam finds the measure of the artwork's authenticity, not in a transcendent Other, but in the unique, pre-existing form of the poem itself, which the artist must divine and embody: "The poem lives by that inner image, by that resounding cast of form [tem zvuchashchim slepkom formy], which precedes the written poem. There is not yet a single word, but the poem already sounds. It is the inner image that sounds, it is this which the hearing of the poet grasps [osiazaet]" ("The Word and Culture" ["Slovo i kul'tura," 1921]).[36] And herein, unexpectedly, lies a notable debt to the preceding generation – a conception of the creative process as receptivity. Ivanov writes:

> We believe that the theurgic principle in art is the principle of least force and most receptiveness. Not to lay one's will on the surface of things – this is the highest precept of the artist, rather to discern and herald the hidden will of essences. As a midwife eases the process of birthing, so [the artist] ought to ease in things the emergence of beauty; with sensitive fingers he is called on to remove the film which hinders the birth of the word.[37]

For Ivanov, the artist, through anamnesis, seeks the Platonic ideal, the *realiora*. He rejects invention that is not supported by an intuition of this greater reality.[38] Mandelstam, just as vehemently, rejects (at least for himself) the artist's individualistic, purely imaginative creativity. The great poet, for Mandelstam, is not a writer, but a scribe ("Conversation about Dante" ["Razgovor o Dante," 1933]):

> Dante and fantasy – but that is incompatible! [...] He writes from dictation, he's a copyist, he's a translator ... He's bent double in the pose of a scribe, glancing with fright at the illuminated original lent him from the library of the prior. [...]
>
> ... Here, let me work a little longer, and then I have to show the folio, doused with the tears of a bearded schoolboy, to most strict Beatrice, who radiates not only glory, but literacy.[39]

Thus, at the root of Mandelstam's memorable image of poetry as dictation lies Ivanov's concept of receptivity. Mandelstam seeks to recall not a metaphysical or spiritual ideal, but a pre-existing artistic prototype, a "resounding cast of form," for which he must listen, and which he must fill.[40] His "poet" also answers for his authenticity to a Fair Lady – one gifted with preternaturally impeccable literary taste.

"A lack of measure and tact, a lack of taste – is falsehood," opined Mandelstam.[41] But what determined that taste as concerns sincerity? One might argue that two key factors were the poet's attitudes towards histrionics, or "vocal strain," and irony. Mandelstam deemed Symbolist art as it existed for the most part in Russia "theatrical" in a negative sense: "That which is objectively valuable hides under a heap of stage-prop, pseudo-Symbolist trash [pod kuchei butaforskogo, lzhe-simvolistskogo khlama]." He wrote in "Letter on Russian Poetry" ("Pis'mo o russkoi poezii," 1921) that the Symbolists "struck the highest, most tensile note right away, deafened themselves and did not use the voice [in its] organic capacity for development." Their histrionics is a "[…] hypertrophy of the creative 'I'."[42] Blok is different; in this latter article (in which Mandelstam is at his most generous regarding the older poet), Blok's voice is "living mercury. He has it both warm and cold, while there it is always hot."[43]

Mandelstam's recognition of the incomparably greater affective power and organicity of Blok's poetry did not, however, exempt that poet from misgivings regarding histrionics and disingenuousness or the possibility of individual tragedy in his poetry. Nor was Mandelstam the sole doubter. Others included the idiosyncratic Innokenty Annensky, a key arbiter of taste for the Acmeists, as early as 1909, and Boris Eikhenbaum, who vividly described what it was like to experience the transfiguration of Blok's tragic *pose* into real tragedy at the moment of his early death.[44]

We can hear hints of Mandelstam's scepticism as early as his ecstatic and intricate entry in a playful collective crowning of Blok as "king of poets" in December 1911:

Блок
Король
И маг порока.
Рок
И боль
Венчают Блока

(Blok
Is king
And magus of sin.
Fate
And pain
Crown Blok.)

An ethereal irony, though uninsistent, is to be sensed in the overweening tone, the too-evident artistry,[45] the one-sided, if still expressive, vision of Blok's persona, the way the poem says immodestly (though in the mould of the Symbolists themselves) what ought to be understood – and, what is worse, says it *in miniature*,[46] and finally, in the poem's implicit link to the restaurant atmosphere in which it was penned. It could hardly have appealed much to Blok.

Mandelstam's ambivalence in regard to Blok's theatrical pose is particularly visible in regard to the latter's "Don Giovanni" poem "Steps of the Knight Commander" ("Shagi Komandora," 1910–12), which Mandelstam accorded the status of "civic equality with myth," but which was subject to polemical deconstruction in poems such as "Let, in the stuffy room, where there are clumps of grey cotton" ("Pust' v dushnoi komnate, gde kloch'ia seroi vaty," 1912) and "We shall gather anew in Petersburg" ("V Peterburge my soidemsia snova," 1920). The polemical positioning in relation to Blok's lyric hero in these poems becomes clear only on the basis of extensive exegesis of Mandelstam's difficult and densely allusive poetry.[47] However, we can observe similar doubts in a more accessible and compact context in Mandelstam's "Venetian life, morbid and barren" ("Venitseiskoi zhizni, mrachnoi i besplodnoi," 1920). Blok had concluded the first poem of his "Venice" cycle with not uncharacteristic pathos:

Адриатической любови –
Моей последней –
Прости, прости!

(To my last –
My Adriatic love –
Farewell, farewell! [or: Forgive, forgive!])[48]

Mandelstam recasts Blok's farewell verses to the maiden Venice – who is also the Adriatic, bride of the Doge, and even a (purportedly) last hypostasis of the poet's Heroine – in the key of melodrama, thus underscoring Blok's tragic pose:[49]

Только в пальцах роза или склянка –
Адриатика зеленая, прости!

(In the fingers but a rose or phial –
Green Adriatic, farewell!)

A second element defining the new taste as concerns sincerity was the attitude towards irony. For Blok, in "Irony" ("Ironiia," 1908), condensed and reprinted in his 1918 collection *Russia and the Intelligentsia*, irony is destructive: it subjects everything dear and sacred to cruel deflation.[50] This seductive, derisive nihilism was applied by the poet himself to consummate artistic effect in a poem like "The Fair Booth" ("Balaganchik," 1905). Irony for Blok is, moreover, destructive to sincerity not only through its active undercutting of positive belief, but because sardonic laughter itself nullifies personhood: "The demon of laughter wracks me; and I myself am naught."[51] Blok's tone in his poems is more complex than this radical ideological rejection of irony might seem to imply.[52] Kornei Chukovsky notes in Blok's antithesis the poems' "pathos, eaten away at by irony; irony vanquished by lyricism; blasphemy and glorification simultaneously."[53] Still, the conceptual opposition between irony and sincerity remains. In such a world view, one speaks truth through irony only in spite of oneself (Heinrich Heine, "Nun ist es Zeit").[54] Such irony differs qualitatively from the irony of Mandelstam, who strikingly embodied in his poetry the Acmeist ideal of "luminous [svetlaia] irony, not undermining the roots of our belief."[55]

The closest analogue to Blokian Romantic irony in Mandelstam's poetry is perhaps "I will say to you with brutal [directness]" ("Ia skazhu tebe s poslednei," 1931), in which images dear to the poet in previous years are subjected to bitterly ironic deflation, and an outward, desperate blitheness does not veil radical disenchantment.[56] More frequently, however, in Mandelstam's works, belief and scepticism, seriousness and humour, the elevated and the ironic coexist in a single text. What is more, belief is "shored up" through scepticism. Oleg Lekmanov remarks on the "equilibrium between irony and metaphysical pathos" in Acmeism and notes that "The Acmeists gained the possibility to speak about the esoteric [sokrovennoe] without forcing their voice in the process, having looked at the outside world through the prism of irony."[57] In my monograph *Mandelstam, Blok, and the Boundaries of Mythopoetic Symbolism*, I examined in detail the tendency of Mandelstam's irony to affirm ideals seemingly dethroned after Symbolism through the device of only *ambivalent* irony.

In Mandelstam's second book, *Tristia*, particularly the second half, there is a constant tension and wavering between such "luminous irony" and lofty pathos. For instance, Mandelstam's elevated, culture-centric reading of the topos of parting in the strikingly beautiful lines of "Tristia" (1918) greets ironies and indignities of existence and creativity in the following sister poem "On the rocky spurs of Pieria" ("Na kamennykh otrogakh Pierii," 1919), with its ironically intoned middle stanzas. The original concluding poem, "Saint Isaac's under a veil of milky white" ("Isakii pod fatoi molochnoi belizny," 1921), with its elevated consummation of a Christian Eucharist of memory and faith, yields its place to a new irony-laced ending in the version of the book included in *Poems* (*Stikhotvoreniia*, 1928) – "I, into the circle dance of shades, trampling a tender meadow" ("Ia v khorovod tenei, toptavshikh nezhnyi lug," 1920), and in this new version the final poem itself presents an ironic counterpoint to the elevated preceding cycle of poems on Stygian themes (though these too vary in tone).[58]

One of the most potent of Mandelstam's ironic counterpoints is to be found not his original poetic texts, but in a translation. It presents an interesting case for comparison to Blok, in whose poetry the Eternal Feminine is displaced in the "antithesis" by various manner of "fallen" women. The beautiful, majestic lines of "Sisters – weightiness and tenderness" ("Sestry – tiazhest' i nezhnost'," 1920), which aspire to the expression of deep truths about the asymmetrically dualistic nature of life and the cosmos, can be seen as one of the pinnacles of the almost ceremoniously serious pole of the poetics of *Tristia*. The aura of depth and gravity only increases when we take into account the poem's allusion to Vasily Zhukovsky's "Roses" ("Rozy," 1852), noted by Omry Ronen: "Радость и скорбь на земле знаменуют одно: их в единый / Свежий сплетает венок Промысел тайной рукой" (Joy and grief on [this] earth bespeak one thing: into a single fresh wreath / Providence weaves them with hidden hand).[59] In Zhukovsky's poem, which is pervaded by religious imagery, the roses (sent to him shortly before his death in a drawing) are an "Образ великий, для нас бытия выражающий тайну" (A great image, for us expressing the secret of existence).[60] However, in 1925 in his translation of *bouts-rimés* (a game in which a poem is composed on given rhyme words) from Jules Romains's novel *Les copains*, Mandelstam plays on and ironically deflates central images of his poem: the "slow whirlpool" (medlennyi vodovorot) of existence becomes the "funnel of a urinal" (voronka pissuara). The deviations of the translation from Romain's original leave no doubt that the echo is purposeful.[61] In "Sisters" we read:

У меня остается одна *лишь* забота на свете:
Золотая забота, как *времени бремя* избыть.
[…]
В медленном водовороте тяжелые, нежные *розы*,
Розы тяжесть и нежность *в двойные венки заплела.*

(Just one care remains for me in the world:
A golden care – how to cast off the *burden of time*.
[…]

In a slow whirlpool heavy, tender *roses,*
The roses weightiness and tenderness are *braided into double wreaths.*)

In the translation of Romains:

О, *годы!* О, *часы!* О, *бремя* Иссуара!
Проточная вода *в воронке писсуара!*
В прорывы *бытия* брось *лилию,* Амбер!
Амбер! Кто *вплел в твой герб* позорный камамбер?[62]

(*O, years! O, hours! O, burden* of Issoire!
Running water in *the funnel of a urinal!*
Into the breaches *of existence* throw a *lily,* Ambert!
Ambert! Who has *braided into your coat of arms* disgraceful camembert?)

In this self-irony, however, we fail to sense a threat to the integrity of the original context. The lines' puerility doesn't allow Mandelstam's play to crystallize into delegitimization. At the same time, particularly given the uses of irony more broadly in Mandelstam's poetry, Mandelstam's irony here appears to function as an ex post facto inoculation against the vulnerability of "Sisters" to overseriousness. Seriousness, in Mandelstam's poetry, is subject to and fortified through irony and humour.[63] As we will recall, these elements of the Acmeist taste – diversity of tone, modulation of voice, and, conversely, suspicion of vocal strain and overseriousness – are all characteristics of our second pole in understanding sincerity.

Parallels in Anglo-American Modernism

T.S. Eliot famously and polemically claimed that "The progress of an artist is a continual self-sacrifice, a continual extinction of personality" and "the more perfect the artist, more completely separate in him will be the man who suffers and the mind which creates."[64] However, among the Anglo-American modernists, particularly of the Imagist and Objectivist camps, there were authors unwilling to part in their discourse with the value of sincerity – despite the boon of artistic freedom one might obtain in the jettisoning of sincerity as a norm. The authors quoted below are more explicit than Mandelstam about their understanding of the functioning and nature of sincerity in poetry – at times, distinctly akin to his. It is, therefore, possible in light of their ideas to trace with greater clarity the logical connectedness of certain aspects of the modernist sincerity we have been discussing. Direct influence on Mandelstam, whose English was poor enough that he experienced a reading of Edgar Allan Poe as a senseless seraphimic phonetics, is highly unlikely. Rather, it seems, a similar cultural moment and common influences from Francophone European culture are paramount in generating the parallels.[65]

Perhaps the most fundamental shift in this modernist sincerity is from a seeking of the evidences of sincerity in a relation internal to the poet-*subject* (but with external and supposedly apparent traces in speech) to a seeking of evidence of sincerity in the verity of the art *object* itself.[66] For Mandelstam, this verity is the field of action of the poet, who must exert an uncompromising will in feeling out the "resounding cast of form" that predates the poem. In its focus on the object rather than the subject, this modernist sincerity represents, according to Bonnie Costello, "almost a turnabout to classical sincerity, which was attributed to objects that were free of impurities."[67] It is clearly this shift and the particular set of demands it puts on the poet that makes it possible for Ezra Pound to see "technique as the test of man's sincerity," Louis Zukofsky to recognize "sincerity as craft."[68] In the work of a later poet of similar spirit, Elizabeth Bishop, Susan Rosenbaum sees the precision of the poems' details, their "honest craftsmanship," as that which "articulated the poet's ethical stance."[69]

Mandelstam's image of the "resounding cast of form" is echoed uncannily on various planes in the Anglo-American context, and in ways that clearly reinforce its connection to the concept of receptivity. T.E. Hulme writes that "[…] the big artist, the creative artist, the innovator, leaves the level where things are crystallized out into these definite shapes,[70] and, diving down into the inner flux, comes back with a new shape that he endeavours to fix. He cannot be said to have created it, but to have discovered it, because when he has definitely expressed it we recognize it as true."[71] Zukofsky, with a greater emphasis on the "reality" of what is described than is operative in Mandelstam, opines that "In sincerity shapes appear concomitants of word combinations, precursors of (if there is continuance) completed sound or structure, melody or form. Writing occurs which is the detail, not mirage, of seeing, of thinking with the things as they exist, and of directing them along a line of melody. Shapes suggest themselves, and the mind senses and receives awareness."[72] Though the focus, in the next case, is on process, rather than result, there is also an analogy in "'sincerity' as Marianne Moore uses the term (and its analogues, integrity, genuineness, authenticity)" as "'a magnetism, an ardor, a refusal to be false' (*Predilections*, vii) which 'precipitates a poem' (*Predilections*, 18)."[73] Finally, Pound's concept of "absolute rhythm" also implies an ideal form that must be intuited, though his emphasis is on authenticity, the truth to personal emotion of the poem's found rhythm as the "uncounterfeiting, uncounterfeitable" signature of the poet.[74]

As is made explicit in Hulme's exposition of Henri Bergson (whose lectures Mandelstam may have attended in Paris in 1908), this faculty of receptivity that differentiates the true artist is inextricably linked to the rare and demanding overcoming of convention and cliché. The latter are not only the prevailing mode of literary production, but the essence of human perception in general, which depends on classification for its pragmatic function since the need for "action" governs perception.[75]

Pound's concept of technique as a test of sincerity is likewise announced in immediate connection with a demand for "the trampling down of every convention that impedes or obscures the determination of the law or precise rendering of the impulse."[76] And he, in a passage reminiscent of Mandelstam's comments on the Derzhavin ode in "The Word and Culture," recognizes that "No good poetry is ever written in a manner twenty years old, for to write in such a manner shows conclusively that the writer thinks from books, convention and *cliché*, and not from life [...]"[77] William Carlos Williams writes that "the mask is smooth coin: – slimed their water, fish dung, a stinky, soupy liquid, endearing terms [...] The birth is in a nest of dead words slimed over [...]"[78] Gumilev and Mandelstam expressed in similar terms the need to rejuvenate moribund language: "И, как пчелы в улье опустелом, / Дурно пахнут мертвые слова" (And, like bees in an abandoned hive, / The dead words reek); "Abstract concepts, at the end of a historic era, always stink of rotten fish."[79]

For Hulme, it was this breaking down of convention that allowed for both precision and the real communication of emotion: "Ordinary language communicates nothing of the individuality and freshness of things [...] The excitement of art comes from this rare and unique communication." Zukofsky, however, insists that "sincerity, even in isolation, persists," which is to say, in the face of a "'literary market' not interested in sincerity as craft."[80] This eliding of the attempt to communicate with a contemporary reader echoes conceptually Mandelstam's "On the Interlocutor," which posits an ideally attuned reader in posterity as the addressee of the poet's speech.[81]

Writers like Hulme, likely in 1911 or 1912, and Zukofsky, in 1931, insist on the importance of sincerity, in this modernist understanding, no less than Blok or the Romantic Grigoryev: "If it is sincere in the accurate sense, when the whole of the analogy is necessary to get out the exact curve of the feeling or thing you want to express – there you seem to me to have the highest verse, even though the subject be trivial and the emotions of the infinite far away"; sincerity is "that ability necessary for existence if one *is* a writer."[82] For Pound, "In depicting the motions of the 'human heart' the durability of the writing depends on the exactitude. It is the thing that is true and stays true that keeps fresh for the reader."[83]

Finally, the aspects of vocal modulation and irony so important to Mandelstam's sincere voice are also at the fount of Anglo-American modernism, which reacted against Victorian statement and sentiment. According to Pound, William Butler Yeats, a key precursor, "has made our poetic idiom a thing pliable, a speech without inversions," and the poetry of the future, twentieth-century poetry, "will not try to seem forcible by rhetorical din, and luxurious riot."[84] Pound, moreover, finds in recent poetry a new modality – *logopoeia*, "'the dance of the intellect among words,'" a mode that "takes count in a special way of habits of usage, of the context we *expect* to find with the word, its usual concomitants, of its known acceptances, and of ironical play."[85] *Logopoeia* was of course a major component of Mandelstam's poetics. Note his dense play with intertext and early affirmation of the importance of Logos in contradistinction to Symbolist music – *melopoeia* in Pound's terms.[86]

That flexibility of tone, incorporating irony, which could be a mark of modernist *taste*, is conveyed well in the litany of those against whom Wallace Stevens set out guardians in "Architecture" (published 1918): "For no one proud, nor stiff, / No solemn one, nor pale, / No chafferer, may come [...]."[87] Here, the unabating seriousness of the first pole of sincerity finds itself under siege, recast as commerce (which a priori eviscerates sincerity).[88] The potential function of irony in generating an Anglo-American modernist sincere voice can be briefly illustrated through E.E. Cummings's "now that fierce few," a poem evocative of the Great War from his *is 5* (1926). We find there an ironically distanced, "hollowed-out" (but simultaneously, as an echo, serious) repetition of "requiescat" (from the Catholic prayer for the dead). The playfully scabrous description "[...] six / feet of Breton big good / body, which terminated / in fists hair *wood* // *erect* cursing hatless [...]" graces a poem with simultaneous pretensions to power and dignity: "once upon a / (that is / over:and the sea heaving / indolent colourless forgets)time." And the ending inextricably blends irony and pathos: "carry / carefully the blessed large silent him / into nibbling final worms."[89]

As we have seen, Mandelstam and Blok espoused radically differing visions of what sincerity, or authenticity, in poetry ought to mean. However, below, I have chosen not to examine the most divergent (and perhaps iconic) examples of these poets' work. It will not be my goal here to analyse Blok's charismatic conjuring with the sincere voice and its impact on the general reading public as a broader phenomenon. I will briefly conjecture, however, about some of the factors that helped sustain Blok's success. First, there is what one playfully might call the *chutzpah* factor. The ambitious theurgic/historiosophic poetry of the mythopoetic Symbolists can devolve into silliness or patent falsity if reduced on reception to *solely* an art object. Blok's charismatic poetry thus, in effect, dares the reader to take it seriously *in at least some frame of reference.* Second, in Blok's poetry, there is a rejection of *metaphoricity*, yielding through a bold and pervasive metaphorical poetics, a profound conflation of self with hero/mask. Thirdly, there is an epic, recognizable consistency (in whatever hypostasis) of Blok's mask itself. And finally, there is verbal charisma – Blok's consummate flare with the poetic word, without which all of the above is meaningless. All this combines with a dizzying of array of shades of belief and doubt, deflating irony and pathos, which help construct the hero's "path," and which in their diversity and subtlety perhaps imply to the reader a consciousness and not a construct.

Tynianov wrote the year Blok died: "In this image [of Blok's lyric hero] [people] personify the whole art of Blok; when they speak of his poetry, almost always behind the poetry they inadvertently substitute *a human face* – and it is this *face*, and not the *art*, that everyone loved."[90] (Of course, there were also contemporaries, particularly among writers who knew Blok, who related with deep scepticism to Blok's tragic-Romantic masks. Sergei Solovyov, for one, wrote, after Blok's "psychic asphyxiation" had retrospectively rewritten for him the poetry: "We did not believe in the sincerity of his 'snow pyres,' but now he has proven that the theme of death was not, for him, 'literariness.'")[91]

Similarly, I will not be examining one of those many poems by Mandelstam in which the lyric "I" is most characteristically effaced – for instance, that poem that Mandelstam called his best, the diptych to Natasha Shtempel, and in which only the words "mozhet stat'sia, iasnaia dogadka ..." (it may be, a lucid guess ...) underscore a subjective element to the vision presented.[92] Nor will I be trying to illustrate the full extent of Mandelstam's "vertiginous" (Karabchievsky) and ethereal irony, which ranges from the more outwardly apparent to the more attenuated (the more elevated the diction), and which does not undermine the inspired pathos of his verse, but rather supports it.

Rather, in an attempt to feel out the irreducible difference between Blok's and Mandelstam's sincere voices, I have chosen poems that "lean" towards each other and share elements like a thematic focus on epistemology and a tension between kenosis and prophetism. It is to these poems I now turn.

Two Poems

1. Blok's "To Vl. Bestuzhev. An Answer" ("Vl. Bestuzhevu. Otvet," 1912)

In the poem to which we now turn, the key device generating a human presence and projecting sincerity, is a "kenotic" abnegation of the trope of the poet-prophet's insight, but from within a context of stubborn belief.[93] The younger or mythopoetic Symbolists, of whom Blok was a key figure, had a dualistic and often apocalyptic world view. Their desire was to welcome the divine Wisdom (Sophia), or the Eternal Feminine, into our flawed world, initiating a universal transformation. For these poets, this world's reality and words served as symbols relating to a Neoplatonic, noumenal Other – hence an all-encompassing split in their world view and poetry between *here* and *there*. This program, as one might imagine, simultaneously generated doubts and disillusionment.

In 1909, Blok had written a particularly blunt poem in the mode of Nietzsche's heroic pessimism – "All in the world will die, [your] mother, [your] youth" ("Vse na zemle umret, i mat' i mladost'"). Vladimir Gippius, writing under the pen name Bestuzhev, took umbrage at the final words: "Chto b bylo *zdes'* ei nichego ne nado, / Kogda *ottuda* rinutsia luchi" (So [your soul] would need nothing *here*, / When the rays rush *from there*).[94] In Gippius's understanding, the divine light was already streaming invisibly through our world:

> Ты думаешь – они оттуда ринутся?
>   Мне кажется, что – нет:
> Но в час назначенный все опрокинутся –
>   Все зримые в незримый свет –
>
> Незримый свет, который в зримом стелется [...][95]

> (You think – they'll rush from there?
>   It seems to me – they won't:
> But in the appointed hour everyone will be toppled –
>   All the visible into the invisible light –
>
> The invisible light, which spreads throughout the visible [...])

Gippius's poetic challenge to Blok was thus devoted in significant part to what, for an outsider, can read as "sectarian" hair-splitting. (The abstruse discourse about the divine light, the location of the noumenal Other in relation to the phenomenal world, did, however, have some

deeper implications for pessimism or optimism, acceptance or rejection
of the world.) Blok answered:

Да, знаю я: пронзили ночь отвека
    Незримые лучи.
Но меры нет страданью человека,
    Ослепшего в ночи!

Да, знаю я, что в тайне – мир прекрасен
    (Я знал Тебя, Любовь!),
Но этот шар над льдом жесток и красен,
    Как гнев, как месть, как кровь!

Ты ведаешь, что некий свет струится,
    Объемля всё до дна,
Что ищет нас, что в свисте ветра длится
    Иная тишина …

Но страннику, кто снежной ночью полон,
    Кто загляделся в тьму,
Приснится, что не в вечный свет вошел он,
    А луч сошел к нему.[96]

(Yes, I know: from of old invisible rays
    Have pierced the night.
But there is no measure to the suffering of a person,
    Gone blind in the night!

Yes, I know in secret the world is beautiful
    (I knew You, Love!),
But this globe above the ice is cruel and red,
    Like anger, vengeance, blood!

You know that some such light flows,
    Encompassing all to the core,
That in the whistle of the wind another quiet
    Seeks us, persists …

But the pilgrim who is full of snowy night,
    Who's stared his eyes out peering through the dark,
Will dream not that he has entered the timeless light,
    But that a ray has descended to him.)

Blok responds to Gippius's tendentiousness in the mode of Wordsworth's "man speaking to men" – beginning his poem in medias res with a colloquial "Da, znaiu ia." "Yeah, I know ..." might better convey the vital feel, the idiomatic indivisibility of the phrase, which is reinforced by a colloquial inversion for emphasis and the fact that "Da" here is relatively, or wholly, unstressed, subordinated rhythmically to "znaiu." A surly worker might answer thus. *What* is so obvious is conveyed in contrastingly lofty stylistics: "pronzili noch' otveka / Nezrimye luchi" (from of old invisible rays / Have pierced the night). The catechism, we sense, has gotten old. (And catechism, here, can be quite literal. In Blok's rendering, even more than Gippius's own words, this image is reminiscent of John 1:5.)[97]

In lines 3 and 4, Blok makes a pivot from acknowledgment of this dogma to personal experience. It is of course the speaker of the poem who has "gone blind in the night" of our existence, and Blok's most recent books of lyric poetry had been entitled *Night Hours* (*Nochnye chasy*, 1911) and *Snowy Night* (*Snezhnaia noch'*, 1912). In the context of Blok's emergent lyric trilogy (first published as such in 1911–12), the descent into blindness can read as a reference to the *shared* Symbolist (and, more broadly, Romantic) path from early intimations of the Divine to loss, wandering, and doubt, hence an expression of not only the lyric hero's anguish, but that of a whole cohort of seekers. Still, at the same time, and more saliently, the *acknowledgment* of blindness represents an implicit challenge, with Blok taking a stance of relative humility in relation to others' (and particularly, Gippius's) more sanguine claims.[98]

Line 3 in particular balances at the edge of vocal overstrain, tempered by the transparently self-referential, but still broadening third person, but also by the context. The immeasurable suffering referenced is generated by the fact that the person cannot *feel*, which is here to say, perceive, what he *knows*. In other words, and particularly in light of the preceding evocation of John, the lines write themselves into a venerable tradition of despair experienced by the would-be believer not graced by God, despite an ardent desire, with spiritual vision.[99]

In the second stanza, however, with the parenthetical "(Я знал Тебя, Любовь!)" the speaker indicates that he (again, in contrast to his interlocutor?) has indeed had an intimation of knowledge within the world of that esoteric truth he and Gippius acknowledge. Conveniently, much of Blok's first book of lyric poetry, *Poems about the Fair Lady* (*Stikhi o Prekrasnoi Dame*, 1905), serves as testimony to such intimations, which, like the blindness and suffering of the first stanza, are part and parcel of Blok's mythopoesis. Simultaneously, the line allows for a playful diversity of readings. The speaker knew terrestrial Love, which is divine;

and/or he knew divine Love; and/or he knew Liubov (lit., Love), his estranged wife, who remains evidence enough that the world is beautiful; and/or he knew his wife Liubov who was (at least then, for him and others) the incarnation of the Divine (hence the capitalized familiar "You"). This playfully pointed double- or multiple-entendre diversifies and notably lightens the poem's tone, generating an inertia that cuts somewhat the sharpness of Blok's following, unnerving assessment: the cruel red globe of the sun hovering over the ice is, it would seem, *all* humanity has empirically, in this world, by which to judge the light. That the second stanza too ends with a raised voice, what we might call in interpersonal terms these days "extreme language," is mitigated not only by the contrasting tone of lines 5–6, but also by the conceptual structure of the poem as a whole, which frames this observation as explicitly subjective.

The opening words of the third stanza both recall and contrast stylistically with the opening two. *Da, znaiu ia* → *Ty vedaesh'*. *Vedat'*, a holdover from Church Slavonic, is somewhat archaic and often retains a connection to the religious sphere. Subtly, but unquestionably, it elevates the interlocutor's knowledge, which the poet conveys powerfully, welding conversational diction (*"nekii* svet struitsia"; "ishchet nas") with capacious concepts: "Inaia tishina …" (another quiet), the subtle spatial aporia of "ob"emlia … do dna" (encompassing … [lit.] to the bottom). The conceptual crescendo organizing this stanza is reinforced by intensifying sound play (n'e̱ki̱ **sv'e̱t** s*trui̱tsᴀ̱* → fsvist'e **v'e̱t̲rᴀ̱** dli̱tsᴈ; i*lnayᴈ* ti*lshylna*). Blok, it seems, gives Gippius (or at least the dogma) a best possible hearing.

But this is only to set up the aphoristic concluding turn. By calling himself in the final stanza a *strannik* (pilgrim, wanderer), also a word borrowed from the religious vocabulary, Blok now subtly elevates his own lyric subject as a determined, if vain, seeker of enlightenment. The following phrase, "full of snowy night," by evoking the vast poetic landscapes of his books *Snow Mask* (*Snezhnaia maska*, 1907) and *Night Hours*, simultaneously enlarges and reduces him. We are reminded of the colossal disenchantments of his "Terrible World," of a persona that can encompass vast blizzards and night.[100] However, by reducing this vastness to a single plaintive phrase, equated, moreover, in the following appositive, to an all-too-human disorientation, Blok performs an act of kenosis, an emptying out of his, if not quite godlike, then still larger-than-life, persona. (Godmanhood had, in fact, been the telos of Blok's favourite philosopher, Vladimir Solovyov, and in 1907 he had called himself, at least in metaphor, "an unresurrected Christ.")[101]

This diminution of his lyric hero is continued in the poem's finale, in which Gippius's spiritual knowledge (*vedenie*) is contrasted not to a more secular and human *znanie*, but to the even lesser epistemological certainty of a dream. Within this dream, the all-pervading eternal light is reduced to a single visible ray (evocative visually of those that might split the darkness of a prison).[102] This vision, however, seems enough, given the speaker's apparently demanding epistemology, for the receptive reader to construe him as having had access to a special grace.

There is no question, of course, that Blok's poem is a highly composed and rhetorical structure.[103] By its concept and purpose, it is an explicitly polemical response.[104] However, the poem intimates a "human" voice not through avoidance of the language of poetry, with its inherent perlocutionary power, but through a shunning of the *gratuitously* poetic in combination with gestures towards everyday speech and intonations in the opening, the parenthetical, and the "decrescendo" of the final turn. When we look at the poem's form, in fact, we see how Blok gives Gippius a masterclass in subtlety of rhetorical structure. Where the second half of Gippius's poem was constituted of a hard-to-miss anaphora built of four logically and, mostly, syntactically parallel arguments (with slight variation and concision only in the finale), Blok's parallels and repetitions are varied and interwoven.[105] Moreover, the graceful development of the poem's argument allows for the terse, six-syllable even-numbered lines to strike the reader as embodying an economy of speech. A seeming avoidance of digression and amplification (with the exception of "Kak gnev, kak mest', kak krov'" [Like anger, vengeance, blood]) was further emphasized in the context of the poem's original publication in *The Hyperborean* (*Giperborei*) through posterior framing with Gippius's baggy sixty-four-line rejoinder.

The potent agnosticism of Blok's poem, which contrasts, it should be said, to the self-assured (if also self-directed) didacticism of that poem which Gippius had initially challenged, crowns an oeuvre in which the poet had tried every point of the epistemological compass, from belief to doubt (in regard to metaphysical assumptions) and from the destruction of the illusion of meaning ("The Fair Booth") to, in this poem, an assumption of meaning in a world bereft of the certainty of vision. In sum, Blok, here, performs an exigent, open-eyed revision of his personal epistemology. And the sincere resonance that adheres is undergirded by the poem's range of vocal inflections, which meld the tragic elevation of the mythopoetic Symbolist voice with more approachable modulation, and by the adequacy of these inflections to the poem's discursive framing – a "person's" answer (within the scale of Symbolist writing) to Gippius's self-assured and somewhat nitpicking criticism. It is also shored up by the poem's laconic referencing of personal experience, in terms that collapse key contexts of Blok's poetic works, familiar to readers across Russia.

We should keep in mind as well that Blok's poem makes not only claims about epistemology or personal experience, but also a subtler claim that it is precisely subjective experience which is the sphere of interest of the poet, that subjective perception, at least with regard to the metaphysical, is all the poet can rightly (which is to say, truthfully) speak of.[106] That is, it constructs a conceptual framework within which its own subjectivity can be recognized as more honest than purported "objectivity." But this still leaves the question – does the reader accept the *acuteness* of the speaker's subjective experience as conveyed in good faith? Or rather, which readers are or are not inclined to? The answers have to do not only with reader world view (for instance, a trust in the existence of extraordinary individuals, possessors of uncannily rich and acutely sensitive inner worlds), but also with literary proclivities. The receptive reader of Blok's poem has to have a degree of tolerance for personal and vocal excess ("Mery net stradan'iu cheloveka" [There is no measure to the suffering of a person]; "No etot shar nad l'dom zhestok i krasen" [But this globe above the ice is cruel and red]).[107]

As a strategy for projecting the sincere voice, Blok's act of "kenosis" is analogous, in certain ways, to Derzhavin and Mandelstam's self-deprecating irony, Lermontov's proactive "disarming," and Akhmatova's rejection of prophetism (in a poem to be discussed below). Still, any parallel with Mandelstam only goes so far. The ennobling here of Blok's personal experience, which is raised to the level of dark tragedy – pierced by a single ray of light – structures a voice quite unlike any that the mature Mandelstam might have produced.[108]

The "literary genre of tragedy" has the power "to activate, by the representation of suffering, a faith quite unrelated to hope, a piety that takes virtually the form of pride."[109] And thus, even if the reader does not question the authenticity of Blok's suffering, Blok's "humility" can read, for those sceptical of tragedy, as self-serving. At the same time, Blok's poem betrays a fundamental seriousness (despite its double-entendre) and understated confessionality; gestures at immediacy ("Da, znaiu ia ..."); and maintains a pervasive, if modulated, intensity. In all of this, it continues to strongly engage our first, "expressive" pole in the conceptualization of sincerity. And one might assume it will be readers of similar bent who will be most swayed by its formidable sincerity devices.

2. Mandelstam's Final "Octave": "I will say this in draft, in a whisper" (1937)

Mandelstam's "Octaves," completed mostly in 1933, were eleven fragmentary and subtle eight-line poems mixing philosophical exploration of physical space coming to life with meta-artistic observations.[110] Mandelstam brings a palpable intimacy and urgency to this form in the following poem. It was written in his Voronezh exile in 1937, where he arrived after having written a suicidally frontal and potent epigram about Stalin. (He was to die after a second arrest in a transit camp in the Far East at the end of 1938.) The poem engages a sensibility, as concerns sincerity, or authenticity, quite different from that active in Blok's poem. Mandelstam's poem is pointedly sotto voce, directly challenges Romantic notions of immediacy, makes no personal confession, and tempers its seriousness, even profundity, with a pointed "quirkiness" of vision and language. It is no less, however, in concert with our definition of the sincere voice. As we will recall, this definition demands inflections or devices capable of insinuating a thinking and speaking subject constituted outside the frame of the artwork and projecting speech in good faith (though not necessarily direct or immediate expression) as well as aspiration to convey a truth about self or world that is experienced not as a given, but in a manner that demonstrates its being personally experienced, interrogated, lived.

Here is the text of the poem:

Я скажу это начерно, шопотом,
Потому что еще не пора:
Достигается потом и опытом
Безотчетного неба игра ...

И под временным небом чистилища
Забываем мы часто о том,
Что счастливое небохранилище
Раздвижной и прижизненный дом.[111]

(I will say this in draft – in a whisper
Because the time's not yet come:
Through sweat and experiment* is attained
The play of unaccountable heaven ...

Opyt retains the additional sense of "experience," but next to *potom* (through sweat) leans strongly toward "trial, experiment."

And beneath the temporary sky of purgatory
We oftentimes forget
That the joyous reservoir of heaven
Is an expandable and not-posthumous home.)[112]

The poem begins with an understated, but potentially powerful sincerity device. In the initial line, through the word "shopotom" (in a whisper), Mandelstam intimates a *sonorous* voice and generates an iconic, almost physical proximity to the reader, forced, as it were, to lean in close to listen and, simultaneously, privileged with the ability to hear. The proximity of this voice is charismatic. It collapses, on different planes, hundreds of kilometres and intervening decades. The first, spatial axis of distance is anchored in the second stanza by an implicit image of big sky evoking the geography of the steppe.[113] The second axis, the ever-expanding temporal distance from the reader, is also part of the poem's implicit pragmatics and was well within the conscious purview of the author.[114]

In lines 3–4, "Достигается потом и опытом / Безотчетного неба игра …" (Through sweat and experiment is attained / The play of unaccountable heaven …), the poet describes specifically that paradoxical process of the active achievement of a patina of immediacy which I assert is the nearly inevitable, if not always evident, foundation of resonant poetic sincerity. These lines are also "iconic," but now in a different sense: their form mirrors (and thus, perhaps, subliminally corroborates for the reader) their content. The phrase "potom i opytom" (pronounced: pótəm y ópytəm) epitomizes, in its paronomasia, the result of poetic labour. It is quite apparently, forcefully (note the multiple plosives "contained"), and elegantly sculpted. "Bezotchetnogo neba igra" (the play of unaccountable heaven), in contrast, seems to flow unforced. In particular, the word "bizatch'ótnəvə"(unaccountable), with its four symmetrically balanced unstressed syllables, feels contrastingly unencumbered in the immediate wake of the preceding phrase's almost tongue-twister-like articulation.[115]

Mandelstam's poet speaks not only in a whisper, but, returning to lines 1–2, "in draft," though it is "not yet time." The implication is that we readers have access – *despite, paradoxically, the nature of what is asserted below* – to the particularly immediate, unfinished expression of the poet, and, moreover, that this glimpse granted to us of his poetic workshop is to be understood as access to a secret, that which it is too early to announce to the world. Thus, "nacherno" and "eshche ne pora" together reinforce the sense of the reader's privileged contact established through the word "shopotom." At the same time, they together intimate what is for the at times self-deprecating Mandelstam a potentially winning amalgam of prophetism (elevation) and imperfection (deflation). In addition, the question is begged, at least implicitly – what necessitates a whisper? And the most obvious answer points towards that "perishability" of poet and poem, which, in Clare Cavanagh's words, underwrites the "civic authority" of Mandelstam and Akhmatova.[116]

The second stanza shifts from the metapoetic to a paradoxically grounded philosophical or metaphysical thought that further embodies the "play of unaccountable heaven." That we are dealing with what is to be seen as a particularly charged and fundamental truth is conveyed in line 6, "Zabyvaem my chasto o tom" (We oftentimes forget). Known in some Platonic sense to all, this truth is forgotten by most and thus, it is implied, hermetic at the same time it is simple and universal.

In order to get at the full resonance of the "reveal" of the second quatrain, it is necessary to provide some glosses, linguistic and subtextual. First, "Reservoir of heaven" (line 7) translates a neologism, *nebokhranilishche*, formed in parallel with two words in particular – *vodokhranilishche* (a resevoir, literally, a holder of water) and *zernokhranilishche* (a silo or granary, literally, a holder of grain). Second, the final line's two unexpected epithets subtly diverge from what would be a commonplace. The poet's assertion is that we forget that the inexhaustible (as implied by "reservoir") joyous heavens are with us *in this life* (*prizhiznennyi* being the antonym of *posthumous*), and that these heavens are expandable, and perhaps by their nature capable of offering a glimpse of something beyond. *Razdvizhnoi* refers primarily to physical objects that open up by sliding apart (like a leaf table), often to reveal something beyond (as with doors, in more recent structures ceilings/roofs).[117] One can also in Russian expand (*razdvigat'*) metaphorical horizons. Subtly nodding to Mandelstam's elevation of Hellenic *domesticity*, the final line gathers a powerful positive charge. [118]

At the same time, a commonplace is retained in the roots and morphological structure of these words, from which Mandelstam *departs* to express a deeper and more personal understanding of the metaphysical and phenomenological relation between the "temporary sky of purgatory" and "joyous heavenly reservoir." This commonplace is the idea of the native sky (and frequently stars, since they are identifiable) which remain above one, no matter one's travels, hence a mobile (the root, *dvigat'sia*) and lifelong – *pozhiznennyi* – home.[119] The juxtaposition of these roots is sufficient to evoke this commonplace, despite the direct sense of the phrase, because the reader *expects* this to be the truth conveyed, and the echo of *pozhiznennyi* is particularly strong, likely because of its use in the phrase *pozhiznennyi srok* (life sentence). The poem was even published in the much-cited 1967 Filippov-Struve edition with the word "pozhiznennyi," though all contemporaneous copies show "pri-" and the poet's widow even underscored this prefix (likely because of its unexpectedness) in a copy made for the poet during his lifetime.[120] Mandelstam, in keeping with his rejection of cliché grounded in language, actively subverts the commonplace, but he does not entirely cancel it out. Instead, he gazes at and beyond it in the same way one might be able to gaze past a *razdvizhnoe nebo* (partable sky). Thus, the structure of expression in the poem seems to imply a truth that arises through the interrogation of received wisdom, through the sort of resistance to cliché which, for Mandelstam, is essential for authenticity.

The poem's subtexts, cued by the Riffaterian "agrammaticality" of the final line ("razdvizhnoi ... dom" [expandable/partable ... house]), reinforce this conceptual structure. A short prose text (*krichal'*) by Khlebnikov describes a future in which the house accompanies the traveller. This is a future with mobile, inter-combinable houses of transparent glass, some of which are also "razdvizhnye."[121] The piece is called "My i doma" (We and [our] houses), but this can also be read as "My i dóma," as in "[vot] my i doma" (here we are, home).[122] Khlebnikov, that is, rebirths our commonplace, but justifies it not through the well-worn trope of native stars, but through an innovative and quirky image of travelling, expandable, see-through houses. The Khlebnikov subtext also potentially triggers the other unexpected epithet, *prizhiznennyi*. Khlebnikov's houses reach Mandelstam in posthumous publication and his future-oriented (*budetlianskoe*) vision turns out also to be a posthumous one. Thus, Mandelstam subtly corrects Khlebnikov, who figures as part of the forgetful "we" (along, presumably, with the poet himself in other moments of consciousness).[123]

The second major subtext (or the third, if the second is Dante's emergence from Inferno into Purgatory, with a sudden revelation of sapphire-blue sky), is Leonardo da Vinci's *The Last Supper* in its context on the wall of the refectory of the Convent of Santa Maria delle Grazie (Milan).[124] This subtext activates the sense of *nebokhranilishche* as a silo or granary, since Mandelstam had earlier called the great churches of St. Peter and Sophia granaries of universal good.[125] The deep perspective of da Vinci's mural turns the refectory visually into an "expandable" edifice, whose wall reveals hidden space and, at the far reaches of that space, windows onto an only glimpsed, but limitless, sky. This subtext, once we recognize it, also becomes the earnest of the metapoetic assertion about creative labour and "unaccountability" above. It turns out that this observation is drawn not, or not only, from Mandelstam's praxis, but from the creative genius of all ages, Leonardo, in whose paintings ineffable presence and charm is founded upon untiring sweat and experiment, as is well known.[126]

It would be wrong, however, to understand "the joyous reservoir/ granary of heaven" in "I will say it" as limited to an image of the church. Likely birthed in that visual paradox, the final lines analogously expand, in typical Mandelstam fashion, beyond their semantic boundaries, generating a "play of *unaccountable heaven*" that retains a visual immediacy within the poem and allows for the poem's "home," for poet and reader, to be experienced as accessible, present *during life* and far from the culturally charged space of a convent in Milan. This visual immediacy is supported by the context of exile in the Voronezh steppe, with its, for Mandelstam, oppressively unbounded expanse of grass and sky: "O etot medlennyi, odyshlivyi prostor" (O, this halting, short-of-breath expanse).[127] The Voronezh sky is quite literally, for him, the "sky of purgatory."[128]

The function of the expandable space of the "Supper" is to reveal for Mandelstam a similar characteristic of the purgatorial world as a whole – a new way to look at and through, in order to experience the hidden *presence* of an inexhaustible joyous beyond. In true modernist mode, this revelation about the world emerges through the midwifery of art. It is through sweat and experiment – and through a subtle ekphrasis – that the "unaccountable play of heaven" and with it the patina of immediacy enters Mandelstam's poem. Ultimately, that one can suffocate and feel imprisoned under the broadest skies of our world, and that this imprisonment cannot take from us from us our birthright of the world's hidden joy – a sentiment of rare optimism for Mandelstam in these days – does not have to be experienced as original in order to ring sincere. As readers, we have little doubt that it is a truth, if contingent and maybe fleeting, which is lived and earned by the poet, and at a price few would wish to pay.[129]

The elucidation of these subtexts helps illustrate how Mandelstam is even here, in a deceptively simple and straightforward poem, true to self, to his art, which was from the beginning intended as a monstrous compacting of sense ("Morning of Acmeism" ["Utro akmeizma"]). Multiple seemingly divergent vectors ("Conversation about Dante") link and compound themselves, forging the poem's architectonics of sense and subordinating irreconcilables – like an image of a granary and a reservoir, a church and the sky, the aporia of the *nebokhranilishche* itself, which both is sky and holds sky – and the paradisal, which is both in it and beyond it; like prophecy and imperfection, palpable immediacy and just as palpable madeness, a whisper and the uncanny carrying of this voice. In other words, the elucidation of the subtexts answers a need to be fully honest with the poem and its voice, a need to try to get back to "Mandelstam" – to a reading adequate, or close to adequate, to what Emma Gershtein called his "edinstvennyi v svoem rode intellekt" (his unique intellect).[130]

But we don't, in fact, have to get all the way there, or even recognize the primary subtexts, to hear the sincere resonance of these lines – because the poetic devices Mandelstam uses to generate this voice exist at the level of text and pragmatics. We need only not be put off by these lines' complexity, their compactness, their slight awkwardness, their aporias, their quirkiness. And then the poem's sincerity devices – the iconic proximity of Mandelstam's whisper, his convincing and internally coherent framing of a mediated poetic immediacy, his expression of bitterly earned but joyous truth, which in its very existence on the page is a triumph over circumstances[131] – can work their magic on the reader ... which is to say, on at least some subset of critical, engaged, and informed readers.

It may be that by subtly drawing, in both cases, on at least some elements of the competing pole in the understanding of sincerity (vocal modulation and kenosis for Blok; prophetic elevation of voice and implicit appeal to a biographical "pedestal" for Mandelstam), these poems generate sincere voices more robust and more stably audible for a broader range of readers than they would have otherwise. Tangential evidence for such a possibility can be found in the poet's qualified recognitions of each other. The pathos of Mandelstam's "Venetian life ..." evidently harmonized sufficiently with Blok's own tastes to finally win for him the older poet's stingy recognition. Blok's diary entry from 22 October 1920 reads:

> The highlight of the evening – I[osif] Mandelstam, who arrived having spent time in one of Wrangel's prisons. He has grown greatly. At first it's unbearable to listen to the Gumilev-brand sing-song. Gradually you adjust, the "little yid" hides, the artiste is visible ["zhidochek" priachetsia, viden artist]. His poetry arises from highly original dreams, lying in the sphere of art alone. Gumilev defines his path: from the irrational to the rational (the opposite of mine). His "Venice."[132]

Mandelstam's "growth" here clearly relates at least in part to aesthetic categories, to a poetic maturation, the perception of which might have been eased for Blok by a shift in Mandelstam's poetics – a second wave of Symbolist influence on him during this period.[133] However, this recognition of Mandelstam's poetry comes – despite the fact that the verse itself remains hardly confessional – at that moment when the charismatic persona of the poet-artiste bleeds through and Mandelstam's life experience ("arrived having spent time in one of Wrangel's prisons") has suddenly become capable of serving for Blok as a secondary and indirect, but still palpable, pedestal for that charisma.

That work which Mandelstam praised to Gershtein as "Blok's poem of greatest genius" foregrounds the tragic ethos of the poet and, as in Blok's comments about sincerity, projects a poetry where the speaker has burned to ash. "Tam chelovek sgorel" (There a person burned up) reads its epigraph from Afanasy Fet.[134] However, it also foregrounds an architectonic logical structure and openly recognizes the need to account for the poetic medium:

Как тяжело ходить среди людей
И притворяться непогибшим,
И об игре трагической страстей
Повествовать ещё не жившим.

И, вглядываясь в свой ночной кошмар,
Строй находить в нестройном вихре чувства,
Чтобы по бледным заревам искусства
Узнали жизни гибельной пожар![135]

(How hard it is to walk among the crowd
And give a show of not yet having perished
And tell those who have not yet been alive
About the tragic play of passions.

And gazing into dark, nocturnal dreams,
To find structure in the disorderly whirl of feelings,
So that by the pale afterglows of art
Others might know life's devastating [*or*, a self-destructive life's] fire!)

While Ivanov, the leading theoretician of Symbolism, recognized that in art Dionysian inspirations must be followed by moments of Apollonian structure, what is described by Blok is more radically antithetical to the concept of poetic immediacy. Blok's poet is forced to be *false* to his inner chaos, but the art that is thus produced allows the reader to recognize by its "pale afterglows" the underlying real, and devastating, "fire."[136]

Presumably, at least in part by recognizing the conventionality and mediated quality of art, and that this conventionality is, in fact, the only path to expressing truth, as well as through the poem's step back from the drama of salvation and history, Blok produces a work which remains true to his own ethos, but which appeals to Mandelstam. Mandelstam, in his poem "Pedestrian" ("Peshekhod," 1912), had implicitly criticized the insincerity of the Symbolists' flirtations with their "abyss."[137] One imagines that here he might have recognized Blok's lyric persona as, for a Symbolist, maximally honest before his own.

Despite any similarities, "To Vl. Bestuzhev" and "I will say it" present a qualitative contrast between the straightforward and serious on the one hand and quirkiness of vision and language on the other; between intensity and a certain lightness of being; between cliché as bearer of old and deep emotion (e.g., the single ray of light) and cliché as barrier to truth that necessitates overcoming;[138] between the seeming immediacy of a "man speaking to men" (even if these men are Symbolist poets) and open recognition of the work essential to achieve the critical impression of the independent life of the image. Two things are perhaps most irreducible. The first is the poets' ethos, which affirms or spurns personal tragedy; the second, the connected, underlying sense of what is the proper theme of poetry – truth (artistic, social, ethical, metaphysical), or the poet's experience of it.[139]

This shift in outlook has potentially far-reaching implications. If the locus of authenticity is within the poet, then the soundness of the work's ethics is not essential to its validity (as opposed to the precision with which it conveys the poet's privileged vision). For Blok, individual poems patently "erroneous" in their outlook retain their validity and importance as genuine stages of his poetic path. Their truth remains specific to the poet. If, in contrast, the authenticity of the poem is external to the poet and the mark of sincerity is the "audible" veracity of the artwork itself, then ethics, conscience, as an active and searching faculty, is liable to emerge as a key arbiter and marker, in any given present, of authenticity.[140]

5 Poetic Sincerity in the Totalitarian and Post-Totalitarian Context

What did poetic sincerity mean in the context of the totalitarian and post-totalitarian Soviet Union? This is a question far larger than can be addressed in the following pages, where I will turn my attention to two specific examples of the navigation of poetic sincerity in this context.[1] As a preliminary, however, it is possible to sketch out two prominent divergent and competing, but at times also entangled, contemporary conceptions of how sincerity functions, or ought to function, in literature.

On the one hand, there was a concept of sincerity linked to "correct" political thought. Inquisition-style enquiries into the extent of citizens' sincerity, based of necessity in part on the tangential evidence of biography and class, were a feature of professional and political life, the logic being that enemies are lurking *dvurushniki* (double-dealers).[2] This application of sincerity rhetoric permeated the official and public sphere and in regard to literature "consisted of assessing: is artist X or Y sincerely dedicated to official ideology?"[3] A "sincere" artist was one who from inner conviction unambivalently supported the current orthodox doctrine.

This approach to sincerity was not an entirely new invention. In Russia, a related understanding of sincerity, which was to be recognized in the expression of correct political emotion, had been prevalent in the relations between court and panegyric poets of the early eighteenth century.[4] Nor was a politicized understanding of sincerity limited to those who supported the regime and its politics. The flip-side of this vision of sincerity was a demand for sincerity expressed in coherent, consistent resistance (or, at the least, in a refusal to be compromised by engaging in unworthy, opportunistic, or accommodating speech). The reverberations of such a construction of sincerity can be detected in the cognitive dissonance that emerged among some in the late Soviet period when poets judged active resistors and martyrs of the regime were discovered to have written poetry that did not fit neatly into this narrative.[5] Subscribers to this approach to sincerity on both sides of the ideological divide tended to view the expression of contrastingly unstable or ambivalent political ideologies as a priori failures of sincerity.

Within the public sphere, however, there existed another, competing model for literary sincerity. A glance at three articles will help illustrate this other sort of mid-century consensus, visible despite differences in the authors' temperament and the political contexts in which they wrote. Each brought on a similar barrage of often virulent criticism from those aligned with the regime and defending opposing models – explicitly, of literary production, and, implicitly, of sincerity.

The first, written by critic Elena Usievich, criticized poetry crudely versifying the latest slogans or addressing the passing preoccupations of the Communist Party and defended a broader conception of the lyric. Occasioned by the Pushkin jubilee, it was published in 1937 at the height of the purges and not long after the arrest of Nikolai Bukharin, an advocate for and patron of poets of literary consequence. (Usievich, in her article, throws Bukharin, together with poets Boris Pasternak and Ilya Selvinsky, under the train, not that this aids her with her critics.)[6] The second, "A Conversation about the Lyric" ("Razgovor o lirike"), was published the month after Stalin's death by Olga Berggolts, an accomplished lyric poet, arrested, tortured, rehabilitated in 1939, radio voice and poetic chronicler of blockade Leningrad. It defended lyric "self-expression" and the necessity of a personal lyric "I."[7] Eight months later, Vladimir Pomerantsev, a middle-aged unknown, declared that "the level of sincerity, that is, the level of immediacy of a work" is "the first measure of its valuation" in his article "On Sincerity in Literature," which was to have broad societal resonance.[8]

The first quality uniting these three authors, besides greater or lesser degrees of civic courage, is that they all demonstrate "universalizing" concepts of sincerity.[9] The assumption behind such a mode of sincerity is that the poet's efforts at adequate, introspective self-expression will yield universal experiential truths. In the Soviet context, this is the expression of "our truth," the experience of those living in a socialist (as opposed to bourgeois-capitalist) society.[10] Berggolts expresses this ethos with the greatest clarity:

> There is no need to articulate proof that our reader will pronounce the "I" of the poet as his or her own "I," will make the psychological state of the poet his or her own, only if the poet expresses and formulates (moreover, passionately expresses and masterfully formulates) the fundamental, best, leading emotions of the epoch, lives by what the people live by, that is,

expresses feelings near and dear to the people, *typical feelings*. However, this does not mean the rejection by the poet of his or her own "I," of individuality, but, quite the opposite, presupposes [individuality].[11]

"Individuality" is good, bourgeois "individualism" and decadence bad. In this universalizing approach to sincerity, Berggolts enlists the support of Belinsky, who wrote about Lermontov: "'A great poet, speaking about himself, about his *I*, always speaks about what is common [...]."[12]

Pomerantsev writes: "[books'] sincerity [...] ought to be the result of long thought [dolzhna [...] byt' vynoshennoi]. Their sincerity ought also to be intrepid ... Don't write until it's white hot ... Know what you are struggling for ... [...] don't allow a single line that doesn't breathe [with the greater idea] ... Be independent ... *And then my truth will merge with our common [truth]*."[13] Usievich is also implicitly a universalist. Her thesis is that, for the poet who is genuinely concerned with the life of the people and the nation, "political content organically permeates *all* his creative work," and thus it is not necessary to limit oneself to specifically political themes.[14]

The three authors also agree that sincerity is a critical capacity; that it rejects "cheerful," "self-satisfied" varnishing of reality; that it requires independence and will; that it infuses all parts of the work with a unified, mature thought or ethos.[15]

Pomerantsev's parable of an investigator writing a report about the chairman of a collective farm who violates laws, but tactically and with a clear intent to serve the greater good, gives us the most detailed vision of a mid-century conceptualization of literary sincerity.[16] Pomerantsev's sincerity is thoroughly "Realist" (as opposed to Romantic or naturalist). As in the Russian nineteenth-century Realist tradition, chance details should not distract from the essence of a situation.[17] Nor can a sincerity worthy of emulation be based on a passing mood. (The investigator's transitory moods are strongly linked to nature and weather and thus implicitly construed as Romantic pathetic fallacy.)[18]

The description of the investigator's struggle to adequately and honestly formulate his report teaches that understanding the world means forming a mature relationship to it, which demands work to understand the self.[19] Sincerity is reached through this protracted inner work to find that deeper truth which reconciles apparent, contradictory *truths* arising from contradictory sets of facts about the world.[20] At the same time, one cannot let bare facts speak for themselves – that is, fail to establish a personal viewpoint.[21] However, once the inner struggle yields a synthetic conclusion, this personal, but no longer solely individual truth will not need to be spelled out. It will infuse with its "breath" every line the author writes.[22] Finally, the author should not aim to please his various readers (here represented by the Prosecutor, Secretary of the Regional Communist Committee, Head of the Regional Financial Department, Head of the Regional Land Department), each of whom will "imbibe from the report only what is near to his own circle of interests and inclinations."[23]

The sincerity thus constituted is clearly more than simply a true, thoughtful, and honestly derived political position. It is a manner of presenting the world in the text that is integral, does not shy from complexity, and bears the stamp of individual thought.[24] But it is also simultaneously, perhaps utopically, of the broadest resonance, because people of good faith and intrepid thought living in the same historical context cannot help but struggle with the same sets of contradictions.

While Berggolts and Pomerantsev's articles were published during the post-Stalinist period and had broad impact during the Thaw, the views they expressed clearly matured during the late Stalinist period when they could not be openly expressed in print.[25] Their broad resonance implies that significant swaths of the population either subscribed to such views or to views similar enough that they could project onto these texts their own vision of what sincerity meant.[26]

These two conceptualizations of sincerity of course do not only compete but also intersect and interact, particularly when we are talking about speakers and listeners inclined to oppositional rather than regime-supporting speech. Speakers, depending on individual temperament, could draw in various doses upon both uncompromising, unmasking approaches to contemporaries and events and on the critical, ultimately humanistic relation to self and world implied in Berggolts and Pomerantsev.

At the same time, in the highly charged speech context of the Soviet Union, the figure of *parrhesia*, as described by Michel Foucault, provides a useful touchstone.[27] *Parrhesia*, in its classical meaning, was the frank speech of the democratic Athenian Greeks and their cultural descendants. The *parrhesiastes* (frank speaker) was defined and recognized not so much by the fact that he spoke his mind in full and holding nothing back (the etymological sense of the word), as by the pragmatics of his speech act. The truth he spoke and his sincerity in its expression was guaranteed through the risk he took in speaking and the courage it implies. To be *parrhesia*, his speech had to be 1) critical (of self or, especially, of those to whom it is addressed), 2) addressed to an interlocutor or interlocutors who have the power to harm the speaker, and 3) offered freely out of a sense of moral obligation or duty.

Importantly, truth in *parrhesia* was not dependent on indubitable evidence and the subjecting of claims to a presumption of doubt (as in Cartesian philosophy). "[…] the *parrhesiastes* says what is true because he *knows* that it is true; and he *knows* that it is true because it is really true." In *parrhesia*, "there is always an exact coincidence between belief and truth."[28] In the Soviet context, as in Russian culture and history more broadly, the power of this constellation of danger, criticism, free will, and conviction in ratifying for the hearer the sincerity of the speech act, and thus its truth value, cannot be overestimated, particularly given that the stakes in entering the "game" were indeed often most extreme.

At the same time, sociopolitical realities excluded the possibility of *parrhesia* in the Athenian sense. For, while the Athenian "Assembly speaker risked fines, ostracism, and execution,"[29] his was the speech of the enfranchised. Aliens, slaves, children, and women were deprived of the use of *parrhesia*, as were, in a direct sense, the vast majority of speakers in the Soviet Union.[30] For Mandelstam to compose his Stalin epigram was, in the eyes of Pasternak, an act of suicide (even though he never wrote it down and only recited it to a small circle of acquaintances). Akhmatova, similarly, considered the potential publishing or circulation of her *Requiem*, prior to the Thaw, suicide and not resistance.[31] For these reasons, in the Soviet context, public speech acts in which *not all is said*, but which are undertaken out of a sense of duty and at some risk to the individual, could occupy a middle ground between venal and base speech and potentially suicidal principled truth-telling. Moreover, an absence of compromising speech could not infrequently be read as an act of courage.[32]

The analyses that follow focus on the late 1930s and 1940s and consider not confessional poetry,[33] but two poems that purport to embody sincerity on the higher, and more demanding, if less literal, plane that Pomerantsev posits.[34] The first of these is Akhmatova's *Requiem: 1935–1940* (*Rekviem. 1935–1940*, written 1935–62).

Anna Akhmatova's *Requiem* at the Crossroads of Sincerity Expectations

Akhmatova may seem a strange choice for a central poet through whom to explore mid-century sincerities, given that she began her career in the early-twentieth-century modernist period. However, her poetry is well situated for an exploration of issues central to this book as they relate to the mid-century totalitarian and post-totalitarian context. *Requiem* draws upon reader expectations linked to both mid-century and modernist conceptualizations of sincerity. It generates its charge both from an outward directness of voice and from a simultaneous complication and fracturing. Its reception has been complicated by shifts in the conceptualization of sincerity as that reception transitioned from a mid-century to a late-twentieth-century context.

Given that, on the surface plane, the conceptual thrust of *Requiem* is highly straightforward, while the text's significant complexities on other levels have been the object of extensive scholarly analysis, my goal will not be further explication. I will argue that *Requiem* inscribes a sincere voice through a specific strategy that cannot be reduced to the aura of political resistance and biographical martyrdom surrounding the work. I will also consider, at the end of this section, the issues Alexander Zholkovsky raises regarding the poem's epilogue.[35]

Requiem works, on one level, through the clarity and unambiguousness of its ethical stance regarding the Stalinist terror. On another, it is composed of intricate, multilevelled complexities and contradictions. At the same time, these subtexts, complexities, and contradictions, rather than complicating sense, as is typical in modernism, almost always generate a deepening resonance for the poem's underlying ethos and new types of unity to synthesize its emergent fracturing.[36]

A courageous and entirely straightforward voice protesting the dehumanization of the Stalinist terror could, one assumes, resonate as authentic and sincere to a broad swath of readers who embody the "liberal" public, functioning as the inverted analogue to that "orthodox" sincerity demanded by Stalinist officialdom. Adolf Urban, for instance, writes, following the publication of *Requiem* in the Soviet Union during the period of glasnost, of a "civic, conscience-driven uncircumspect candour" in the work.[37] At the same time, oversimplification was even in the 1930s seen by some public advocates of the lyric as an impediment to sincerity.[38] And more importantly, this voice, it seems, would hardly register as authentic for Akhmatova herself.

As we will recall, Lermontov, in Powelstock's reading, first developed a paradoxical public "authenticity that was unsatisfying to the poet himself and was then at pains to develop a private, deeper authenticity which could satisfy the poet and his most discriminating readers. Akhmatova in *Requiem* appears to chase codependent surface-level and deeper authenticities. The poem's resonance is grounded, in the first place, upon an illusory straightforward simplicity. A "sincere" and personal voice emerges concentrated particularly in a series of conspicuous emotional/conceptual/ethical foci or peaks. At the same time, the authenticity of the voice for Akhmatova and "coeval" readers would appear to be based on a complexity that is true to her voice as modernist poet (however much the horror of the chronotope may seem to relieve her of a demand to function as a traditional "poet").[39] In other words, we may theorize that for *Requiem* to read as a sincere/authentic text to Akhmatova herself as modernist poet, its apparent "immediacy" and "directness" of statement must loom above and take root in a rich and contradictory complexity.

Requiem – a lyric cycle, or long poem constructed of lyrics – bridges the lyric and epic in evoking the experience of the mothers and wives of those repressed in the Stalinist purges largely through the experience of Akhmatova herself. The biggest group of texts was written in the period of just over two years following the arrest of Akhmatova's son, Lev Gumilev, in March 1938, with the earliest of these marked 1939. However, the poem took its final, or almost final, form, depending on which edition is taken as canonical, with the addition of two texts written during Khrushchev's Thaw.[40] The body, on which we will focus, is made up of ten brief numbered lyrics ranging from four lines and one word to twenty lines and is framed by "paratexts" (epigraph, dedication, epilogues, etc.) occupying nearly half the length of the cycle.[41]

Requiem has a cohesive emotional unity and a strong narrative arc built on the development of emotional experience rather than a coherence of events.[42] Akhmatova complicates this unity and dramatic coherence in ways both veiled and demonstrative, noted as follows:

1 Fracturing/disunity of voice
Akhmatova uses stylistic means as well as confusion of geographical and historical references to evoke a series of voices, or a splintering of voice, in the main texts. Two ends are achieved: a fracturing of the psyche as a portrait of trauma and the emergence of a composite speaker through multiplicity of voice.[43]

2 Deformation of chronology
The narrative of the main poems, while referencing some concrete biographical details, clearly presents a mythopoetic generalization of the poet's and others' experience. Akhmatova includes enough dates of composition and internal time indicators to make it clear to anyone who knows the date of Lev's arrest (10 March 1938) that even the poems seemingly contemporary in setting and style cannot be read as a diary of her experience during her son's incarceration. (This is despite the superficial chronology of the dates included in the text, which misleadingly imply that the poems are in chronological order.) What is more, poems 5 and 6, the two central narrative poems according to Efim Etkind,[44] could easily have been reversed, yielding a timeline

more reconcilable with biography. Akhmatova herself is clearly aware of these dates and, moreover, references the highly specific span of seventeen months from Lev's arrest to their prison meeting before his ultimate departure for the labour camps. However, she allows this time frame to relate in the poem rather to the period before his sentence is revealed. It is clear that, for her, the cycle's narrative structure transcends factual biography.

3 Use of subtext

The cycle's resonance is deepened through the use of multiplicitous and multilayered subtexts.[45] For instance, the first line of poem 2, "Тихо льется тихий Дон […]" (Quiet flows the quiet Don […]), potentially evokes multiple contexts on different levels, with an elegantly complementary functionality.[46] Rhythmic associations evoke a nightmarishly out-of-place lullaby, underscoring the grotesque position of the bereft mother in an empty house.[47] A distant echo of Blok's cycle "On Kulikovo Field," reinforced by potential allusion to that work elsewhere in *Requiem*, sets up a contrast with the too sanguine vision of history and the individual's place in it in Blok's work.[48] Yet more obliquely, the subtle evocation of Blok may hide an entirely personal reference to lines by Blok from that same work recited by Lev to his mother in the prison meeting – lines that evoke, through a Blok citation on a postcard sent to Akhmatova during the First World War, Lev's father Nikolai Gumilev, executed by the State.[49] The quite obtrusive, by contrast, nod to Sholokhov's novel *Quiet Don* (*Tikhii Don*) may also point to Lev, as Akhmatova told Emma Gershtein this was his favourite novel.[50] The sonic qualities of differing parts of the line can evoke a whispering or sighing of "Lyova" (cf. lyotsa) and the ring of a funeral bell (Don[-don-don]), associations reinforced in the commentaries of Lydia Chukovskaya and Akhmatova herself.[51] Finally, and most importantly, it seems these words allude specifically to the lines from Cossack folk songs given as epigraphs to Sholokhov's novel, thus introducing an epic historical backdrop of slaughter and the suffering of the bereaved:

Украшен-то наш тихий Дон молодыми вдовами,

Цветен наш батюшка тихий Дон сиротами,

Наполнена волна в тихом Дону отцовскими, материнскими слезами.

Ой ты, наш батюшка тихой Дон!

Ой, что же ты, тихой Дон, мутнехонек течешь? […][52]

(Our quiet Don is adorned with young widows,
Our father the quiet Don is embellished with orphans,
The wave in the quiet Don is filled up with fathers' and mothers' tears.

Oh you, our father quiet Don!
Oh why do you, quiet Don, murky flow?)

4 Pregnant displacements

To take one prominent example, while a requiem is a Mass for the *dead*, who are only obliquely referenced in Akhmatova's cycle, and while the text and constituent parts of a requiem as musical form are evoked only most obliquely in Akhmatova's work, another Latin, religiously inspired musical form, the Stabat Mater, is pointedly present, including through the words "Mat' stoiala" (the Mother stood) in the final, tenth poem of the body. The archetypal Mother's role as witness to her child's torments, moreover, provides the overarching context of the work as a whole.[53] At the same time, in *Requiem*, the arrested are conceived as dead and their "mourners" as living dead. Kees Verheul notes multiple links to the Orthodox *panikhida* (funeral, or memorial, service),[54] while the title as synecdoche brings into the work the here *unarticulated* prayers for mercy and rest for the souls of the dead of which a requiem consists.[55]

5 Achitectonic construction

Abundant connections and echoes among the poems allow for competing visions of its highly architectonic construction. Thus, Etkind and Crone each illustrate series of symmetries but oriented around a slightly different centre.[56] It is also possible to see the main poems as arranged according to the structure of an inverted odic stanza (AABCCBDEED; cf. Lomonosov's "First War Trophies of His Highness Ivan III" ["Pervye trofei ego velichestva Ioanna III," 1741]). The first "tercet" is made up of poems linked by a potential theatrical aspect, with the first two "rhymed" through the shift of voice occurring in their final two lines (see below). Poems 4 and 5 are rhymed through their express invocation of Akhmatova's biography, poems 3 and 6 through their sotto voce quality, while a contrasting contemporary aspect unites the second "tercet." The final four poems are conjoined as explorations of four well-defined and nameable phenomena, with a distinct "rhyme" emerging between Death (8) and Insanity (9) – two potential fates of the traumatized speaker – and another between Sentence (7) and Crucifixion, or *Kazn'* (Execution; 10).

These characteristics underscore for the careful reader the made-ness of *Requiem*, which emerges as a saliently constructed artefact. At the same time, as Michael Basker notes, *Requiem* "indeed seems readily accessible and intensely moving. In lines such as: 'Ia zhdu tebia – mne ochen' trudno' [I wait for you – it's very hard, S.G.] it achieves a pathos-laden directness and an absolute simplicity at the very limits of poetic art."[57]

As noted above, I will argue that this impression of "pathos-laden directness" and "absolute simplicity" emerges from a series of emotional/ethical/conceptual foci, or peaks – one- or two-line forays into a particularly palpable immediacy – which loom, by design, above the texture of the work as a whole, imbuing it with an overarching personal authorial voice. This personal voice emerges at the same time that the complicating tendencies in both texts and subtexts broaden the resonance of individual experience and elevate it as an expression of repeated trauma and national tragedy. To illustrate this dynamic, I will analyse examples from the first seven of the numbered poems.

Poem 1 is the most emphatically stylized of the first-person lyrics:[58]

Уводили тебя на рассвете,
За тобой, как на выносе, шла,
В темной горнице плакали дети,
У божницы свеча оплыла.
На губах твоих холод иконки.
Смертный пот на челе ... Не забыть! –
Буду я, как стрелецкие женки,
Под кремлевскими башнями выть.

(They took you away at dawn,
I followed behind you as at a funeral,
In [their] dark chamber, the children wept,
The candle in the icon corner guttered.
On your lips the cold [touch] of the icon.
Mortal sweat on your brow ... Who could forget! –
Like the [poor] wives of the *streltsy*,
I will wail beneath the Kremlin towers.)

The stylistics initially hampers the reader from drawing an equivalence between the speaker and the biographical Akhmatova. The *gornitsa* (chamber) and *bozhnitsa* (icon corner) can refer either to a historical or to a peasant dwelling. The former sense is intensified by the reference, in the final lines, to the *streltsy*, or musketeers, executed by Peter the

Great en masse after their latest rebellion in support of his sister in 1698. The possibility arises that this speaker is conceived as separate from Akhmatova, or that the speaker should be conceived as a mask of the lyric persona. However, Akhmatova's modernist roots point to another possibility, a "shimmering" or diaphanous ontology of the lyric subject, who is both "Akhmatova" and "not Akhmatova" simultaneously.[59]

This ambiguity of voice in the first six lines has two divergent, but ultimately complementary, artistic functions linked to the problem of sincerity and the sincere voice. First, the modernist character of the cycle's presentation, which is in constant tension with a straightforward biographical context, I would argue, is important to the author's own sense of what constitutes artistic "truth." (On modernist sincerity, particularly that practised by Mandelstam and the Anglo-American Imagists and Objectivists, see chapter 4.) Second, it is precisely this distancing of the lyric voice in the opening six lines that sets up a subtle, but still striking, shift to a more immediate voice in the poem's conclusion.

The final two lines are marked and set apart through a strong syntactic and intonational break; punctuation (the exclamation point-dash at the end of line 6); colloquial syntax (the inversion "Budu ia"); and especially through a discursive shift from past-tense and implied past-tense *narration* to a future-tense *first-person reaction* to the fiercely imagined and feared outcome of the morning's events. The lines are also marked by the rhetorical figure of chiasmus (a crossing), implemented through sound orchestration:

Budu ia, kak s*triletskie* zhon*ki*,
Pod *kriml'ovskimi* **ba**shniami vyt'.

The anchoring *v* of the final word *vyt'* (wail) has, at this point, not appeared for six lines, but was (together with *t*) the dominant phoneme of the opening two lines: "Uvodili *t*ebia na rass*v*e*t*e, / Za *t*oboi, kak na *v*ynose shla." This creates a subtle sense that the final line's visceral "wail" is preordained when it arrives. The force of expression is also intensified through the familiarizing and deflating, sociolinguistically marked diminutive *zhenki* (wives), which underscores the degrading force of this imagined behaviour.

In these concluding lines, the poet takes a familiar but historically distant image (Vasily Surikov's painting *The Morning of the Execution of the Streltsy* [*Utro Streletskoi kazni*]; Mussorgsky's opera *Khovanshchina*)[60] and makes it strikingly concrete and personal. Most importantly, because the comparison to the "wives of the *streltsy*" is made through *simile*, these final lines no longer must be experienced as either a historical mask or a radical use of metaphor (the inseparability and unfusedness of time frames). Suddenly they can function equally well as the direct speech of the "poet." This shift can be experienced as a subtle dropping of a stylized mask or literary stance, an uninsistent but potent transition to a more present and personal "I." For this reason, despite the unlikeliness of a literal enactment of the speaker's words in the contemporary historical context, these lines have the potential to register as an immediate and potent expression of the "poet's" emotional state.

In the second poem of the cycle proper, a parallel device is mounted:

Тихо льется тихий Дон,
Желтый месяц входит в дом,

Входит в шапке набекрень,
Видит желтый месяц тень.

Эта женщина больна,
Эта женщина одна,

Муж в могиле, сын в тюрьме,
Помолитесь обо мне.

(Quiet flows the quiet Don,
A yellow moon enters the home,

It enters in a cocked hat,
The yellow moon sees a shadow.

This woman is not well,
This woman is alone,

Husband in the grave, son in prison,
Pray for me.)

As noted above, the opening registers as a layered cultural reference. It does not intimate a physical setting or speaker-mask but rather evokes through subtext a broad traumatic context. Lines 2–6 sketch impressionistically an ominous picture. The cocked hat is reminiscent of the angled rays of the moon, but also of the menacingly familiar manner of an intruder. Don Cossaks wore their caps cocked.[61] The shadow is both the woman (a shadow of her former self) and the shadow she casts. The poem's trochaic tetrameter rhythm is unusually monotonous –

one might say, demoralized. Not only are all four stresses realized in four of eight lines, with a caesura after the second foot in five of eight, but in lines 1, 2, and 4, which set the tone, each ictus is filled with a separate trochaic word, aligning word breaks with ictuses.[62] Syntax is simplistic, almost childlike (the stuff not only of lullabies, but of nursery rhymes [cf. Russian *shchitalki*], sublimated nightmares),[63] and each line is syntactically self-contained.

The final two lines, as in the previous poem, stand markedly apart. The features Akhmatova employs to engrave this particular couplet with such relief are maximally laconic brevity – reduction to bare, desperate facts;[64] parallelism of construction (capping the parallelisms of the first three couplets); dense paranomasia (**Muzh v mo**g*ile*, sy*n* v tiur*'me* / **Pomo**l*ites'* **obo** *mne*), and a sudden shift from the third to the first person.[65] Moreover, as Alexandra Harrington notes, the reader is suddenly addressed directly; the second-person verb "'gestures across the ontological divide separating the speaker of the poem (the poet?) from those of us sitting "out here" in the world beyond the text.'"[66]

These structural elements combine to violently impose the author's words on the reader at that very moment when the heroine is defined as someone whose betrayals by history and the Soviet state firmly align with the poet's own biography. And yet, in contrast to the preceding poem, these nine simple words could be spoken by many women of Akhmatova's generation, overheard (if not in such sculpted form) all too easily in the Leningrad prison lines.[67] Thus, in this moment when a maximally arresting first-person voice emerges, the double-voicedness (or choral mulitvoicedness), which, by design, elevates the speaker of these lyrics, holds steady, reinforced by the expansive image of suffering subtly introduced in line 1.

In the third, very brief poem, the strikingly intimate words come, rather in the beginning:

Нет, это не я, это кто-то другой страдает.
Я бы так не могла, а то, что случилось,
Пусть черные сукна покроют,
И пусть унесут фонари …
        Ночь.

(No, this isn't me, this is someone else suffering.
I couldn't [suffer] so, and what has happened
Let black felt cloths cover
And the lanterns be carried away …
        Night.)

The opening "Net" (No) cannot be in answer to a question or mistaken supposition (as in Lermontov's "No, I am not Byron, I am another" ["Net, ia ne Bairon, ia drugoi," 1832], for instance). Rather, despite the subdued punctuation, this "no" is an internal protest. Its force and syntactic independence, together with the strong caesura after the fifth syllable, help prevent the reader from sensing any organized metrical pulse in the first line.[68] The vernacular feel is also potentially reinforced through the repetition, which, though it simultaneously creates an "incantatory" emphasis, can equally be experienced as betraying the redundancy of natural speech, as if the speaker were feeling her way forward.

As we proceed further, existence itself appears sucked into a funnel as, line by line, beats and syllables diminish. The expansive white of the page surrounding the poem's sparse text becomes a functional element.[69] However, this white is also contrasted *theatrically* to the encroaching blackness – first of the black felt cloths that are to be brought and then of the all-encompassing night that remains when lanterns (or, alternatively, street lamps) are carried away. The theatrical associations, particularly in light of Akhmatova's well-established typecasting in the culture of the 1910s as an ersatz tragic actress, a Russian Mlle. Rachel, cannot be ignored.[70] "Night" signals an end to the drama, and perhaps to life, sanity, civilization.[71] In its place here, it functions as the only adequate word to describe the looming horror in which culture and self end. However, it can only function as such because it is a word hallowed in culture. Paradoxically, the theatrical masquerades as the breakdown of art.[72]

The upshot of these clearly intentional complications in Akhmatova's formulation of a tragic and non-monologic but simultaneously lyric, immediate, and personal voice in *Requiem* is that she herself recognizes and does not try to elide the difficulties and contradictions involved in speaking *artistically* about a personal and national calamity. Whether or not this embrace of contradiction and acknowledgment of her own theatricality is a winning move in terms of generating a voice reverberating as sincere for Akhmatova's readers (those who recognize these intimations) will depend on their attitude towards and conceptualization of sincerity. Pre-revolutionary flame Boris Anrep called *Requiem* "a great tragic work" and "written in your blood" (napisano vashei krov'iu), which are emphatically not the same thing, and which in their contradictory coexistence nod to the work's complex negotiation of authenticity.[73] While these words are directed to the poet, Anrep talks in the next paragraph about Akhmatova's other recent poetry, which he finds uncompelling, suggesting he is not intentionally flattering. If so, a reader of Akhmatova's own generation and cultural background indeed experienced the overarching voice as sincere.

Anrep's aesthetics were moderate, however. Readers with a strongly *modernist* bent appear to have had distinct difficulty accepting the poem. Roman Timenchik notes the initial reactions of the modernist composer Arthur Lourié ("'a forgery'"), publisher of the Acmeist poets Boris Filippov ("'uneven in its artistic achievement'"), and expert on Russian Futurism Vladimir Markov ("'weak poetry, not on the level of A.'s best' [...] egocentrism, preoccupation with herself'"). All three were, at the time, living in emigration.[74] One might conjecture that they were turned off, in part, by the "concessions" made to achieve the more immediate "face" of the poem.

The fourth poem concludes: "[...] а сколько там / Неповинных жизней кончается ..." ([...] but how many / Innocent lives end there ...). In this poem, more than in any of the other poems of the cycle proper, the lyric subject speaks from a voice that is biographically demarcated as and limited to Akhmatova's own. Devices of reserve help generate the impact of the ending, quoted above. "*Skol'ko* tam" is, outwardly, one of the intensifiers so common from Akhmatova's earliest poetry.[75] However, its tone here in light of the actual biographical circumstances is paradoxically reserved, so that instead of striking the reader as a melodramatic cry, it registers as understatement. Understatement is similarly characteristic of the word *konchaetsia*. Clearly, the "innocent lives" do not simply end, but palpably *obryvaiutsia* (are unnaturally broken off), as one might, indeed, say of the final quatrain. The preceding "Not a sound" is embodied in the prematurely ensuing silence of the final ellipsis and missing twelfth line.[76] This iconic breaking off is itself a figure of reserve – a strategy which we have seen time and again in embodiments of the sincere voice, evoking the choice not to speak that which cannot be spoken without *fal'sh* (falsity). The curtain is dropped before the speaker dares to imagine for us or to put into words the horror experienced not by those bereaved or reduced to subhuman wait and worry, but by those physically repressed.[77]

These figures (understatement and breaking off of speech) having a chilling effect, which contrasts particularly with the poem's opening six lines, spirited in tone, even as they diminish the earlier, carefree heroine: "Показать бы тебе, насмешнице / И любимице всех друзей [...] Как трехсотая, с передачею [...]" (If one could show you, carefree mocker / And favourite of all your friends [...] How three-hundredth, with a parcel [...]).[78]

The opening lines of the fifth poem are called by Urban an "image of piercingly personal pain":[79]

Семнадцать месяцев кричу,
Зову тебя домой.
Кидалась в ноги палачу,
Ты сын и ужас мой.

(Seventeen months I've been screaming,
Calling you home.
I threw myself at the feet of the headsman,
You – son and horror of mine.)

They strike one immediately with their extremity of language and situation. Their functioning is more complex, however. The four lines are constructed as intonational counterpoint. The first, with its striking time frame and present-tense verb with no object, conveys, with powerful immediacy, an utter impotence.[80] We picture a screaming at the walls (throttled, if we feel a need to adjust for the realities of a 1930s communal apartment). The imperfective verb "Kidalas'" (I threw myself) in line 3 similarly connotes impotence, activity without strategic sense or particular belief in a successful outcome.[81] The intervening line, "Zovu tebia domoi" (I call you home), in contrast, evokes, through its strong secondary connotations, a normalized context in which a mother calls her child from the door or window of the apartment building. These two intonational vectors merge in the fourth line, "Ty syn i uzhas moi" (You – son and horror of mine), which can be read as chillingly literal but also evokes the loving "horror" of a mother chastising her unruly son.[82] These four lines thus unite intensity with a complex modulation of voice and play not to one (the expressive) but to both of our poles in the conceptualization of sincerity.[83]

Juxtaposition of lines from poems 5 and 7 with earlier lyrics by Akhmatova demonstrate how the extremity of the poet's biographical situation allows her to translate vocal intonations that previously might have registered as melodrama into the material of tragedy:[84]

От любви твоей загадочной,
Как от боли, в крик кричу,
Стала желтой и припадочной,
Еле ноги волочу. (1918)[85]
            vs.
Семнадцать месяцев кричу,
Зову тебя домой. (*Requiem*)

(I scream out loud as from pain
From your enigmatic love,

I've become jaundiced, given to seizures,
Barely drag my legs. [1918]
> *vs.*

I've been screaming for seventeen months,
Calling you home. [*Requiem*])

Пусть камнем надгробным ляжет
На жизни моей любовь. (1912?)[86]
> *vs.*

И упало каменное слово
На мою еще живую грудь. ("Sentence" [Prigovor], *Requiem*)

(Let love sprawl like a gravestone
Upon my life. [1912?]
> *vs.*

And the stone word fell
Onto my still living breast. ["Sentence," *Requiem*])

The striking first stanza of "Sentence" is constructed on a clash of styles. Lines 1–2 raise the tenor and consequence of the poet's experience to a near impossible height. Then, from this height, we crash to the reality of a life that goes on:

И упало каменное слово
На мою еще живую грудь.
Ничего, ведь я была готова,
Справлюсь с этим как-нибудь.

(And the stone word fell
Onto my still living breast.
I'm okay, after all, I was ready,
I'll get through this somehow.)

The elevated, even biblical stylistics of the opening extends beyond the initial "And" (И)[87] to a generally "pared down," severe and simple diction. The use of singular "slovo" (word) is evocative, uniting the abstraction of myth with the biographically concrete (for instance, the weighty word "prigovoril/a" [has condemned] in official sentences). The epithet "kamennyi" (stone) connotes a general severity, hints of a gravestone, a sense of suffocation (in combination with the "breast" from the next line).

And could Akhmatova have known the *process* of stoning in ancient Israel?

> The place of stoning was as the height of two men. One of the witnesses pushed him down [...] *If he died thereby, that was sufficient; but if not, the second [witness] took a stone and set it* [editorial note: "*i.e.*, dropped it"] *on his heart*. If he died thereby, that sufficed; but if not, the stoning [had to be carried out] by all Israel [...] (Sanhedrin, 6, 4)[88]

The first two lines are thus, whether intuitively or by design, a precise metaphorical description of the experience of being stoned. These severe "biblical" lines are effectively contrasted to the highly colloquial and exceedingly human reaction given in the remaining two lines of the first quatrain ("Nichego" [here, I'm ok]; "Spravlius'" [I'll get through this]). A single impactful stanza again weaves contrasting instantiations of the sincere voice – as persuasive verbal encoding of maximally intense emotional experience and as a subtly modulated, human voice that is true to circumstance. The latter "sincerity" holds precisely because we understand that the speaker is not honest with herself here. The *truth* is rather to a deeply convincing pattern of human thought that incorporates the need for self-deception – "a to ..." (or else ...), as she says later in the poem.

The above passages demonstrate not only a broad range of emotion – the "stages of grief" of wives and mothers – but also a broad diversity of intonations and discursive orientations. Passages like these gather much of the subjective emotional experience of the lyric poems of *Requiem* in tensely focused and intuitively lucid bundles. It is, it seems, this characteristic that leads Naiman to assert: "Akhmatova's language [in *Requiem*] is almost newspaper simple, clear to the people [i.e., a broad reading audience], the majority of her devices are frontal."[89] The fact is not, however, that a "majority" of the poetic devices in *Requiem* are frontal, but that the frontal devices conspire to present the "face" of the work. In counterpoint to the poem's complexities and to elements generalizing the experience or elevating it through less immediate mythical, literary, and religious resonances, these emotional "peaks" aid in defining for the reader a more direct authorial "voice" that hovers above the totality of the work's subjectivity.[90]

The Second Epilogue: Confession of Hubris?

Akhmatova's *Requiem* ends with the following lines:

> А если когда-нибудь в этой стране
> Воздвигнуть задумают памятник мне,

Согласье на это даю торжество,
Но только с условьем – не ставить его

Ни около моря, где я родилась:
Последняя с морем разорвана связь,

Ни в царском саду у заветного пня,
Где тень безутешная ищет меня,

А здесь, где стояла я триста часов
И где для меня не открыли засов.

Затем, что и в смерти блаженной боюсь
Забыть громыхание черных марусь,

Забыть, как постылая хлопала дверь
И выла старуха, как раненый зверь.

И пусть с неподвижных и бронзовых век
Как слезы струится подтаявший снег,

И голубь тюремный пусть гулит вдали,
И тихо идут по Неве корабли.

(And if ever in this country they think
To erect to me a monument,

I give consent for this triumphal event
But with a condition – that it not be placed

Either by the sea, where I was born:
[My] last bond with the sea is torn,

Nor in the tsar's garden by a dear stump,
Where an inconsolable shade seeks for me,

But here, where I stood for three hundred hours
And where they didn't open the bolt for me.

Because even in blessed death I fear
To forget the rumbling of the Black Marias,

To forget, how the insufferable door slammed
And an old woman howled liked a wounded animal.

And let, from [my] motionless and bronze eyelids,
Flow like tears the just-melted snow,

And a prison pigeon coo in the distance,
And ships pass quietly down the Neva.)

Akhmatova wrote to Anatoly Naiman that Lydia Chukovskaya "found an epigraph to all of my poetry: 'Na pozornom pomoste bedy, / Kak pod tronnym stoiu baldakhinom [On the ignominious scaffold of misfortune, / I stand as under a regal canopy].'" "But then maybe it's not to all of it?!" (No kazhetsia eto ne ko vsem?!), she added, it seems, beseechingly.[91] Alexander Zholkovsky finds the invariant of her poetic world in analogous figures of "power through weakness."[92]

In the context of a broader assault on hagiographic biographies of Akhmatova and the poet's "authoritarian" relation to her poetic and iconographic legacy and its meanings as well as a sophisticated study of her life-creating and mythopoetic strategies, Zholkovsky levies a challenge to the sincere resonance of *Requiem*.[93] In summary, the poet's preoccupation with her own posthumous glorification, expressed particularly in a peculiarly material embodiment of the Horatian monument topos in the second part of the epilogue, belies Akhmatova's attempts to associate herself with the simple women of the Petersburg prison queues. She is outwardly oppressed and diminished, surreptitiously regal and full of pride. The epilogue displays "a sophisticated technique of manipulative unfurling-veiling of her narcissism."[94]

Zholkovsky's reading of the second epilogue is seductive but, at least inasmuch as his emphasis remains on the unmasking of a *veiled* narcissism, in this reader's view, imprecise. Zholkovsky writes: "Behind the tactful unassumingness of this discourse, constructed according to the formula, beloved by Akhmatova – *skromnost' pache gordosti* [humility is greater than pride; an idiom frequently meaning "excessive or feigned humility is worse (or a greater hubris) than hubris," S.G.] – the author's requisition for a monument is clearly legible."[95]

I would argue, however, that Akhmatova's *outward* (if still unstated) posture as regards poet, state, and monument is not, in fact, falsely unassuming. The logic runs thus, in my rendering:

Despite my indignation regarding the state's (possible? inevitable?) hypocritical appropriation of my legacy (in some hypothetical future), I pre-emptively demand that any statue erected to me (as poet) be placed in such a way that it stands instead as a timeless witness to the State's crimes, thus not allowing the state to elide the memory of the purges (and what it did to me).

Akhmatova, after all, is writing just three years after the monstrously hypocritical and blatant co-opting of Pushkin's legacy by the Soviet state at the height of the purges during the Pushkin jubilee of 1937.[96] That we are *intended* to understand her "consent" as given only despite palpable indignation is conveyed, in lines 17–20, through the unambiguously negative "Vozdvignut' *zadumaiut*" (*think to* erect) coupled with the ironic echoes of "torzhestvo" (triumph, but also gala event, celebration).

True, the poet gives her permission rather quickly in the face of this indignation. The composition of the second epilogue works to elevate Akhmatova and, in relative terms, to occlude the simple women to whom she dedicates her work: twelve initial lines relate to the other women, the final twenty-two to the poet and her monument. The monumental image of resistance and martyrdom evoked by the hypothetical statue at Kresty – a statue was, in fact, erected on the opposite embankment on the fortieth anniversary of Akhmatova's death in 2006 – yields a figure more powerful, and perhaps also more flattering, than those more personal monuments she rejects.[97]

And notwithstanding this, a question remains whether one can apply here the formula "skromnost' pache gordosti." Where is the pose of modesty in "moi [...] rot, / Kotorym krichit stomil'onnyi narod" (my [...] mouth / Through which screams a 100-million-person nation)? To this reader, moreover, it seems manifestly clear and not at all masked that the monument at issue is a monument to Akhmatova as poet, rather than as representative victim of Stalin's abuses.[98] It is her request, whether coy or not, that this secular (literary) monument be transfigured into a monument to her and her cohort as victims, that is, into a testament to the memory of the purges.

What is more, Akhmatova acquiesces – even, in a sense, *confesses* – to her hubris within the text of the second epilogue. True, she inscribes this self-accusation through subtext, but that is to say, she does it in her own mature poetic idiolect. And the allusion is so transparent, with its classical, archetypal referent, that it seems only the potentially offputting, and hence dissonant, nature of the character traits it underscores explains why it has never been central to readings of the poem in the past. The allusion is, moreover, "ratified" through what appear to be additional references elsewhere in the cycle. I am speaking of the image of Niobe in the penultimate couplet: "И пусть с неподвижных и бронзовых век / Как слезы струится подтаявший снег [...]" (And let, from [my] motionless and bronze eyelids, / Flow like tears the just-melted snow [...]).

Robert Bird has written about the image of Niobe in *Requiem* but assigns the role of key pre-text to the passage about Niobe from the *Iliad*, which, however, is not particularly telling, being part of a Homeric simile bent by Achilles to specific contextual needs.[99] The key texts in regard to *Requiem* are rather the sixth book of Ovid's *Metamorphoses*, where the tale is told in vivid detail, and, secondarily, Sophocles's *Antigone*, where the heroine compares her fate to that of Niobe.[100] Niobe, as is made excruciatingly and repeatedly clear by Ovid, is punished by Latona (Leto) for the hubris that causes her to affront this goddess. All of her fourteen children are slaughtered by Latona's son and daughter Phoebus and Diana (Apollo and Artemis); she loses her husband Amphion, who commits suicide; and, left utterly alone, she is turned to stone by her grief.[101] In *Antigone*, the rain and snow "never leave her," dripping from her stone eyes like tears. A figure of the paradigmatic bereaved mother and, in Ovid's telling, a *statue*, rather than a crag, "within also her vitals are stone. But still she weeps [...] And even to this day tears trickle from the marble."[102]

Niobe is a *mat'-geroinia* (Soviet for "mother of many children"), and her hubris in regard to this great maternal abundance is what gets her in trouble with Latona, a *mat'-odinochka* (single mother) with only two children, though they are Olympian gods. Akhmatova had only one child. Nor could she boast, like Niobe, of wealth and power as the literal Queen of Thebes. Akhmatova's imagined monument is made of bronze (like Falconet's monument to Peter the Great), not of marble. But as if in compensation for these, in truth, not so crucial divergences, there are additional eloquent echoes to back up the fundamental image connection. For one, Niobe's husband, Amphion, together with his twin brother, built the walls of Thebes. Amphion's role in this endeavour is that he moves the stones into place by playing on a lyre given him by Hermes.[103] In other words, he is a Poet-Mason, a fine calque for Akhmatova's executed former husband, the Acmeist poet Nikolai Gumilev.[104] Niobe can boast not only of high birth, but, like the young Akhmatova, of beauty and a striking presence: "*thronged about* with a numerous following, a *notable figure* in *Phrygian robes* [compare Akhmatova's always elegantly striking dress] [...] and beautiful as far as anger suffered her to be [Akhmatova's when desired fear-inducing *regal* presence];[105] and *tossing her shapely head* [...]."[106]

In this latter element, we have potential evidence that Akhmatova had specifically Ovid's Niobe in the back, or even forefront, of her mind as she wrote the second part of the epilogue. The phrase "movensque decoro cum capite" is reproduced, perhaps playfully, almost verbatim in the opening of the poem, displaced to an anonymous woman: "ta, chto, *krasivoi triakhnuv golovoi* [...]" (that one that, *having tossed her pretty head* [...]). [107]

To push the parallels further, Niobe's pride is also a vanity ("I have beauty worthy of a goddess").[108] Niobe has, according to Latona, "her father [Tantalus's] unbridled tongue," and she continues her prideful speech even after the death of her sons (calling down doom on her daughters as well). "Misery made her bold."[109] The passage "Alas, how different now was this Niobe from that Niobe who had but now driven the people from Latona's altar, and had walked proudly through the city streets, enviable then to her friends, but now one for even her enemies to pity"[110] is notably reminiscent of the structure and logic of the opening of poem 4 of *Requiem*, "If one could show you, carefree mocker" (Pokazat' by tebe, nasmeshnitsa). After Niobe has lost all but one daughter, "The mother, covering her with her crouching body and her sheltering robes, cried out: "Oh, leave me one, the littlest! [...] I beg you – just one!" – words perhaps reminiscent of Akhmatova's self-abasing letter to Stalin of 6 April 1939, and with it, poem 5 (cf. "Kidalas' v nogi palachu" [Threw myself to the feet of the executioner]).[111]

What seems clear is that Niobe and her fate were not far from Akhmatova's mind and that she uses the image of this epically bereaved mother from a mythological context to close the epilogues of *Requiem* in concert with but also in contrast to the sacred image of the Virgin that closes the main texts. Niobe is deployed, however, not only as the paradigmatic image of the grieving mother, but also as a nod to an in some ways kindred soul subject to analogous travails and weaknesses. Surely, Niobe figures in the epilogue – written in March 1940 – not outside of the context of her hubris, but because Akhmatova senses that her own ambition and pride, perhaps given new life by that winter's unexpected, temporary, radically positive turn in her literary fortunes, may be her tragic flaw.[112]

The image of Niobe, *immortalized* in her sorrow, does not dissonate with Akhmatova's overarching strategy of "power through weakness" (Zholkovsky).[113] Moreover, it is precisely the inscription of a *tragic flaw* that can accord Akhmatova's literary heroine the status of tragic hero in the classical mode. Akhmatova hardly shields from view the hubris potentially inhering in her projected monument and

even advertises – subtextually, but in no uncertain terms – her aware-
ness of her own potential pride and vanity.

Lionel Trilling, in the opening pages of *Sincerity and Authenticity*,
takes Polonius's advice to Laertes in *Hamlet* – "This above all: to thine
own self be true [...]" – as a central example of the emergence of an
ethic of sincerity in modern Europe.[114] Nikolai Nedobrovo, writing in
1915, had noted:

> [...] Akhmatova's vocal arrangements [golosovedenie] themselves, firm
> and rather self-assured, than not, [her] very calmness in confession and
> pain and weakness, finally, the very abundance of poetically transfigured
> torments – all this testifies not to a delicacy [or, tearfulness] on account of
> everyday trifles, but reveals a lyric soul sooner rough than too soft, rather
> cruel than tearful, and manifestly commanding [gospodstvuiushchaia]
> and not oppressed.[115]

So, if this was the essence of Akhmatova (or "Akhmatova"), apparent
to the most sensitive of her readers as early as 1915, if one perceives the
poet as "true to her own self" in dutifully betraying this dominating
self to others, might this not strike the reader as human to a fault, and,
indeed, sincere? For Zholkovsky, this argument – shared with him –
falls flat. The epilogue still reads, after my claims, as manipulation –
brilliant, modernist manipulation, inconspicuously "naturalized" au-
thorial play with established topoi – but manipulation none the less.

Nikolai Bogomolov, after constituting the nature of Akhmatova's
"life-creation" in terms consonant with Zholkovsky's, writes:

> The change of generations, chronological distance, shifting of the bound-
> aries of aesthetic categories led to the fact that in the [publicly presented]
> image [of Akhmatova; her *oblik*], internally complex and simultaneously
> directed toward a singular goal, it became possible to differentiate "hu-
> man, too human" features. And this gave birth, in turn, to the possibility
> of understanding all of Akhmatova's artistic and life creativity as artificial,
> in some way most unpleasant, and in part even self-parodic. [...] Akhma-
> tova is not at fault in such an impression [...]. The turn of the twentieth
> and twenty-first centuries has come to dictate different demands on po-
> etry that is perceived as contemporary, and here the meticulously con-
> ceived and harmoniously constructed edifice came to seem pompous and
> uninviting.[116]

Resonant sincerity, as I have argued throughout this study, is depend-
ent on reader communities possessing cultural codes suited to its

decoding. *Requiem* now potentially coexists in several reader universes that presume divergent understandings of how sincerity is encoded in literature, only some of which existed at the time of its writing. If, in "Monument," Pushkin seemed able, almost miraculously, to generate a sincere resonance for competing readerships in radical disagreement about the poem's meaning and focused on different, alternatively salient elements, Akhmatova's self-positioning in *Requiem* has turned out to be less durably advantageous. Her posture can register as sincere to one subset of readers who perhaps thirst after a heroine of resistance and memory – a model or paragon inherently elevated even as she shares the demeaning and capricious fate of her fellow women. One could easily imagine that this group might include some of the women to whom the poem itself is dedicated. No less a reader than Vladimir Toporov saw *Requiem* "not only as a fact of history and literature," but, through its pragmatics, its "synchronous, constant" years-long memorization and repetition "in a whisper or under the breath" as a "memorial rite in the strict sense of this word – for all the victims [...]."[117] But *Requiem* is poetry – as Akhmatova herself insisted – and the same posture has turned out to be off-putting for other, and particularly more recent, readers.[118] That one of these groups displays a lesser tolerance for the internal contradictions that challenge Akhmatova's ethical maximalism does not mean, however, that the text does not also encode those markers of sincerity salient to the other group, and still audible, it seems, to intermediary readerships.

Konstantin Levin: An Ironic Mid-Century Sincerity

How can one write a thematically ambitious poem touching on Stalin in the post-war period, write it with open eyes, write it not "for the ashtray" (as Akhmatova wrote her *Requiem*), and yet attain a durably sincere voice? How can one write sincere *poetry* in the immediate aftermath of the Second World War's horrors at all?[119]

The following poem, by Konstantin Levin, a highly original writer of the war generation, was recited "passionately, with enthusiasm" (goriacho, uvlechenno) to Konstantin Azadovsky by Joseph Brodsky in the 1960s. I cite it at length, in part because of its limited accessibility:

Нас хоронила артиллерия.	The artillery was laying us to rest.
Она сначала нас убила	First it killed us
И, не гнушаясь лицемерием,	And, not shying from hypocrisy,
Клялась потом, что нас любила.	Swore afterwards it loved us.

Она раскаивалась жерлами,
Но мы не верили ей дружно
Всеми искромсанными нервами
В руках полковников медслужбы.

Мы доверяли только морфию,
По самой крайней мере – брому,
А те из нас, что были мертвыми,
Земле неверной, но знакомой.

[...]

Нас поздравляли пэры Англии
И англичанки восковые,
Интервьюировали б ангелы,
Когда б здесь были таковые.

[...]

Один из нас, случайно выживший,
В Москву осеннюю приехал.
Он брел по улицам, как выпивший,
Он меж живыми шел, как эхо.

Кому-то помешал в троллейбусе
Ногой искусственной своею.
Сквозь эти мелкие нелепости
Он приближался к Мавзолею.

Там все еще ползут, минируют
И отражают контрудары,
А здесь уже иллюминируют,
Уже кропают мемуары.

И здесь, вдали от зоны гибельной,
Лиловым лоском льют паркеты,
Большой театр квадригой вздыбленной
Следит салютные ракеты.

И здесь, по мановенью Файера,
Взлетают стати Лепешинской,

It regretted with the maws [of guns],
But we gave no credence all as one
With all our shorn and mangled nerves
In the hands of the colonels of the medical ward.

We trusted only morphine,
Bromide as a very last resort,
 – And those of us [already] dead –
The earth, unfaithful though familiar.

[...]

Peers of England greeted us
And waxlike English girls;
Angels would have interviewed us
If any angels were around.

[...]

One of us who survived by chance
Arrived in autumn Moscow.
He wandered the streets like a drunken man,
He walked among the living like an echo.

He inconvenienced someone on the trolley
With his artificial leg.
Surmounting these minor absurdities,
He approached the Mausoleum.

There [men] still crawl, lay mines
And fend off counterattacks,
While here they're already lighting up the city,
Already puttering away at memoirs.

And here, far from the danger zone,
They swash parquet with purplish gloss,
The Bolshoi with its rearing foursome
Follows the firework rockets' flight.

And here, at the wave of Fayer's hand,
Fly up the forms of Lepeshinskaya,

И фары плавят плечи фрайера	And the headlights smelt the shoulders of [some] chump
И шубки женские в пушинках.	And women's fur coats [all] in snowflakes.
Солдаты спят. Им льет регалии	The soldiers sleep. At night the mint
Монетный двор порой ночною.	Is pouring them decorations,
А пулеметы обрыгали их	As the machine guns showered them
Блевотиною разрывною.	With [their] explosive vomit.
Но нас не испугает ненависть	But we'll not be cowed by the animosity
Вечерних баров, тайных спален.	Of evening bars, of secret bedchambers.
У нас защитник несравненный есть –	We have an incomparable defender –
Главнокомандующий Сталин.	Commander-in-Chief Stalin.
И отослав уже к полуночи	And having sent off by midnight
Секретарей и адъютантов,	The secretaries and the adjutants,
Он видит: в серых касках юноши	He sees: in grey helmets youths
Свисают с обгорелых танков.	Hang from burnt out tanks.
На них пилоты с неба рушатся,	Pilots plummet towards them from the sky,
Костями в тучах застревая.	Lodging among the clouds their bones.
Но не оскудевает мужество,	But fortitude does not run dry,
Как небо не устаревает.	Just as the sky does not get old.
Так пусть любовь и независимость	So may love and independence
Нас отличат от проходимцев,	Distinguish us from the scammers,
Как отличил Генералиссимус	As the Generalissimus has distinguished
Своих неназванных любимцев.[120]	His unnamed favourites.

"The artillery was laying us to rest," when published, posthumously, in the 1980s, was substantially rewritten.[121] Azadovsky's text, despite its problematic history, provides what access we are afforded to the original 1946 version.[122]

Azadovsky writes that "redaction of this sort – even with the acquiescence and participation of the author – deprived the poem of its central merit: sincerity."[123] He then outlines what he sees as the essence of this sincerity:

At that time, in 1946, Levin was able to convey in his poem the feelings of many thousands of soldiers from the front. The general exultation that had

> seized the victorious nation and still fresh grief for the perished united then, it seemed, the peak and base of the state pyramid: the infantryman and the Generalissimus [...] and it is not surprising that his image crowning the poem sounds like an apotheosis!

This is accompanied by a sensitive grasping by Levin of the

> incipient division of the "united Soviet people" into participants of the war and its "memoirists" [...] Soldiers from the front, maimed by the war, already sensing their "superfluousness" [...] yet hoped for recognition of their contributions and, duped more than once, sincerely believed that this recognition could be obtained only from Stalin himself. The author seems to share in their faith. But in the final chords, nonetheless, wafts a doubt, still vague, emerging little by little [or, surreptitiously, S.G.], intonationally. Grief for those who died (one of the main motifs of Levin's war lyrics) is stiffened by deeply hidden disenchantment. All of this makes "The Artillery" (of course, in its initial, authentic state) an immortal poetic testimony of the epoch.[124]

Levin's tone in the original version is indeed remarkable. He is critical without defiance, fraternal without indiscriminacy, enthusiastic without blindness, disappointed without losing touch with a fundamental individual optimism and vitality. A palpable sincerity is founded throughout upon various modes of irony, and a subtle complexity of outlook is perceptible even in the final "apotheosis." In the end, I will argue, Levin evinces quite concretely, if not demonstratively, a tugging scepticism directed at Stalin. At the same time, the poem is constructed such that the bulk of its original audience was apparently so struck by the boldly negative image of the home front that occupies the centre of the poem as to miss the yet more brazen question it poses.[125]

Azadovsky's version of Levin's text shows a clearly thought-out composition (replaced in the later versions): six stanzas about the front and hospital, six describing the visit of the soldier who "randomly survived" to the incongruous "home front" of wartime Moscow, and four relating to Commander-in-Chief Stalin, who from the capital experiences visions of and a connection to the front. The idiosyncratic, deadpan tone of the opening lines was surely a source of the poem's appeal. Although the ontology of the artillery's burial rites is not entirely clear, it is apparent that the opening lines represent to us a false service. The pity rendered by the artillery in burying the dead is belied by its role in the soldiers' deaths and becomes an act of open hypocrisy when the artillery professes its love for them.

Most likely, we should understand the role of the artillery as oblique. The artillery kills the soldiers inasmuch as they take a role in the suicidally dangerous artillery attack. (Levin's deployment took out German tanks at short range with the small 45 mm artillery gun artfully nicknamed "goodbye, Motherland!" [proshchai, Rodina!]. In just four months, he was wounded twice, losing a leg, and decorated twice, the order for a third decoration having been lost while he was in hospital.)[126] The ontology of the speaker is also not immediately clear. He seems, particularly in line 2, to speak from the dead, though it soon becomes clear that he speaks for the dead and living and is rather in hospital. The strangeness of this opening – which certainly fits the definition of formalist critic Victor Shklovsky's *ostranenie* (defamiliarization, as a central device in literature) – calls the hearer to heightened attention in order to process the situation.[127] After lines 5–6, the poem settles into a more realistic mode of description, still, however, deeply informed by the speaker's ironic view of the world.

The somewhat detached situational irony of the opening, despite the potency of "ne gnushchaias' litsemeriem" (not [revolted by and hence] shunning hypocrisy), avoids any descent into personal bitterness. The tightrope-walking tone is illustrated in the second stanza in the tension between "ne verili ei *druzhno*" (gave no credence *all as one*) and "Vsemi *iskromsannymi* nervami" (With all our *shorn and mangled* nerves). ("Iskromsannymi" potentially implies a rough cutting job by the Soviet surgeons.)[128]

The irony continues near the front as the wounded soldiers present an interest for English lords and ladies and documentary cameramen, who are wishfully jeered by owls, and then the ironic eye travels with a surviving soldier to the streets of Moscow, where a constant contrast is drawn between the experience of the front and the oblivious and even unscrupulous home front. In this section, the irony shifts its character, becoming not philosophical and resigned but indignant and assailing in a way that hardly seems necessary to illustrate.

After these latter six stanzas, the tone suddenly becomes elevated: "zashchitnik nesravnennyi" (incomparable defender), "Glavnokomanduiushchii Stalin" (Commander-in-Chief Stalin), "ne oskudevaet muzhestvo" (bravery is not depleted), "nebo ne ustarevaet" (the heaven does not get old), "liubov' i nezavisimost'" (love and independence), "Svoikh nenazvannykh liubimtsev" (His unnamed favourites), the "Generalissimus." Many of these words sound like they could come straight out of the official lexicon, as does the image of the great leader, who, a modern-day *tsar'-batiushka* (Tsar-father [to all]), spends his nights agonizing over the unavoidable but gruesome fate of his beloved "sons." However, as we listen more intently to the passage, the tone begins to drift. The deaths of the soldiers are depicted in more gory, even phantasmagoric, detail than is necessary. Of course, this is presumably to the virtue of Stalin, who cannot help but picture so vividly the deaths of his soldiers. "Muzhestvo" – "military valour, courage" when used in official contexts – can also mean a more general resolve, the strength and presence of mind to press on, to suffer through hardship and calamity, and in this meaning can depict a different kind of individual strength.[129] "Ne ustarevaet" (does not get old) also tends towards ambivalence in the wartime context, potentially calling to mind the soldier killed in battle who does not grow old (ne stareet). "Nezavisimost'" (independence), while its usage is justified in light of the contrast with the sycophantic "scammers" who populate the capital, also perhaps hides a challenge to the state or leader to accept this autonomy. And "Generalissimus" is a title, not a rank – a particularly pompous one, which can, at times, be presented, or self-presented, to the unworthy. Because of this, it lends itself to ironic and figurative usages. In the most immediate context, "Generalissimus" was a cliché from the official congratulatory speeches of 1945 and had not been used during the war. It thus makes for a potential stylistic contrast to the severe, simple, and familiar "glavnokomanduiushchii" (Commander-in-Chief) above. Likely, these are some of the markers of a sneaking ambivalence that struck Azadovsky.[130]

Yet more crucial, however, is the question that is inescapably posed, I would argue, through the poem's composition, and which becomes perceptible only when we juxtapose the closing of this quite long poem with the opening six lines. The final and initial lines form a ring linked by the word root *-liub-* (to love). The artillery first sends the soldiers to their death, then takes care to bury them, expressing its regret with the barrels of its guns and stooping to the baseness of open hypocrisy ("ne gnushaias' litsemeriem") when it declares its love. Stalin, in the poem's finale, having sent millions of soldiers to their deaths, similarly seems troubled by regret. We are told in the final line that these soldiers are his favourites – etymologically, in Russian, those he loves. And, thus, the poem implicitly asks us to make a judgment: is the parallel between the artillery and Stalin one of contrast or is it one of analogy? If the latter, the poem intimates Stalin's hypocrisy in his supposed love. Hypocrisy in appreciation of and love for the fallen is, of course, not a crime. However, callously reckless expense of human capital – if we push the parallel with the artillery to its extreme conclusions – is more serious.

Note that I am not arguing that Levin, in the 1946 version, is creating an Aesopian text within which to express condemnation of Stalin. Rather, the precise constellation of subtle stylistic and compositional elements collectively insinuating doubt in Stalin functions as a gauge of the speaker's underlying ambivalent feeling in the final stanzas. Stalin is here, as makes sense in the context of the time, something of the soldier's "holy of holies," that on which he cannot encroach, possibly even in conscious thought.[131] But the structural logic of the poem raises the "sacrilegious" question. And, in any case, the apotheosis of the finale does not exist in isolation from the challenging opening and, in this context, does not sound as it might in another's hollowly celebratory poem.

To what extent does the poem fit our definition for a sincere voice and particularly one that leans towards the second pole in the conceptualization of sincerity, the pole of modulated and mediated sincerity?[132] First, Levin's poem is imbued with a wide range of vocal inflections – particularly the shifting tonalities and types of irony in the opening six lines, the remainder of the first section and the second section, and then the pathos and latent doubt of the finale. Together, these can imply a human complexity and ambivalence of experience and outlook.

Second, Levin's readers of all stripes seem to have understood the poem as spoken in good faith – misguided maybe, but always an expression of personal conviction. This impression is abetted by the poem's biographical framing. The voice positions itself as a humble but astute participant in events. Its credibility derives from its lack of social capital, and the physically palpable ("inconvenienced") and anatomically undeniable wound the speaker manifests – written into the poem obliquely, precisely such that it is not made an outward basis for any claim – can only strengthen its authority. The irony in the first two sections is experienced by the reader as this speaker's very personal pain and offence. And this occurs despite an outward reticence of self-presentation: the lyric "I" subsumes itself to a "we" in parts 1 and 3 and, in part 2, to an imaginary double, who, however, can, like the poem's author, inconvenience riders on the trolley with an artificial leg. Moreover, given the striking concreteness and freshness of vision, it is difficult to picture the reader who would not imagine the poem forged in the crucible of individual experience and individual reflection – even one who knows nothing of Levin's actual biography.[133]

I would argue that the biographical framing and freshness of vision collude with the singular, unconventional *voice* of the poem, audible particularly in the opening stanzas, to assert, for the reader, an unstated claim to authenticity. What is more, the reserve of trust accumulated in the first two sections drives the reader's reception of the apotheosis, whether the reader perceives these final stanzas as straight or laced with subterranean doubt.

At the same time, the sincerity evinced is, like that in the articles surveyed at the outset of the chapter, universalizing rather than individualist and betrays the application of a critical faculty to a socially and historically concrete reality. We have here another interesting hybrid – an ironic mid-century sincerity.

6 Case Studies in Turn-of-the-Millennium Sincerity

1 BORIS RYZHY'S RENEWAL OF TRADITIONAL SINCERITY

Boris Ryzhy (1974–2001) presents a test case for a traditional turn-of-the-millennium sincerity. As the guitar bard Grigory Danskoy, a sophisticated reader from similar circles, put it: "[…] Boris is that poet who at the turn of the [twenty-first] century somehow found a voice and spoke authentically, at full force and with a kind of highly convincing, sometimes very pained intonation."[1] Highly educated and deeply versed in the poetic tradition (Pushkin's circle, the modernists, Soviet poetry, Brodsky and his circle, contemporary Petersburg poets),[2] but a native of the provinces who spent a significant portion of his childhood in a particularly depressed, dirty, and dangerous factory neighbourhood, Ryzhy combines the voices and impressions of Sverdlovsk with poetic sophistication and self-awareness.[3] One layer of his projected authenticity – that which is most superficial – relates to the shady company he keeps (in his poems at the least), the marginality and (in bourgeois terms) "asocial" behaviour of his lyric hero.[4] More important is Ryzhy's versatility in the language of this milieu. Also crucial is a life-creating plane:

> Ведь я заслужил это, не правда ли, сделал шаг,
> отравил себя музыкой, улицами, алкоголем,
> небом и северным морем. «Вы» говори, дурак,
> тому, кто зачислен к мертвым, а из живых уволен.[5]

> (After all, I've earned this, isn't that true, taken
>   the [decisive] step,
> poisoned myself with music, the streets, alcohol,

the sky and northern sea. Use "vy,"* fool,
with one enlisted with the dead and dismissed
    from among the living.)

At the same time, Ryzhy's metapoetic musings on his hero plainly debunk any naïvely uncomplicated approach to his poetic sincerity. Ryzhy's verse, in Sergei Gandlevsky's carefully chosen words, "has a direct relationship to the maximally confessional poetic tradition."[6] This, however, does not imply essential identity. Ryzhy thirsts for and depends upon the liminal space between truth and invention. Only this space accords with a desire to "remain oneself":

Мальчишкой в серой кепочке остаться,
самим собой, короче говоря.
Меж правдою и вымыслом слоняться
по облетевшим листьям сентября.[7]

(To remain the young boy in the grey cap,
oneself, in short.
To traipse along betwixt truth and invention
on the stripped leaves of September.)

Some of Ryzhy's poems most pointedly playful in terms of the lyric subject come from his publication "Geological Engineer" ("Gornyi inzhener"; *Znamia*, no. 3 [2000]), which inspired Kees Verheul to write him: "I rejoiced, having seen how consciously, with elusive cunning, the poet approaches the formation of his image. This means he won't be the victim of this process of transformation; something (the most important?) he keeps to himself [za dushoi] [...]."[8] In one, the poet playfully kills off his lyric hero, but dons another mask, the criminal authority, to do so ("My [lyric] hero slips into the dark" ["Moi geroi uskol'zaet vo t'mu," 1998]). Another sketches a scene of the "poet's" interaction with naïve listeners from his Sverdlovsk milieu. With a knowing wink, the poet relates the reactions of older criminals (cf. "bratva") or workers (cf. "rabochie ruki") to his verse, their supposedly naively literal understanding ("Eto vse prikliuchilos' s toboiu" [All this stuff happened to you]) and their appreciation, their verdict that he is indeed "v nature poet" (a poet for real [slang]). He has successfully deceived his listeners 1) because of their unpreparedness as "readers," but also presumably 2) because of the compelling authenticity of the voice he presents in his poems, which is natural enough to fool not only the capitals, but also the very people whose stylized portraits populate his verse.

---

*Formal address

Notably, he swipes the glass when they drink to his success. His stories may be fiction, but he is not, at least in his own not necessarily trustworthy telling, without a real, if playful, streak of kinship to his listeners.[9]

However, this fraught relationship between hero and author does not mean that there is no truth value to poetry or that truth is unimportant. On the contrary, Ryzhy says to and of Aleksandr Kushner, most admired by him among living poets, "It seems that today only you answer for your words."[10] Ryzhy too aspires to answer for his words.

Many of Ryzhy's poems are not metapoetic and indeed powerfully incite the reader to equate author and hero:

Дай нищему на опохмелку денег.
Ты сам-то кто? Бродяга и бездельник,
дурак, игрок.

Не первой молодости нравящийся дамам,
давно небритый человек со шрамом,
сопляк, сынок.

Дай просто так и не проси молиться
за душу грешную, – когда начнет креститься,
останови.

... От одиночества, от злости, от обиды
на *самого*, с которым будем квиты, –
не из любви.[11]

I have allowed some small liberties with the translation:

(Give the beggar a buck for his hangover.
Just who are you? Good for nothing, wanderer,
bit player, cad.

Attracting ladies not so fresh at heart,
that long-unshaven fellow with the scar,
mom's snot-nosed lad.

Give just because. Don't ask for a prayer
to save your soul. And when he signs the cross,
just shrug it off.

… Out of loneliness, from anger, from offence
at that *selfsame* with whom we'll settle debts,
not out of love.)

I have purposely avoided mentioning Ryzhy's suicide up to this point. His authenticity stands (or falls) apart from it and prior to it. It is not of course Ryzhy's measure of pain, nor its ratification in his suicide, that gives his poetry resonance, but how it is written. Only the words can carry the burden of their own authenticity. At the same time, suicide as a ratifier of the seriousness and sincerity of words has an ancient pedigree.[12] The noose with which the heroine has hanged herself and not the imprint of her signet ring is the true seal of Phaedra's *false* words in Euripedes's *Hippolytus*.[13] The act of suicide thus has an awesome potency to shape or endorse a personal narrative, true or false. As concerns Ryzhy, his good friend Oleg Dozmorov notes how his poems were written to shift their tonality at different moments and depending on how the still open biography developed. At the time, the poems evoking suicide seemed to him to encompass rather a bravado that could read as jest.[14] The biography and its ending have, however, introduced a rather inescapable framing for the words.[15]

"Give the beggar" is written in an of-the-moment stylistics, but cleansed of some of the excesses of criminal slang that marked Ryzhy's work as he first gained notoriety. How precisely does the poem generate its palpable aura of authenticity? Our definition of the sincere voice demands that it manage *by its inflections* to imply a thinking and speaking subject constituted outside the frame of literature. The opening of Ryzhy's poem, through its pragmatic framing, works effectively and economically in this direction. The leading, self-directed imperative implies not simply the internal monologue characteristic of the lyric broadly, but rather internal dialogue, tension of competing impulses – because its hortative quality insinuates potential resistance, and the imperative form carries within itself the possibility of non-fulfilment.[16] This dialogic quality – inasmuch as we believe it is non-trivial – hints at a matrix of competing values, motivations, impulses, which helps us envision a complex, ontologically real subject.

Ryzhy departs here from a simple and universally familiar situation, a field of conflicting values charted, to generalize greatly, by the pity and Christian (or other ethically normative) duty foregrounded in the word "nishch[ii]" (indigent) and the squeamishness and manifold rationalizations for inaction implicitly present in "na opokhmelku" (for alcohol to "cure" his hangover). At the same time, the subtle divergence from this blueprint of the specific sort of inner tension and motivations the lyric subject here experiences, which become clearer as the poem develops, also works in favour of a richly developed individuality.

The opening line also demonstrates a subtle resistance to the gravitational pull of ready-made poetic forms through its diction (lack of inversion; the colloquial "na opokhmelku") and, especially, its rhythmic realization. While its underlying pulse is iambic pentameter, the uncommon rhythm it generates through hypermetric stress followed by consecutive pyrrhic feet ($\acute{\,}\,\acute{\,}\,\_\,\_\,|\,\_\,\_\,\_\,\acute{\,}\,\_\,\acute{\,}\,\_$), gives it, at least prior to continuation, an aura of colloquial, non-poetic speech. In this way, it can hint subliminally at immediacy of expression, one of the secondary traits evocative of "sincerity" and "authenticity" for authors and readers leaning towards our first pole.

Within the same model of sincerity, we might also expect to see confessionality. The not entirely rhetorical question that follows the first line ("Ty sam-to kto?" [Just who are you?]) draws an implicit parallel between the hungover street beggar and the lyric persona who encounters him. The lyric persona is, or so he asserts to himself, hardly better or more worthy than this figure. The reader is, moreover, led to assume that the speaker's empathy is founded on a deep personal acquaintance with the phenomenon of "hangover" – implying both the romanticized ability to give oneself up to personal abandon (cf. Ryzhy's poem "From a Photo Album" ["Iz fotoal'boma," 1998]) and the physical and psychic doldrums that follow.[17] Indeed, the poses through which the lyric persona defines himself here waver between the self-deprecating and potentially romanticized: vagabond, player, loafer, fool/clown.

The individual human presence pointed at beyond the frame of the poem through the internal dialogism of the opening stanza is reinforced in the second, which begins as an ersatz look in the mirror. The "feedback" reinforces the ambivalencies of self-image of the first stanza. The hero, apparently too worn to attract young girls, catches, however, the eye of more experienced women. His long unshaven face speaks to dissipation and perhaps a faltering of will.[18] The scar, clearly visible in many photographs of the poet, is a marker of the individual par excellence. While the reader is told nothing of its form or placement, it marks the speaker as a physical body with a past, and it serves as an a priori identifier.[19] The final line integrates into this physical image a psychological past, indicating the vestigial identities, childish vulnerability, and childish neediness (*sopliak, synok*), which are concealed by an indurate surface. (Ryzhy often returns to such childhood identities in his verse.) These identities are contrasted to the socially demarcated (outward facing) roles that occupy the analogous position in the first stanza.

The third stanza conveys a shunning of transactionality ("dai prosto tak" [give just because]), of grace and gratitude ("ne prosi molit'sia [...] kogda nachnet krestit'sia, / ostanovi" [don't ask for a prayer [...] when he starts to sign the cross / stop him]). The lyric persona, whose inner trials remain unspoken, rejects transcendent aid and, perhaps even more, does not wish to be taken for the hand through which God works charity.

The contradictory emotions of the opening of the final stanza (loneliness, anger, offence) lead into the double pronged *pointe* that closes the poem in a manner highly conducive to the sincere voice. First, the fact that the lyric persona's act of "charity" is to be motivated by a wallowing in personal pain (*odinochestvo, zlost', obida*) rather than founded on Christian love or humanistic empathy ("ne iz liubvi" [not from love]) reinforces a sense of candour. Second, a particularly chilling potency is introduced by the pseudo-performative in the second half of the penultimate line: "ot obidy / na *samogo*, **s kotorym budem kvity**" (from offence / at that *selfsame* **with whom we'll settle debts**). The phrase "na *samogo*" (at that *selfsame*) balances between implied direct objects: "na *samogo* sebia" (at myself) and "na *samogo* Boga" (at God himself). Both are implicated by the context and by idiomatic usage. The device appears to be borrowed from Brodsky's "From nowhere with love, teenth of Martuary" ("Niotkuda s liubov'iu, nadtsatogo martobria," 1975–6): "Ia liubil tebia bol'she, chem angelov i samogo" (I loved you more than angels and myself/God himself), but the double-voicedness is cemented in Ryzhy's case because the act of settling debts is of necessity an accounting with both entities – payback to the self for its inadequacies and a returning to the deity of that which has been given.[20]

"s kotorym budem kvity" is a performative in the sense introduced by J.L. Austin in that "budem kvity" (lit., we'll be even), despite its indicative mood, functions as an implied oath – such is its illocutionary force.[21] It is not descriptive of an oath, but in the particular pragmatic instantiation internal to the poem actually constitutes one. The pronunciation of a performative, when the conditions for its felicitousness are met (for instance, the speaker has the status to enact the deed which the speech act represents), has impact within the world, changes a state. Pronunciation of a non-empty oath commits the speaker to what is undertaken.[22]

The power of a performative in lyric poetry is that it directly challenges the boundary between art and world.[23] Consider: during performances of Christopher Marlowe's *Doctor Faustus* in the Elizabethan era, the scripted incantations that conjured demons on stage were titillating in that on any given night they always had the potential to call extra, actual, non-stage demons into the theatre. On multiple occasions actors and audience fled the theatre believing this had indeed happened.[24] These words pronounced by the actor were, then, not "empty" or "unhappy" (per Austin's reckoning) but highly effectual, though they were spoken, both actor and audience knew, without inner conviction or intention, even in fear of the result. Analogously, "dangerous" words in poetry *threaten* to be the words of the extraliterary poet.

This effect is perhaps heightened in the Russian poetic tradition, within the deepest and most central stream of which words have often been accorded an extrapersonal, even fatal power.[25] In this tradition – without a descent into simplistic and banal equation of poet and lyric voice – words in poetry are understood to retain extraordinary power and tension within the world. This power is related, not always consciously, on a philosophical plane to the poetic word's birth in the Logos, a Word which is more than just words,[26] and, on a pragmatic plane, to its birth into a social sphere where words have been and continue to be deeds. The charged power of the poetic word is, moreover, ratified for poetry's audience by the procession of tragic real-world outcomes of speaking or simply being as a poet – censorship, imprisonment, exile, starvation, illness, suicide, violent death (the theme of Khodasevich's "Bloody Repast" ["Krovavaia pishcha," 1932] and Roman Jakobson's "On a Generation that Squandered Its Poets" ["O pokolenii, rastrativshem svoikh poetov," 1931]), and has been thoroughly conceptualized within the culture.[27]

The power of the dangerous word, so familiar to the Russian reader, is, moreover, if anything, intensified in formally structured poetry. In the Anglo-American tradition from Milton to Lowell, readers and writers have often come to think of rhymed and metred verse as a Procrustean bed, form as a structure to which words, thoughts, feelings must be adapted, a force distending or crucifying to a greater or lesser extent, ever inciting the author to bend truth.[28] However, when readers, and particularly Russian readers, experience powerful formally structured poetry, there competes a countervailing sense that the "right" word becomes welded in place ("iz pesni slova ne vykinesh'" [one can't drop a word from a song]), or even that, as the poet encounters form – which among forms for the major poet always represents a choice – there is at work a play between individual authorial will and extrapersonal fate.[29] For even if the poet has been incited (inspired, pressured?) to utter the dangerous words by his or her encounter with form, for the poet who "answers for his words" (as, we will recall, Ryzhy says of Kushner) there is always a choice in play – to *write* these words, or not. Ryzhy, one of the last Russian poets (so far?) who by his temperament to such an extent functions within and exploits this paradigm, writes the words.

Ryzhy leans strongly towards our first pole in the evocation of sincerity, though with some caveats. It is hard to question the fundamental

seriousness of tone of the poem, which makes a flaneuristic encounter the platform for questions of existential import – even if a subtle self-deprecating irony colours the first two stanzas. **Immediacy** of expression is reinforced through repeated instances of colloquial diction and syntax that collapse the distance between the poem and everyday speech (*na opokhmelku*; *sam-to*; *bezdel'nik*; *nebrityi*; *sopliak*; *synok*; *prosto tak*; *budem kvity*).[30] Immediacy is also gestured at through the framing, which makes the entire brief poem the thoughts running through the lyric persona's head as he approaches a panhandler (even if we simultaneously recognize that such a gesture cannot be taken literally). The poem's **intensity** is not so much an intensity of speech, as one of experience, of heightened being within the world. The poet's speech is pointedly not overstrained. Emotions course under the surface and are, if anything, somewhat deadened. Still, the very experience of reading the poem is an intense one, linked in no small part to its self-positioning, in the final lines, as an instantiation of unusually *reckless* **candour**.[31]

Ryzhy's poems engaging suicide or directly taking suicide as theme are generally written from the perspective of an "I" at no obvious state of remove from the poem's speaker. The poet's frequent winking recognition of the invention and posing that goes into the production of the hero is absent. However, even in the poem we have just looked at, there is a subtle way in which the roles that define the poet, particularly those in the first stanza, are clearly also roles or faces presented to the world (in the sense explored by sociologist Erving Goffman). These prefabricated roles underscore, paradoxically, the superficial inadequacy of the poet's own *definition* of the person encountered as "nishchii" (an indigent), and this inadequacy of role to essence becomes one of the key understated "truths" purveyed by the poem, an example of that "earned" truth which undergirds the sincerity effect.

In sum, we see at work in "Give the beggar ..." an updating of a highly traditional sincerity, unobtrusively cognizant, in the subtlety of its play with roles and self-deprecating irony – both transcended – of "what we know now." This is often the trajectory of Ryzhy's poems – from winking irony to a transcendence of this irony in lyric pathos, though here the centre of gravity throughout leans towards the serious and earnest.

Before moving on to the second poet of our chapter, I would like to look briefly at one more of Ryzhy's sincerity devices. Ryzhy is hardly the first poet to incorporate a signature into his poetry. We can look for the roots of this device at least as early as the opening of the "Small

Testament" ("Le lais," 1456) of François Villon, an early potent practi-tioner of the personal and biographical in lyric poetry:

> L'an quatre cens cinquante six,
> Je Françoys Villon, escollier,
> Considerant, de sens rassis,
> Le frain aux dens, franc au collier,
> Qu'on doit ses œvres conseillier [...][32]

> (In this four hundred fifty-sixth year,
> I, François Villon, student,
> with settled mind and bridled humor,
> sincere and zealous, believing
> That one's works must be judged [...])

Ryzhy updates this device to particular effect in the postscript to his poem "Elegy" ("Elegiia," 2000). The poem starts out nondescript and begins to get more interesting when the poet proposes a devil's deal: he will write himself out of the past and memory in exchange for this past's preservation in his verse. The deal is, however, disingenuous. He is retained in the poem proper as the intrusive gaze that forces the heroine, perhaps too facilely called Liubov (thus some desirable Liuba, but also "Love herself"),[33] to cross her arms defiantly over breasts re-vealed through a rain-soaked summer dress. Then, his verse signature completes with his name the rhyme left unfinished in the poem proper.

What is effective here, however, is not this wily feint, but the quality of the signature itself, which positions itself for the future as an artefact of the poet. A signature in poetry is a formalized group of components (name, date and sometimes place) which insinuate a link – however tenuous or indirect – between the text and an author with an extra-textual biography. Ryzhy's verse "signature" here works not only by recalling and deautomatizing this practice, but by recreating, or at least hinting at, these formalized elements in a way that gives each broader resonance: name becomes status, time – situation, place – material cul-ture (and hence time), date – a nod to its own irrelevance.

> [...]
> Пусть даже так: меня не будет в нем,
> в том прошлом, только чтоб без остановки
> лил дождь, и на трамвайной остановке
> сама Любовь стояла под дождем
> в коротком платье летнем, без зонта,

скрестив надменно ручки на груди, со
скорлупкою от семечки у рта.
12 строчек Рыжего Бориса,
забывшего на три минуты зло
себе и окружающим во благо.
«Olympia» – машинка, «КУМ» – бумага.
Такой-то год, такое-то число.[34]

(Even if thus: I won't be in it,
in that past, just so that without cease
the rain would pour, and at the tram stop
Liubov herself would be standing in the rain
in a short summer dress without an umbrella,
crossing her thin arms haughtily across her chest with
the shell of a sunflower seed hanging out her mouth.
12 lines by Boris Ryzhy, who
For three minutes put troubles out of mind,
To the good of self and those around him,
The typewriter – Olympia, the paper – KYM,
Such-and-such a year, such-and such a day.)

Ryzhy initiates his lyrical signature with an "inaccuracy." The main portion of the poem consists not of twelve, but of fifteen lines.[35] Ryzhy's "12 lines" – which is simply a conventional length for a lyric poem – speaks wishfully to rounded completion.[36] However, what is tangibly absent in the main poem, to which this number plainly refers, is, again, the rhyme which will close the quatrain by introducing the poet. In the postscript, Ryzhy supplies the missing rhyme, but signs himself in the manner not of a poet ("Boris Ryzhy"), but of a class roll ("Ryzhy Boris"), divesting himself of exceptionalism.[37] Such self-diminishing, as we have seen, has often been employed as a sincerity device. Lines 2 and 3 of the italicized signature laconically signal the context of Ryzhy's troubled inner life, projecting this as a moment of brief transcendence. The fourth line of the signature, "'Olympia' – mashinka, 'KYM' – bumaga" (The typewriter – Olympia, the paper – KYM) gives us a tantalizingly material window into the artist's personal world and establishes his milieu, dating the poem.[38] Together, these two images have an almost archaeological feel.

   In the final line, which displaces the poem's date, the lyric "I" leaps into an enduring, "mythic" present. But this is achieved through a descent into conversational tone and in words that convey a cavalier attitude towards the, in truth, only indifferent main poem created, an attitude consonant with the mildly kenotic aura attached to the poet's name above.[39]

At the same time, the lyricism that has been gathering runs aground of an escalating prosaicism in the last two lines, and the enclosing rhyme shuts down the forward motion of the signature with a subtle and somehow unexpected finality (AbCCb). The impact of this postscript, with its amalgam of the concrete (lines 1 and 4) and the self-diminishing and familiarizing (lines 1, 2, and 5), is the inscribing at the end of the poem of a human trace (or, at least, of its profound illusion).

It would be wholly inappropriate to see Ryzhy as a representative of the "New Sincerity" in contemporary Russian poetry. The "New Sincerity" is, in its various guises, a development of and/or reaction against postmodernism and Conceptualism.[40] And while it is true that philosophical postmodernism, with its focus on the mediated nature of the artistic text, raises the bar for sincerity for all poets by changing the contours of "what we know now," postmodernism and Conceptualism are not relevant for Ryzhy. He comes straight out of the main lyric tradition, including Soviet poetry – one poem imagines the hero with a prison tattoo of Boris Slutsky – and was impacted by and consciously distanced himself from Brodsky, Mayakovsky, and Pasternak.[41] Ryzhy is a representative not of a New Sincerity movement, but of an old lyric sincerity tradition, one which lives on through recalibration and invention.

2 THE "PRODIGAL" SINCERITY OF TIMUR KIBIROV

Я верую – ибо абсурдно
Абсурдно, постыдно, смешно […]

(I believe – because it is absurd,
absurd, shameful, laughable […])

Отточенные лясы
все тщусь я прицепить и к Правде, и к Добру.

(I struggle always
to hitch (my) sharpened banter to the True and Good.)[42]

Timur Kibirov has been a particularly potent practitioner of second-pole, "modulated" sincerity in the most recent past and can serve as an exemplar of how this pole in the conceptualization of sincerity develops in our day.[43] Authors and readers with such sincerity proclivities tend to find evidence of sincerity in the diversity of mood and modulation indicative of a "human" voice and are suspicious of vocal strain and excessive seriousness and focus on the self; they are apt to take as a given the mediated nature of literary expression and integrate irony into the fabric of the sincere voice.[44]

So, largely, Kibirov. He is suspicious of Romantic individualist posture, which in his own retelling becomes the original sin of his youthful first steps as poet,[45] and he was occupied, especially in the early years of his mature art, with the fixation of the fast-disappearing Soviet world in all its sensory, experiential, and linguistic richness (in contradistinction to an excessive focus on self). While raising the banner of a new sentimentalism – his earliest collected works, released in 1994, was called *Sentimentalities* (*Santimenty*) – his poems do not gravitate to the reflective exploration of the poet's inner world.[46]

Kibirov's quite recognizable "voice" is a composite of a broad diversity of moods, modes, and modulations. He prevailingly leavens serious topics with irony and humour. Moreover, his "human" voice (and "humanity" is, it seems, a principal value for Kibirov) emerges from a pastiche of pre-existing styles, registers, genres, and quotations.[47] "Just this way in kitchens we spoke with one another in wall-to-wall quotations from Galich and Mandelstam, peppered with clichés from the songs of Lebedev-Kumach and Matusovsky – Dolmatovsky … [i.e., Soviet mass and popular song]," writes a younger contemporary.[48] This cultural idiom common to the late-Soviet generation, and deployed with virtuosic aplomb by Kibirov, should be viewed as a language, with its own lexicon and expressivity.[49] What is more, if Mandelstam's rich intertextuality combined with suspicion of linguistic inertia and cliché (see chapter 4), Kibirov, in his intertextuality, appears indifferent to such concerns.

Kibirov evinces a clear comfort with the poetic and verbal media of his art.[50] The illusion of immediacy is not central to his voice, even if, particularly at an early stage, an air of graphomania and the rejection of polish were important to the self-differentiation of his *poetry* from the empty, overly polished "poeticity" of Soviet literature.[51] The question of intensity of voice in Kibirov's poetry is a complex one. Sergei Gandlevsky writes of Kibirov's "'indecorous' ardor [pylkost']," and ascents to pathos are frequent and programmatic. However, these are, again, leavened and transmogrified both from within and without the individual poems by humour and self-deprecating irony.[52]

A key constituent of this authorial stance is the relation it presupposed between citationality, irony, and sincerity. Mikhail Epstein attributes to Kibirov a "'post-postmodern,' neo-sentimental aesthetics" that actively challenges "that emphatic distancing, impersonality, citational quality, which is characteristic of Conceptualism [a major current within Russian postmodernism, S.G.]."[53] Analysing "To L.S. Rubinstein" ("L.S.

Rubinshteinu," 1987), Epstein points to a "movement of sense simultaneously in both directions, an enclosing and removing of quotation marks" with the removing occurring "from within the depth of quotation." The voice thus constituted receives a "renewed status [as the] possible, [...] 'may-be-sincerity.'"[54] At the same time, some of Kibirov's most compelling poems, particularly of a slightly later provenance, read as quite lyrical, if with a playful undercurrent, or ironic, with a lyrical undercurrent, but in stable scenarios and doses that don't cause the reader cognitive dissonance regarding Kibirov's lyric subject.[55]

In this sense, Kibirov's poetics are compatible with the American new sincerity movement, which, in its most artistically meaningful and influential manifestations, aims at the complex restructuring and rejuvenation of sincerity as a value and artistic method, but after and with an awareness of Theory and postmodernism.[56] For Kibirov, in order to generate lyrical, emotional texts, an awareness must be maintained of the watchful sardonic eye that punctures all such traditional subjectivity:

> Suddenly, I recognized that if I want to stubbornly pursue my intention to write traditional texts – lyrical, emotional texts with pathos [...] then I *must remain aware* that [Conceptualist confrere] Dmitry Alexandrovich [Prigov] watches mockingly over this and in general the practice of traditional literature, and under his gaze everything becomes comical, pathetic, provincial [...] After Prigov one can either come to terms with what he has introduced to literature and forgo traditional lyricism [pesnopenie]. Or one can do one's own thing with audacity and abandon [s derzost'iu i otchaianiem] and decidedly *in such a way* that the reader also realizes that this is serious, that there exists another literature.[57]

It seems clear (and not least on the basis of Kibirov's praxis) that by "doing one's own thing" he does not mean writing without irony (he is after all a person "with a playful streak") or simply adopting a naively traditional lyricism, closing one's eyes to what Conceptualism has introduced to culture.[58] Rather, these words describe a strategy that would allow for the poet, using irony, provocative sentimentalism, and other means, to signal awareness of "what we know now," and thus to carve out space to continue to project an extraliterary subjectivity, even for a reader who has passed through the school of Conceptualist mockery and scepticism.[59]

As stated throughout this book, I believe we can look for the specific factors that underlie the success of individual texts in generating a sincere voice. To that end, in the remainder of this chapter, I will look in detail at how, in the final two bravura poems of his collection *Kara-baras* (online pre-print, 2005, publ. 2006), Kibirov constructs a sincere voice grounded in and transcending irony. In the first of these poems, "Kara-baras!," there are more than enough gestures to support readers' impressions of the domination of either irony or sincerity – depending on reader proclivities, sensitivities, and preparation, though I would argue that the text, more precisely, first foregrounds a prophylactic irony masking and sugar-coating serious content (in the body), then emergent seriousness half-heartedly undercut by playful irony (in the apotheosis), and finally (in the closing) harbours rich possibilities for alternative tonal readings. The following poem, "Epilogue" ("Epilog"), departs into a radically different and more stable tonality, using the "slippery"-ironic quality of "Kara-baras!" as a platform to support the emergence of a still-playful but now stable sincere voice.[60]

How the Sincere Voice of "Kara-baras!" Is Structured

"Kara-baras!" is a sharp-tongued meditation on the postmodern condition cast as an equimetric retelling of Kornei Chukovsky's classic densely rhymed children's poem, "Moidodyr" (roughly, Scrub-Right-Through, publ. 1923).[61] The poem's hero, after sullying himself in postmodern rejectionism, overcomes relativism in art and ethics, returned to the bosom of meaning not by Chukovsky's "Great Washbasin," but by the Logos.[62]

Not surprisingly, given their dissimilar cultural contexts and the divergent auras of their prototexts, "Kara-baras!" is quite different from a poem like Prigov's "Broad Is My Native Land" ("Shiroka strana moia rodnaia," 1974), another experiment in the interpretation of a classic text (the subtitle of Kibirov's poem). In Prigov's poem, through an ironically naïve identification with the official discourse expressed in Vasily Lebedev-Kumach's 1935 Soviet mass song, a taking of its every phrase at face value and a "not-noticing" of the contradictions it presents, these contradictions are amplified.[63]

But "Moidodyr," in Kibirov's poem, is *instrument*, not object or metonym. What the constant, audible presence of Chukovsky's charming didactic tale of a Pig-Pen–like child's return to hygiene does bring is 1) a highly potent rhythmic-compositional-narrative structure that can be applied by Kibirov to his new material;[64] and 2) a substratum of prophylactic irony in relation to Kibirov's own project in the poem. That project is a negotiation between relativism and Christian values, imagined through a distant recasting of the story of the prodigal son, a recurring paradigm and reference point in Kibirov's poetry of this period:[65] "Как пустился я по улице/ бежать, / Прибежал к Порогу Отчему / опять" (And I took off running down the street, ran back to [my] Father's Doorstep).[66]

Relativism is a long-standing issue for the poet. In his playfully poignant and magnificent poems to his toddler daughter, "Twenty Sonnets to Sasha Zapoeva" (1995), Kibirov, "S mladykh nogtei alkavshii Absoliuta" (Having from the cradle thirsted for the Absolute) – no, not that kind, he goes on – when confronted with the reality of a child, finally knows that there exists

> хоть что-то, неподвластное ухмылкам
> релятивизма, ни наскокам пылким
> дионисийских оголтелых муз![67]

> (at least something not subject to the smirks
> of relativism, nor the hotblooded onslaughts
> of Dionysian muses run amok!)

The body of "Kara-baras!" is a story of the reining in of a "poet"-lyric hero who, through his human weaknesses and inevitable embeddedness in his cultural milieu, has fallen into such "temptations." After a flailing attempt to chase down his scattering ideals, this lyric hero laments:

> Боже, боже,
> Что случилось?
> Отчего же
> Всё кругом
> Завертелось,
> Закружилось
> И помчалось колесом?
> *(в смысле ницшеанского вечного возвращения или*
> *буддийского кармического ужаса, дурной бесконечности –*
> *вообще всякой безысходности)*
> Гностицизм
> За солипсизмом,
> Солипсизм
> За атеизмом,
> Атеизм
> За гностицизмом,
> Деррида
> за
> М. Фуко

> *(Деррида здесь помещен более для шутки,*
> *М.Фуко – более для рифмы) –*

Всё вертится
И кружится,
И несётся кувырком!..

Вдруг из сей всемирной склоки
Позабытый, чуть живой,
Возникает древний Логос
И качает головой:

«Ах ты, гадкий, ах ты, грязный,
Безобразный греховодник!
Ты чернее фарисея,
(*вариант –*
ты наглее саддукея),
Полюбуйся на себя:
У тебя на сердце злоба,
На уме одна стыдоба,
Пред тобой такие виды,
Что сбежали аониды,
Аониды, пиэриды
Убежали от тебя.
Рано утром на рассвете
Умиляются мышата
И котята, и утята,
И жучки, и паучки.

Ты один не умилялся
А кичился и кривлялся [...][68]

(Lord, o Lord,
What's happened?
Why has
All around
Gone a-spinning,
And a-whirling
And a-rushing like some spokes
(*in the sense of Nietzschean eternal return or*
Buddhist karmic terror, bad infinity –
in general all manner of hopelessness)
Gnosticism
Chasing solipsism,
Solipsism
Chasing atheism,

Atheism
Chasing gnosticism,
Derrida
Chasing
M. Foucault

(*Derrida is placed here more in jest,*
M. Foucault more for rhyme) –

Everything's a-spinning
And a-whirling,
And turning head-over-heels!..

Suddenly from out this worldwide squabble,
Left forgotten, half-alive,
Arises ancient Logos
And shakes his head:

"Akh, you nasty, akh, you filthy,
Deplorable sinmonger!
You are blacker than a Pharisee,
(*variant* –
You're more brazen than a Sadducee),

Get a load of yourself:
You have spite in your heart,
And nothing but sin on your mind,
Before you are such views
That you've chased away the muses,
The Aonides, the Pierides,
Have run away from you.

Early, early in the morning
All the mouselings ooh-and-aah,
And the kittens, and the ducklings,
And the beetles and the spiders,

You alone did not feel tender wonder,
But puffed yourself and clowned [...])

The Logos, which unites both cultural and religious spheres of
meaning, returns the prideful and clowning protagonist to its bosom,
aided by the six-winged seraphim of Pushkin's "The Prophet," who

stands in for Chukovsky's crocodile. (The seraphim is accompanied by a contemptuously derisive and somewhat infantile Pushkin himself, replacing the crocodile children. Pushkin, despite the complementary Christian associations facilitated by his poetry of the 1830s, is always a playful spirit for Kibirov.)[69] The prominence for the poet of the expressly Christian aspect within the ongoing dualism of the Logos is affirmed in its self-description, quite precisely echoing John 1:2–3, just a few lines after the passage quoted above.

The poem's lyric subject, though he is to an extent personalized through his snarky prose commentaries, also feels throughout the body of the poem substantially generalized or distanced due to the poem's narrative character (despite the first person) and the constant echo of Chukovsky's prototext.[70] The substantive questions for our purposes will be:

1 does the *lyric voice*, in parallel to the plot, overcome or transcend its cheeky clowning (*krivlianie*) in this poem, and
2 to what extent does the poem allow for an *unambivalent* answer to this question?

To address these issues, we must examine the poem's ending in detail.

After the "poet"-hero's return to the Logos, the poem's apotheosis pronounces:

> Да здравствует Истина чистая,
> И Красотища лучистая,
> Истое наше Добро,
> Вечное наше перо!

> (Long live undefiled [or, unalloyed] Truth,
> And radiant, bodacious Beauty
> Our genuine Good,
> Our enduring plume!)

Particularly in the thirteenth line from the poem's end (which parallels the seventh to the last line of Chukovsky's poem), a more audibly serious voice seems to break through:

> Давайте же, братцы, стараться,
> Не злобиться, не поддаваться
> В тоске, в бардаке и во мраке,
> В чумном бесконечном бараке –[71]

И паки, и паки,
И ныне и присно –
Вечная слава –
Вечная память –
Вечная слава
Жизни!

(Let us then, brothers, strive,
Not hold anger, not give in
In dejection, the grand mess, in the dark,
in the pestilent, interminable barracks –

Anew and anew [Church Slavonic],
And now and evermore [Church Slavonic] –
Eternal glory –
Eternal memory –
Eternal glory
To life!)

Kibirov here stretches Chukosky's finale, intensifying its pathos. The progress of the poem through the prototext is suspended after "Vechnaia slava" (Eternal glory), adopted verbatim from Chukovsky, and only two lines later do we reach that word which ought to parallel the final word of Chukovsky's poem. When we do, its reversed foot breaks more noticeably than anything yet in this long poem the pattern of equimetrical, and often equirhythmic, equivalence to "Moidodyr." Supplanting with a trochee Chukovsky's final iambic word and thus distorting the series of dactyls that structure the last line of the earlier poem ("Véchnaia sláva vodé!" [Eternal glory to water!]), this detached word – "Zhízni!" (To life!) – falls with solidity and weight.

In the five preceding lines, however, there are new potential markers of irony. While "I paki, i paki / I nyne i prisno – / Vechnaia slava" (Anew, and anew / And now and evermore – / Eternal glory) are not nonsensical in an Orthodox Christian context, they can *sound* like a conglomeration of Church Slavonic buzzwords – particularly given the use of "paki, paki" as just such a senseless marker of Church Slavonic in a beloved late-Soviet comedy. And note how, more subtly, "I paki, i paki" seems to sprout phonetically from "barake" (the barracks) which itself is a more distant offshoot of "bardake" (the shit show, lit. brothel).

In addition, the line "Vechnaia pamiat'" (Eternal memory) can seem absurd. "Vechnaia pamiat'" is said in reference to the dead! We can, however, if we *really* try, understand "Vechnaia pamiat' [...] Zhizni" awkwardly as "Eternal memory [...] *of* life" (not dative, but genitive) and thus this line as the apotheosis of Logos as art and memory in the poem.

Further, there had been an element of proto-*stiob* to Chukovsky's "Moidodyr" itself, particularly notable in the ending. (*Stiob* is, in a narrow sense, irony through overidentification with a dominant ethos, discourse, language. In a broader sense it refers to various ironic strategies of late-Soviet youth and underground cultures.)[72] There are justifications for Chukovsky's extreme enthusiasm. Clearly the issue of hygiene was of heightened importance in the anti-sanitary conditions of a largely agrarian and illiterate society with crumbling social and physical infrastructure following years of revolution and civil war. And on a wholly different level, Chukovsky with his deeply perceptive feel for young children and their psychology captures here the sheer physical joy of bathing for a young child. But still, what Chukovsky writes is an *apotheosis* of hygiene, bookended by the publicistic clichés "*Long live* the fragrant soap" and "*Eternal glory* to water!" (emphasis mine). Surely, subtle Chukovsky was having some fun here, as was illustrator Yuri Annenkov, whose self-aware drawings grace the first edition.[73] This susceptibility to and pre-existing aura of *stiob* is likely part of what makes the poem particularly attractive to Kibirov as the canvas for his poem.[74]

Despite these intimations of irony, however, the lines of Kibirov's apotheosis stand out from what went before. This, it seems, is particularly due to the capaciousness of "life" as a concept, which insinuates a broader perspective of what the Christian truth is and brings.[75] This capaciousness contrasts to the narrower thrust of some earlier lines:

Надо, надо Бога славить
По утрам и вечерам,

(One must, one must praise God
Every morn and eve,)

By repeating not the expected "Praise God!" – "Hallelujah!" – but the childish/didactic-sounding "one must," these lines refuse to link the author with the Christian ethos through *non-ironic* statement.

Similarly, when Kibirov not only overlays a reference to the influential Christian author G.K. Chesterton on children's poetry, but updates

"Ia khochu napit'sia chaiu" (I want a drink of tea) to "Mertvykh voskresen'ia chaiu" (I long for the resurrection of the dead), he projects an awkwardly doctrinaire ethos. The psychological distance of this purported longing from the everyday human wants and needs underscored through the subtext cannot help but cue a playfully ironic tone, even if we suspect, and have more and more evidence in Kibirov's later work, that it is intended as – almost – serious.[76] These sorts of tonal "interference," however, are absent as the lyric persona of "Kara-baras!" halts us on the word *Zhizni*.

Another yet more radical tonal bifurcation occurs, however, within the final lines, which are wholly Kibirov's:

Подымайте
Медный таз!

С нами Бог! Кара-барас!

(Raise up
The copper washtub!

God is with us! Kara-baras!)

Earlier in the poem, Kibirov's lyric hero has reinterpreted Chukovsky's lines ("On udaril v mednyi taz / I vskrichal: 'kara-baras!'" [He struck the copper washtub / And cried out: "kara-baras!"]) through the idiom "(vse) nakrylos' mednym tazom" (lit., [everything] is covered with a copper washtub), which means "we're up shit creek," "it's the end of the world." Thus, to raise the copper washtub in the final lines should presumably be to uncover one's head to see that what appears to be darkness and a grand mess is *not* the end of the world. "God is with us," however we may have become blind to his presence. Kibirov, when he reads these lines, pronounces them in a calmly matter-of-fact intonation and with an emphatic pause after "Podymaite" that seems to support this reading.[77] In this light, the confusingly "senseless" word "Kara-baras!" could even become re-encoded as an inscrutable embodiment of the trans-sense Logos.[78] In any case, its playful "mystery" remains unworrisome.

At the poem level, pragmatic framing neither supports nor undermines such a reading, in which an audibly earnest voice emerges quite directly from amidst the irony of "Kara-baras!" In fact, as in a purely postmodern mode, pragmatic framings at the poem level are largely absent. While the poem has a dedication to the mainstream and well-respected

critic Andrei Nemzer and makes broad-brush references to a lyric sub-
ject's prodigal abandonment of higher meaning while mired in sin and
rejectionism, it avoids psychological or biographical detail as well as
the construction of a projected addressee.[79] Laying bare its device of
rewriting of the children's poem, it asks, as it were, to be viewed as a
self-standing art object, existing in the sphere of verbal and conceptual
play. However, the reader with access to the entire collection – which
repeatedly problematizes the abandonment of an "unshakable scale of
values" with decidedly Christian markings[80] – and, all the more so, to
Kibirov's poetry as a whole, which from his first high-profile publica-
tion had woven Christian motifs into ironic contexts,[81] is quite well pre-
pared to accept such a position as reflecting the attitude of Kibirov-poet.

And still, there is good reason why the opening of the "Epilogue"
which follows asks:

Короче – чего же ты все-таки хочешь?
Чего ты взыскуешь? О чем ты хлопочешь,
лопочешь, бормочешь и даже пророчишь
столь невразумительно, столь горячо?[82]

(So what is it you really want?
What are you seeking? What are you fussing about,
mumbling, babbling and even prophesying
so obscurely, so heatedly?)

This passage speaks to a very real "slipperiness" of "Kara-Baras!"

For one, the poem's final lines contain a visual double-entendre.
There is a strong counterpull to understand the washtub here not in
Kibirov's earlier professed sense, but in Chukovsky's, inverted and
held aloft to be struck like a drum or tambourine.[83] The concluding
lines can then – perhaps even primarily in the absence of Kibirov's
voicing – sound like a call to lift the copper washtub like a timbrel,
raising the wild and meaningless cry "kara-baras!" – a sentiment
seemingly coming from the realm of Dionysiasm. The last three lines,
taken *this* way, sound gratuitous and deflating. This, again, is not the
manner in which Kibirov intones them aloud. Yet there are additional
indications that this image is not simply a reader fantasy or decon-
structionist "gotcha."

The poem's final tonal bifurcation occurs within the implied image
of the timbrel itself, iconically raised overhead. The predominating to-
pos for this image within Russian culture is that of the wild, orgiastic
Dionysian dance – from the "bowdlerized," Sentimentalist images of

Batiushkov's "Bacchante" ("Vakkhanka," 1815) and Pushkin's "Triumph of Bacchus" ("Torzhestvo Vakkha," 1818) to Annensky's classic translation of Euripides's *Bacchae* to the openly syncretic, modernist (and, from a Christian perspective, relativist and antinomian) visions of Ivanov ("To the Unknown God" ["Nevedomu bogu," by 1903]) and Merezhkovsky (*Resurrected Gods. Leonardo da Vinci* [*Voskresshie bogi. Leonardo da Vinchi*, 1900]):

> [...] raising / The Phrygian timbrel overhead [...] Let the loud blows
>   gather / Here the Thebians
> The timbrel sounded wildly: [...] Resonant hide has driven them to
>   madness. (Euripedes through Annensky)[84]

> The slaves, expiring in blood, crashed to the slickened floor slabs ...
> Lovely daughters of Mylitta call to the charity of love ...
> "Evan" Egipanus will cry and "Evoe," prancing in a mask;
> "Evan" in an intoxicating howl they strike the sistrum and mad
>   timbrel ... (Ivanov)[85]

> And at that instant the satanic sabbath was transformed into a divine orgy of Bacchus [...] Satires, bacchantes, striking the timbrels, wounding their nipples with knives, pressing out the crimson juice of grapes into golden kraters and mixing it with their own blood, danced, twirled, and sang: "Glory, glory to Dionysus! The great gods are resurrected! Glory to the resurrected gods!" (Merezhkovsky)[86]

That this specific pseudo-Dionysian context is deeply marked for Kibirov in his negotiation between relativism and Christian truth is affirmed in his *Graeco- and Roman-Catholic Songs and Amusements* (*Greko- i rimsko-kafolicheskie pesenki i poteshki*, 2009), which is almost entirely and quite frontally devoted to the Christian idea. In this brief collection of forty-four poems, two, including the opening poem, reproduce as a signal of the anti-Christian, relativist ethos the cry of the bacchantes: "Evan evoe!"[87] The overturned washtub, raised with a wild cry of "Kara-baras!" is thus, potentially, a clownish embodiment of the relativist topos – a subversive unravelling of the poem's ethos.

However, the timbrel is simultaneously linked to another, radically opposed cultural sphere – that of the Bible. (As with the English word, the Russian *timpan* is used in both cases.) Clearly, raising the timbrel in praise of God is quite the opposite of raising it in the context just discussed.

One particular passage, by design or coincidence, helps further elucidate some of the tensions at play in the closing of "Kara-baras!" This is David's self-debasing dance as he leads the ark of the covenant to Jerusalem (2 Samuel 6). Though the timbrel is mentioned only early and in passing here, it is strongly connected with dance (cf. Exodus 15:20, Psalms 149–50), and some visual respresentations of David's dance have stressed its presence, for instance, those by Melchiorre Cafà and James Tissot:

> And David and all the house of Israel played before the Lord on all manner of instruments made of cypress-wood, on harps, on psalteries, on timbrels, on sistrums, and on cymbals. [...] And David danced before the Lord with all his might [...] So David and all the house of Israel brought up the ark of the Lord with shouting, and with the sound of the horn. [...] And Michal the daughter of Saul came out to meet David, and said: "How the king of Israel has distinguished himself today, going around half-naked before the eyes of the slave girls of his servants as any vulgar fellow would!" And David said unto Michal: "Before the Lord [...] I will [play and dance]. And I will be yet more vile than thus, and I will be base in mine own sight; But by these slave girls you spoke of, I will be held in honour." (2 Samuel 6:5, 14–15, 20–2)[88]

This protonarrative of kenosis and *iurodstvo*,[89] the emptying out by the poet-king of his majesty and parting with all propriety to dance wildly, "half-naked" before the Lord, a debasement that is honour for those who will see, resonates with the ending of "Kara-baras!"[90] In a similar fashion, from out of the self-debasement of even our most ironic reading of the final lines, from the potential *iurodstvo* of the final wild cry "Kara-baras!" winks the possibility of profound belief and the desire to be one of those who leads the, in truth, never-departed Covenant back to the forgetfully bereft community, one who heralds an awakening of Christian belief and memory: "God is with us!" (S nami Bog!).[91]

And yet, it is impossible to deny that the poem "Kara-baras!" retains an overarching ironic sensibility and is dominated by an ironic tonality.[92] Its sincere resonance, to the extent one perceives it, is recognizable through and on the platform of irony and is, moreover, not only liable to, but dependent on a tonal "slipperiness." The sincere voice of "Kara-baras!" indeed remains a "may-be-sincerity," if a potent one, since the text refuses to unambiguously corroborate its good faith. These thickets of irony experienced in "Kara-baras!" define, in their sudden dissipation, the starting place of the following text.[93]

The "Epilogue"

The "Epilogue" positions itself immediately as a summing up, a no-nonsense distilling and clarifying of what has come before. Such, after all, is the import of the parasitic filler word "Koroche –" (roughly, long story short) from which the poet starts and which, in its repetitions, loosely demarcates the poem's compositional structure. In contrast to "Kara-baras!" the poet here establishes both discursive and biographical framings supporting a more traditional sincere voice. From the self-directed questions of the opening lines, he shifts to a thou-orientation: "*Ty znaesh'*, my zhili togda na Urale" (*You know*, we lived back then in the Urals).[94] This "you" can seem gratuitous, a bit of perfunctory colloquial filler, and the interlocutor remains unnamed. However, the recounting of Kibirov's childhood anecdote indeed presupposes another who can empathize, perhaps even commiserate – even if the collection's "target audience" (tselevaia auditoriia), as per the dedication, consists of two women too young to remember that time. Hence the need to mention that mandarins were a rarity in the stores.

In addition, the utterance is expressly situated in relation to a biographical context. The childhood described is represented as the real childhood of the poet and is manifestly plausible in both its psychological and biographical detail. This pragmatic and biographical framing forms the girding for the middle part of the poem, which consists of a well-developed narrative of a feverish childhood illness and the father's brief appearance during a turn as duty officer to check on him and dump a large packet of ice-cold mandarin oranges into his bed.

The poem is composed almost entirely in amphibrachic tetrameter. However, a casually prosaic feel is introduced to the main narrative through Kibirov's use of rhyme, at turns casual (series of contiguous grammatical rhymes), absent, or camouflaged through the use of distant off rhymes and enjambment:

> А чем я болел, и куда наша мама [closest rhyme "prodmagakh" –
>   twelve lines earlier]
> уехала – я не припомню … Наверно, [closest rhyme "merzko" –
>   six lines later]]
> на сессию в Нальчик. А папа в ту ночь [closest rhyme "zamok" –
>   eleven lines later]
> как раз оказался дежурным по части … [unrhymed]

> (And what I was ill with and where our mom
> had left for I can't remember … Most likely

exams in Nalchik. And papa that night
happened to be duty officer.)

At the same time, this story, and this colloquial prosaicism, does not constitute the poem's acutely sincere voice, but rather serves as yet another intermediate platform for its emergence in the final lines, where the story is reconstrued:

Сестре я почти ничего не оставил …

Короче –
вот это, вот это одно –
что мне в ощущениях было дано!

Вот эту прохладу
в горячем бреду
с тех пор я ищу
и никак не найду,
вот эту надежду
на то, что Отец
(как это ни странно)
придет наконец!
И все, что казалось
невыносимым
для наших испуганных душ,
окажется вдруг так легко излечимым –
как свинка, ветрянка,
короче – коклюш!

(I left my sister next to nothing …

Long story short –
Just this, just this alone –
of all sensations was given me!

That coolness
amidst fevered delirium
I seek from that time
and can't ever find,
that hope
that the Father
(strange as it seems)
will show up in the end!

> And all that seemed
> unendurable
> for our affrighted souls
> will suddenly turn out so easily curable –
> like chickenpox, mumps,
> you know – whooping cough!

And so *Kara-baras* ends with a yet more undeniable appeal to Christianity as refuge as well as, for this reader, if one reads the collection from beginning to end, with goosebumps, which are impossible to reproduce here, in the absence of the carefully erected, multistage platform the collection provides.

This ending repays deeper scrutiny. The poet's search here parallels the labyrinth or quest topos of medieval Christianity, but with a twist. The knight's path to the Grail is conceived as a moral and physical labyrinth in which, after a deceptively quick approach and a vision of the close but unattainable goal, the path winds ever further away before the final approach – for the worthy.[95] However, what the lyric persona experienced in childhood was not a vision of God's grace, however incomplete or fleeting, but only its secular analogue – the care and affection of the this-worldly father. And it seems that only retrospective reflection makes this a prefiguration of the experience of grace. Still, the transferred desire for God's reassurance and healing is so potent perhaps precisely because it mirrors a very accessible desire to recapture the this-worldly father's unexpected, timely presence.

Crucially, Kibirov is able to achieve here an effect that is ambivalent, tentative, and full-throated simultaneously and in this way reads as fervently experienced but also honest in its self-knowledge – a powerful sincerity ferment. In part, this relates to the logical and syntactic structure of these lines. There was a sensation (coolness amidst fevered delirium), which the lyric persona seeks from that time. But, in a crafty substitution, this sensation is equated syntactically to only a *hope* that the Father will come at last, a hope that is itself only *sought*. Simultaneously, however, the earlier phrase "bylo dano" (was given), spoken in an incontrovertible indicative mood and following the emphatic repetition, "vot eto, vot eto odno" (just this, just this alone), continues to resonate through these lines, and this is particularly true, it seems, regarding "nadezhdu" (hope), despite the fact the case usage does not allow us to connect these phrases syntactically. Another "crafty" substitution is the economical shift in perspective from personal to universally human in "*nashykh* ispugannykh dush" (*our* affrighted souls). This structure inoculates against hubris, dogmatics, posturing, while also generating an irrational but powerful countervailing sense of assuredness.

The sense of catharsis and emotional uplift is supported through the passage's language, which is uncommonly simple and deceptively direct, as well as through a sudden shift from prosaicizing verse form to an aspect of unassuming poetry. Kibirov, in this section, divides the mostly amphibrachic tetrameter lines. The rhyme scheme runs Xaa XbxbXcXcXDeDXe (X/x = unrhymed; the first X here, however, is the second to last repetition of *koroche*, the A-rhyme of the entire poem). Despite the fact the rhyme can technically be simplified to aabbccDeDe, additional phonic echoes in the interstitial rhyme positions (prokhládubredú-ishchú-nadézhdu;   stranno-kazalos';   dush-[mid-longer-line] vdrug) and minor irregularities in the division of lines and in the rhythm (the expressive syncope of "nevynosímym" [unbearable]) generate an impression not of simple mechanical division, but intensifying *verse organization*. The resulting "column" that ends the poem thus has an impact not merely visual.[96] This verse intensification, which feels something like a runner shifting onto his toes, adds to the gathering pathos.

Simultaneously, however, the burgeoning pathos is softened through the slightly outlandish sound of the litany of children's diseases, accentuated particularly by the playful phonetics of the final line: "koroche – kokliush!" (karóchi kakl'úsh). The phonetic overtones introduced through the filler word *koroche* (in its sixth and final appearance) thus help reduce the threatening whooping cough (kokliush) to children's nonsense play, distantly echoing the ending of "Kara-baras!" and reinforcing iconically the semantic thrust of the last six lines.

Had the poem been published separately, as indeed the final lines are distinctly orphaned above, it would have been overwhelmed by the weight of its sentimentality and the reach of its metaphysics. The ending would never have struck its mark. Another reader of my generation, Oleg Lekmanov, in his review called the "Epilogue" "wonderful" (prekrasnym) and "illuminated" (prosvetlennym), the latter having connotations of both an overcoming of inner darkness and an inner living radiance that inhabits the poem.[97] I would argue that this radiance is, in part, a concomitant of the sincere voice.

In what terms can we summarize the nature of the shift we observe as we move to and through the "Epilogue?" In "Kara-baras!" we have a poem that provides, at least internally, minimal pragmatic framing, presenting itself as a personal statement and appeal, but also as an art object, existing in the sphere of verbal and conceptual play. It seemingly declines to corroborate the good faith of its final transcendence of irony and posturing, and it balances the "may-be" sincere voice that does emerge on a slippery platform of shifting, playful ironies. The "Epilogue," in contrast, carefully establishes discursive and biographical framings that not only establish its function and place within the collection, but also inscribe it more forcefully in the context of a "fleshed-out" extratextual life. It draws upon a contrast with initial prosaicism to generate burgeoning pathos in the finale and draws on a contrast with the preceding poem's irony to establish its bona fides as "post-sceptical" and mark its conclusions as a product of experience and introspection, lending it a more immediate, and adult, backstory. The epilogue's finale, moreover, preserves in its logical structure a modicum of salutary and believable self-doubt, even as its self-assured tone drives a sense of achieved catharsis. In its crowning move, it softens and humanizes its metaphysical flight with the litany of somewhat silly-sounding childhood illnesses.

Through this trajectory, Kibirov's collection *Kara-baras* presents the Father's *presence even in apparent absence* as an earned truth, one which can be reached only by way of a "straying" (irony, doubt, prodigal wandering) or "exile." And this is as it should be – for the absence is at least half the truth. In the title of this section, I called Kibirov's sincerity "prodigal," intending two senses. On a more superficial plane, Kibirov is given to moments of *lavish* sentiment, which retain a sense of their own extravagance. It is the poet's implicit nods to this extravagance that recuperate these emotional excesses into a second-pole, "modulated" sincerity. On a deeper one, I believe we can talk about ironic scepticism and relativism in Kibirov, at least in this period, as constituents of a master trope of prodigal rebellion and delayed return. Irony and sincerity are factually synchronous, but, unlike for Derzhavin or Mandelstam or Levin, these qualities participate in a mythology that has a narrative arc.[98]

Paradoxically, when the Christian idea finally takes undeniable centre stage in Kibirov's collection *Graeco- and Roman-Catholic Songs and Amusements* (2009), it will not form the earned truth of the collection. The Christian truth, after all, is a matter of faith and communal values. At the heart of Kibirov's poem "Theodicy" ("Teoditseia") are the stigmata on Jesus's hands.[99] One cannot argue for or against this, and Kibirov does not even attempt to bring the sceptical reader to an understanding of how he has arrived here. I suspect that the very personal earned truth of this later collection concerns at least as much how the poet should bear himself – and bare himself – within the cultural field. Christian truth, we see, can be stated unambiguously and openly, if still with a varied and, at the collection's best, subtle tone – not couched in irony or dispersed among and thus camouflaged by other poems but gathered into an aggregate easily recognizable to all.[100] But this truth is also a continuation in another cultural space of Kibirov's old determination to speak through "tastelessness," through a claiming of what has been deemed uncouth for poetry by cultural consensus: "I understood that it was possible either to reject lyricism entirely or just as [strongly] to emphasize all this, a sentimentality so indecorous in contemporary culture and so on, so that this sentimentality itself underscores that I know that it is indecorous. [...] I know that this looks silly [eto smeshno], but let's try it just the same, dear reader."[101]

Conclusion

The open-endedness of literary history, the malleability of the sincere voice, and the diversity and unpredictability of potential reader conceptions of sincerity mean that it is and will always remain too early to round off a story of the sincere voice in poetry. We can, in any case, affirm that the sincere voice has remained an elusive but valued quality through many different periods, including some, like modernism, generally seen as antagonistic to sincerity. For this reason, the issue of how the sincere voice emerged in Russian poetry and how it is produced and renewed is a vital one for poetics. The readings in this book have striven to illustrate that, despite the philosophical and linguistic barriers, poets have achieved meaningful successes in the stable inscribing of sincerity in their poetry and that it is possible to analyse and tentatively reconstruct the factors underlying this achievement. Moreover, the insights here into the ways in which readers process and evaluate sincerity may also have broader import for understanding how sincerity is encoded and "read" – as well as why it can misfire – in "real-world" communication.[1]

These insights centre, first, around two idealized poles in the conceptualization of sincerity – one more familiar, which prioritizes the baring of the self and sees this confirmed by attendant qualities such as seriousness, intensity of expression (pointing to intensity of experience), immediacy, candour, reflection, and confessionality. The other pole is less familiar and its adepts less outspoken about sincerity, but it is no less crucial to an understanding of how sincerity has been negotiated in poetry and how this process has impacted literary history. This second pole is suspicious of heated emotional displays, vocal strain, and excessive focus on the self. It values, rather, diversity of tone and mood and subtle modulations of voice that imply a broader range of human experience and acknowledge human complexity in a different way. This pole tends to see the self reflected particularly through its outward gaze and its dialogue with other voices. Often, it values the acknowledgment of epistemological doubt inherent in irony as a component of sincerity, and it tends to recognize and remain unfazed by the mediums of language and poetry that necessarily intercede between subject and expression, to recognize the need for performativity and triangulation if meaningful communication and meaningful art are to happen. Second, the insights of this study concern the way pragmatic framings and poetic devices can conspire to intimate a sincerity in harmony with individual author-reader conceptions, which, while idiosyncratic and often hybrid, seem to gravitate in important ways to these two poles.

An awareness of the tension between the two poles helps us to see anew processes that drive change in the cultural sphere. Thus, in the moment when Derzhavin emerges as Russia's pre-eminent eighteenth-century poet by writing his ode to Catherine, "Felitsa," within that central space in Russian literary life which is occupied by the ode, Derzhavin's second-pole sincerity, structured around modulation and irony, is perceived as revolutionary, challenging the high-blown rhetoric and overheated sentiment of the mid-eighteenth-century ode and its epigones. In the Romantic period, voices drawing upon qualities like seriousness (and self-seriousness), intensity, reflexivity, purported immediacy, and candour will come, in important ways, to hold the literary high ground. However, a Pushkin, still reared in a genre-based poetics and well aware of the ironies of literary subjectivity, presents a powerful image of resistance to these tendencies – at the same time that he effectively harnesses and plays upon the sincerity expectations of readers schooled by Sentimentalist and Romantic poetry.

In the modernist period, some poets value a neo-Romantic subjectivity as well as intensity of experience and expression, others the downplaying of the subject, modulation of voice, and self-deprecating irony. In Russia, scepticism directed at the Romantic-tragic posture, self-directedness, and "vocal strain" of Symbolism produces a reaction uncannily similar to that spurred earlier by the high-pitched ode, in part supporting the shift in taste necessary for high modernism. (In the Anglo-American context, the "offending" poets are the Victorians.) Historical conditions, and prevailing tastes, help elevate the serious and earnest in the Stalinist and post-Stalinist mid-century context. However, the poles remain in tension: we see that elements of modernist poetics complicate a first-pole sincerity in Akhmatova's *Requiem* and diverse ironies underly a sincere resonance in the poetry of Levin. At turn of the millennium, we again observe competing sincere voices, which draw upon expressive and ironic poles, respectively, in the poetry of Ryzhy and Kibirov. Moreover, Kibirov's sincere voice, which builds upon ambivalent amalgams of irony and pathos, simultaneously transcends postmodern nihilistic irony and the self-seriousness of Soviet mid-century poetry. Each of these types of "sincere voices" can read as questionable in its sincerity given inconducive reader codes but will resonate as sincere only if codes align *and* there is a felicitous convergence of pragmatic framings and poetic devices. No previous study has looked at the tensions that drive change in lyric poetry through the prism of conduciveness of different poetics to emergent models of sincerity.

Though this has not been my point of focus, we have also seen, in the readings, that sincerity and authenticity inevitably connect the subject to problems of epistemology, ontology, and axiology, at the centre of which stands the question of truth. In even the "smallest," most detached, least ontologically "ambitious" poem, how poetry expresses and engages with truth and how the poet's mode of expression can contribute to or detract from that process remain at issue. If sincerity is to be meaningfully negotiated in poetry, these problems must be faced while the poet simultaneously runs up against and bends to the good the intransigence of language.

While I believe this work has much to contribute to our understanding of lyric poetry more broadly, it should be underscored that the sincere voice, in all its diversity, is only one subset of poetic voice. And this, inevitably, raises questions about the boundaries of the phenomenon of the sincere voice. As I look back at the choice of poems read, I see that some phenomena have remained outside of my purview serendipitously, while others, indeed raising pointed questions about the margins, have been consciously set aside during this first attempt to get at the heart of the issue as I have framed it. One of these latter phenomena is poetry that does not struggle to embody a sincere voice but plays with and problematizes this phenomenon and the expectations it generates, and which incorporates elements undermining a sincere resonance or the "presence" of a subject in tension with competing elements projecting these qualities. Though one could certainly point to earlier examples, a context in which we see this – one much in scholarly vogue today – is the poetry of conceptualist Dmitry Alexandrovich Prigov.[2] Another phenomenon testing the boundaries of the sincere voice is poetry projecting dialogic, fractured, and other experimental subjectivities. This has been a powerful current in recent Russian poetry, as evidenced, for instance, by the November-December 2019 special issue of *Russian Literature*.

In both these instances, one can meaningfully ask whether the poets (or, rather, some poets and some poems) are engaged in a process of forming a readership prepared to experience such radical and problematic subjectivities as sincere, in part through their implicit acknowledgment of a prevalent *what we know now* deeply sceptical of traditional poetic subjectivity. This indeed seems to be the case.[3] A third area in which the boundaries of the sincere voice can be fruitfully explored is what I might term "popular sincerity," sincerities resonating with broad reader groups with a substantially lesser or only indirect knowledge of the literary tradition. This is not to say that popular sincerities cannot appeal to "sophisticated" readers or "literary" poets to "naïve" readers. Indeed, the poetry of Akhmatova or Sergei Esenin handily confirms that they can. But where such appeal draws strongly upon the commonplace and *poshlost'* (philistinism), this has remained outside the bounds of the current study. (Prigov's experiments with sincerity, incidentally, often explore this latter territory.)

Two additional phenomena have fallen outside the choice of readings, though I see them as unquestionably well suited to exploration within the theoretical framework developed here. One of these is poetry entirely forgoing an explicit, grammatically or contextually implied "I" (or "we") and other deictic markers – poetry that implies a subject solely through that subject's auditory impressions, gaze, or vision (more broadly understood). I could, however, have chosen a poem by Mandelstam illustrating this type of poetic speech, and the pretensions to sincerity of such poetic utterances are broadly recognized in the Imagist/Objectivist context.[4]

A final phenomenon that has remained, perhaps surprisingly, outside my examples is free verse. The same frameworks for understanding how sincerity is written and read should be applicable to any free verse that answers our definition for a resonantly sincere voice – even if the poetic resources for foregrounding the poems' "indwelling voices" in some ways differ.[5] At the same time, analysis of the Russian context, which retains formal aspects like metre and rhyme more vigorously over a longer stretch of the post-Romantic era than Anglo-American poetry, including in many contemporary poets, has helped to illustrate that there is no inevitability in the gradual withdrawal of poetry to freer and freer forms in the face of the demand for sincerity, that the abandoning of any given formal stricture is only one potential strategy for renewing poetic language, and that free verse is no more or less inherently capable of expressing sincerity than more formally circumscribed poetry. In both contexts, particularly in our day, there are manifold obstacles, formal and philosophical, to be overcome.

In this book, I have striven to present a fundamentally new, methodologically sound approach to the study of sincerity and authenticity in poetry through introducing the concept of the *sincere voice* and through demonstrating two competing, historically developing poles in the conceptualization of sincerity. To the competing poles are linked clusters of secondary traits that stand in for sincerity (since the truth value of the expressed in relation to an inner world is not, of course, readable), thus allowing reader recognition, but also, because the two poles are in tension, inciting telling conflicts of opinion. This, in turn, has empowered a framework within which one can tease out, in historically grounded case studies, the pragmatic framings and poetic devices that have made possible the inscription of relatively stable, "audibly" sincere voices. Collectively, through these interventions, it has been possible to chart a more fine-grained picture than previously of how sincerity has been written and read in Russian and, by extension, Western poetry from the late neoclassical or proto-Romantic period to post-postmodernism.

The traditional lyric participates in two sets of pragmatic relations. There is a cluster of relations internal to the poem – those among speaker(s), the utterance, "world," and addressed and implied audience(s). But these are overlaid on a separate cluster of relations from our world, between author(s), the utterance, world, and reader(s), however inchoate the latter relations. Among these two sets of coordinates, only the utterance has complete identity with itself. The lyric subject is reducible neither to the speaker, nor to the author.[6]

The true subject of the poem is rather the amalgam that emerges from this double-exposure and out of these pragmatic tensions. And this subject, which constitutes the speaking voice in its complex, indeterminate, shimmering connection to our lived world, is a part of the aesthetic charge of traditional lyric. How do we adequately incorporate the subject, thus understood, into the field of poetics? And how can we speak responsibly about how some poems intimate an unusually powerful bond, running through the axis of the subject, with the extratextual world? Ultimately, how does the poet, when it is desirable, generate the powerful sense of presence connected to the feeling that he or she speaks *through* the poem? And why does this resonate or fail to resonate for which competent readers? These, I believe, are potent questions to be asking, questions which can be illuminating for readers and writers, as well as scholars of the lyric, to pose. They are the core questions that inspired this book. They are questions that, I hope, will enrich our conversations about sincerity and about poetry.

Appendix
Another Vista on Pushkin's "Monument"

What happens when we attempt to look at Pushkin's "Monument" from the perspective of his own circle? As a starting point to enter this specialized reader code, we might note that the final words, "I ne osporivai gluptsa" (And don't dispute a fool), and their immediate context represent not only a well-trodden topos ("Не отвѣщай безумному по безумію его" [Answer not a fool according to his folly; Proverbs 26:4]), but also a topos relevant to Pushkin's formative literary milieu. Three contexts bear particular relevance and help explain the notable deviations of the fifth stanza from the Horatian model.

In Pushkin's early years, he was strongly connected to the playful Arzamas society, which, through multilevelled parody and protest, contested the Slavophilic and archaicizing influence of the competing Colloquy of Lovers of the Russian Word (Beseda liubitelei russkogo slova). Derzhavin, though not active in the polemics, was co-chair and host of the Colloquy. The "brethren" of Arzamas took as their banner particularly the linguistic and genre innovations of two older authors, Nikolai Karamzin and Ivan Dmitriev.

Dmitriev, in 1810, had published a loose imitation of Horace's ode 2.16, which ends "et malignum / spernere vulgus" (and to scorn the spiteful rabble). Dmitriev's version concludes: "I ravnodushie k suzhdeniiu / Tolpy zoilov i gluptsov" (And indifference to the opinions / Of the crowd of [harshly unjust] critics and imbeciles).[1] Horace's ode 2.16, it should be noted, in contrast to ode 3.30 ("Exegi monumentum …"), is made up, like Pushkin's poem, of four-line stanzas with a shortened final line.

This potential source in Dmitriev/Horace is mediated by a second context that does not appear to have been mentioned previously in connection with Pushkin's poem. Zhukovsky's epistle "To Prince

Viazemsky and V.L. Pushkin" ("K kn. Viazemskomu i V.L. Pushkinu," 1814) was part of an extensive poetic exchange between the three, published in *Russian Museum* (*Rossiiskii muzeum*), nos. 2, 3, 7 (1815).[2] Pushkin would certainly have followed this exchange, given his acquaintance with the participants (including the "poet-uncle," who "matched him with the muses") and that he and friend Anton Delvig published a series of early poems in the same journal that same year.[3] The catalyst for the epistles was a rumour that the intrigues of the Colloquy's Alexander Shakhovskoi had led to the failure of *Polyxena* (*Poliksena*, 1809) and, ultimately, the mental and physical breakdown of tragedian Vladislav Ozerov. Departing from V.L. Pushkin's epistle to Viazemsky on the poet's (and particularly Ozerov's) suffering on account of the envy, dimwittedness, and pseudo-learning of the critics from Colloquy and Viazemsky's reply that the appropriate response is silence, Zhukovsky writes:[4]

> Друзья, тот стихотворец – горе,
> В ком без похвал восторга нет.
>
> ....
>
> Презренью бросим тот венец,
> Который *всем* дается светом; [5]

> (Friends, that poet is a wreck,
> In whom there is no rapture without praise.
>
> ....
>
> We cast to scorn that crown,
> Which is given by the *whole* world.

Zhukovsky in his epistle combines the theme of indifference, not only to the persecution of critics, but to public praise and glory (as in Pushkin's stanza 5) with a locating in oneself of the poet's "pokoi, i chest', i naslazhden'ia" (calm, and honour, and enjoyments – very Pushkinian values) and, in the conclusion of the epistle, a contrasting of incorruptible posterity, which will give answer for the poet, to the frail *edifices* of the enviers (evoking the Horatian monument topos). Early on, he adduces the image of Memnon, both monument and metaphor for the poet, who, with his "elevated head," scorns those of lowly spirit:

> Один, среди песков, Мемнон,
> Седя с *возвышенной главою*,
> Молчит – лишь *гордою* стопою
> Касается ко праху он;

(Alone, among the sands, Memnon,
Sitting with an *elevated head*,
Keeps silence – but with his *proud* foot
Does he touch the dust.)

Pushkin would interpolate within the monument framework: "*Voznessia vyshe on glavoiu nepokornoi*" ([My monument] has *raised* its *unbowed head* up higher). This image, like the fifth stanza's call for indifference to praise as well as blame, is absent in both Horace and Derzhavin.

The thrust of the Memnon topos is the transfiguration of inert substance (and, by extension, the poet) through inspiration, so we are not talking about a direct conceptual echo in Pushkin's monument "not-of-human-hands."[6] However, there is a potential associative connection between the Colossus of Memnon at Egyptian Thebes (an image of which graced the frontispiece for the volume of Zhukovsky's works that he gave to the young poet in 1815); the Egyptian/African topoi of the pyramids (Horace and Derzhavin's monument poems); and Pompey's pillar at Alexandria (in a literal understanding of Pushkin's initial stanza).[7] Zhukovsky's frontispiece also perhaps provided an impulse towards Pushkin's interpolation in "Monument" of a "narodnaia tropa" (path of the people). A column of tiny human figures is seen approaching the remote Colossus from the right. And yet more tangential evidence for an associative riff on Memnon in the first stanza of "Monument" can be found on the final page of the rough draft of "Autumn" ("Osen'," 1833), where thoughts of the pyramids, Egypt, and eternity – all *displaced* from the opening stanza of Pushkin's "Monument" – surround a drawing of a parodic Memnon-like seated Colossus.[8]

Zhukovsky's epistle had been republished four times in different editions of his *Poems* (*Stikhotvoreniia*) by the time "Monument" was written, and, thus, the allusion cannot be construed as the sort of Pushkinian gesture literally comprehensible only to his closest circle.[9] However, unlike Derzhavin's "Monument," with which Pushkin's poem entered into an obvious implicit dialogue, the subtle allusion to Zhukovsky's text, even for the contemporary who knew and remembered the epistle, might have passed under the radar. And only for a quite narrow readership, largely circumscribed by the outlines of the Arzamas society, would the subtle allusion to Zhukovsky's epistle have evoked its full cultural, personal, and polemical context.[10]

Is this text necessary to read "Monument?" Does the allusion add any *semantic* facets to Pushkin's masterwork? No. But might Zhukovsky and Viazemsky upon reading "Monument" have recalled their epistles and this episode, central to the immediate prehistory of Arzamas? And, in that case, might they not have savoured the irony that Pushkin returns to his roots in his monument poem not only with a recollection of Delvig's prophecies in the loftily intoned and Horatian/Derzhavinian "To Pushkin [Who, like the swan of flowering Ausonia]" ("Pushkinu [Kto, kak lebed' tsvetushchei Avzonii]," 1815?),[11] but that, in fact, he closes his poem with a set of proto-Arzamasian motifs, elevated in their placement and the economy of their diction to the level of the most serious and high-stakes poetry.[12]

That Pushkin, in the last stanza of "Monument," engages a circle poetics is also underscored in light of the private resonances of the final line. Andrei Dobritsyn, following Alekseev and others before him, notes Pushkin's earlier reference in "Onegin's Album" ("Al'bom Onegina," 1828) to a "Koranic" source of this topos: "V Korane myslei mnogo zdravykh, / Vot naprimer: [...] Chti Boga i *ne spor' s gluptsom –*" (In the Koran there are many sound thoughts, / For instance: [...] Revere God and *don't argue with a fool* –).[13] However, Pushkin had not included this passage in the published version of his novel in verse. Nor would his intimates have had to learn of the connection from "Onegin's Album." It was already a part of their common, exclusive language. Thus, Dobritsyn demonstrates that the phrase "sviataia zapoved' Korana" (a sacred commandment of the Koran) is used in an 1824 letter to Viazemsky to mean, do not enter into polemics with low-brow and unscrupulous journalists. He also notes that in a contemporaneous letter to his brother Lev, Pushkin had remarked: "One ought to have respect for oneself. You, Delvig, and me can all three of us disregard [lit., spit on] the dregs of our literature – this is my whole advice to you."[14] Pushkin's reference to the intimate collective in the letter to his brother and his expectation of understanding on the part of Viazemsky indicate the role that the concept "don't dispute a fool" played within Pushkin's closest circle and the fact that it had, by 1824, a private shorthand. The commandment is "sacred" in the letter to Viazemsky not because it comes from the Koran, but because it is fundamental for, or at least deeply aspired to, by Pushkin.[15] Not the Koran's *commandments* are sacred, but *this one*, sacred enough, in fact, to become the final words of his monument poem.

So, where might the reader attuned to this context locate the sincere voice in "Monument?" Perhaps, for Pushkin's Arzamas brethren, it was conveyed in a playfully discrete revisiting of an anti-Colloquy and, hence, implicitly anti-Derzhavin episode within the most stodgy, serious, and Derzhavinian of endeavours, a subtle nod that reassured them – this is *our* Pushkin.

Notes

Introduction

1 van Alphen and Bal, "Introduction," in *Rhetoric of Sincerity*, 3, 2.
2 See Roman Jakobson's model of the speech act, "Closing Statement," 353. See also Lotman, *Struktura*, 35–8 (trans., *Structure*, 23–5).
3 Cf. Hans Robert Jauss on literature's shifting "horizon of expectations" ("Literary History").
4 Cf. Yuri Tynianov's use of the concept of "worn" (*stertye*) words, images, metres, etc. in *Arkhaisty i novatory*.
5 Lecture, Emory University, Decatur, GA, 2 November 2007.
6 See the epigraphs to this chapter, which are intended to highlight, in something of a dialectic, a few of the founding assumptions of this study. Eikhenbaum's comment underscores the inescapable constructedness of what strikes the reader as most organic and immediate – the voice. The quote from Grigoryev honours the concept that truth can be a central value in poetry (however we come to understand or approach that truth). Mandelstam's words are chosen to emphasize that "direct" speech, in poetry, is not sufficient, or even necessarily suited, to generate the charge of sincerity.
7 Cf. Wordsworth's "Essay upon Epitaphs": "But it is required that these [common-place, S.G.] truths should [...] be uttered in such connection as shall make it felt that they are not adopted, not spoken by rote, but perceived in their whole compass with the freshness and clearness of an original intuition" (*Literary Criticism*, 117–18). (On the universalizing aspect of Wordsworth's conception of sincerity, which values *common* truths, see Forbes, *Sincerity's Shadow*, chapter 2.)

    In the case of poetry constructed of imperatives or of what J.L. Austin called "performatives," our definition will stand if we break it off at the words "in good faith," the felicity of a performative being in that it is not "empty," rather than that it conveys any truth outside of itself. Searle, however, sees even this felicity as a truth value, arguing that the truth of a promise consists in its being intended as a promise ("How Performatives Work," 545). One could additionally argue that "performatives" often imply an *axiological* foundation which can constitute a truth in relation to a self projected in the poem.

8 Trilling, *Sincerity and Authenticity*, 2. For Trilling's influential definition of authenticity, see *Sincerity and Authenticity*, 11–12, 92ff.

9 Cf. Pickett on the overlap between these terms (*Rethinking Sincerity*, 8). Milnes and Sinanan see in Romantic literature an emergent "binding" of authenticity and sincerity, the former understood as state, the latter as practice ("Introduction," 2, 4, 17). In any case, a philosophical distinction between the "inward self-relation" of authenticity and outward directedness of sincerity (Pickett, *Rethinking Sincerity*, 162–3) is of limited utility in the consideration of poetry, where all modes of being are accessible only through some form of verbalization.

10 These are Grigoryev's "On Truth and Sincerity in Art" ("O pravde i iskrennosti v iskusstve," 1856, discussed in chapter 3, part 2) and Pomerantsev's "On Sincerity in Literature" ("Ob iskrennosti v literature," 1953, discussed in chapter 5).

11 *Merriam-Webster* (accessed online 7 July 2018). Though this usage of "authenticity" has become second nature to us, the *Oxford English Dictionary* demonstrates how relatively recent it is in English as well, traceable to Heidegger's *Sein und Zeit* (*Being and Time*, 1927; first English usage in this meaning, 1948). Johann Herder, however, had already formulated in the eighteenth century a modern concept of a self that could be the measure of authenticity ("Each human being has his own measure, as it were an accord peculiar to him of all his feelings to each other"; cited in Charles Taylor, *Sources of Self*, 375).
On the historical and etymological roots of the word *iskrennost'* (sincerity) , see Kozlov, *Readers*, 63; Rutten, *Sincerity after Communism*, 412.

12 On post-postmodern ironic sincerity, see, for instance, Zorin, "Chtoby zhizn'," 17; Epshtein, *Postmodern*, 254–94; Yurchak, "Post-Post-Communist"; Magill, *Sincerity*; Kelley, "Dialectic of Sincerity"; Rutten, *Sincerity after Communism*; MacDowell, "The Metamodern, the Quirky." A rare voice acknowledging irony's function in some earlier rhetorics of sincerity is Rosenbaum, *Professing* (see esp. 60–1, 160, 222). Authors such as R.D. Timenchik, Sergei Averintsev, Clare Cavanagh, Oleg Lekmanov, and myself have written on the subtle ironies underpinning the serious in Russian Acmeism (Modernism). For this literature and analysis of the phenomenon, see Goldberg, *Mandelstam, Blok*, esp. 227n57–8, 14, 20, 56–64, 216. Cf. the concept of affirmative doubt in Manning, *Rhétorique*

de la sincérité, 403ff. See also Gluck on the potential sincerity of irony in post-Stalinist Soviet prose ("'I Want to Be,'" 119–20ff.).

13 See, for instance, Handwerk, *Irony*, 18–43, on Friedrich Schlegel's Romantic irony.

14 These are roughly those forms implying irony in its "oppositional" or "assailing" functions as per Hutcheon (*Irony's Edge*, 52–6).

15 To be clear, I am using belief and doubt in a secular sense here, one which admits religious contexts, but is broader, concerning all manner of potential truths about the world and self.

16 Gumilev, *SS*, 4: 173; on Derzhavin, see chapter 1.

17 See Hutcheon, *Irony's Edge*, esp. 89–101.

18 Within a particular cultural context, and, given a specific set of more or less well-defined "readerships," the adept poet or other speaker is capable of tuning an utterance consciously or subconsciously to evoke particular emotional responses, and sometimes multiple simultaneously divergent responses (not that an artwork's function and meaning are limited to such foreseeable responses).

19 Despite parallels between the social constructedness of emotions and emotional regimes and the social constructedness of sincerity, the latter is not an emotion. While individuals may experience varying degrees of certainty (and varying levels of emotionally tinged concern) regarding their own sincerity in a given instance, the quality of sincerity itself does not have variable "intensity" like emotions. If we take the terms given in William Reddy's influential *Navigation of Feeling*, we can see that while sincerity partakes of his universals (effort, uncertainty, and [deep] goal-relevance [60]), it is completely at odds with his descriptive definition (top of 111). In addition, inscriptions of sincerity have only two of the three features of Reddy's "emotives" – "relational intent" (i.e., illocutionary force) and "self-exploring and self-altering effects" (i.e., potential self-directed perlocutionary impact), ibid. Recognition of these aspects of sincerity is crucial to a proper understanding of how sincerity functions in the world. However, for Reddy, emotives also have "descriptive appearance," and herein lies a distinction with implications for methodology. While "emotion claims" often play a key role in analysis of the history and cultural embeddedness of emotion, our gaze has to be turned otherwise, primarily towards indirect indicators, to observe the functioning of sincerity in poetry. Difficulties arise in analysis of these planes of self-presentation because indices of indirect expression are multifunctional and, therefore, resist explication. But it is for this reason that Besnier, in an article reviewing research into affect from the field of linguistic anthropology, calls for analysis of micro-contexts ("Language and Affect," 429, 438–9) – central here. At the same time, Besnier rejects

as unfruitful the question "How do members of different social groups distinguish 'true' from 'deceitful' affective displays [...]?" (430), a capitulation I hope to prove unwarranted.

20 For sources in Romantic aesthetics of the connection of these qualities to sincerity, see chapter 2. For their continuing relevance, cf., for instance, the assumption that seriousness is a key characteristic, even a calque, for sincerity in de Vries, "Must We (NOT)"; the reflection of the criteria of intensity and immediacy in Davie's exasperated rhetorical questions ("Are we to believe a poet sincere because [...] he shouts at us? Or [...] because he writes a dishevelled poetry [...]?" ["Sincerity and Poetry," 8]); the way candour, in poet Ilya Selvinsky's aphorism, both subsumes and drives past sincerity: "A talented poet is sincere; a major poet is candid" (quoted in Mikhail Gasparov, *Zapisi i vypiski*, 245).

21 My initial recognition of this competing mode of sincerity grew out of the comparative study of the early twentieth-century poets Alexander Blok and Osip Mandelstam and was strongly reinforced by parallels discovered in Derzhavin and Pushkin.

22 We will hazard this word ("self"), despite, for instance, John Keats's radical rejection of selfhood in a letter in which he disdains the "wordsworthian or egotistical sublime" ("To Richard Woodhouse," 27 October 1818).

23 Pushkin, *PSS16*, 12: 93. All translations are my own unless otherwise noted.

24 Cf. Reddy on the difficulties posed by the extreme emotional regime of Sentimentalism (*Navigation of Feeling*, 429, 438–9, 252, 256).

25 Thomas, *Collected Poems*, 116.

26 The May 1951 letter containing the poem included the note, "The only person I can't show the little enclosed poem to is, of course, my father, who doesn't know he's dying" (Thomas, *Collected Letters*, 800). David John Thomas died in December 1952 "in great pain & blind" (860).

27 Heaney, "Dylan the Durable?" 78, 85.

28 Cf. the not inaccurate, but still irksomely misleading footnote in the *Norton Anthology of Poetry* – "written in May, 1951, during the final illness of Dylan Thomas's father" (Allison et al., 1181). The *verses* of the poem begin to make cogent sense precisely when we let go of the image of the poet bedside with a dying father and posit Thomas's anxiety rather that his father will pass *suddenly* and quietly, without father, particularly, but also son (writing abroad) having had the chance to confront the transitional moment and its meaning. The "misreading," placing the son next to the father, and incited by Thomas through the difficulty of determining the level of metaphoricity of the phrase "proud height," brings with it in tow powerful emotional memory through its familiarity and long cultural lineage (descending ultimately to the image of the aged and blind Isaac's blessing, and blessing-curse, of his sons).

29 Cf. Heaney on the "genuinely desperate rhetoric" that immunizes the villanelle's "fantasy and extravagance of imagery and diction" from "rant and posturing" ("Dylan the Durable," 79).

30 In Southern Welsh English the vowel is a true long vowel (Penhallurick, "Welsh English," 108, 112–13). Note, in any case, the obvious incongruity of any attempt to subordinate the pronunciation of these two syllables to the verse rhythm. The complexity of the poem's tone is of course greater than is conveyed in this particular line.

31 One should keep in mind that we are speaking of excess to semantics here, not emotional excess (despite the emotional urgency which becomes, in part, the content of this excess in the above instance). For examples of excess to semantics cueing rather vocal modulation and representing our second pole, see the readings of Derzhavin in chapter 1.

32 The quotation is from Esterhammer, "Scandal," 105. On sincerity and the history of its reception in Western culture, particularly as concerns literature and poetry, see esp. Ball, "Sincerity"; Perkins, "Challenge"; Abrams, *Mirror*; Trilling, *Sincerity and Authenticity*; Guilhamet, *Sincere Ideal*; McGann, *Byron and Romanticism*; Forbes, *Sincerity's Shadow*; Rosenbaum, *Professing Sincerity*, van Alphen, Bal, and Smith, eds., *Rhetoric of Sincerity*; Milnes and Sinanan, eds., *Romanticism*; and Manning, *Rhétorique de la sincérité*. A selection of works critically engaging issues linked to sincerity in the Russian context might include Lotman, "Teatr i teatral'nost'"; Ginzburg, *O lirike*; Epshtein, *Postmodern*; Schönle, "Scare"; Powelstock, "Burying the Elegiac" and *Becoming*; Fishzon, "Operatics"; Harrington, "Melodrama"; Golburt, *First Epoch*; Klein, "Istina i iskrennost'"; Rutten, *Sincerity after Communism* and "Sovetskaia ritorika"; Gluck, "'I Want to Be.'" See also note 12 above and chapter 4, note 10.

33 My own approach is sufficiently distant from prevailing previous ones that my observations are almost always in a relation of complementarity to the best scholarship. Ellen Rutten's *Sincerity after Communism* is the most substantial study engaging the Russian context. It contains an excellent chapter-length overview of the history of sincerity as a concept, comparing and contrasting Western and Russian traditions. However, the body of her study is devoted primarily to the contemporary period and centres on the relation of sincerity to traumatic memory, commodification, and new media, concerns distant from my own. Moreover, Rutten's methodological focus on "sincerity talk," which she derives from history of emotions (cf. "emotion talk" [Plamper "Fear," 281]), is antithetical to mine. Tellingly, in Rutten's informative chapter on the phenomenon of Dmitry Alexandrovich Prigov, no poetic text or performance is subjected to analysis. Trilling's *Sincerity and Authenticity* is the seminal overview of sincerity as a phenomenon in Western culture, and it was he who

brought to light the productive connection and contrast between sincerity and authenticity. At the same time, Trilling's lectures are not concerned with issues of poetic sincerity and are, to an extent, informed by their vantage point at a moment of counterculture looking back on earlier rebellions. For instance, Trilling's vision of an "authenticity" antagonistic to "culture" and civilization fits Symbolist Alexander Blok's mature poetry but cannot explain the sources of Osip Mandelstam's authenticity a half-generation and sea change in poetics later. Deborah Forbes's fine study *Sincerity's Shadow* subtly distinguishes a series of contrasting Romantic sincerities as engaged in poetry. This differentiation of Romantic *sincerities* strongly influenced my thinking and is reflected (together with Trilling's work) in my title. However, Forbes explores these sincerities in a synchronic rather than diachronic framework (stressing the parallels between nineteenth- and twentieth-century writers), and the overarching question which organizes Forbes's approach to the material – "what responses does the structural impossibility of sincerity [*per se*] permit?" – differs radically from my own. Susan B. Rosenbaum's *Professing Sincerity* takes a crucial step forward in recognizing sincerity as a performative rhetoric. She also avoids the reflexive opposing of sincerity and irony. However, her overarching focus on sincerity's interdependence with commerce and commodification can be overly determinative. Also, even when looking at phenomena that complicate the Romantic model, both Rosenbaum's and Forbes's point of reference remains British Romantic and American confessional poetry. *The Rhetoric of Sincerity*, edited by Ernst van Alphen, Mieke Bal, and Carel Smith, has driven recent scholarly conversations about performative sincerity. The authors consider the phenomenon of sincerity in a broad range of cultural spheres and from varied approaches. Still, few places in the volume attempt to analyse *how* sincerity is conveyed. (A notable exception is Katherine Bergeson's excellent article on vocal performance in Republican France.) Nicholas Manning, in *Rhétorique de la sincérité*, defines a cluster of modernist approaches to sincerity constructed in opposition to the "Romantic, expressive" mode (a mode he greatly and polemically oversimplifies). Manning's extended and serious focus on modes of sincerity in Western European and Anglo-American Modernism is both unique and very welcome. At the same time, he does not contextualize this shift within a broader historical perspective; he frames these modernist approaches differently from my second pole; and our understanding of the object of study and how to approach it could hardly be more divergent.

34 See Barthes on the Russian church bass ("Grain," 505). Cf. Cavarero, reading Calvino ("Multiple Voices").

35 Calvino, *Under the Jaguar Sun*, 54.

36 Dolar, "Linguistics," 541. More broadly, see 540–4; cf. also Cavarero, "Multiple Voices," 526–7. This dualism is paralleled, in Barthes, by the distinction between the "pheno-song" (encompassing the elements that are transparent to cultural codes) and "geno-song," which in its un-encoded materiality bears traces of significance transcending the structure of communication/meaning, "Grain," 506–7.

37 Cf. Dolar, "Linguistics," 542.

38 For an overview of the semantics of voices in cultural context, see Bulgakova, "Znaki differentsiatsii," in her *Golos*. The book's preceding section outlines some key semiotic binaries in which voice participates.

39 Mandelstam, *PSSP*, 2: 155–6.

40 Cf. "ordinary speech, which gives way to a trivial transparency that hides its sounded significance" (Ihde, *Listening*, 167). This is not to generalize that "New Sincerity" poetry is prosaic, or that, when lacking in irony or obvious formal structuring, it cannot find its own innovative devices for generating the charge of sincerity.

41 Paul de Man wrote, in a comment that has received much attention lately, that "The principle of intelligibility, in lyric poetry, depends on the phenomenalization of the poetic voice." In regard to the "sincere voice" in lyric poetry (and leaving aside any broader theoretical generalizations), I can indeed concur that – when successful – such an "actualization of the speaking voice" is a fundamental element of the reading process and is grounded in language and "poetic labor." I depart from de Man, however, in posing rather more seriously the question of how poets convince readers (and not readers convince themselves, as in Jonathan Culler's reading of de Man) of the presence of a voice. See de Man, "Lyrical Voice," 55; Culler, *Theory*, 85; cf. de Man, "Anthropomorphism," 256.

42 Cf. Jakobson's reflections on the intuitive in poetry (*Language*, 250ff.).

43 Cf. Booth, on a similar facet of the identification of irony, *Rhetoric of Irony*, 79–82; Egerton Brydges (1824), quoted in McGann, *Fiery Dust*, 27.

44 One can of course lie vehemently, without inhibition, in a serious and earnest tone, making all manner of false or calculating "disclosures."

45 Consider the following example from outside of poetry. At the end of the film comedy *Ivan Vasilyevich Changes Profession* (*Ivan Vasil'evich meniaet professiiu*, 1973), the hero, Shurik, awakens from what appears now to have been a dream, and he and the viewer are confronted with a different version of his wife, Zina. The viewer is clearly intended to experience her denials of an affair and her surprise at Shurik's questions as sincere. While some of this is conveyed through contextual narrative framing (the vulgarly frivolous Zina of the body of the narrative is presumably as unreal as the time-travel depicted), a whole series of visual traits translate to us the real Zina's sincerity. These include contrastively simple dress and

hairdo, a lack of heavy cosmetics, her body language and facial expressions. In a first close-up, she looks straight into Shurik's eyes with eyes wide open and slightly raised to meet his, generating an impression not only of openness, but of a certain defenselessness, ingenuousness. All of these elements of course represent evidence of sincerity that is circumstantial at best, but they function effectively to unambiguously *communicate* her sincerity to the film's viewer.

46 I speak here neither about the maximally naïve reader who *assumes* every poetic "I" to be the poet and needs no further confirmation, nor about the maximally poststructuralist reader who *assumes* no cohesive authorial "I" can exist. Succinctly, on "naïve biographism" and "naïve bio-skepticism," citing Jakobson and Bakhtin, see Khitrova, *Lyric Complicity*, 104, 256n71. At more length on the problem of the biographic subject, examining (and, in the first two cases, critiquing) lenses provided by Freud, Bloom, Jakobson, and Lotman, see part I of Bethea, *Realizing Metaphors*.

47 The universality of this definition of sincerity is perhaps brought into question in the Modernist context, in which some speak about the "sincerity of the poem" as opposed to the sincerity of the poet and in which verity often seems, in important ways, externalized. However, it is, even here, the poet's individual perception (of world, language), a "sense of one's own rightness" (Mandelstam) that structures the poem, which is checked against a purportedly outer authority by an inner instance (see chapter 3).

48 Jane Taylor, "'Why Do You," 19.

49 Cf. Hutcheon: "pragmatic theories [of irony] claim that something has to invite response, has to trigger interpreters to seek alternate meanings" (*Irony's Edge*, 149, citing Peter L. Hagen); as well as Hutcheon's paradigm of "frames" and "markers" in her analysis of the attribution of irony (141–59). My usage of "framing" here is, however, closer to Hutcheon's notion of circumstantial, textual and inter-textual context (143–4) than her own use of the term "frame."

50 While individual poetic devices can draw upon grammatical (encoded, conventional) and pragmatic (contextual, ad hoc) elements in support of the sincere voice, I do not intend this specialized linguistic meaning of "pragmatic." Nor will I be focusing here on the social pragmatics of the text, its situational uses by writers and readers, compellingly explored in a Golden Age context by Khitrova (*Lyric Complicity*). What I am interested in is the author's pragmatic situating of the text, implied on a variety of levels.

51 Lermontov's authorship has been disputed, but this does not change the resonance of the poem when printed as one of his canonical texts.

52 Merezhkovskii, *Dve tainy*, 109.

53 Tiutchev, *PSSP*, 2:137.

54 There are multiple reasons why poetic devices contributing to the inscrip-
   tion of the sincere voice often lean towards the iconic – when the form
   itself expresses or echoes the content. Iconic devices have a way of func-
   tioning as potent, subliminal italics. They are both particularly "striking"
   because of the artistic virtuosity needed to generate a resonance between
   thematic elements and elements of the code, and usually "'swallowed'
   by the reader almost imperceptibly, subliminally," due to the presumed
   muteness of the code as it functions in natural language (Zholkovsky,
   "How to Show," 220). This makes iconic devices also subtle and, gener-
   ally, individual in ways that are conducive to poetic sincerity. Moreover,
   just as iconic devices are dependent on parallel referential "concretiza-
   tion," which can suggest an interpretation and link disparate elements of
   the code (ibid.), extra-semantic verbal gestures or markings of sincerity
   are dependent on support from the referential plane (semantics) and
   pragmatic framings.

   A wholly different sort of "iconic" device relevant to sincerity (with
   apologies for the potential terminological ambiguity) are those *sui generis*
   devices that intimate vocal sonority or bodily and facial corporality.
55 On this stance, see especially Leibov, "*Liricheskii fragment*," 30–43.
56 Ritualized aspects of mourning, a long poetic tradition (cf. Petrarch;
   David in 2 Samuel 1), and inherent conflicts between private and public
   space add to the challenge of finding in the modern era an uncompro-
   mised and personal voice adequate to the situation of mourning.
57 F. [F.] T[iutchev], "Tiutchev. (Materialy k ego biografii)."
58 Cf. "one of those scenes which drove us – her, to Volkovo field [i.e., the
   cemetery], me to something which has no name in any human language"
   (*PSSP* 6:89).
59 Wordsworth and Coleridge, *Lyrical Ballads*, 157. While Wordsworth does
   not here explicitly connect this quality, which he attaches to "all good po-
   etry," to sincerity, it has very much been linked to sincerity by others. Cf.
   in *The Prelude*: "Emotion which best foresight need not fear, / Most worthy
   then of trust when most intense" (Wordsworth, *Thirteen-Book Prelude*, 316).
60 See Besnier's extensive catalogue of levels at which languages can be
   marked for affect ("Language and Affect," 421–8) and his discussion
   of the limitations on markers' interpretation, including cross-cultural/
   linguistic divergences (429). My own brief examples make no pretence of
   comprehensiveness.
61 Tsvetaeva, *SS7*, 3:24.
62 Mandel'shtam, *PSSP*, 2:272.
63 Tsvetaeva, *SS7*, 3:24.
64 I have borrowed a few words from Alyssa Gillespie's wonderful trans-
   lation, which, unfortunately, is insufficiently literal for my purposes

(Marina Tsvetaeva, "*Poem of the Mountain* and *Poem of the End*," *The Silver Age Journal* 2 [1999]: 52–111).

65 Without breaking a rule (as Russian versification allows for any number of pyrrhic feet), Tsvetaeva turns a simple trochaic tetrameter into a quasi-logaedic torpedo of a stanza. As logaedic verse (combining varied metrical feet in a regular pattern), one might parse it: anapaest | iamb | iamb / peon I | trochee | peon I ×2. Note that Tsvetaeva's preceding "Dedication" is unambiguously logaedic. On Tsvetaeva's logaedic rhythms, see Etkind, *Tam, vnutri*, 371–91. (Though a weakened stress falls on the first syllable of the odd lines, the first full stress is on syllable three. Cf. Zhirmunskij, *Introduction to Metrics*, 102, 104.)

66 On the paradigmatic and syntagmatic axes of the artistic text, see Lotman, *Struktura*, 89–203.

67 We can speak perhaps of general categories of device like accumulation, repetition, juxtaposition, hyperbole, but these become too broad to have interpretive value in individual contexts.

68 In Tsvetaeva's own translation: "[…] Все расстающиеся говорят как пьяные и любят торжественность …" (*SS7*, 3:24; original German: "nehmen gerne sich festlich"). *Torzhestvennost'* resists translation in the single word. However, *affect* conveys well the salient sense of slightly affected exaltedness of speech.

69 Volkov, *Dialogi*, 58–9.

70 For someone working in the Slavic field, it can feel like Culler, in *Theory of the Lyric*, works too hard to make the important point that the subject is reducible neither to speaker, nor to the author. (This goes especially for his repeated contesting of reading through the prism of dramatic monologue.) Culler cites the work of Käte Hamburger, whose 1957 book, *Die Logik der Dichtung* (trans. as *The Logic of Literature*, 1973), preceded Lydia Ginzburg's *O lirike* (1964, expanded 1974). (Ginzburg, however, develops a conception of the lyric hero first introduced by Yuri Tynianov in relation to the poetry of Alexander Blok in 1924.) Ginzburg writes: "The specificity of the lyric is that the person is present in it not only as an author, not only as the object of depiction, but also as its subject, included in the aesthetic structure of the work as an active element. At the same time, direct speech of the lyric 'I' is not in any way mandatory […] The lyric knows various degrees of distance from the monological type, various means of […] enciphering the author's consciousness – from masks of the lyric hero to all manner of 'objective' narratives, personages, things, enciphering the lyric personality (*lichnost'*) specifically in such a way that it shows through" (*O lirike*, 7). Ginzburg's book, read together with the broadly conceived, culturological semiotic approach of Yuri Lotman and others, has had a very broad influence in Slavic studies. These theories

incorporate concepts like the coherence of the artistic persona within some poets' oeuvres and the prevalence, certainly within the Russian context, of life-creation (*zhiznetvorchestvo*), the artist's construction or simply navigation of biography and persona outside the text, in order to approach the complexity of relation between poem and subject.

71 Boym convincingly situates readings of Tsvetaeva as "high-pitched" within a gendered aesthetic deriving from classical and Kantian concepts of "taste" ("Loving," 160–5), demonstrating how Tsvetaeva herself embraces and integrates within her poetics the intensity of excess. (For a corrective to Boym's reading of Mandelstam's reading of Tsvetaeva, however, see Ronen, *Poetika*, 150–7.)

   Is lyric poetry, in fact, hyperbolic in its essence, in the fundamental strangeness of its function as a speech act, as Culler argues in *Theory of the Lyric*? Maybe indeed. But then we must ask why such speech has been accepted by readers as a mode of sincere expression (and thus as expression perceived, presumably, as natural *in its context*)? And, further, what degree of such "hyperbolism" harmonizes with the temperament of what readers, failing to trigger alarm bells as staged, exaggerated, overwrought?

72 Cf. Wierzbicka on the distinction between the iconic meaning of "facial displays" and what this meaning "happens to convey to various addressees in various communicative situations" (*Emotions*, 181).

73 Cited in Abrams, *Mirror*, 126.

74 In this light, perhaps the popularity of the Romantic fragment can be linked to a productivity in terms of the sincere voice.

75 On the functioning of prosaicisms in various poetic contexts and periods, see Ginzburg, *O lirike*, esp. 214–21.

76 Cf. Adorno, "Curves"; Fishzon, "Operatics"; Rutten, *Sincerity after Communism*, esp. 59–62, 182–94.

77 The personal idiom of a poet may also be stylized, oriented to a particular non-contemporary linguistic milieu, and this medium may not read as an impediment to "sincerity" for the given poet or a particular readership. Cf. Pound, *Literary Essays*, 11. Even the medium of a not entirely mastered foreign language can form a basis for an emergent sincere voice, as Psoi Korolenko's remarkable, sensitive, and pointedly-not-overtly-ironic song setting of the young Rainer Maria Rilke's not quite grammatical Russian poetry demonstrates ("Ril'ke," on *Russkoe bogatstvo*).

78 At the same time, it is necessary to negotiate a fine line below between immanent and socially contextualized, reader-aware approaches to the "resonance" of the text. We can ignore neither since poets write both for themselves (or no one, or "ideal readers" in posterity) and for concrete reader communities envisagable from their present moment.

79 Perhaps it is worth articulating that, while each individual resonantly sincere passage must discover its own means of establishing a sincere voice, and while, given the challenges, moments of durably inscribed resonant sincerity are a testament to the talents of the author, neither originality nor quality is an identifier of sincerity. It should be quite obvious that all manner of poetic intonation or undertaking, including those neutral or antithetical in regard to sincerity, can display both innovation and quality.

80 Cf. Booth, *Rhetoric of Irony*, esp. 47–86; Hutcheon, *Irony's Edge*, 143–59.

81 This cultural myth has deep roots. Cf. Milton, "The Verse," in *Paradise Lost*, 4.

82 Western pre-Romantic poets like Edward Young and Friedrich Gottlieb Klopstock did, however, influence a magnificent speculative religious ode by the hero of our first chapter, Gavrila Derzhavin. His "God" (Bog, 1780–4) had been translated, by the mid-nineteenth century, into nine languages, including Japanese. See Grot, notes to Derzhavin, *Sochineniia* (1864–83), 1:189–90, 201–2.

1 The Problem of Sincerity and the Poetic Device in Gavrila Derzhavin's Odes

1 Habermas, *Theory*, 1:15–17.

2 On the tension between corporate and individual authorship in the first half of the eighteenth century, see Pogosian, *Vostorg*, 55–91. When one looks at the mix of signed and unsigned publications in the *Companion* and in Derzhavin's oeuvre (pamphlets), it becomes clear that the bounds of individual and collective authorship remained fluid later in the century as well. On the role of Catherine and her court in contemporary cultural life, see esp. Proskurina, *Mify imperii; Imperiia pera*.

3 See Klein, "Istina i iskrennost'," 198–9, 201–3. The previous model of sincerity, prevalent in the early eighteenth-century panegyric, incorporated formally a rhetoric of sincerity (the need to protest against intimations of flattery was already felt) and pragmatically an equation, dictated by the genre itself, of sincerity with "correct" political emotion (see Pogosian, *Vostorg*). The assumptions undergirding sincerity in this former model were, however, inadequate for Derzhavin's generation. Even if Derzhavin, in "Felitsa," told Catherine a truth which was not bitter, but sweet (Proskurina, *Creating*, 207), he had to do it in a way that implied an independently speaking and thinking subject, what Harsha Ram calls "the workings of an ethically self-reflexive mind" (*Imperial Sublime*, 8).

4 Klein, "Istina i iskrennost'," 215–18.

5 Cf. Shcheglov, who finds the key to the poem's rhetoric in the fact that the "liturgical" and ecstatic (in the poet's relation to Catherine/Felitsa) is integrated with "elements of 'human,' disarmingly sincere and lightly humorous speech [element[y] 'chelovecheskogo' podkupaiushche iskrennego i slegka iumoristicheskogo obrashcheniia]" ("Igrovaia ritorika," 169).
6 Shcheglov, "Igrovaia ritorika," 196–7; Pogosian, "Uroki imperatritsy."
7 On the readership, see, for instance, Derzhavin, *Sochineniia* (2002), 558, citing Osip Kozodavlev. On the *Companion*, see Klein, "Istina i iskrennost'," 215–17. Cf., however, Vera Proskurina, whose emphasis, in reading the same texts, is on the equivalency drawn by these authors between "truth" and praise of Catherine (*Mify imperii*, 224–6). What becomes clear through Proskurina's deep dive into the contemporary cultural milieu in *Mify imperii* is the vast gravitational web of the Empress within the *Companion* and the way that not only was Derzhavin's praise inevitably suspect, but also the acclaim of his supporters, who, in recognizing the "truth" of his flattering portrayal *in Catherine's chosen playful mode*, were potentially ingratiating themselves with the Empress. This does not, however, erase the cultural dynamics of the moment or the uniqueness of Derzhavin's achievement in "Felitsa" in adapting that playful mode to generate a sincere *voice* within the odic frame. It is not the *that* of Derzhavin's poem which implicitly validates these authors' praise, however clumsy, but the *how*, and that how is synthetic, complex, practically inimitable. Presumably, Derzhavin's text became such a focus of attention – negative and positive – at least in part because the way it sounded implied sincerity (or masked flattery) successfully enough to be perceived as a challenge to the uneasy equilibrium between servility and service in the bureaucracy.
8 Pogosian, "Uroki imperatritsy." On the courtiers' reactions, see 247–8; cf. Klein, "Istina i iskrennost'," 196. Obviously, Catherine's initial reaction as reported by Dashkova ("kak dura plachu" [I'm weeping like a fool; cited in Derzhavin, *Sochineniia* [2002], 558) was extremely positive. The gift may have been playfully ambiguous from the beginning, however. In 1777, Vasily Ruban received from the Empress a gold snuffbox with 500 *chervonnykh* (10-rouble pieces) as a gift for his openly flattering ode to then favourite S.G. Zorich (Zapadov, "Problema literaturnogo servilizma," 68, 70). Derzhavin's snuffbox, however, was encrusted with diamonds – and given in a witty and playful manner underscoring Catherine's enjoyment of the unique game of masks he had initiated.
9 Derzhavin, *Sochineniia* (1864–83), 629–31. On this letter as it touches upon issues of sincerity, see Klein, "Istina i iskrennost'," 187–92.
10 Derzhavin makes "Felitsa" (1782), along with "Bog" (God, 1780–4), central to his legacy in "Pamiatnik" ("Monument," 1796), accentuating

particularly these odes' sincerity: "V serdechnoi prostote besedovat' o Boge / I istinu Tsariam s ulybkoi govorit'" (In simplicity of heart to chat about God / And to speak truth to Tsars with a smile). Compare also his "Lebed'" ("Swan," 1804). Derzhavin's poetry is cited from *Sochineniia* (1864–83) unless otherwise indicated.

11 Continuities between modernism and the eighteenth century were evident to early twentieth-century poets and critics. For a recent scholarly consideration, see Smoliarova, *Three Metaphors*, 232–52. My claim looks at previously unnoted parallels as well as an underlying analogy in the dynamics of literary evolution, which drives similarities in poetics.

12 On the second pole in the conceptualization of sincerity, see the Introduction, pp. 7–8.

13 Mandel'shtam, *PSSP*, 2:57.

14 Mandel'shtam, *PSSP*, 2:79.

15 Gumilev, *SS4*, 4:173. On the ironies deployed in Acmeism, see the Introduction, note 12.

16 Tynianov, *Arkhaisty i novatory*, 54ff.

17 Lomonosov, *Izbrannye proizvedeniia*, 61. Compare Golburt: "Odic historical time includes only the high points" (*First Epoch*, 45).

18 *Russkaia literatura. Vek XVIII*, 173, 174, 177.

19 Pumpianskii, "Ocherki," 120.

20 Klein, "Istina i iskrennost'," 215–17.

21 "Pis'mo k tvortsu ody, sochinennoi v pokhvalu Felitsy, Tsarevne Kirgizkaisatskoi," in Kostrov, *Sochineniia*, 109.

22 Kostrov, in this passage, to a large extent reflects the rhetoric of naturalness and, implicitly, sincerity, including criticism of *gromkost'* (loudness), which had been deployed by classicist theoretician and writer Alexander Sumarokov in his arguments with Lomonosov. Compare Gukovskii, *Russkaia poeziia XVIII veka*, 21, 23–4, 202n24. However, the terms engaged by Sumarokov are used by Kostrov to recognize in "Felitsa" the successful *emergence* of a new taste, its concrete exemplar. This new taste is, in the poem's finale, appreciated by "sincere hearts" (Kostrov, *Sochineniia*, 111), a phrase perhaps not solely limited to its traditional loyalist connotations.

23 Derzhavin, *Zapiski*, 379.

24 See also Shcheglov's cogent analysis of the rhetorical strategies underlying Derzhavin's achievement in "Felitsa" ("Igrovaia ritorika," 174–84).

25 Derzhavin relies on the eastern colour of Catherine's moralistic fairy tale, "Tale of Tsarevich Khlor" ("Skazka o Tsareviche Khlore," 1781), the borderlands location of his own land holdings, and his descent from a fifteenth-century Tatar nobleman, Bagrim. For historical/ideological contextualization of the eastern motifs of the "Felitsa" cycle, see Ram,

Imperial Sublime, 100–15. Derzhavin's "familiarity" with the Empress, while bold in the odic context, echoed Catherine's public posture in this period. Cf. Proskurina, *Mify imperii*, 200–1.

26 See, for instance, Crone, *Daring*, 129ff. This answered the Horatian call for *dulce et utile* (Harris, "Creative Imagination," 165).

27 See Gukovskii, *Russkaia literatura*, 93–5; Klein, "Istina i iskrennost'," 215, citing Bogdanovich.

28 For a particularly perceptive analysis of the dynamics of this stylistic innovation, see Uspenskii, "Iazyk Derzhavina," 781–806. On the conformity of Derzhavin's stylistic innovation to the fashion for the amusing (*zabavnyi*) promoted by Catherine, see Proskurina, *Mify imperii*, esp. 222, 226–8; cf. also her *Imperiia pera*, 204–6.

29 Golburt, in her excellent recent reading of "Felitsa," evinces a similar sense of Derzhavin's tone (without reference to sincerity): "Derzhavin relishes perspectival and tonal shifts, moving with expert, often tongue-in-cheek agility between the public and private spaces of poetic utterance" (*First Epoch*, 27).

30 Tynianov, *Arkhaisty i novatory*, 77.

31 The word *pyshno* (luxuriously) is negatively intoned for Derzhavin, as, it seems, for any man of his century and bent. Compare Lomonosov's 1759 translation of Jean-Baptiste Rousseau's "Ode à la Fortune" or Derzhavin's own "Grandee" ("Vel'mozha," 1794) and "Peacock" ("Pavlin," 1795).

32 The *murza* is, according to the full original title, on business in Petersburg.

33 For a differing take on these passages, see Shcheglov, "Igrovaia ritorika," 176–7.

34 Crone, *Daring*, 132. Cf. also Harris, "Creative Imagination," 167.

35 I thank Kirill Ospovat for pointing out that the eastern mask Derzhavin has adopted here is precisely that of the flatterer. Cf. Ram on the tension between sycophancy/despotism and enlightenment already implicit in Derzhavin's choice of masks (*Imperial Sublime*, 7); Golburt's fine reading of this stanza's opening (*First Epoch*, 59).

36 *Daring*, 6–7, 116.

37 *Sochineniia* (1864–83), 1:270–1.

38 Lappo-Danilevskii, "K istorii."

39 "Kak poddannykh rvala okovy / V nikh dushi poseliala novy" (How she tore the fetters of her subjects / Imbued them with new souls); "sego osmogo diva […] podvigi" (the feats […] of this eighth wonder [of the world]). Cited in Lappo-Danilevskii, "K istorii." 218, 217.

40 Khodasevich, *Derzhavin*, 159.

41 Klein, "Istina i iskrennost'," 204; compare Harris, "Creative Imagination," 169.

42 Raphael was Derzhavin's *alter ego* already in a 1783 letter to Kozodavlev
(*Sochineniia* [1864–83], 5:369). That his instructions are also orders to self
underscores his inner ambivalence.

43 Derzhavin, in Kononko, "Primechaniia," 81–2.

44 Derzhavin, in Kononko, "Primechaniia," 82; *Sochineniia* (1864–83), 1:287.

45 Golburt offers an appreciative reading of "Felitsa's Portrait" as a classi-
cist mirror for Catherine underscoring precisely the impossibility of en-
compassing her countless merits within a surveyable frame (*First Epoch*,
59–71).

46 Derzhavin, in Kononko, "Primechaniia," 84; *Sochineniia* (1864–83), 9:238.

47 This is how the note originally appeared in 'Rukopis' 90-kh' (Manuscript
of the 1790s; Arkhiv Derzhavina, IRLI, f. 96, op. V, no. 4, l. 78 ob.). This
is the earliest extant copy of the poem and that which was, as per Grot's
assertion, used to prepare Derzhavin's 1795 calligraphic volume for
Catherine ("Predislovie," in *Sochineniia* [1864–83], 1:xii–xiii). The phrase
is crossed out, with "pisannaia na maslenitse" (written on Maslenitsa)
written in above. On the poem's genre, see Pumpianskii, "Lomonosov,"
11–13; Proskurina, "Mezhdu," 130 and *Imperia pera*, 208–9; and Klein, *Pri
Ekaterine*, 181–2. This "candour" and "freedom" is not realized on a polit-
ical plane. In relation to Derzhavin, one is speaking not of radicalism or
even liberalism, but rather a provocative independence of voice that tests
the boundaries of the permissible but without departing from a politi-
cally conservative worldview.

48 Lomonosov wrote fourteen of twenty odes in this strophe (one with re-
versal of masculine/feminine rhymes). His most common other strophe
was its inversion, tercet/tercet/quatrain: AAbCCbDeDe.

49 *Arkhaisty i novatory*, 54–8.

50 Compare the strophe of Derzhavin's "My Graven Image" ("Moi istukan,"
1794), which foregrounds a closing couplet: AbAbCdCdEE. In ten stanzas
of twenty-four, this couplet encapsulates the preceding lines' sense in an
aphorism.

51 "On Fortune" is cited from *Sochineniia* (1864–83) with some emendations
on the basis of "Rukopis' 90-kh," ll. 78 ob.-84, where stylistics, declama-
tion or sense are implicated.

52 On his copy of *Sochineniia Derzhavina. Chast' I* (1798), Derzhavin revised
this stanza in a way that smooths its syntax and virtually eliminates any
irony in relation specifically to Catherine – precisely by changing three of
these key words. (The fourth, "krasivo" was in the more difficult to revise
rhyme position.) This post-1798 text, noted by Zapadov ("Neizvestnyi
Derzhavin," 46–8) and printed in the errata of the 1798 edition (p. 400),
but not reproduced in the authorial 1808 edition, displays a natural sof-
tening of the poet's evaluation of Catherine in hindsight. During Paul's

notoriously arbitrary and capricious rule, the irony of this strophe, which contrasted Catherine's spoken ideals to the practices which graced her reign, likely sounded too caustic.

53 Lomonosov, *Izbrannye proizvedeniia*, 156; Radishchev, *PSS3*, 1:2.

54 Derzavin uses the orthography here to convey his choice of the Russian colloquial, rather than the expected Slavonic/poetic pronunciation ("inago") (Ionin, in Derzhavin, *Sochineniia* [2002], 549). "Rukopis' 90-kh" showcases the poet's dynamic use of orthography as a component of style. Connecting hatcheks over "io" alternate with "e," demarking colloquial and Slavonic high-style pronunciations (some of the latter in contrastively low-style contexts).

55 *Sochineniia* (1864–83), 5:865–6.

56 Crone, "Deržavin's," 19, 26; Harris, "Creative Imagination," 233–5.

57 Crone, "Deržavin's" and *Daring*; Proskurina, "Oda"; *Creating*; *Imperiia pera*. It is difficult to imagine, however, that Derzhavin could have *presented* this poem to Catherine in 1789 in the spirit of persiflage, as Proskurina has implied ("Oda," 139, and *Creating*, 254, where the poem is described as a "literary gambit"; cf. *Imperiia pera*, 210, 236–7). Derzhavin could barely get a letter into her hands at the time, and the letter he did send with Tersky was full of detailed documentation of the corrupt progress of his case. He could hardly have risked the Empress's distraction or, more to the point, the tonal dissonance between the letter and the poem with its risqué and pointed, personally directed insinuations, unlike anything included in "Felitsa" (cf., for instance, strophe 19 on the backdrop of the story with hot air balloon conveyed in Pogosian, "Uroki," 244–6, 260–2, 264; Proskurina, *Imperiia pera*, 242–3). Moreover, the markings in "Rukopis' 90-kh" seem to underscore concerns Derzhavin and/or his co-editors had even years later about provocative passages. Among those marked with a large "X": "V glaza patriotizma pliuesh'" (You spit in the eyes of patriotism) and "Parizhu pukli razbivaesh'" (You bust Paris's ringlets; now sounding quite different in connection with the recent guillotining, in 1793, of Louis XVI) as well as the beginning and end of strophe ten, analysed above. Strophe 7 (beginning "In these days, when everything everywhere is in a [drunken] revel") was given a redundant and unconvincing footnote relating it specifically to Maslenitsa, it appears, in Derzhavin's own hand (l. 80). The decision to include "On Fortune" in the volume given to the Empress in 1795 reflects the boldness in defining his legacy of a far more secure Derzhavin.

   Also, if the writing of the poem was a bold gambit which led to his exculpation, why would Derzhavin have demurred from telling the story in in his expansive, often self-aggrandizing "Notes" and "Explanations"?

58 *Sochineniia* (1864–83), 8:577.

59 Although in "Rukopis' 90-kh" the year has been crossed out in the editing process, Derzhavin both retained the exact date in the calligraphic volume for Catherine (with "Pisannaia na Maslenitse" [Written on Maslenitsa] inscribed on the ribbon and "1789" on the soap bubble in Aleksei Olenin's opening emblem; *Sochineniia. Chast' I* [1795], Otdel rukopisei RNB, Arkhiv Petra Petrovicha Dubrovskogo, F.XVI.16, l. 109 ob.) and printed the poem in the first edition with the correct date ("Pisano na Maslenitse 1789 goda" [Written on Maslenitsa 1789]; *Sochineniia* [1798], 179). The authorial copy of this edition, to which Zapadov refers in "Neizvestnyi Derzhavin," likewise shows "1789" (RGALI, f. 180, op. 1, ed. khr. 14, l. 96). Thus, Zapadov's citing of "1790" in Derzhavin, *Stikhotvoreniia*, 384, implying Derzhavin's falsification of the date, is in error. The phrase appears to have misled both Ionin (Derzhavin, *Sochineniia* [2002], 575) and, through him, Proskurina (*Imperia pera*, 201, 208).

60 Proskurina thoroughly, with expert facility, confirms the emergence of the poem in winter of 1789 through reference to the current international situation (most recently, in *Imperiia pera*, 212–35). However, despite the success of "patriotic" parties on the world stage around 1789 (218, 225–7), the word "patriotism" was used broadly at the time in its primary sense: a lover and supporter of one's fatherland (cf. the contemporary usages of *patriotizm* and *patriot* in the Russian National Corpus [www.ruscorpora.ru]; Derzhavin's later commentary to this strophe: "contempt of love for the fatherland" ["Primechaniia," 84]). Note also that the phrase about patriotism occurs in a strophe relating to Russia and not international circumstances.

61 See Kulakova, "O spornykh voprosakh," 26ff.

62 For the stylistics of "vcheras'," compare Derzhavin's letter to his wife, *Sochineniia* (1864–83), 5: 812.

63 Derzhavin could, for instance, recall at least one incident of quite notable luck at cards, when he was able to turn 50 roubles into 40,000 over the course of several days in 1776 (Khodasevich, *Derzhavin*, 91–2). However, here, description is generic, rather than specific. Nothing is included that would differentiate the lyric subject from any other fortunate player.

64 It is worth noting the felicitous play with the names of the odes' addressees. "Schast'e," or Fortuna, the Roman deity of *fickle* fortune, is the treacherous double of "Felitsa," or Felicitas, deity of blessed/happy fortune.

65 *Sochineniia* (2002), 506. On Potemkin in "On Fortune," see also Proskurina, *Imperiia pera*, 208, 227–32.

66 See Linda Hutcheon's analysis of the "self-protective" ironic mode, which often expresses itself in self-deprecating irony (*Irony's Edge*, 50).

67 This development is clearly parallel to the processes of assertion of the poet's independent authority and persona described in Crone, *Daring*. On

the importance of biographical deed within poets' mythologies of self in early nineteenth-century Russian poetry, see, for instance, Lotman, *Pushkin*; Bethea, *Realizing Metaphors*; and Powelstock, *Becoming*.

2 Romantic Sincerities I

1 See Todd, *Familiar Letter*, 64–5, 102–3.

2 Batiushkov, *Opyty*, 22. The idea to live as one writes is rehearsed and then twisted through a self-deprecating witticism at the end of his programmatic "To [My] Friends" ("K druz'iam," 1817). Cf. Khitrova, *Lyric Complicity*, 51.

3 Zhukovskii, *PSSP*, 13:91, 63. Note the similar relationship between life and poetry implied in the final lines of part 2, chapter 10 of Madame de Staël's *Germany* (*De l'Allemagne*), published just prior in 1813. One might wonder if, despite direct German influence on Zhukovsky, this concept took root in Russia thanks to de Staël.

4 Fleishman, "Iz istorii elegii," 35.

5 Lotman, *Karamzin*, 16. Khitrova stresses the opposite aspect of reader behaviour in the Golden Age, the tendency of readers to adapt and repurpose verse for their own pragmatic needs (*Lyric Complicity*).

6 Boileau, *Oeuvres complètes*, 164. Cf. Abrams, *Mirror*, 71–2; Boileau's eighteenth-century Russian adept Sumarokov: "Our thoughts accompanied only by feeling are represented in better words than by art, though art also is much needed for nature" ("O stikhotvorstve kamchadalov," 63).

7 This represents a subtle shift from the 1794 essay "What Does an Author Need?" ("Chto nuzhno avtoru?") by these poets' mentor and Russia's leading Sentimentalist author, Karamzin: the writer must have a "good, tender heart" because "The creator is always depicted in his creation, and often against his own will" (*Sochineniia*, 2:60). Karamzin, at least here, suggests that unfeeling authors give up the enterprise, not transform themselves.

8 See Lotman, "Teatr i teatral'nost'," 618.

9 One might add to this list – sincerity.

10 Todd, *Familiar Letter*, 102–3.

11 Todd, *Familiar Letter*, 65. "'Poets must pour their soul into manifold vessels,'" wrote Prince Viazemsky (cited in Khitrova, *Lyric Complicity*, 108).

12 Note, however, Pushkin's integration of elements born out of different genre traditions into a single, constantly developing poetic system, in contrast to the discontinuous genre poetics of his older contemporaries (Boris Gasparov, *Poeticheskii iazyk*, 117).

13 On the history of this term in criticism, see Kulagin, "Pushkinskii proteizm."

14 Cf. the representation of Anna Kern in lyric and correspondence (Lotman, *Pushkin*, 107–9), Peter's legacy in the odic and narrative portions of *The Bronze Horseman* (*Mednyi vsadnik*, 1833), etc.

15 See, for instance, Ginzburg, *O lirike*, 182–4. For two excellent encapsulations of the ways in which Pushkin navigated between Romanticism and Classicism, see Boris Gasparov, "Pushkin and Romanticism," 553, 550; Kahn, *Pushkin's Lyric Intelligence*, 15–19, 85–7. Of course, the situation regarding the lyric subject in Romanticism was complex, governed by esteem of inspiration/insight and subjectivity on the one hand and, on the other, what Luba Golburt calls "a paramount principle of Romantic self-fashioning: [...] the Romantic irony that would underscore the textuality and constructedness of both the poem's lyric subject and its addressee" (*First Epoch*, 143).

   On Pushkin's subtle navigation of the shifting norms of voice, audience, and genre in the 1810s, with reference to flattery and sincerity, see *First Epoch*, 134–9.

16 See, for instance, Lotman, *Pushkin*, 67–71, 180–3; Proskurin, *Podvizhnyi palimpsest*, 59–60.

17 On the difficulty (and, in the case of Bethea, necessity) of grappling with the subject behind Pushkin's literary subjectivities, see Monika Greenleaf, "The Imaginary Subject: From Schlegel to Pushkin," in her *Pushkin and Romantic Fashion*, 38–55; David M. Bethea, "The Problem of Poetic Biography," in his *Realizing Metaphors*, 34–44.

18 Cf. David Powelstock's (non-naïve) analysis of Pushkin's path to and success in generating the "personal lyric" in "Burying."

19 Boris Gasparov, "Pushkin and Romanticism," 555.

20 *Severnye tsvety na 1832 g.*, 274. Note how this formulation curiously fails to conflict with the, for Pushkin, maximally Romantic image of inspiration developed in "Poet" (1826). Cf. also Pushkin's near-translation of André Chénier, "Near the parts where golden Venice reigns" ("Bliz mest, gde tsarstvuet Venetsiia zlataia," 1827).

21 Pushkin, *PSS16*, 13:243, letter to Viazemsky, November 1825. Note that Pushkin before this point has been talking specifically about Byron's *Don Juan*. I thank Alyssa Dinega Gillespie for bringing this passage to my attention.

22 Cf. Ginzburg, "Pushkin i liricheskii geroi," 146. Gillespie has conjectured that Pushkin allows his persona to emerge more fully precisely in the context and under the mask of his narrative and dramatic works ("A Dangerous Feminine Force: Pushkin's Abstract Muse in the Major Works of the 1830s" [ASEEES, 2016]). Cf. Mikhail Gasparov on Catullus: "In some way, these [mythological] poems allow one a deeper glimpse into Catullus' soul than the self-reflexive ones" ("Katull," 392).

23 *PSS16*, 12:93.

24 The fact that Pushkin was aiming here particularly at the Sentimental and
     Romantic *elegy* is reinforced in the draft versions of this passage (*PSS16*,
     12:377). Pushkin's comment gives the lie to Manning's generalization
     that poets and critics have been unaware of sincerity's engagement in the
     battles of literary schools (*Rhétorique*, 78–9). Pushkin is clearly aware (and
     long before Manning's modernists and late-twentieth-century critics) of
     the way the term is contested.

25 Cf. Boris Gasparov on the ethos of Arzamas: "Laughter was for the
     [brethren of] Arzamas not only a weapon of criticism, directed against
     their opponents, but also a means of affirmation of positive values" (*Poet-
     icheskii iazyk*, 143, see also 146).

26 Some support for these associations is provided by Pushkin's own early
     recasting of Gresset's poem, ("Town [To ***]" [Gorodok (K ***), 1815]),
     within which he devotes to Voltaire an embedded sonnet emphasizing the
     latter's range (greatness in diverse genres) and his "naughty," mocking
     playfulness (fused with wisdom): "Syn Moma i Minervy [...] sedoi *shalun*"
     ("Son of Momos and Minerva [...] Grey-haired *imp*"). It goes without say-
     ing that Pushkin's engagement with and attitude towards Voltaire is more
     complex than conveyed in these passages. On "The Cloister," see, for
     instance, Dobritsyn, *Vechnyi zhanr*, 498–503; Bogdanovich, "Druzheskoe."
     The vision of sincerity Pushkin presents here can, in concept, even encom-
     pass *shalost'* / *shalosti* (playful pranks), a poetic genre and, more broadly,
     sphere of behaviour analysed in Peschio, *Poetics of Impudence*.

27 See M.L. Gasparov, "Katull."

28 Pushkin's taste echoes a broader suspicion of "grandeur" and "sublimity"
     in the Golden Age culture from which he emerged. Khitrova writes of the
     "thematic megalophobia of Golden Age poetry," its rejection of "ideals too
     lofty, heroes too dignified, or palaces too opulent" (*Lyric Complicity*, 48).

29 This claim to sincerity must be seen as conditional. In regard to the pas-
     sages in question, unsurprisingly, given their publication history, we
     do not have contemporary reader reactions expressly underscoring a
     perceived sincerity – one possible "gold standard" in terms of reception.
     At the same time, even if the collective body of literature on Pushkin and
     his milieu can help to approximate in an informed way the "horizon of
     expectations" (Jauss, "Literary History") of the poet's contemporaries,
     Pushkin's poetics complicate the privileging, in regard to the reception
     of his work, of any given set of readers, contemporary or future (Boris
     Gasparov, "Pushkin and Romanticism," 551–2).

30 On the development of the elegy, see, e.g., Fleishman, "Iz istorii"; L.G.
     Frizman, *Zhizn'*; Vatsuro, *Lirika pushkinskoi pory*; Proskurin, *Podvizhnyi
     palimpsest*.

31 Pushkin, *PSS16*, 3:257.

32 P.V. Annenkov, *Materialy*, 188. Annenkov wrote that Pushkin made the change "right away," Gofman that Pushkin wrote out a full clean copy of the poem before making changes ("Neizdannye rukopisi," 370). Both are, it seems, correct. The new words in lines 1–2 are interpolated in the same brown ink used to copy out the full initial version of the poem and with which the date, 27 Nov. 1830, is recorded. However, the poet appears to have hesitated before deciding affirmatively on this change – as the original words "чужбины" and "родной" are crossed out in a different, blacker ink, the same ink with which most of the changes to the rest of the poem, including the changes to the final lines, were made. Given that we can likely conclude that the changes in black were made at a different sitting from those in brown ink, we cannot for certain ascertain the moment in which the poem achieved its relatively final form, which was still, as has been noted, not a clean copy. There were two mistakes ("томленья страшное" and "с нимъ и"), and line 19 remained incomplete, with words stricken but not replaced (IRLI, f. 244, op. 1, no. 146, ll. 1 and 1ob).

33 Shchegolev, "Amaliia Riznich," 272–4, esp. 274*n*1; Makogonenko, *Tvorchestvo*, 51, 82–3. Cf. also B.V. Tomashevskii's commentary in Pushkin, *PSS10*, 3:512.

34 Gofman, "Neizdannye rukopisi," 372; Bakhtin, *Iskusstvo i otvetstvennost'*, 74–5; Broitman, *Poetika*, 35–6. Wachtel concurs with this view (*Commentary*, 215).

35 In Shchegolev's article on the subject, such logic is represented in the coarsest form ("Amaliia," 272). The history of Derzhavin's "Swallow" ("Lastochka," 1792, 1794), for instance, demonstrates quite powerfully that sincerity does not have to be undermined by the repurposing of poetic material. See note 141 below. The same can be said of the collective epistolary revision of early nineteenth-century poetic texts (with suggestions then adopted or rejected) which Khitrova describes in *Lyric Complicity*.

36 Bakhtin, *Iskusstvo*, 76.

37 Cf. also Ovid, *Tristia*, Book 1, 3. On Batiushkov's influence on Pushkin more generally, see esp. Eliash, "K voprosu"; Gershenzon, "Pushkin i Batiushkov"; Proskurin, *Podvizhnyi palimpsest*. Eliash finds in the description of "Lila's" death in "To a Friend" ("K drugu," 1815) a source for "For the shores" (34–5).

38 Batiushkov, *Opyty*, 206.

39 *PSS16*, 12:259. On the role of idyllic topoi in the development of the Russian elegy, see Vatsuro, *Lirika*, 126–37.

40 A similar situational (and also emotional) inversion, playing on Batiushkov's topoi and phraseology, is executed by Pushkin in "Pod nebom

golubym strany svoei rodnoi," as described by Proskurin (*Podvizhnyi palimpsest*, 199–203).

41 Cf. Vinogradov, *Stil' Pushkina*, 117; Tynianov on the function of Blok's use of traditional imagery in *Arkhaisty i novatory*, 517; Proskurin, *Podvizhnyi palimpsest*, 200, 236–7.

42 This situational "narrowing" can be seen as a productive – at least in terms of the sincere voice – departure from the classic Golden Age elegy, which, as Khitrova argues, "was two things at once: an emotional address in which 'I' and 'you' were spaces for a user to fill in, like blanks in letter-writing manuals; and a line from a pre-existing dramatic dialogue, in which the speaker represents the specific, recognizable type of amatory behavior [...] The blanks for 'I' and 'you' were both blanks and masks" (*Lyric Complicity*, 168). Of course, susceptibility to use as "blanks and masks" did not preclude a sincere *emploi* for the speaker (or for the redeployer, as in the reader E.B.'s album appropriation of Pushkin's "I have outlived my desires" [Ia perezhil svoi zhelaniia]). Nor did it preclude an insincere one, as in Evgeny Baratynsky's "Confession" ("Priznanie"), laced, as Khitrova shows, with libertine tropes (81–3, 184–91).

43 Cf. Grekhnev, *Mir*, 330–1; Broitman, *Poetika*, 38, 41; Antiokh Kantemir in Batiushkov's "An Evening with Kantemir" ("Vecher u Kantermira," 1816): "Ia *nepritvorno* liubliu goluboe nebo i vechno zelenye olivy stran poludenykh" (I *without affectation* love the blue sky and perennially green olive trees of southern lands; *Opyty*, 42, emphasis mine).

44 Grekhnev, *Mir*, 332–3; Broitman, *Poetika*, 38.

45 Broitman, *Poetika*, 43–4.

46 Cf. Batiushkov's "A Last Spring" ("Posledniaia vesna," 1815?) in which the young hero dies on the backdrop of *spring/summer*, inverting Charles Hubert Millevoye's paradigmatic "The Falling of the Leaves" ("La Chute des feuilles"). On Millevoye, see Savchenko, "Elegiia Lenskogo," 75–6; Vatsuro, *Lirika*, 203–12; Proskurin, *Podvizhnyi palimpsest*, 70ff.

47 Batiushkov, *Opyty*, 231.

48 Batiushkov, *Opyty*, 232.

49 Batiushkov, *Opyty*, 326, 327.

50 Batiushkov, *Opyty*, 208.

51 Batiushkov, *Opyty*, 342. Pushkin's knowledge of this latter text, published only in 1834, is unlikely, though not excluded (Igor Pilshchikov, private correspondence). See Pilshchikov on the multifarious French translations and imitations of Janus Secundus's "Kiss II" ("Basium II," by 1536) which inspired Batiushkov's imitation in "Elysium" ("Simvolika," 99–107, cf. also 91–3). If Pushkin was aware of these texts, most prominently by Pierre de Ronsard, Claude Joseph Dorat, and Pierre François Tissot, it may not be irrelevant that they form a tradition of poetic "kisses" (*Basia*, *Baisers*).

52 Schiller, *Werke*, 1:123.

53 On the Elysian idyllic topos of the elegy, see Vatsuro, *Lirika*, 131–7; Pil'shchikov, "Simvolika."

54 Bakhtin sees the "real [real'naia] intonation of the heroine" refracted through the axiological system of the hero and aesthetic prism of the author (74–5); Grekhnev, a "deep psychological collision" between hero's (proto-Realist) and heroine's (Romantic) world views (*Mir*, 332–3); Broitman, the "incomplete unity and incomplete separation" [nesliianost' i nerazdel'nost'] of their world views (*Poetika*, 42). All imply a heroine whose psychology is presented with more depth than is actually suggested by her speech.

55 Broitman, *Poetika*, 43–4.

56 Cf. Batiushkov, *Opyty*, 214; Karamzin's 1796 elegy "To One Unfaithful" ("K nevernoi").

57 "Bakhchisaraiskii fontan" (1821–3), *PSS16*, 4:159. Cf. also Baratynsky's usage within the stylistically marked elegiac context of his "Kiss" ("Potselui," 1822).

58 Note that while Pushkin, in his revisions to the final stanza, removes the inversion at the beginning of line 24, establishing a natural, conversational tone, in the first stanza, where he is operating with elegiac cliché, he introduces in his revisions an additional trope (Я умолял [I begged] → Мой стон молил [My moan implored]), *increasing* the literariness of this passage.

59 Cf. Batiushkov's sensual Elysium, analysed in Pil'shchikov, "Simvolika," 86–99. By 1815, Batiushkov himself had become disillusioned with the "'crude, earthly pleasures'" with which poets had filled their depictions of Elysium (Pil'shchikov, "Simvolika, 112–13).

60 On the editorial conjecture, see *PSS16*, 3:1223.

61 Taranovskii, *Russkie dvuslozhnye razmery*, 39–40, 46.

62 The idiom "Ochered' za *kem, chem*" (one's turn has come; "Chem chashche prazdnuet litsei" [The more often [our] lyceum celebrates, 1831]) is differentiated under a separate heading in *Slovar' iazyka Pushkina*, 2:14.

63 Cf. the finale of Andrei Turgenev's well-known "Elegy" ("Elegiia," 1802), which expresses an in ways analogous, but more discursive consolation through belief in the afterlife, "Gde tsarstvo vechnoe odnoi liubvi sviatoi" (Where [lies] the eternal kingdom of nothing but sacred love) (*Russkaia elegiia xviii-nachala xx veka*, 129). One can also see Pushkin here *overcoming* the "ubiquitous preciousness of posthumous, elegiac reunions in Russian poetry in the early 1810s" (Irina Semenko, paraphrased in Peschio, *Poetics of Impudence*, 77) and the stylized images of dear shades (*teni*) in his own poetry (as in the contemporaneous "Incantation" ["Zaklinanie," 1830]).

64 Feinberg, *Chitaia*, 583–5; Proskurin, *Podvizhnyi palimpsest*, 275–88.

65 On the semantics of this word, see esp. Mur'ianov, "Dva etiuda," 206–14.

66 Derzhavin had previously introduced the concept of an "immortal soul" to his Horatian "Swan" ("Lebed'," 1804), another major source for Pushkin's poem. However, the "soul" in Pushkin's "dear lyre" not only conveys a potential Christian note, but implies, in a more forceful way than Derzhavin's "chast' menia bol'shaia" (a large part of me), from his "Monument" ("Pamiatnik," 1795), a belief that the poet's feelings, convictions, his intellect – his personal essence – lives on in his poetry.

67 Pumpianskii, "Ob ode," 136.

68 *PSS16*, 3:424.

69 Gershenzon, *Mudrost'*, 51; Solov'ev, "Znachenie"; Pumpianskii, "Ob ode," 149; Solov'ev, "Znachenie," 702–8 and Gershenzon, *Mudrost'*, 53–61; S.A. Vengerov, cited in Gershenzon, *Mudrost'*, 64; Evlakhov, cited in Gershenzon, *Mudrost'* , 66 (cf. Pumpianskii, "Ob ode," 149); Veresaev, *V dvukh planakh*, 117, 121. All but Pumpiansky are dismissively catalogued in Alekseev, *Stikhotvorenie*, 45–52. On this stanza, see also Feinberg, *Chitaia*, 578–83, 586–9.

 In light, particularly, of Pushkin's well-known ironic self-portrait as "Dante" in laurels, drawn in 1835 or 1836 (see Alekseev, *Stikhotvorenie*, 132–6), it seems not much of a stretch to imagine that a "vertiginous" and unstable irony (or simply its potentiality) contends in these middle stanzas with seriousness, in fact enabling the high seriousness of Pushkin's monument poem.

70 Alekseev, *Stikhotvorenie*, 49.

71 Bondi, *O Pushkine*, 467.

72 Bondi, *O Pushkine*, 468–75.

73 Bondi, *O Pushkine*, 475.

74 On the poem's bolder archaisms, see Viacheslav [Vs.] Ivanov, "K issledovaniiu."

75 Bethea, *Realizing Metaphors*, 74–5, 78–81, 163–4, 219n192.

76 Horace, *Odes and Epodes*, 216, literal translation mine.

77 Lomonosov, *Izbrannye*, 255; Derzhavin, *Sochineniia*, 224. "Vozgordit'sia" carries the meaning "gordym, nadmennym, spesivym sdelat'sia" (to become proud, haughty, arrogant), *Slovar' Akademii Rossiiskoi*, 2, col. 241–2.

78 Cf. Pumpianskii, "Ob ode," 150.

79 Bethea, *Realizing Metaphors*, 233.

80 Alekseev, *Stikhotvorenie*, 122.

81 This effect of rhythmic dissociation becomes salient on the backdrop of the pre-rhyme-syllable euphonies that accentuate the masculine rhymes in each of the preceding stanzas: *tropa – stolpa*: t-a-liquid (r/l); *ubezhit – piit*: labial stop (b/p)-i; *drug stepei kalmyk – sushchii v nei iazyk*: vowel series u-i-ʲei; *probuzhdal – prizyval*: identical prosody and alliteration. Cf. Briusov, "Levizna Pushkina v rifmakh," *SS7*, 5: 171, 178, 179, 183.

82 Cf. Bethea, *Realizing Metaphors*, 233.

83 Zholkovskii, "Prevoskhoditel'nyi pokoi." Perhaps the secret (beyond raw poetic talent) to the success of Derzhavin and Pushkin's monument poems, in contrast to others, is to be located in Horace's "sume superbiam," which expresses in kernel "aloof calm." When Derzhavin remade Horace, and Pushkin, Derzhavin, they were translating into their own idiom sentiments that fit their poetic paradigms. (Cf. the final strophe of Derzhavin's "On Fortune.")

84 See Zholkovskii, "Prevoskhoditel'nyi," esp. 240–1, 246; "Invarianty," 7–8.

85 Cf. Lotman, Pushkin, 67–71, 180–3; Proskurin, *Podvizhnyi palimpsest*, 59–60; Bethea, *Realizing Metaphors*, 137–8.

86 Ginzburg, "Pushkin i Benediktov."

87 Cf. Pushkin's prominent publication of those works where he continued to implicitly call for a pardoning of the Decembrists (Bondi, "Pamiatnik," 470–4) with the unpublished "personal lyrics" (Powelstock, "Burying," 88–91). Cf. also Bethea, *Realizing Metaphors*, 221–2.

88 Alekseev writes of the fourth stanza: "Thus *he himself understood* his work, and thus he defined its meaning; and this final *self-evaluation* casts a light on the entire path he took. 'Monument' *with complete clarity unveils* for us which conscious goals Pushkin set himself in his creative work" (*Stikhotvorenie*, 49, emphasis mine). Bondi explains thus the necessity of his apology for the "traditional" understanding of stanza 4: "[…] all the more necessary, given that […] *very important, culminating thoughts* about his works are expressed […]" (Bondi, "Pamiatnik," 443, emphasis mine). Cf. Kathleen Manukyan: *"an honest enumeration* of what the poet considers his virtues" ("Poet and His Readers," 22, emphasis mine). Another passage, from yet a third period, affirming this perspective can be found in Gornfel'd, *Muki slova*, 5.

89 Pumpianskii, "Ob ode," 150.

90 Vladimir Odoevskii, letter to Mikhail Pogodin (1828 or earlier), cited from Barsukov, *Zhizn' i trudy*, 2:91.

91 Venevitinov, *Sochineniia*, i–ii, vi; Polevoi, *Literaturnaia kritika*, 23; N.I. Nadezhdin, cited in Piatkovskii, "Biograficheskii ocherk," 30.

92 Ginzburg, "Opyt filosofskoi liriki," 78–81, 99–101. Andrei Nemzer writes of the "elegiac, Byronic and Schellingian banalities of his polished lines" (*Pri svete*, 190). Larry R. Andrews more generously notes the "attractive clarity and vigor" that he combined with the "diction of sensibility" ("Sketch," 382). Ginzburg, however, underestimates the extent of the influence of German Romanticism in Venevitinov's poetry, particularly in the period immediately preceding the Decembrist uprising: 1824–5. Ginzburg additionally argues that, given the breakdown in the 1820s of the genre system, within which the lyric voice had been a product of

the given genre and the elegiac voice of different poets more alike than the voice of a particular poet in different genres, the fairly homogeneous "type" of poems penned by Venevitinov and their repetitive content made the thoughts and themes expressed more easily taken as a necessity, thus facilitating a breach of the boundary between literature and life in which the lyric "I" was taken as the voice of the poet ("Opyt filosofskoi liriki," 95–7).

93 See, for instance, Dmitrieva, "K istorii sozdaniia."

94 Cf. Mann, *Russkaia filosofskaia estetika*, 37. Given the constant and serious attention to the journal in Venevitinov's letters, it is hard to agree with Nemzer that the enterprise was "not so important" for him, though easy to agree to the tactical nature of Pushkin's participation (Nemzer, *Pri svete*, 188); mercantile as well – Pushkin was to be paid 10,000 roubles.

95 Letter to his brother, the poet Aleksei Khomiakov, 3 December 1826 in "Pis'ma k A. S. Khomiakovu," 224.

96 Barsukov, *Zhizn' i trudy*, 90. Cf. also A. I. Del'vig, in Venevitinov, *Polnoe sobranie sochinenii*, 396.

97 See Pogodin's diary: "I bawled hysterically" (revel bez pamiati), "Sobolevsky [...] 'burst out sobbing'" (Barsukov, *Zhizn' i trudy*, 91); Venevitinov, *Polnoe sobranie sochinenii*, 406–8; Polevoi: "Pushkin and [Polish poet Adam] Mickiewicz followed Venevitinov's coffin to the grave and cried for him as for a friend" (*Literaturnaia kritika*, 26).

98 Ginzburg calls the "archaistic [stylistic] tendencies of the Liubomudry" (she refers here, it seems, primarily to Khomiakov and Shevyrev), their turn towards the odic and Lomonosovian "some sort of feebleness in finding their own form for the new Romantic histrionics (novaia romanticheskaia patetika)" (*O lirike*, 165). However, one might also consider both the need for and the direction of their search an outgrowth of a return to an understanding of sincerity linked to the expression of intense emotion.

99 I borrow this felicitous expression from Alyssa Dinega Gillespie's translation of the letter to Viazemsky cited in the previous section.

100 Staël, *Germany*, 1:195, 194; *De l'Allemagne*, 142, 141.

101 Wordsworth continues and qualifies his thought: "but though this be true, Poems to which any value can be attached, were never produced [...] but by a man who being possessed of more than usual organic sensibility had also thought long and deeply" (Wordsworth and Coleridge, *Lyrical Ballads*, 157). In other words, for Wordsworth's "spontaneous overflow" to be of value, the poet, gifted with a proclivity for organic synthesis, has to have previously undergone the *mental work* of reflection.

102 Abrams, *Mirror*, 89. The philosopher J.G. Herder similarly deemed "the natural overflow of primitive feelings [...] the condition of all genuine poetry" (90).

103 Emphasis mine. Venevitinov's poetry is cited, unless otherwise noted, from Venevitinov, *Stikhotvoreniia. Proza.* "Immodest laughter" (neskromnyi smekh) is from the initial publication in the *Moscow Herald* (291).

104 Cf. Shelley's "Skylark" that "Pourest [its] full heart / In profuse strains of unpremeditated art" (*Poetry and Prose*, 226). Venevitinov is often close to Shelley's positive strain of Romanticism.

105 Note that this artlessness would be a simplification of F.W.J. Schelling, who asserts in *System of Transcendental Idealism* the necessity in art (for him, inherently the work of a genius) of the mutual, separate but indivisible work of unconscious intuition ("poetry") and conscious and diligent craft ("what is ordinarily called *art*," i.e., serious application, industry and thought) (Part 6, 223–4). In "Anaxagoras. A Conversation with Plato," however, Venevitinov presents a more complex artistic process. Here, the three stages "Plato's" artist passes through distinctly parallel Schelling's path from unconscious unity with nature / the Absolute through division to unity, consciously reachieved (*Stikhotvoreniia. Proza*, 126–7). On this aspect of Schelling's Philosophy of Identity, see Pratt, *Russian Metaphysical Romanticism*, 17–18.

106 "Poet" itself, however, bears no clear defects that would point to a lack of craft and was, moreover, intended for publication. See "Pis'ma k A. S. Khomiakovu," 224; Venevitinov, *Stikhotvoreniia. Proza*, 370. The French inscription on a copy of Venevitinov's "To My Goddess" ("K moei bogine," 1826 or 1827) reads: "This piece is very imperfect […] but it is one of the works one doesn't touch twice" (*Stikhotvoreniia. Proza*, 492).

107 Cf. Ginzburg, *O lirike*, 164–5; Maimin, "Venevitinov i ego nasledie," 444–5.

108 Alexander Odoevsky described the young poet at a ball in Moscow: "[…] a wholly elegant face […] and a smile full of sadness, the inaptness of which he tried to mask with a tone of light irony […]" (Venevitinov, *Polnoe sobranie stikhotvorenii*, 191).

109 *Stikhotvoreniia. Proza*, 379, dated by the editors.

110 "Pis'ma k A. S. Khomiakovu," 224; Cf. Venevitinov's letters to Pogodin: "Today I'm moving into my apartment, which will be my hermitage"; "I am always somehow in a reverie of verse […]" (*Stikhotvoreniia. Proza*, 365, 370).

111 M.A. Venevitinov, "K biografii," 123.

112 The vaudeville referred to in the epistle may, however, be a separate earlier work. See Venevitinov, *Stikhotvoreniia. Proza*, 469–70.

113 Cf. Ginzburg on the lyric subject of Kondraty Ryleev as a "still transitional phenomenon" since "Unity of personality (edinstvo lichnosti) is an inalienable characteristic of Romanticism" (*O lirike*, 138).

114 Cf. Venevitinov, "Anaxagoras. A Conversation with Plato" ("Anaksagor. Beseda Platona, "1825), *Stikhotvoreniia. Proza*, 123.

115 On the unconscious in German Romanticism, see Abrams, 201–13.

116 "I feel, in me burns" ("Ia chuvstvuiu, vo mne gorit," 1826 or 1827).

117 "Pis'ma k A. S. Khomiakovu," 224.

118 "A Defence of Poetry," in *Poetry and Prose*, 480.

119 On the philosophical roots of the problem of the inexpressible, see Seifrid, *Word Made Self*, 13–17, cf. also 26–7; in the context of Russian Romantic poetry, see Mann, *Russkaia literatura*, 27–33; Khagi, who prefers the term "Romantic verbal skepticism," *Silence*, 40–74.

120 If Venevitinov read this passage from *Childe Harold*, it appears to have left little trace on the much more conservatively thought and optimistic "Solace." Viazemsky's "Byron (A Fragment)" ("Bairon [Otryvok]"), which includes a prose translation of Byron's strophe as an epigraph, was published, like "The Inexpressible," in 1827 (*Moskovskii telegraf*, ch. 13), concurrent with or after Venevitinov's death. Khagi traces the topos to a different, and less radical, passage from Canto IV of *Childe Harold*, which influenced Batiushkov and later Tiutchev, and also cites a compelling prose remark from Herder (*Silence*, 41). A passage Khagi cites from Mme de Staël (42) is, in its proto-Romanticism, very close to "Solace": "The gift of revealing by speech the internal feelings of the heart is very rare; there is, however, a poetical spirit in all beings who are capable of strong and lively affections: expression is wanting to those who have not exerted themselves to find it" (*Germany*, 193; *De l'Allemagne*, 140).

121 *Stikhotvoreniia. Proza*, 23.

122 Cited in Ginzburg, *O lirike*, 134, my emphasis.

123 Abrams, *Mirror*, 73.

124 Abrams, *Mirror*, 134, 135.

125 *Stikhotvoreniia. Proza*, 155–6. On the influence of Byron in Venevitinov's predilection for intensity (in contrast, for instance, to Schelling), see Mann, *Russkaia filosofskaia estetika*, 27–8.

126 "Dukh" ("Spirit") is capitalized as per the first printing.

127 Cf. Wilhelm Küchelbecker's use of a similar phrase in 1823: "Gremite zhe, sviatye struny" ("Thunder, sacred strings"; *Polnoe sobranie stikhotvorenii*, 119–20). Küchelbecker's usage however, is actively supported by his poem's imagery as well as its more thoroughly archaizing (odic/psalmic) stylistics and combative tone.

128 "Calm" predates poetic inspiration in the latter sonnet. Cf. a note inscribed on the autograph: "'Calmly' is a false expression for the bard so filled with passion that the ferocity of raging waves, or the cracking of thunder, or the howling of the tempest cannot be likened to his ardent transports" (*Stikhotvoreniia. Proza*, 472).

129 This shift perhaps reflects a desire to achieve a subjective-objective synthesis in art (cf. Mann, *Russkaia filosofskaia estetika*, 22–6) as well as the influence of Pushkin's *Boris Godunov* and the second chapter of *Eugene Onegin*.

130 *Sochineniia. Chast' pervaia*, ii.

131 *Sochineniia. Chast' pervaia*, ii.

132 Pogodin, years later, compared the place of Venevitinov in his circle as the lost "favourite, treasure," "as if […] an expiatory sacrifice," to that of Alexander Petrov, Andrei Turgenev, and Nikolai Stankevich for their generations (Barsukov, *Zhizn' i trudy*, 2:92–3). Andrei Turgenev entered Russian literary "mythology" as an unrealized poetic genius who died at the age of twenty-two of a sudden illness, carelessly contracted – not unlike the final illness of Venevitinov, who ran perspiring and underdressed across a frigid courtyard. Karamzin had mourned his friend Alexander Petrov using the literary name Agaton in an essay that made his greatest virtue "artistism of nature" (Kochetkova, "'Ispoved',"' 77). Venevitinov's friend Platon Obodovskii in an 1829 memorial poem called the poet a "krotkii Agaton" (meek Agaton) (Venevitinov, *Polnoe sobranie stikhotvorenii*, 153).

133 See Barsukov, *Zhizn'*, 2:92–3. A letter by Khomiakov is also richly telling in this regard ("Pis'ma k A. S. Khomiakovu," 224).

134 Inspiration and truth are linked, for instance, by Schelling, for whom the "product" of the integration of conscious and unconscious impulses is ultimately the expression of an objective reality that the artist "does not fully understand himself, and whose meaning is infinite" (*System of Transcendental Idealism*, 222–3).

135 Mann demonstrates how Venevitinov alone, among contemporary critics, is able to grasp the essence of Pushkin's development beyond the frameworks of Romanticism in *Eugene Onegin* (Mann, *Russkaia filosofskaia estetika*, 30–47, esp. 46–7).

136 Not counting the suicide motifs in "To My Ring" ("K moemu perstniu," 1826 or 1827) and "To My Goddess," these include "Testament" ("Zaveshchanie," 1826 or 1827), "Poet and Friend" ("Poet i drug," 1827), "Sacrifice" ("Zhertvoprinoshenie," likely 1826; a contemporary read the poem precisely this way in *Damskii zhurnal* no. 7 [1827]; see *Stikhotvoreniia. Proza*, 488) and, as we will see below, "<On the New Year (1827)>." This presentiment was not without some underpinning. Note Venevitinov's chronic painful cough (predating the move to Petersburg), his quite severe illness in late fall, and a comment his superior made, having seen him for the first time (not long after his brief stay in the Peter and Paul fortress): "[…] we won't use him for long, he has death in his eyes (il a la mort dans les yeux) […]" (M.A. Venevitinov, "K biografii," 122–3).

137 See "Several Thoughts for the Plan of a Journal" ("Neskol'ko myslei v plan zhurnala," 1826), *Stikhotvoreniia. Proza*, 131. Cf. Shelley, *Poetry and Prose*, 482. This understanding of the failings of poetic expression *in the present* appears to have developed in Venevitinov's final year. His answer to Merzliakov had been contrastingly sanguine. Even so, while Venevitinov questions the effectuality of the poetic speech of his day and indeed calls for a time when writing will be put on hold (cf. Khagi, "Silence and the Rest," 48–50, 58), in regard to the greater possibilities of poetic language, he is not pessimistic. It is a specific poetic language that is deficient, and this can be corrected in Russia, he goes on to make clear, through a period of introspection and maturation, much like, it should be noted, what goes on in the poet before he is ready to speak ("Poet"). Silence, for Venevitinov, bounds and prepares true poetic speech, rather than replaces or stands witness against it.

138 Russian National Library (RNB), Saint Petersburg, Arkhiv V. F. Odoevskogo, f. 539, ed. kh. 1484.

139 Odoevsky wrote a fantastic tale disputing the Romantic inspiration of "The Improviser" ("Improvizator," 1833). However, Venevitinov's visible "performance" of Romantic creativity should not have registered as suspect "improvisation" for Odoevsky. First, it was free of mercantile motives (the notorious greed of a Sgricci; see Weintraub "Problem of Improvisation," 129n34). Second, the performance was an expression of inner necessity, while the work of the *improvisatore* was launched from topics proposed by the audience (cf. Caesar, "Poetic Improvisation," 701–2). Third, its written form – even if the text were not actually saved – implied a different ontology, an innate value pertaining to individual words that was lacking in improvisation. (Note Mickiewicz's ban on recording the improvisations with which he thrilled onlookers – including Prince Viazemsky [Weintraub, "Problem of Improvisation," 124; Borovkova-Maikova, "Mitskevich," 218–20].) Fourth, the poem's modest scope was in scale with Romantic conceptions about the brevity and intensity of the moment of inspiration (Abrams, *Mirror*, 133–4). The *improvisatore*'s compositions awed through their seemingly endless productivity (Caesar, "Poetic Improvisation," 702). In Odoevsky's tale, Kipriano is not only gifted with inexhaustible poetic flow, but also cursed with the inability to see synthetically, making him the *antipode* of the Romantic genius.

140 Text is from the draft but in modern orthography; title, date, and interpolated punctuation (in angle brackets) are taken from the first publication in *Moskovskii vestnik* 5 (1828), 3–4. There, the poem is followed by an answer written by Aleksei Khomiakov, "Na Novyi 1828 god" ("On the New Year 1828"). In this context, the parentheses can only mean that "1827" was not part of Venevitinov's title. This, in turn, ought to imply

that Venevitinov somehow or somewhere expressed the intention that his poem take the title "Na Novyi god" ("On the New Year"). One cannot, however, be certain that the title was not added purely at the editors' behest.

141 Derzhavin could rework just the final lines of his existing poem "The Swallow" ("Lastochka," 1792, 1794) creating a highly resonant poem of memory dedicated to his wife – one of the lyric masterpieces of the late eighteenth century. Pushkin could (hypothetically) readdress his "For the shores of a distant homeland," among other revisions, and, in doing so, attain its remarkable sincere "resonance." As a corollary, Mikhail Gasparov's readings of Mandelstam's opaque poetry through his clearer drafts ("'Za to, chto ia ruki'"; "'Solominka'") betray a logical fallacy. The poet began with a more circumscribed and limited meaning and re-worked his poems to be radically open-ended and multivalent. It is thus wrong to locate the plot of these finished artworks in their initial impulse.

142 A careful look indicates that the plural "оправданій," which likely emerged automatically from the rhyme with "обещаній," has been hast-ily changed to defective "оправданья"; thus, the final reading should presumably be taken as the singular, "оправданья." The poet thus goes in this word from more "automatic" to less automatic, and *seemingly* more natural, "unmediated" speech, which, in truth, is actively generated in resistance to the automatic. Venevitinov's publishers, however, resur-rected the original, more conventional rhyme.

143 Cf. Shelley: "'When composition begins [...] inspiration is already on the decline,' and poets must fill the gaps between the incandescent moments by an 'intertexture of conventional expressions'" (*Poetry and Prose*, 504).

144 Cf. B.V. Smirenskii in the notes to *Polnoe sobranie sochinenii* (1934), 438.

145 *Stikhotvoreniia. Proza*, 399–400. Cf. Khomiakov: "Strange that with all this he hardly believes that he has poetic talent" ("Pis'ma k A. S. Khomiak-ovu," 224).

146 *Stikhotvoreniia. Proza*, 400.

147 Dmitry Potapovich Shelekhov, known mostly for his agricultural school and essays, participated in the almanac *Mnemosyne* (*Mnemozina*, 1824), published by Odoevsky and Küchelbecker. Fedor Stepanovich Khomi-akov was, as noted above, Venevitinov's housemate. Vasily Ivanovich Obolensky, a philologist and teacher, knew Odoevsky (and Venevitinov) from Raich's circle. This identification (as opposed to one of Venevitin-ov's Obolensky relatives) is strongly supported by his authorship of an article that appeared in the correctly timed second issue of the *Moscow Herald* for 1827.

148 The chronology does not conflict with Venevitinov's letter to his sister of 8 January. While *Stikhotvoreniia. Proza*, 353, gives a translation placing

Venevitinov at "a masquerade, given by the Court on New Year's" (na Novyi god), the original French reads "bal masqué que la Cour a donné le 1-er jour de l'an" (a masquerade ball given by the Court the first day of the year), hence the *following* evening. At the same time, the poem itself demonstrates that imputing to Venevitinov's contemporaries a consciousness of the moment of midnight as the start of the New Year (and, hence, cause for celebration) is not anachronistic.

3 Romantic Sincerities II: Late-Romantic Sincerities

1 Lermontov, *SS4*, 4:413, my emphasis.
2 Ginzburg, *Tvorcheskii put'*, 86ff. and *O lirike* (1974), 160–4. The careful reader of his diversely intoned late poetry can, however, question the thoroughness with which this unity is constructed.
3 In the former regard, compare the scandals regarding the poet's alleged flattery that arose around Pushkin's "Stanzas" ("Stansy," 1826) and "To [My] Friends" ("Druz'iam," 1828; see Pushkin, *PSS10*, 3:486) and "To a Grandee" ("K vel'mozhe," 1831; Vatsuro, "'K Vel'mozhe,'" 177–81; Golburt, *First Epoch*, 142–3ff.). In the latter, compare Khodasevich on Lermontov's work as "the poetry of suffering conscience" ("Fragmenty," 442, 443).
4 See below on Belinsky and Grigoryev's contrasting reactions to "Meditation" ("Duma," 1838). Cf., on the 1837 "Prayer" ("Molitva"), Rozen ("Stikhotvoreniia," 149); Shevyrev ("Stikhotvoreniia," 132, 137); and Pumpianskii, the latter not explicitly defending the sincerity of the poem, but methodically deconstructing that reader code and reception of the poem's stylistics, which leads Rozen to criticize it as insincere ("Stikhovaia rech'," 391–3). It is telling the Prigov makes Lermontov a paradigmatic figure of maximally "straight" and thus maximally suspect poetic sincerity in his 1980 "advertisement" to the cycle "Sincerity on a Contractual Basis or the Tears of a Heraldic Soul" ("Iskrennost' na dogovornykh nachalakh ili slezy geral'dicheskoi dushi"): "And I cried. And I understood that there is nothing more decorative than a sincere and suffering poet (Lermontov, Esenin)" (*Sovetskie teksty*, 206).
5 Powelstock, *Becoming*, 69.
6 See Powelstock, *Becoming*, 172–5.
7 See esp. Powelstock, *Becoming*, 190–5.
8 Powelstock's book, one of few studies of pre-Conceptualist Russian poetry to consider sincerity in its performative aspects, contains more insights into Lermontov's struggle for sincerity and authenticity than can be acknowledged here. Its attempt to demonstrate the achieved "fierce authenticity" of Lermontov's final poems places the author soundly

within a readership that acknowledges his accomplishments in this re-
gard: "[…] the poems themselves, in all their dynamic complexity – were
utterly unique instantiations of personality, authentic traces of a unique
self whose essence remained outside of language" (402).

9 Lermontov uses this term in an 1835 letter to Alexandra Vereshchagina,
explicitly in regard to success in society and in life, implicitly in regard to
poetry. See Powelstock, *Becoming*, 118.

10 Though "verbal charisma" is difficult to quantify, a lack of recognition
of this quality is a weakness of Forbes's analysis of Byron in *Sincerity's
Shadow* (chapter 4). While the tension between fictive and biographical
aspects of Byron's heroes that Forbes attests as the foundation of his
charisma was indeed qualitatively new and an essential element of his
poetics (cf. McGann, "Hero with a Thousand Faces"), and while the am-
biguous identification of Lermontov by contemporaries particularly with
Pechorin (*Hero of Our Time*, 1840) and the Demon of the eponymous long
poem lent a scandalous allure both to his figure and to these works, it
is not difficult to see that *verbal* charisma – which cannot necessarily be
equated with generally recognized poetic virtues – is also an essential ele-
ment without which such texts fall flat.

11 See Ginzburg, *Tvorcheskii put'*, 65; *O lirike* (1974), 158. On Lermontov's be-
latedness in relation to Byronic Romanticism, see Allen, *Fallen Idol*.

12 Even Belinsky, who Ginzburg notes was first to recognize the unity of
Lermontov's lyrical voice (*Tvorcheskii put'*, 99), asserts that in his book are
to be found "vse stikhii poezii" (all modes of poetry) ("Stikhotvoreniia,"
158). Works such as "Borodino" (1837) and "Testament" ("Zaveshchanie,"
1840), in which Lermontov inhabits a voice distinctly separate from his
own, speak to the author's keen observation and empathy and have the
potential to register, paradoxically, as fictional but sincere.

13 See Serman, "Sud'ba," 932–4; Ginzburg, *Tvorcheskii put'*, 88; cf. Belinskii,
"Stikhotvoreniia," 178–80, 183.

14 Powelstock's concept of "intimacy" seems tied primarily to Lermontov's
ability to envision and write an implied reader into his poems, while
"disarming" emphasizes the author's devising of ways to relate to his *self*
that reciprocally put his reader at ease. Compare the poet's conversation
with Pushkin's widow, as conveyed by Natalia Nikolaevna's daughter,
which Powelstock views in terms of a "growing willingness to reveal
himself" and "a sympathetic readiness to see others as they really were,"
but which also parses perfectly as a strategic "disarming": "'in order to
gain her trust, [Lermontov] began himself to initiate her into thoughts
and feelings that had so agonizingly poisoned his life, repenting of the
sharpness of his opinions, of the mercilessness of his judgments that had
so often repelled from him people who were in no way worthy of his

blame … A lively sympathy instantly awakened [in my mother]'" (*Becoming*, 403–4).

15 See Eikhenbaum, *Lermontov*, esp. 107–13; Pumpianskii, "Stikhovaia rech'," 391–403, esp. 399–403.

16 Lermontov's poetic works are cited from *Polnoe sobranie stikhotvorenii.*

17 Cf. Maksimov on "Farewell, unwashed Russia" ("Proshchai, nemytaia Rossiia," 1840 or 1841) as "an act of […] resistance" (*Poeziia Lermontova*, 172).

18 See chapter 1, note 3.

19 In the late eighteenth and early nineteenth century in Russia, not the advent of copyright and literary professionalism (cf. Rosenbaum, *Professing*), but the emergence of a new quasi-religious concept of the "poetic Word," the idea of the poet as a "prophet of truth" in a far more literal sense than applied in Western Europe (Lotman, *Karamzin*, 57–8) transformed the relation between self and word, placing new demands on the poet's sincerity.

20 See, for instance, Rutten, "Sovetskaia ritorika." See also chapter 5, pp. 143–4.

21 Rozen, "Stikhotvoreniia," 154.

22 Powelstock, *Becoming*, 6.

23 Grigor'ev, "Lermontov," 211.

24 Belinskii, "Stikhotvoreniia," 178–80. On the "universalist" mode of poetic sincerity, see Forbes, *Sincerity's Shadow*, chapter 1.

25 *Lermontovskaia entsikopedia* (hereafter, *LE*), s.v. "Ne ver' sebe," 337 (E.E. Naidich); Powelstock, *Becoming*, 265.

26 On the poem's ironies, see also Powelstock, *Becoming*, 324–7; Khagi, *Silence*, 73.

27 Vatsuro, "Chuzhoe 'ia,'" 317. Individually, as Vatsuro demonstrates, many of these evaluative statements parallel commonplaces of late 1830s epigonic Russian Romanticism (318–20).

28 See Naidich, "'Est' rechi,'" 157.

29 *Stikhotvoreniia N. Iazykova* (SPb.: V tip. vdovy Pliushar s synom, 1833), 1.

30 Cf. Khagi on this "icy word" (*Silence*, 71).

31 See Naidich, "'Iz plamia …'" 157–8. Naidich, developing L.A. Bulakhovskii's observations (cf. his *Kurs russkogo literaturnogo iazyka*, 5th ed., v. 1, 206n2), notes similar usage in Kantemir, Radishchev, Derzhavin, and Krylov (all of whom reached adulthood in the eighteenth century), as well as three other poems by Lermontov, and points to roots in dialectical and colloquial speech.

32 Cf. Powelstock's somewhat divergent takeaway in *Becoming*, 445.

33 On Lermontov's choice not to immediately publish the intimate poems of his prison cycle, written contemporaneously to the "rhetorical" poems, see Powelstock, *Becoming*, 178.

34 Serman, "Sud'ba," 937, who sees evidence of this in the poem's great popularity: "'whoever comes to us [from Moscow] inevitably knows [this poem] by heart and praises [it]'" (Nikolai Elagin, cited in Serman, "Sud'ba," 937).

35 For a succinct comparison of Lermontov's poem and Goethe's original, see Fedorov, *Lermontov*, 261–3; see also M.L. Gasparov, *Metr i smysl*, 52–3.

36 Cited from *Stikhotvoreniia M. Lermontova* (SPb.: V tip. Il'i Glazunova i ko., 1840), 119–20.

37 *LE*, s.v. "Iz Gete," 183 (R.Iu. Danilevskii); M.L. Gasparov, *Metr i smysl*, 52–3.

38 Cf. Serman: "the hero, for whom rest and calm are possible only in death" ("Sud'ba," 938).

39 See Fedorov, *Lermontov*, 262–3.

40 On the connection with the latter, see *LE*, 183.

41 Cf. Bukhshtab, "Blagodarnost'," 406–7.

42 Khodasevich, "Fragmenty," 435.

43 To be precise, while Lermontov unobtrusively holds in reserve the *content* of his passions, sufferings, and betrayals, he makes *public* his quarrel with God. On the personal reserve of Lermontov's mature verse, cf. Ginzburg, *Tvorcheskii put'*, 72–3.

44 Unauthorized publications appeared in 1801 and 1803 (Goethe, *Sämtliche Werke*, 1:1072).

45 Goethe, *Sämtliche Werke*, 2:64; translation, http://gutenberg.spiegel.de /buch/3670/92 (accessed 3 November 2017). Cf., among other places, "Bored and sad ..." (I skuchno, i grustno, i nekomu ruku podat', 1840).

46 Lermontov, *PSS*, 616–17.

47 Bukhshtab, who uncovered the echo, no doubt rightly sees in Lermontov's poem a bitterly ironic answer to Krasov ("Blagodarnost'," 407).

48 Goethe, *Sämtliche Werke*, 1:229; translation, http://gutenberg.spiegel .de/buch/3670/92 (adapted to reflect the earlier version). "Ein Gleiches" to an even lesser extent implied that the sought-after rest was the peace of death.

49 Goethe, *Sämtliche Werke*, 2:64; translation slightly modified from http:// gutenberg.spiegel.de/buch/3670/92.

50 On the structure of the poem, see Maksimov, *Poeziia Lermontova*, 173–5; Powelstock, *Becoming*, 405–7.

51 See Ginzburg, *O lirike*, 233–4. Cf. Gogol's "The Lost Charter" ("Propavshaia gramota"; pub. 1831).

52 Maksimov's patriotically tinged Soviet-era discussion fails to reproduce this diminutive! See his *Poeziia Lermontova*, 174–5.

53 Nechaeva presents a credible argument that the title was added by the author, not his posthumous editors, as generally asserted ("K istorii," 70–1).

54 For the influence on Lev Tolstoy, see, for instance, Semenov, *Lermontov i Tolstoi*, 58–75; Durilyn, "Na putiakh," 187, 193. Notable predecessors to Lermonotov in the criticism of war include Voltaire's *Candide* (pub. 1759); Byron's *Don Juan*, Canto VIII (1823) with its ironic deconstruction of the "heroism" of conquest (specifically "Suwarrow's" taking of Ismail), though not necessarily valour; Stendhal's demythologization of battle as initiation in *Charterhouse of Parma* (1839).

Vladimir Golstein has written a study on narratives of heroism in Lermontov, in which he stresses Lermontov's "rejection of all patriarchy, authority, tradition, and existing social conventions and connections." However, he defines heroism substantially differently from what is intended here, linking it to the "embodiment of the spirit of autonomy, dignity and self-reliance." Golstein sees Lermontov's position in "Valerik" as emblematic of stoicism (*Narratives*, 20, 6, 179).

55 Powelstock, *Becoming*, 208. See also Viskovatov, *Lermontov*, 137–8. On Davydov, see, for instance, Leighton, "Davydov's Hussar Style."

56 Lermontov, *PSS*, 1:76.

57 Kropotkin, *Ideals*, 57, my emphasis. Semenov's 1914 comparison to Tolstoy (primarily "The Raid" ["Nabeg"]) is more serious and penetrating, but I would argue that he too, in equating the two works, fails to truly appreciate the radicalism of "Valerik." For instance, while Tolstoy rejects *molodechestvo* and clearly demonstrates the senselessness of the campaign and its human loss, the captain is shown as quietly competent, and his compassion and fortitude under fire have meaning and impact. Nothing so redeeming is sketched by Lermontov here.

58 Cf. Fussell on the residual romanticism of the cavalry still operative at the beginning of the Second World War (*Wartime*, 5).

59 Cf. Pumpianskii, "Stikhovaia rech'," 419–20, 429.

60 Cf. Pumpianskii, "Stikhovaia rech'," 421; Maksimov, *Poeziia Lermontova*, 169–70.

61 Trilling, "The Meaning of a Literary Idea," cited in Allen, *Fallen Idol*, 118. The maximum extent of a warrior ideology within the main battle narrative is perhaps the muted reverberations of such words as "usachi" (mustachioed [soldiers]; both endearing and conveying an unquestionable "Russianness") and the dignifying "boevye" in "ostatki boevye" (approx., *war-tested* remains). *Ostatki*, however – literally, remains – subtly displaces *ostanki* (a person's remains), pulling in the opposite direction.

62 Imperial ideology: "Miatezhnik, khishchnik neporkornyi" (Mutineer, unsubmissive predator) vs. "Kazach'ia buinaia otvaga" (unruly Cossack bravery); "Zakon i pravdu okhraniat'" (To protect law and truth); "Zveropodn[yi] narod[]! / Ego stikhiia – krov' i boi, / Nasil'stvo, khishchnost' i razboi, / I beznachal'naia svoboda" (Beast-like people! /

Its element is blood and battle, / Force, predation and banditism, / And freedom without control"; "Zakon i mech! – Vot dobrodetel'!" (Law and the sword! – That is virtue!); "Ne trat'te [...] zariada [...] Dlia [...] stada / Dovol'no sabli i shtykov" (Don't waste a [...] cartridge [...] On the [...] herd / Sabre and bayonets suffice). Confession-based ideology: "Velen'e Moshchnogo sbylos'" (The charge of the Almighty has been fulfilled); "Gremit uzhasnoe 'Alla!'" (A terrible "Allah!" resounds); "chechenets, / Khristovoi very palach[]" (the Chechen, / Executioner of the Christian faith); "smel[ye] voin[y] Zaveta" (bold soldiers of the Covenant). "Chir-Iurt" is cited from Polezhaev, *Stikhotvoreniia i poemy*, 295–322.

63 Layton's explanation of the inconsistency of Polezhaev's critique of war and apology for a Russian massacre through "moral turmoil" is unsatisfying ("Aleksandr Polezhaev," 568).

64 Viskovatov, *Lermontov*, 309–10. A request was made for a decoration – the order of St. Vladimir, 4th degree – but cancelled "at the highest levels" (Semenov, *Lermontov i Tolstoi*, 58; Powelstock, who cites Nicholas's personal veto, *Becoming*, 341).

65 Viskovatov, *Lermontov*, 305.

66 Russian slang from Tatar, lit. "guest."

67 Cf. Polezhaev: "the heroic exploits of the preceding battle, worthy of notation in the chronicles of the Caucasus" ("Chir-Iurt").

68 Lermontov, *SS4*, 4:450. Viskovatov notes that Lermontov's estimate of the Chechen dead is strongly exaggerated (*Lermontov*, 309).

69 On Ekaterina Sushkova and Varvara Lopukhova as stand-ins for quintessential types of reader confronting Lermontov, see Powelstock, *Becoming*, 174–5.

70 Hutcheon, *Irony's Edge*, 50, 53–4.

71 Cf. Powelstock, *Becoming*, 243, 267. Soviet scholarship tends to put the poet into a teleological framework that observes the markings of a (not fully realized) turn in the poet's final works from Romanticism to the preferred modality of Realism. "Valerik" has, unsurprisingly, served as a useful data point in some of these arguments.

72 Cited in Vittaker and Egorov, "Zhizn' Grigor'eva v pis'makh," 318.

73 The use of this word below, often without quotation marks, reflects the perspectives and linguistic usage of Grigoryev's milieu. For an emic perspective on Russian Roma, see Lemon, *Between Two Fires*. Lemon's book "treats images of Gypsy Song or street life" (contrastingly positively and negatively coded but similarly pigeonholing images of Roma) "not as organizing truths, but as threads of encounter ... that Roma alternately internalize, reject, or are indifferent to" (2). Lemon is also deeply concerned with issues of authenticity and performance, categories which continue to challenge and inform the identity of contemporary Russian Roma.

Other of Grigoryev's poems tend more to the confessional and self-reflexive, as in his long poem "Up the Volga" ("Vverkh po Volge," 1862) or his lyric "The tragedy is close to its dénouement" ("Tragediia blizka k svoei razviazke," 1855). For a theoretically well-grounded look at sincerity in Grigoryev on different material, see Iufereva, "Eshche raz."

74 *Besnovanie* derives etymologically from the concept of demonic possession and initially described insanity, potentially implying a different circle of associations, but nineteenth-century usage centred on lack of self-control, self-limitation.

75 Carlyle, with his great enthusiasm for sincerity, would exert a strong influence on Victorian attitudes towards sincerity in the West as well as on Grigoryev. See Wright, "Sincerity's Repetition"; Grigoryev's "O pravde i iskrennosti," 57, 59, 438n8; Egorov, *Apollon Grigor'ev*, 119.

76 Grigor'ev, "O pravde i iskrennosti," 51. The full title is "On Truth and Sincerity in Art. In Regard to One Question of Aesthetics. Letter to A. S. Kh[omiak]ov" ("O pravde i iskrennosti v iskusstve. Po povodu odnogo esteticheskogo voprosa. Pis'mo k A. S. Kh-vu").

77 Grigor'ev, "O pravde i iskrennosti," 51, author's emphasis.

78 Grigor'ev, "Lermontov," 215.

79 Cf. Belinsky, in the article in which he introduced this originally Lockean term to the Russian reading public: "[…] our century is predominantly an age of reflection" ("Geroi nashego vremeni," cited in Ginzburg, *Tvorcheskii put' Lermontova*, 20).

80 On how these competing imperatives function as a dialectic in Romanticism, see Hartman, "Romanticism and 'Anti-Self-Consciousness,'" 46–51.

81 Grigor'ev, "Lermontov," 213.

82 Grigor'ev, *Russkie narodnye pesni*, 45. While Grigoryev operates with ethnic categories and stereotypes that feel to the modern reader naïvely universalizing, there seems little question he approaches Romani musical culture with respect and attempts to understand it from an internal perspective. What is more, he sets out, at least in some ways, to challenge stereotypes of his day (as, in this passage, the equally limiting understanding of "Gypsy" emotion as staged).

83 Grigor'ev, *Stikhotvoreniia. Poemy. Dramy*, 708. It was, naturally, thus that Grigoryev called in his letters the pre-existing song upon which his poem improvised.

84 Blok, *SS6*, 4:224–5.

85 According to twenty-first-century critic Andrei Nemzer, "no one has in Russian expressed" the emotion bound up in the *vengerka* "more terrifyingly and veridically [*dostovernee*] than the affected declamer Apollon Grigoryev" ("O boli," 221). The extent to which the embodiment of "Gypsy" emotion in the poems is compelling is also suggested by the

success of the renditions that have deeply permeated Russian song culture. These recreate the alternation of quiet intensity and ecstatic speech but in most cases drop or replace 95 per cent of the *text* of the ambitious and lengthy "Vengerka" and often combine and rearrange stanzas of both poems. Set to an existing Hungarian Gypsy melody in the arrangement of Romani chorus leader Ivan Vasilyev, they ultimately became, anonymously, and with ever-changing deletions, insertions, and variations, among the most widely recognized "Gypsy" songs in Russia.

86 This organic criticism was to be a "perspective on art as a *synthetic*, holistic, immediate, perhaps, intuitive understanding of life as distinct from *knowledge*, i.e. understanding analytical, particular, collective, empirical" (Grigor'ev, *Estetika i kritika*, 117–18, author's emphasis).

87 Cf. Pushkin's "Gypsies" ("Tsygany," 1823); Franz Liszt, *Des bohémiens et de leur musique en Hongrie* (1859). Prosper Mérimée's ethnographic epilogue to *Carmen* (1845) fights these tendencies to read Gypsies through a Romantic lens. On the Enlightenment roots of the Romantic topos, see Lotman and Mints, "Chelovek prirody," 600ff.

88 "Chelovek prirody," 617.

89 See Fet, "Kaktus," in Grigor'ev, *Vospominaniia*, 330–3.

90 Note, however, his exaggeratedly, even comically Slavophile dress in the 1850s (Fet, "Kaktus," 331, Egorov, *Apollon Grigor'ev*, 99).

91 Gypsies' wild, disharmonious passion is depicted in Derzhavin's 1805 "Gypsy Dance" ("Tsyganskaia pliaska"; see Lotman and Mints, "Chelovek prirody," 608–9). However, there, this passion is foreign to the speaker and ultimately rejected in favour of the measured dance of the "Russian maiden." Stepan Shevyrev's 1828 poem of the same name betrays the Romantic's unadulterated fascination with Gypsy passion, which, however, retains its exoticism.

92 Note the similarities and differences in Grigor'ev's description of *Russian* folk song: "[…] singing broad, powerful, coursing with quiet fire along the veins. The songs flowed, flowed, one broader than the next, one more rhapsodic [perelivistee] than the next. The soul expanded together with the song […]" (*Russkie narodnye pesni*, 43). See also Lotman and Mints, "Chelovek prirody," 614–15.

93 Cf. the unselfconscious "egoism" in love of the heroine of Pushkin's "Gypsies." Mérimée's epilogue, in contrast, stresses Gypsies' loyalty and self-sacrifice.

94 The poet makes a concerted attempt in the fourth poem of the "Struggle" cycle to derive the cycle's name from a struggle of wills between hero and heroine. However, the internal struggle of the hero to maintain control over his passions underlies in a much more pervasive way the dynamics

and plot of the cycle and is made explicit (and called "bor′ba") in poem 10.

95　Grigor′ev, *Russkie narodnye pesni*, 45.

96　In Volkonskaya's poem, the star is soulmate to the female speaker. They are conjoined – "Твой луч, светя, звучит в душе моей […] И жар ее, твой отблеск верный здесь" (Your ray, shining, sounds in my soul […] And its ardour is your faithful reflection here; *Severnye tsvety*, 263), but also separate, such that the star is "empathetic" and the speaker can compare their relationship to the meeting of two conjugal gazes, two answering choruses. While Volkonskaya nowhere indicates the speaker's gender in the words of the poem, she strongly masculinizes the star in the first stanza through its metaphoric and metonymic representations (svet [light], put′ [path], luch [ray], otblesk [reflection]), culminating in the line: "Gori! gori! ne vygorit on ves′!" (Burn! burn! it [masc.] will [never] wholly burn out!). The antecedent of the masculine "on" (it) is the star's terrestrial "otblesk," which is also, in an appositive phrase, the "zhar" (ardour, masculine) of her (feminine) soul. Moreover, Volkonskaya's is "The star of my living melody!" (Звезда моей мелодии живой!). Grigoryev borrows both the *musicality* of Volkonskaya's star and the complex *dialogism* she unfolds to develop his own quadripartite structure, connecting speaker, guitar, star, and implicitly, beloved.

97　Liapina's claim for the overarching peonic rhythm structure of this poem is misleading ("O literaturno-khudozhestvennoi"). While the even lines are indeed overwhelmingly and strikingly structured as second peons (exceptions being line 22 and, with more ambiguity, 18 and 26), of the fourteen odd-numbered lines, only lines 17 and 27 scan convincingly as fourth peon, while in several places strong phrasal stress is at odds with this metre (khot′ tý so mnoi; núzhno ei; Dopói zhe mne; Smotrí: zvezda odna gorit; gotóv s toboi) – this, despite Kirill Taranovsky's law of "regressive dissimilation" for binary metres in Russian, which implies a tendency to generate fourth peons in iambic tetrameter.

98　"Kaktus," 331. Cf. Nemzer, *Dnevnik*, 219.

99　Grigor′ev, *Vospominaniia*, 271; cited in Egorov, "Apollon Grigor′ev," 36. In a letter, Grigoryev calls the "vengerka" a "meteoric tavern poem [made up of] sounds of desperate suffering," Grigor′ev, *Pis′ma*, 178.

100　Cf. *Slovar′ iazyka Pushkina*, s.v. "pokhmel′e."

101　In this latter case, Grigoryev changed the phrase from a draft version that employed a more commonly imitated folk diction "Po bessonnym, po nocham" (see Egorov, "Apollon Grigor′ev," 34), intensifying the sense of an authenticity of language use. On the use of "extended adjectival reflexes" to vary syllabification in authentic folk song, see Bailey, *Three Russian Folk Song Meters*, 124–5.

102 Egorov, "Apollon Grigor'ev," 32; Nemzer, *Dnevnik*, 219.
103 One phrase, early in the poem, "sladostrast'e[] baiaderki" (the voluptu-
     ousness of the *bayadere*) might strike the modern reader as, in contrast,
     highly literary and hence a stylistic malapropism. A *bayadere*, however, is
     more correctly a Hindu dancing girl, and things fall into place when we
     consider how and by whom it was being *misused* at the time. For instance,
     Faddei Bulgarin, a writer known for his lowbrow tastes, used this word
     in regard to Gypsy women in 1843 (ruscorpora.ru). Hence, Grigoryev's
     misappropriation of the word is an example of lowbrow, rather than
     highbrow, stylistics. Grigoryev, the leading theatre critic of his day and a
     lover of Goethe, would surely have been aware of the more precise mean-
     ing of the word, which appears to have entered Russian through Goethe's
     ballad and Daniel-François-Esprit Auber's opéra-ballet, *The God and the
     Bayadere* (1797 and 1830).
104 Liszt, *Des bohémiens*, 73.
105 On the possible Romani antecedents, see Egorov, "Apollon Grigor'ev," 34.
106 Cf. Searle and Vandervenken, *Foundations*, 12–20, 193.
107 This "burgeoning" is perceptible as each of the lines expands the preced-
     ing trochees with an additional interval syllable.
108 Cf. *sibiriak* (Sibir'), *permiak* (Perm'), *tuliak* (Tula). Egorov, though he goes
     back and forth on the issue (cf. *Apollon Grigor'ev*, 131; Grigor'ev, *Vospom-
     inaniia*, 423), sees the lines, quite possibly, as Grigoryev's own based on
     the unexpected and biographically apt image of blue eyes ("Apollon
     Grigor'ev," 37); this despite Fet, who seems to imply that this chorus
     predates Grigoryev ("Kaktus," 331). Note also that Chibiriak is found as a
     Russian surname.
109 In the earlier "Ekh ty, zhizn', moia zhizn' …" we have a similar six-
     syllable line with caesura and phrasal stress on the third and sixth
     syllables. "K serdtsu serdtsem prizhmis'!" follows this stress pattern but
     without a caesura.
110 See Bailey, *Three Russian Meters*, 173–5.
111 Cf. Bailey, *Three Russian Meters*, 93, and its "Glossary of Folk Song Accen-
     tuation," 316–43; additional analogous stress shifts include *sudarúshka*,
     molodúshka, *golubúshka*, *soldatúshka*.
112 *Narodnyia russkiia pesni iz sobraniia P. Iakushkina* (1865), 151. Judging by
     this collection, to which Grigoryev contributed some of his own tran-
     scriptions, the comma preceding "to" in Grigor'ev, *Stikhotvoreniia. Poemy.
     Dramy*, 137, is an editorial overcorrection (note that it does not appear in
     the Blok's edition) and "to li" should be pronounced as an enclitic (i.e.,
     unstressed). One of the songs contributed by Grigoryev himself uses this
     structure four times: "Chto khotiat-*to li* […] / Chto kuiut-*to li* […]" (*Nar-
     odnyia*, 104).

113 See Bailey on contrasting accentuation of the same word or root in folk poetry in contiguous lines, or in the same line, through the introduction of "artificial stress." Artificial stress is non-standard stress not present in archaic, dialectical, or substandard language but applied broadly as an option within authentic folk songs to sustain the metrical structure (*Three Russian* Meters, 44; on non-past verbal forms, 66–7).

114 This does occur in folk songs, including in an object-verb phrase, though stress shift appears to be quite rare in imperatives, to judge by James Bailey's magisterial study. See Bailey, *Three Russian Meters*, 58, 65–75, 94 (note particularly "stúpen' stúpila" and "ídi, mílen'kii"). "Tópi" requires not only a stress shift to the root, but retention of the final *–i*, which normally disappears in root-stressed second-conjugation imperatives without a consonant cluster before the ending. Such a stress shift, though relatively rare, is attested in some northern Great Russian dialects (Sologub, "Formy povelitel'nogo," 375). Thus "tópi" can potentially be either dialectical or artificial stress.

115 On Lermontov's position, from the beginning, as a belated Romantic, see esp. Allen, *Fallen Idol*.

116 Mandel'shtam, *Stikhotvoreniia. Proza*, 276.

4 A Fault Line in Modernism

1 See Goldberg, *Mandelstam, Blok*, esp. chapters 6, 9, and 11.

2 Cf. "The beginning poets published by the Acmeists put out cleaner books than many and were more intrinsically literary, more cultured, more proper; but this is of course hardly praise. The only real exception among them was Anna Akhmatova […] In Gumilev's own poetry there was something cold and foreign that inhibited one from listening" ("'Bez bozhestva, bez vdokhnoveniia' [*Tsekh akmeistov*]" [1921], Blok, *SS8*, 6:180–1). There were other dimensions to the poets' mutual ambivalence – Mandelstam's ethnic identity in light of Blok's antisemitism, Blok's social and political maximalism and *barstvennost'* (aristocratic demeanour) for Mandelstam. For literature on Blok's antisemitism see Goldberg, *Mandelstam, Blok*, 224n19. On Mandelstam's understanding of Blok's *barstvennost'*, see chapter 12.

3 Each of the major Russian post-Symbolist poets wrought an (at times) sincere modernist voice undergirded by a different set of principles, and therefore potentially striking a chord with a different set of readers. For instance, Akhmatova's sincere voice verges on melodrama, gathers prophetic intensity, draws upon the platform offered by the tragic historical backdrop of her times; Pasternak's poetry, at its most charismatic, is powered by a verbal and vitalist enthusiasm, generating a Romantically

subjective voice larger than life because of its context in a world experienced with larger-than-life intensity; Velemir Khlebnikov's voice is grounded in idiosyncratic quirkiness and inspired linguistic "pottering"; while unparalleled verbal and personal intensity marks Tsvetaeva. How each of these voices relates to modernism on the one hand and sincerity on the other is a very large question that cannot be undertaken in the context of this study. In any case, however, it is clear that models of sincerity linked to or mixing both poles elaborated in this book continued to operate in Russian post-Symbolism.

4 The divergence of potential attitudes to text and biography within modernism is vividly encapsulated in Svetlana Boym's presentation of diametrically contrasting proto-modernities viewed through the prism of Stéphane Mallarmé and Arthur Rimbaud, the former representing the limit of the (still incomplete) effacement of the extra-literary authorial "I" in the literary text, the other the limit of the effacement of the literary text and tradition in favour of a "true life" sought outside of and in rejection of writing (Boym, *Death in Quotation Marks*, chapter 1). Cf. Taylor on modernism's simultaneous slide into deep subjectivity and anti-subjectivism (*Sources*, 456, 462). On the terminological difficulties surrounding modernism, see, for example, Calinescu, *Five Faces*; Livak, *In Search*, esp. 38–77.

5 Trilling, *Sincerity and Authenticity*, 6–7. This position, developing the sensibilities of Gautier, Mallarmé, and Wilde, and propounded perhaps most famously by T.S. Eliot, bears strong comparison to John Keats's earlier rejection of the "wordsworthian or egotistical sublime." Cf. his letter to Richard Woodhouse, 27 October 1818.

6 Conflictual meanings are understood not as mutually cancelling, leading to emptiness or kaleidoscopic loss of bearings, but paradoxically additive, one of the key features of modernism and that which most crucially distinguishes it from postmodernist play.

7 This despite the strong contrast with predecessors perceived by contemporaries. Cf. Zhirmunsky (in 1916, having seen only the 1913 and 1916 editions of the poet's first book *Stone* [*Kamen'*]): "In Mandelstam's mature poetry we no longer find his soul, his personal, human moods" ("Preodolevshie simvolizm," 43).

Mandelstam's mode of subjectivity as vision (broadly speaking), rather than auto-reflexive confession, can be compared to Keats's "negative capability" (see Forbes, *Sincerity's Shadow*, ch. 5) and Manning's "perceptive" sincerity (*Rhétorique de la sincérité*, 59–63, 297–361). However, the latter as a term, with the teleological valorization Manning gives it (together with other modernist modalities), is problematic. First, how can one draw a boundary between the perceptive – in which a subject puts into words the world as he or she has seen it – and the "expressive," in which a subject puts into words his or her experience in the world? Compare the unabashed Romantic Tiutchev's "Smotri, kak roshcha zeleneet" ("See how the grove shimmers green," 1857). Can we really not assert that sincerity here is experienced by the poet through the quality of fidelity to perception? Second, "perception" in poetry is – in a way Manning seems reluctant to confront – subject to the same potentially distorting translation into language that confounds "expression." (Cf. esp. his analysis of Louis Zukofsky's optimistic model.)

Manning's broad-reaching analysis of another modernist modality – affirmative doubt (*Rhétorique de la sincérité*, 59–63, 403–38) is particularly illuminating. (Cf. my *Mandelstam, Blok, passim*, on irony and doubt as a path to more subtle affirmation in the wake of the crisis of Symbolism and its epistemology.) It should be kept in mind, however, that what Manning is describing is not a necessarily more compelling mode of sincerity, but a sincerity effect which will be of greatest impact for those with a particular reader code.

8 See below, p. 120.

9 On the analogies between Mandelstam's and Anglo-American modernism, see Cavanagh, *Osip Mandelstam*, 13–28; Rusinko, "Russian Acmeism and Anglo-American Imagism." The Imagist and, particularly, Objectivist context is examined at length in Manning, *Rhétorique*.

10 On modernist sincerities and authenticities, see also, for instance, Adorno, "Curve of the Needle"; Tynianov, "Promezhutok" (on Mayakovsky and Esenin); Benjamin, "Work of Art"; Trilling, *Sincerity and Authenticity* (esp. on Conrad and Freud); Holdsworth, "Some Modernist," 61–2; Costello, *Marianne Moore*, 2–3, 26; Bird, "Envoicing History"; Sharp, "Sincerity and Objectification"; Groys, "Production of Sincerity"; Fishzon, "Operatics" and *Fandom*; Rutten, *Sincerity after Communism*, 59–65; Harrington, "Melodrama, Feeling"; Doak, "Emotion as Such"; as well as Abrams, *Mirror and the Lamp*, 320; and Rosenbaum, *Professing Sincerity*, 252n34.

11 Mandel'shtam, *SS4*, 2:236.

12 Mandel'shtam, *SS4*, 2:363–4.

13 A rough draft to "Conversation about Dante" seems to confirm this understanding: "[Dante] is the instrument itself in the metamorphosis of collapsing and unfolding literary time, which we have ceased to hear, but study both here and in the West as a paraphrase of so-called 'cultural formations'" (Mandel'shtam, *SS4*, 3:181).

14 Tynianov's vision, in regard to the necessity of poetry to continuously transform itself, is largely cognate to that of Mandelstam: "I speak about that novelty of interaction of all aspects of poetry [stikh, a word with

technical/stylistic connotations], which gives birth to new poetic sense [novyi stikhovoi smysl]" ("Promezhutok," 549). Cf. also Hulme: "Those arts like poetry, whose matter is immortal [i.e., recorded and not ephemeral, S.G.], must find a new technique each generation. Each age must have its own special form of expression, and any period that deliberately goes out of it is an age of insincerity" (*Collected Writings*, 51; cited in Manning, *Rhétorique*, 81).

15 Mandel'shtam *SS4*, 2:60.

16 Mandel'shtam, *SS4*, 2:107.

17 "Stanzas" ("Stansy," 1935). Unless otherwise noted, Mandelstam's poetry is cited from Mandel'shtam, *PSS*.

18 A classic expression of the civic poetry topos can be found in Nikolai Nekrasov's, "The Poet and the Citizen" ("Poet i grazhdanin," 1855–6): "Иди в огонь за честь отчизны, / За убежденье, за любовь, / Иди и гибни безупречно – / Умрешь не даром: дело прочно, / Когда под ним струится кровь ..." (Walk into fire for the Fatherland's honour / For principle, for love ... / Go forth and perish irreproachably. / You won't die in vain: the venture is sure, / When under it flows blood ...; (Nekrasov, *Stikhotvoreniia*, 13). Nadson rhymes *krov'–liubov'* and *zakhlebnetsia v krovi–k bezzavetnoi liubvi* (will choke with blood–to selfless love) in "My friend, my brother, [my] weary, suffering brother" ("Drug moi, brat moi, ustalyi, stradaiushchii brat," 1880), a poem of known significance to Mandelstam. Blok too is not averse to this traditional rhyme. (Cf., among many examples, the finale of "Gem Ring-Suffering" ["Persten'-Stradan'e," 1905].) Acmeist Mikhail Zenkevich's poem "The Eternal/Perpetual Rhyme" ("Vechnaia rifma"; pub. *Giperborei* 9/10 [1913]) with its juxtaposition of slaughter and mating in a barnyard presents a purposefully scandalizing extrapolation of the decadent aesthetics of love/blood.

19 Mandel'shtam, *SS4*, 2:347–8.

20 Mandelstam uses this expression in a somewhat different context in regard to Innokenty Annensky, a poet with whom he has more affinities (Mandel'shtam, *SS4*, 3:34).

21 Blok's maturation, however, is implicitly cast by Mandelstam as an outgrowing of Romanticism in the model of Pushkin (*SP*, 526).

22 Cf. "If you insist, it means that you love not me but my mask, which always brings *me* suffering" (Blok, *SS8*, 8:271). This discomfort is also conveyed quite powerfully in Khodasevich, *Nekropol'*, 91–2.

23 Mandelstam too, of course, reacts to a rapidly and radically changing world. Again, the difference is of emphasis, the "specific gravity" so to speak, within their respective poetics of these types of change. Cf. Blok: "I find it painful [...] when [Ivanov] crows about κάθαρσις with the same

tone in 1912 as [he did] in 1905" (*SS8*, 8:386); Mandelstam: "[Pushkin,] the author of Boris Godunov, even if he wanted to, could not repeat the lyceum verse, just like nowadays no one will write a Derzhavin ode. Who likes what better is another thing" (*SS4*, 2:244).

24 Tynianov, "Blok i Geine," 245–6.

25 Blok, *SS8*, 8:344.

26 See Mikhail Gasparov, *Zapisi i vypiski*, 245.

27 From "Doomed" ("Obrechennyi," 1907).

28 Blok, in contrast to some other Symbolists, understood that taste and sincerity demand a certain modesty. Compare: "Briusov hides his knowledge about Her. In this, he is sincere to the extreme" (Blok, *Zapisnye knizhki*, 65). It is another matter that in Blok's poetry humility struggles against hubris, and in his worldview the boundary between these qualities is marked quite differently than in the world view of Mandelstam.

29 Mandel'shtam, *SS4*, 2:99. Boris Bukhshtab admonished: "a portrait accompanying the poetry of Mandelstam would be artistic tactlessness" ("Poeziia Mandel'shtama," 147). We should recall, however, that these words were written in 1929, i.e., they do not reflect either the most immediately "personal" mature poetry of Mandelstam in the early 1930s, nor deeply personal motifs of his early, then-unpublished Symbolist poetry.

30 Building upon the observations of Zhitenev ("'Oskorblennyi i oskorbitel'"), we can say that, through the communicative strategies of "scandal" in "Fourth Prose," Mandelstam achieves indeed that exit beyond the bounds of "civilized" literature that Blok espouses in his essays, and with it an authenticity in the mode of Trilling (*Sincerity and Authenticity*, 11) and Blok himself.

31 Cf. also the non-linearity of Mandelstam and his "street," in which the passer-by divines only a twistedness ("What street is this?" [Eto kakaia ulitsa?, 1935). While not contesting, and in fact affirming, the organicity of Mandelstam's world view (tselostnost' miroponimaniia), I fail to see any indication that Mandelstam himself saw in this "the measure of the authenticity of the poet," as Nadezhda Mandelstam asserts (*Vospominaniia*, 243). She is, however, unquestionably correct when she connects authenticity with the concepts of *pravota* (rightness) and *priamizna* (straightness, directness) and further connects the poet's authenticity to his or her role as "unsettler of sense" (kolebatel' smysla) ("Conversation about Dante") and rejection of pre-existing "proposition-formulas" [suzhdeniia-formuly].

32 Blok, *Stikhotvoreniia*, 1:343. This evidence is an important corollary to Blok's more Romantic statements: "In light of such a consciousness, artists' works themselves become secondary, since to present they are all imperfect creations, fragments of concepts far grander" (Blok, *SS8*, 6:109).

When Blok asks, "why are we moved by Andreev's *Life of Man*, which is distant from art [...]?" (*SS8*, 5:278), he both demonstrates that he recognizes artistry and its absence and makes a compromise unimaginable for Mandelstam.

33 Blok, *SS8*, 5:278, author's emphasis.

34 *SS4*, 2:422. The vision of a complex non-linear poetic directness in the poems in memory of Bely can likely be seen as a literary atonement for these perhaps over-emphatic earlier accusations of falsehood.

35 On music in the world view of Blok and the relation of music to the preceding ideal of the World Soul, see Maksimov, *Poeziia i proza*, 361–4; on the perceptible silence of Blok during the last years of his life, see Pyman, *Life*, 2:365–6.

36 Mandel'shtam, *PSSP*, 2:54.

37 Ivanov, *Po zvezdam*, 250.

38 On receptivity in Ivanov's aesthetics, see Wachtel, *Russian Symbolism*, 64–5.

39 Mandel'shtam, *SS4*, 2:406–7. For Mandelstam, the individual creative will is subverted to a greater power, which, not contained within the poet, also cannot be subsumed in the reflected solipsism of the Romantic poet's "Muse." Cf. his "Not mine, not yours, but theirs" ("Ne u menia, ne u tebia, u nikh," 1936).

40 Mandel'shtam, *SS4*, 2:226.

41 Mandel'shtam, *SS4*, 2:423

42 Mandel'shtam, *SS4*, 2:342; Mandel'shtam, *SP*, 526; See also chapter 1, pp. 27–9, comparing the Acmeists' attitudes with that shift in contemporary taste which elevated as sincerity Derzhavin's overcoming of the strained voice of the Lomonosovian ode.

43 Mandel'shtam, *SP*, 526.

44 Annenskii, *Knigi otrazhenii*, 348; Eikhenbaum, "Sud'ba Bloka," 44–6. On Mandelstam's attitude towards theatricality and tragedy, see also Goldberg, *Mandelstam, Blok*, 185–90.

45 The poem is made up rhythmically of a single trochaic tetrameter couplet, broken by "hyperstanzaic" rhyme into dense tercets of monosyllable-iamb-iambic dimeter (MMFMMF).

46 Compare Blok's "Your face is more pale than it was" (Tvoe litso blednei, chem bylo, 1906); his description of Briusov as "severe magus of my land" (Surovyi mag moei zemli; *Stikhotvoreniia*, 2: 333); Bely's cycle "To Briusov" ("Briusovu") from *The Urn* (*Urna*, 1909).

47 See Goldberg, *Mandelstam, Blok*, chapters 6 and 10.

48 Blok, *Stikhotvoreniia*, 3:119.

49 Melodrama, however, is not necessarily a negative attribute. The lyric persona of Mandelstam's poem is simultaneously drawn and repelled

by the decadence and morbid theatricality of Venetian life, which has a "bright meaning." Blok himself, in "On Theatre" ("O teatre," 1908), saw a positive historical role for melodrama in the development of modern theatre.

50 Zara Mints conducted a detailed analysis of "laughter" in Blok. She studies the chronological development and subtle gradations of his irony but doesn't in the end deny its sceptical "destructive" character and its seriousness. Fittingly, even in the early and late periods in which Blok positively evaluates affirming, constructive laughter, this positive laughter is described, rather than embodied in his texts. Mints, "K genezisu," 428–9, 438–9, 440–1.

51 Blok, *PSS20*, 8:87.

52 One might also argue that Blok's irony in the second book, especially in its less-caustic varieties, re-establishes a lost or wavering authenticity through expressing a "more exigent" (Trilling) relation of the disenchanted poet to self and world.

53 Chukovskii, *Sobranie sochinenii*, 8:141.

54 "Ach Gott! im Scherz und unbewusst / Sprach ich was ich gefühlet" (Oh God! in jest and unbenowst [to myself] / I spoke what I felt). Chukovsky and Heine are cited in relation to Blok in Masing-Delic, "Mask Motif," 90, 93.

55 Gumilev, *SS4*, 4:173.

56 Cf. Cavanagh, *Modernist Creation*, 220–8; Zeeman, *Later Poetry*, 115–18. For examples of "tragic" irony connected to expression of doubt in the poet's own directness/verity, see Ronen, *Approach*, 196.

57 Lekmanov, *Kniga ob akmeizme*, 86, 78. See also Averintsev, "Sud'ba i vest'," 16–17; Timenchik, "Zametki ob akmeizme II" (1977), 184; Karabchievskii, *Voskresenie Maiakovskogo*, 197. Clare Cavanagh explores the related phenomenon of Mandelstam's "powerful insignificance" in the poetry of the 1930s (*Modernist Creation*).

58 Cf. "When Psyche-life descends to the shades" ("Kogda Psikheia-zhizn' spuskaetsia k teniam," 1920).

59 Ronen, *Approach*, 337; Zhukovskii, *PSSP*, 2:348.

60 Zhukovskii, *PSSP*, 2:348.

61 The original reads: "Le temps! Le temps! Issoire, / Il coule et tourne et gire et vire et filtre en ta passoire, / Emmi l'absent décor lilial d'Ambert … / Issoire! Qui a dit que tu faisais des camemberts?" (Romains, *Les Copains*, 30). A majority of the key words linking the translation to "Sisters," and even the image of the flower in the whirlpool, are Mandelstam's, as is, of course, the laying bare of the "pissoir" hiding in Romains's "passoire."

62 *PSS*, 149, 375, emphasis mine.

63 Mandelstam's readings in 1920, in a uniformly inspired lilt and with transfigured, illuminated facial features (Nadezhda Pavlovich, "Vospominaniia," 63), presumably included irony-tinged poems and lines – also for Mandelstam elevated as poetry and poetic "rightness."

64 Eliot, "Tradition and the Individual Talent" (1917), in *Sacred Wood*, 53, 54. These comments do not, it should be noted, exclude sincerity in the modernist mode we have been describing.

65 Cf., i.a., Rusinko, "Acmeism, Post-Symbolism"; Fauchereau, "Ou Pound et Eliot." Here, I make no attempt to flesh out individual authors' conceptualization of sincerity as I did with Mandelstam and Blok. Rather I focus on parallels among different authors' statements touching on sincerity (and outside any judgment regarding success or failure in embodying such ideals).

66 Cf. Zukofsky's definition of the rarer and yet more desirable sister phenomenon of "objectification": "This rested totality may be called objectification – the apprehension satisfied completely as to the appearance of the art form as an object" ("Sincerity and Objectification," 274).

67 Costello, *Marianne Moore*, 2.

68 Pound, *Literary Essays*, 9; Zukofsky, "Sincerity and Objectification," 284.

69 Rosenbaum, *Professing Sincerity*, 34.

70 Hulme is referring here primarily to the unavoidable physiological distortions of non-artistic perception.

71 Hulme, "Bergson's Theory of Art," in *Speculations*, 149.

72 Zukofsky, "Sincerity and Objectification," 273.

73 Costello, *Marianne Moore*, 2.

74 Pound, *Literary Essays*, 9. Hulme even uses the word "mould" in this connection, though he is not speaking of the form of the poem per se, but of a new mould of consciousness/vision (*Speculations*, 150).

75 Hulme, *Speculations*, 147–63.

76 Pound, *Literary Essays*, 9.

77 Pound, *Literary Essays*, 11; Mandel'shtam, *SS4*, 2:244. Cf. also Eliot, *Sacred Wood*, 51.

78 Williams, "Ideal Quarrel," 39–40.

79 Gumilev, *Stikhotvoreniia i poemy*, 328; Mandelstam, *SS4*, 2:104.

80 Hulme, *Speculations*, 162–3; Zukofsky, "Sincerity and Objectification," 284.

81 Zukofsky, in his article, adopts the role of ideal contemporary reader of Charles Reznikoff's "sincere" modernist poetry and translator of that sincerity for a broader reading public ("Sincerity and Objectification"). Note that Zukofsky's ideal of "objectification" as a "rested totality" – a modernist incarnation of Symbolist Apollonian form – differs from Mandelstam's emphasis on productive tension, equilibrium of counterforces and, in later criticism, an unreconstructable semantic dynamism (e.g.,

"Conversation about Dante" [1933], *SS4*, 2:364–5, 382–3, 403–4, 411–13). More similar in concept – if not necessarily artistic realization – is the poetry of Moore, in which "flux and tension are set in motion by sincerity, which accepts no single-minded description of reality" (Costello, *Marianne Moore*, 3).

82 Hulme, *Speculations*, 138; Zukofsky, "Sincerity and Objectification," 273, author's emphasis.

83 Pound, *Literary Essays*, 22.

84 Pound, *Literary Essays*, 12.

85 Pound, *Literary Essays*, 25, author's emphasis.

86 Mandelstam, a self-proclaimed "sense-worker" (smyslovik; Nadezhda Mandel'shtam, *Vospominaniia*, 195) who wrote of the poem's "monstrously compacted reality" ("Morning of Acmeism," *SS4*, 2:320) and the word's divergence of semantic vectors ("Conversation about Dante," *SS4*, 2:374) could hardly have disagreed with Pound's assessment that "great literature is simply language charged with meaning to the utmost possible degree" (Pound, *Literary Essays*, 23).

87 Stevens, *Harmonium*, 102–3.

88 On sincerity and commerce, see esp. Rosenbaum, *Professing Sincerity*; Rutten, *Sincerity after Communism*, 19–22, 142–58.

89 Cummings, *is 5*, 75, emphasis mine.

90 Tynianov, "Blok i Geine," 240, author's emphasis.

91 Cited in Gaidenko, "Soblazn," 109. I borrow the phrase "psychic asphyxiation" from Bethea, *Khodasevich*, 252. Blok's death, interpreted in this sense (as it was by Eikhenbaum [see above] and, apparently, by Mandelstam as well) is reminiscent of a *literalized* version of the final lines of Heine's "Nun ist es Zeit," in Apollon Grigor'ev's translation: "[…] должно быть […] что, с смертною язвой в груди, представлял / Я сцену: «Боец умирающий»" ([…] it must be […] that I played the dying fencer with a mortal wound in my breast) (*Stikhotvoreniia. Poemy. Dramy*, 552).

92 Mandel'shtam, *PSS*, 287–8. The words "dlia nas" (for us) refer, it seems, not so much to perception as to the underlying reality.

93 My choice of the term "kenosis" in reference to something *poets* enact, an implicit renunciation of stature ultimately allowing for recuperation of authority, is of course influenced by Harold Bloom's usage in *The Anxiety of Influence*. The context of a struggle between poetic fathers and sons is not, however, relevant to the present study.

94 Blok, *Stikhotvoreniia*, 3:220, author's emphasis.

95 *Giperborei. Ezhemesiachnik stikhov i kritiki* 2 (1912), 3.

96 Blok, *Stikhotvoreniia*, 3:164.

97 In the Synodal translation: "I svet vo t'me svetit, i t'ma ne ob"iala ego" (lit., The light shines in the darkness, and the darkness has not

encompassed it). Note Blok's inverted use of *ob"emlia* (encompassing) in relation to the light in line 10.

98   Blok's "Ty vedaesh' …" (You know …) vacates Gippius's "kazhetsia" (seems), denying him this caution and, in a sense, calling his bluff. Why, after all, challenge Blok's vision over a hunch?

99   Cf. Tiutchev's appeal to this topos in "Our age" ("Nash vek," pub. 1851).

100   Note, however, Valery Briusov's scepticism as to the psychological reality of Blok's "snow pyre": "[…] specifically snowiness, eternal cold constitutes the very essence of A. Blok, and […] the fiery whirlwinds of his feelings rise only from the icy fields of his soul. That is why [the book] *Snow Mask*, enchanting us with the grace of its strophes, does not horrify, and we calmly believe that our poet will rise up unharmed from his 'snowy' pyre for new songs" (*Sredi stikhov*, 236–7). This was a scepticism that Blok himself cherished (*SS8*, 8: 195).

101   *Stikhotvoreniia*, 3:283.

102   Cf. Byron's "Prisoner of Chillon": "Dim with a dull imprisoned ray, / A sunbeam which hath lost its way, / And through the crevice and the cleft / Of the thick wall is fallen and left"; in Zhukovsky's translation: "Луч, ненароком с вышины / Упавший в трещину стены / И заронившийся во мглу" (Byron, *Complete*, 4: ; Zhukovskii, *PSSP*, 4:37). Cf. also Blok's Faina, whose name means "radiant," and who, according to Magomedova, "embodies the features of a fallen Sophia, entrapped in a terrestrial body, captive and suffering," and thus a Gnostic understanding of the light (*Avtobiograficheskii mif*, 79).

103   Blok's struggle for the sincere was never a struggle to transcend the linguistic or poetic medium. It is not language he mistrusts, but the "mask." See note 22 above.

104   Blok's argument, however, in elevating the validity of personal truth and subjective perception against objective truth, implicitly challenges the sectarian *polemics* common among the Symbolists.

105   The second stanza echoes the first, but ends with a tripartite comparison (line 8); two parallel claims structure a stanza three that echoes the first half of each of the first two stanzas; and the final stanza echoes the second half of those stanzas and is itself made up of a bipartite first half and contrastingly drawn-out syntagma in the second.

106   This represents, clearly, a radical reversal in relation to the postulates of Viacheslav Ivanov's "realistic Symbolism." Cf. *Po zvezdam*, 278ff.

107   Cf. Manning: "But the reasons according to which a reader decides to believe or not to believe in an emotion, an observation or a concept expressed in a poem are nearly all reasons of an aesthetic order" (*Rhétorique*, 49); Mandelstam, who quipped about Bely's *Notes of an Eccentric* (*Zapiski chudaka*, 1922): "If a person experiences colossal spiritual catastrophes

three times a day [...] we have the right not to believe him" (*SS4*, 2:423). Mandelstam's comment, in turn, bears comparison with Viazemsky's (second-pole) criticism of Zhukovsky a century earlier: "'There was a time when [Zhukovsky] hit upon the idea of death and would end every poem with his own funeral. [...] but when we see someone waiting for death every day [...] the premonition is bound to grow ludicrous'" (cited in Khitrova, *Lyric Complicity*, 108).

108 See note 139 below.
109 Trilling, *Sincerity and Authenticity*, 158.
110 On the "Octaves," see esp. Pollak, *Mandelstam the Reader*, 49–84.
111 Mandel'shtam, *SP*, 246–7.
112 Andrew Davis's subtle translation of the penultimate word as "present" is a bit too distant for our needs here, but it may be of use to the reader without Russian.
113 The connection is reinforced through Mandelstam's appeals to this image in several contemporaneous poems.
114 Cf. "On the Interlocutor" ("O sobesednike," pub. 1913): "It is not about acoustics one has to worry: they will come themselves. More about distance. It's boring to whisper back and forth with a neighbour. It is infinitely tedious to mine one's own soul (Nadson). But to exchange signals with Mars – of course, not in fantasy – is a task worthy of the lyric poet" (Mandel'shtam, *PSSP*, 2:11–12); Mandelstam's comment that Annensky "knew distance, felt its pathos and cold" (75).
115 "Unaccountable" here is intended in the meanings "Not liable to be called to account" (OED); "not responsible" (Merriam-Webster). An example from the OED engages the second relevant set of connotations of *bezotchetnyi*: "All else was ... unaccountable, *by instinct led*" (R. Pollok, 1827), my emphasis. These are precisely the meanings of *bezotchetnyi* given in D. N. Ushakov's fundamental *Tolkovyi slovar' russkogo iazyka* (1935–40).
116 Cavanagh, *Lyric Poetry and Modern Politics*, 118. This "perishability" of the artwork, palpable in the poet and his widows's very real fears regarding the fate of his work, is brought more directly into "I will say it" through the darker counterpoint of "The sky of the supper fell in love with the wall" ("Nebo vecheri v stenu vliubilos'"), composed the same day. In the latter poem, a "beyond" figured as eternity, a night sky and battering ram ("stenobitnaia tverd'") threatens and gradually compromises Leonardo's decaying mural "lacerated with the light of scars."
117 The word can also refer to objects that expand through a separation of seated compartments.
118 Cf. "On the Nature of the Word" ("O prirode slova," 1922), Mandel'shtam, *PSSP*, 2:75–6; Nikita Struve, *Osip Mandel'shtam*, 158.

119 Cf. Mandelstam's own: "No trudno plyt', a zvezdy vsiudu te zhe" (But
     it's difficult to sail, and the stars the same all over; *PSS*, 152 [1920]). In
     fact, in relation to Dante's *Purgatorio* (and Mandelstam mentions Dante,
     his most beloved poet in the 1930s, directly in another poem begun the
     same day), the commonplace turns out to be false. The stars visible from
     Purgatory include those of the unfamiliar southern sky and fail to include
     some always visible in the north (*Purgatory*, Canto I, ll. 18–30).

120 Arkhiv Mandel'shtama (Princeton University Library), Box 2, Folder 23,
     #104, VII. Accessed online at https://findingaids.princeton.edu/collec-
     tions/C0539/c71 (image #312; last accessed 20 July 2020). For the mis-
     print, see Osip Mandel'shtam, *SS3*, ed. Boris Filippov and Gleb Struve
     (Washington: Inter-Language Literary Associates, 1967), 1:256. (Curiously,
     their 1964 two-volume first edition has the correct word.) Cf. Iurii Frei-
     din on Mandelstam's "'Prosvechivaiushchie slova'" (words which show
     through) in his eponymous article.

121 The story was published in 1930. It is extremely likely, though not certain,
     that Mandelstam explored this edition prior to 1937; he borrowed a copy
     to bring to Samatikha in 1938 (Mandel'shtam, *PSSP*, 3:856–7).

122 "A box of warped glass or travelling cabin was invented […] with its own
     inhabitant inside, it [could be] put on a train […] or steamer, and, in it, its
     resident travelled, never stepping outside. Sometimes expandable [razd-
     vizhnoi], this glass tabernacle was fit for overnight stays" (Khlebnikov,
     SS6, 6/1:232).

123 Mandelstam wrote about Khlebnikov's poetry that it is a "vast all-Rus-
     sian prayer book-image book (trebnik-obraznik), from which for centu-
     ries and centuries only the lazy won't draw" (*SS4*, 2:349).

124 Mikhail Gasparov identified the striking visual allusion to da Vinci,
     strongly supported by the mural's near-explicit evocation in "The sky of
     the supper," written the same day (*Grazhdanskaia lirika*, 28–9, 58–9).

125 In "St. Isaac's under a veil," however, these eternal churches existed as
     granaries specifically outside of time and were contrasted with St. Isaac's
     cathedral in Saint Petersburg, which could be a refuge within the world
     in times of calamity. Cf. also: "They say that the cause of revolution is
     hunger in interplanetary space. It is necessary to scatter grain through the
     ether" (Mandel'shtam, *PSSP*, 2:54).

126 Mandelstam would certainly have seen the *Madonna Litta* of the Hermit-
     age, the uncannily radiant skin of which conveys the play of heaven in a
     different sense.

127 Mandelstam, *PSS*, 262.

128 Cf. Adam Mickiewicz's juxtaposition of purgatory and incarceration in
     Forefathers Eve, Part III (*Dziady, Czesc III*, 1832): "Wiem, co cierpią, jeżeli

czyściec jest niewolą" (I know what they suffer if purgatory is captivity; *Dzieła*, 3:252).

129 Mikhail Gasparov's interest in the semantics of metre – usually well-founded and brilliantly executed – here misleads him. Gasparov assumes, on the basis of metre, time frame of composition, and the image of "purgatory," also found in a poem he considers a key subtext of "Verses on the Unknown Soldier," Mandelstam's major larger form piece of the period, that "I will say it" should be understood in the context of apocalyptic war and revolutionary peace (*Grazhdanskaia lirika*, 28–9, 58–9, 23–4). However, the metrical context may be misleading given the potential inertia of Mandelstam's ongoing work in anapaests. Metre in the "Octaves" is not entirely regular, but amphibrachic trimeter with FMFM rhyme dominates – a form, one might argue, not so distant from this poem's anapaestic trimeter with DMDM rhyme. Gasparov would insist of course that they have different semantic traditions and auras. Cf. *Grazhdanskaia lirika*, 48, where anapaestic trimeter DMDM in Russian poetry is said, in passing, to "unambiguously associate with the poetics of [Nikolai] Nekrasov and [be] perceived as doleful, plaintive, heartrending" (though this can hardly be said of the poem at hand) and *Metr i smysl*, 120–51, which examines various threads in the usage of amphibrachic trimeter FMFM, none of which, however, are relevant to the "Octaves." In any case, the thematics of Mandelstam's poem (the "inner excess of space" [prostranstva vnutrennii izbytok; *SP*, 199] and artistic creation) beg a philosophical and metapoetic reading in consonance with his "Octaves."

130 Gershtein, *Memuary*, 12.

131 Nadezhda Mandelstam memorized the entire corpus of the poet's verse of the 1930s and spread copies among trusted friends in order to preserve Mandelstam's poetry for posterity. See Clarence Brown (who smuggled Mandelstam's archive to the West in his luggage), *Mandelstam*, 1–2.

132 Blok, *SS8*, 7:371; full text restored per Mandel'shtam, *Sochineniia*, 1:488.

133 Pavlovich mentions that Mandelstam's "Venetian life" reminded Blok of his own Venetian impressions ("Vospominaniia," 63).

134 For the comment to Gershtein, see Blok, *Stikhotvoreniia*, 3:358.

135 Blok, *Stikhotvoreniia*, 3:30.

136 This occluding revelation is wholly in concert with the mythopoetic Symbolists' understanding of the nature of masks. See Masing-Delic, "The Mask Motif," 81.

137 See Goldberg, *Mandelstam, Blok*, 64–71.

138 On Blok and cliché, see Tynianov, "Blok i Geine," 245–6.

139 Mandelstam's unflinching rejection of *personal* tragedy as worthy ethos is marked with particular clarity at this very time in the powerful image of

the poet's shared fate, "s gur'boi i gurtom" (with the crowd, as a flock [of sheep]), in "Verses on the Unknown Soldier" (*PSS*, 275).

140 This excludes of course neither active, successive ethical searchings in poets of the first type, nor, conversely, problematic ethical framings in the poetry of the latter.

5 Poetic Sincerity in the Totalitarian and Post-Totalitarian Context

1 For an overview of the literature on mid-century Soviet subjectivity, see Pinsky, "Origins," 458–64.

2 These repeated assessments not only condemned, but also excused failings based on political context and biographical and class evidence. See, for instance, Halfin, *Terror*, 220–30; Fitzpatrick, *Tear off*, 14–21, 91–152.

3 Rutten, "No Truer Truth," 494.

4 See Pogosian, *Vostorg*.

5 See Rutten, "Sovetskaia ritorika," 181–2.

6 "Regarding the Arguments about Political Poetry" ("K sporam o politicheskoi poezii"), *Literaturnyi kritik* 5 (1937): 62–102. For the reaction, see articles in *Literaturnaia gazeta* for 30 October, 15 and 20 November 1937. On this incident and related discourse in this period, see Clark and Tihanov, "Soviet Literary Theory," 119–20; Clark's more extensive comparison of the ideas of Berggolts and Usievich in "'Wait for Me.'" On Usievich, see also Timenchik, *Anna Akhmatova*, 323–4.

7 *Literaturnaia gazeta*, 16 April 1953. On the reaction, see Lapushin, "Lyric poetry." On Berggolts see also Gluck, "'I Want to Be,'" 81–3.

8 *Novyi mir* 12 (1953): 218–45 (219). On the societal resonance and responses of readers (positive) and functionaries (negative), see Kozlov, *Readers*, 44–87.

9 Berggolts and Usievich use the term "iskrennost'" (sincerity) only occasionally (Berggol'ts, *SS3*, 2:371, 373, cf. also in a follow-up article, "besstrashneishaia ispoved'" [the most fearless confession, 385]; Usievich: "sincere, passionate feeling," "K sporam," 81). Gluck notes the universalizing aspect of Berggolts approach to sincerity (and its parallel in Evgeny Evtushenko), "'I Want to Be,'" 82, 84.

10 The key distinction here from the "Personal Universal," which Forbes describes in relation to Wordsworth and Adrienne Rich (*Sincerity's Shadow*, 14ff.) is that, for Wordsworth, the universal which is to be accessed purportedly engages feelings common to all humanity, while the Soviet version presupposes a belief that experience is grounded in class and social constructs and thus attempts to access truths common to members of a given society. A similar phenomenon is described in relation to epistemology by Pinsky ("Origins," 461).

11 Berggol'ts, *SS3*, 2:368.
12 Berggol'ts, *SS3*, 2:372. One does not sense that Berggolts strongly distorted her views for the sake of publication, though it was necessary, of course, to calculate the format in which they were expressed. Only the phrase "Our poetry is party poetry, aggressive, active and consciously serving the cause of the building of communism" (371) rings as a distinct concession.
13 Pomerantsev, "Ob iskrennosti," 228, my emphasis.
14 Usievich, "K sporam," 69, author's emphasis. The more ideological Usievich also gives clear voice to the "orthodoxy" approach to sincerity: "Therefore, the poem fulfils its primary purpose, it gives a politically correct response to a topical event, expresses the correct relationship to it" (72).
15 Pomerantsev, "Ob iskrennosti," 219–20, 228; Usievich, "K sporam," 71, 73, 81; on varnishing, also Berggol'ts, *SS3*, 2:370–1.
16 Pomerantsev, "Ob iskrennosti," 221–8.
17 Pomerantsev, "Ob iskrennosti," 227, 240–1.
18 Pomerantsev, "Ob iskrennosti," 223, 227.
19 Pomerantsev, "Ob iskrennosti," 225.
20 Pomerantsev, "Ob iskrennosti," 226, 227.
21 Pomerantsev, "Ob iskrennosti," 226.
22 Pomerantsev, "Ob iskrennosti," 227.
23 Pomerantsev, "Ob iskrennosti," 226.
24 While the necessity of individual personality is less clear in Pomerantsev's prose-oriented text than in that of Berggolts, compare, for instance, the words of his satirized "producer of standard [fare]": "I crudely cropped myself in my books"; his call for books that are "serious and [intimately] warm" (ser'eznye i teplye); the "own world of notions" (sobstvennyi mir predstavlenii) that characterizes the poets of the nineteenth century and the "dactyloscopic lines" that differentiate post-revolutionary poets, unnoted by Soviet critics ("Ob iskrennosti," 232, 233, 236–7). Cf. Gluck, "'I Want to Be,'" 32–4.
25 On continuities of the early Thaw with Stalinist culture, particularly in regard to "sincerity," the "authentic" (Clark translates "podlinnyi" as the "genuine" and "true"), and "lyricism," see Clark, "'Wait for Me'"; specifically on the blurred boundary between ideas expressed shortly before and after the death of Stalin and on speeches made by Berggolts and Margarita Aliger in January of 1953, see "'Wait for Me'," 86–7, 93. For a detailed tracing of the evolution through the Stalinist and post-Stalinist periods of the thinking of Alexander Tvardovsky, poet and publisher of *New World* (*Novyi mir*), see Pinsky, "Origins."
26 Kozlov notes that letters to the periodicals involved in the debate around Pomerantsev's article came from students, junior-rank military

servicemen, and educated professionals, i.e., the Soviet intelligentsia, not the working class (*Readers*, 59).

27 Foucault, *Fearless Speech*, esp. 11–20. Cf. also Markovits, *Politics*, 65ff.

28 Foucault, *Fearless Speech*, 14.

29 Markovits, *Politics*, 68.

30 Foucault, *Fearless*, 12. One might, however, speak of the potential for a "monarchic" *parrhesia* in the interactions between Stalin and his cohort or the writers and citizens that entered into direct communication with him. Cf. Foucault, *Fearless*, 22–3.

31 Naiman, "Slova," 172.

32 There existed a limited array of options for positioning oneself within the political/pragmatic spectrum of potential modes of being for the writer: collaboration, "fellow-travelling," public or private resistance, writing for the desk drawer, escape into translation, scholarship, or children's literature, emigration, silence, suicide. Cf. Zholkovsky, "Obverse," 68.

33 One need only look, for instance, at the literary works of Berggolts herself in this period to find examples of more traditionally confessional poetry.

34 Cf. esp. "Ob iskrennosti," 220–1.

35 See Zholkovsky, "Strakh, tiazhest'," 554–7; and "Mezhdu."

36 Akhmatova's stance vis-à-vis Soviet power melds political resistance and stylistic affinities. Anatoly Naiman described *Requiem* as what Soviet poetry should have been according to its own prescriptions, had it (and they) been sincere: "Requiem is *Soviet poetry* executed in that *ideal* form which all its declarations describe. […] From real Soviet poetry, stilted, pseudo-heroic, false, godless, this poetry is differentiated by the *absence* of these qualities, their refutation through sincerity […]" (Naiman, "Slova," 177, author's emphasis). Zholkovsky goes much further in arguing Akhmatova's "obverse" relation to the style of Soviet empire ("Obverse," "Strakh, tiazhest'").

37 Urban, "'I upalo.'" Cf. also Zaitsev in Akhmatova, *Requiem*, 299; Sam Driver, cited in Basker, "Dislocation," 5.

38 See Clark and Tihanov, "Soviet Literary Theory," 119.

39 Cf. Naiman, who notes Akhmatova's annoyance at a too-politicized reading touting the "blood and tears" of *Requiem*: "[Akhmatova] did not separate these poems, their artistic devices and principles from the rest [of her poetry]," "Slova," 176.

40 One text reacts to events of 1935.

41 See especially Amert, *In a Shattered Mirror*, 30–59; Harrington, *Poetry*, 89–100, who takes the term paratext from Gérard Genette.

42 Cf. Eikhenbaum on the intimations of plot which do not become a concrete *fabula* in Akhmatova's early poetry, "Anna Akhmatova," 144, 140,

146; see also Levin et al., "Russkaia semanticheskaia poetika," 55–7; Toporov, "Ob istorizme."

43 See Levin et al., "Russkaia semanticheskaia poetika," 69–70; Etkind, "Bessmertie"; Basker, "Dislocation," 8, 9, 12, 23; Bird, "Voices of Silence," 336–7; Harrington, *Poetry*, 100–12.

44 Etkind, "Bessmertie," 345.

45 More broadly on the function of subtext in Akhmatova's poetry, see, for instance, Levin et al., "Russkaia semanticheskaia poetika," 70–4; in *Requiem*, esp. Iovanovich; Amert; Etkind; and Basker. For an example of a multilayered complex of autocitation in *Requiem*, see Zholkovskii, "Mezhdu," 130–1.

46 Here and below, *Requiem* is cited from the second edition, Akhmatova, *Rekviem* (1969).

47 See Etkind, "Bessmertie," 348.

48 Iovanovich (who also notes a parallel effect in the following line in regard to Lermontov's "Cossack Lullaby"), "'Chuzhie golosa,'" 170–1; cf. Basker on the similar effect of a possible Blok subtext in poem 3 ("Dislocation," 18). Note also the quite resonant passage Iovanovich cites from Vladimir Solovyov ("'Chuzhie golosa,'" 178n15).

49 Timenchik, "K genezisu." See also Lekmanov, "O dvukhadresnoi." Lekmanov's thesis about dual addressees (private and public) in Akhmatova's poetry presents an interesting parallel to mine about the direct and complicating aspects of Akhmatova's sincerity (which, however, in the ideal, gain potency through their interwovenness, rather than being directed at disparate readers).

50 Etkind, "Bessmertie," 348; Burdina, *Poemy*, 162.

51 Basker, "Dislocation," 17.

52 Sholokhov, *Tikhii don*, 3.

53 Katz, "Unheard Female Voices," 260–3. The connections to the text of the Latin Requiem evinced by Naiman ("Slova," 175–6) seem dubious. Ichin and Iovanovich give more provocative, if at times impressionistic, parallels ("K razboru").

54 Verheul, "Public Themes," 112. Leiderman asserts parallels with the "materinskaia prichet' [*sic*]" (folk genre of ritual keening), "Bremia."

55 See also Basker, who points out a rich array of such eloquent "inconsistencies" ("Dislocation").

56 Etkind, "Bessmertie," 345, 353–4; Crone, "Metabole," 28–30.

57 Basker, "Dislocation," 5.

58 The poem is *marked* 1935, which for Akhmatova's readers, many of whom would have at least a rough sense of her personal history, nods to the simultaneous arrest of then common-law husband Nikolai Punin and her only son, Lev, whose second arrest in 1938 provides the main context for

the cycle. Akhmatova told Gleb Struve that the poem was dedicated to Punin (Akhmatova, *Requiem*, 24), which explains the image of crying children, more evocative of a husband's arrest.

59 Alexander Blok had boldly, and with undeniable charisma, originated a technique of emphatic "inseparability and unfusedness" (nerazdel'nost' i nesliiannost') of lyric subject and historical mask in such cycles as "On Kulikovo Field" and "Venice" ("Venetsiia," 1909). Akhmatova's fellow Acmeist Mandelstam had convincingly followed suit, for instance in his "On a sledge covered in straw" ("Na rozval'niakh ulozhennykh solomoi," 1916). See Goldberg, *Mandelstam, Blok*, 105–9. Akhmatova had developed a diaphanous lyric persona herself, if with less insistence, in her early poems, spoken from the voices of various young women – at least to the extent that we believe her own subjectivity is also implied. Many readers *assumed* that all of these poems were spoken from Akhmatova's personal perspective (Eikhenbaum, "Anna Akhmatova," 146). On Akhmatova and Blok, see especially Zhirmunskii, "Anna Akhmatova i Aleksandr Blok"; Toporov, *Akhmatova i Blok*.

60 Kovalenko, S.A., "Kommentarii," in Akhmatova, *Sobranie Sochinenii*, 3:492; Katz, "Unheard Female Voices," 257.

61 I thank one of the anonymous external readers for this observation. (These caps – *furazhki* – were originally called "furazhnye *shapki*.")

62 For comparison, in the nineteenth century, only 22.6 per cent of Russian trochaic tetrameter lines had four realized stresses (Taranovskii, *Russkie dvuslozhnye*, 79).

63 Cf.: "Вышел месяц из тумана, / Вынул ножик из кармана. / Буду резать, буду бить – / Все равно тебе водить!" (The moon stepped out of the fog, / Pulled a knife from out his pocket. / I will slash, I will hit – / No way you're not it!). The link is noted in Lekmanov, "Nikolai Gumilev," 27.

64 Terseness was a key feature of Akhmatova's poetics from her earliest work (Eikhenbaum, "Anna Akhmatova," 86, 89–92, 102), but here is taken to a particular extreme.

65 Verheul, "Public," 90. Basker refers to the "agonized immediacy of the final line," "Dislocation," 16.

66 Harrington, *Poetry*, 102, citing Brian McHale.

67 In constituting this fact, I do not intend to contest the widespread recognition in the scholarship that the claim in the second epilogue to have woven, in *Requiem*, a "broad shroud" of the women's own, "meagre [...] overheard words," is wildly misleading.

68 Cf. the strong amphibrachic inertia of *No eto ne ia – eto kto-to drugoi stradaet*.

69 Harrington, *Poetry*, 103.

70 Cf. Mandelstam's "Akhmatova" (1914), the opening lines of which are highly evocative of the portrait of Rachel by William Etty (1841–5). Mandelstam would supplant this image with that of a "real" tragic persona, Cassandra, in a poem of 1917. As Crone has noted, "In the missing stanza from 'Reshka' concerning *Rekviem*," Akhmatova unites herself and the women in a "bezmolvn[yi] khor[]" (silent/wordless chorus) of "Obezumevshie Gekuby" (Hecubas gone mad) and "Kassandry iz Chukhlomy" (Cassandras from Chukhloma, i.e., the provinces), "Antimetabole," 28.

71 Cf. the end to her "Voronezh" (1936).

72 Etkind notes that the poem "collides reality and theatre" and sees it as a moment when "an actress who has played alien roles now speaks for herself" ("Bessmertie," 348), which makes some sense in light of the fourth poem where Akhmatova will speak from a biographically demarcated voice. However, the progression thus implied is in conflict with the poem's structure, which moves not from theatricality to immediate self-expression but in reverse.

73 Anrep, "O chernom kol'tse," in Akhmatova, *Desiatye gody*, 208.

74 Timenchik, *Anna Akhmatova*, 621–2n208.

75 Cf. Eikhenbaum, "Anna Akhmatova," 113–14; Blok, letter to Akhmatova of 14 March 1916 (*SS6*, 6:263–4).

76 Basker, "Dislocation," 11.

77 Cf. "About what those executed or interred in camps experienced I don't dare to speak. It can't be named in words" (Chukovskaia, *Zapiski*, 2:137). This silence is thus a partial corrective to the impression of aplomb attaching to the seemingly all-encompassing "Mogu" (I can [describe this]) of "In Place of a Foreword."

78 The transition between these two sections of the poem is the image of the swaying *topol'* (poplar, m.) whose fall is not heard ("I ni zvuka" [And not a sound]). The subtext, which ratifies the morbid sense, is Mandelstam's "I vershina kolobrodit, / Obrechennaia na srub" (And the [tree's] crown sways in a circle, / Doomed to be cut down) from "A chill tickles the crown of my head" ("Kholodok shchekochet temia," 1922).

79 Urban, "'I upalo.'"

80 Seventeen months is the exact time between Lev Gumilev's arrest and Akhmatova's prison visit (referenced also in "In Place of a Foreword"). Whether or not Akhmatova intended to inscribe in this way a record of biographical fact, *semnadtsat' mesiatsev* is also overdetermined in a phonic sense: *Semn*adatsat' *mesiatsev* [...] *syn* i uzhas *moi*.

81 The biographical reference is surely to Akhmatova's letter to Stalin, which quite nearly had a circuitous positive impact on Lev's case (see Golovnikova and Tarkhova, "'I vse-taki'," 122–9).

82 Lev was quick-witted, incautious, obstinate, and a loyal son of his executed father, i.e., his character could well have filled his mother with a mix of appreciation and horror. "You will have a hard time keeping him safe, there is a fatality in him [v nem est' gibel'nost']," Mandelstam told Akhmatova in 1933 (L.V. Iakovleva-Shaporina, "Iz dnevnika," cited in Akhmatova, *Requiem*, 101).

83 Duality (constructedness and immediacy) is also inscribed in the poem's structure – a crypto-sonnet, the form partially masked by an unexpected metre, alternating iambic tetrameter and trimeter. Cf., on the form, Etkind, "Bessmertie," 351. The transition from poem 5 to poem 6 of the cycle reinforces the sense of modulation through the latter's rewriting, largely in a tender, intimate voice, many of the same tropes embodied with vocal intensity in the fifth.

84 On the melodramatic and melodrama in Akhmatova's early lyrics, see Eikhenbaum, "Poeziia Akhmatovoi," 110–14; Harrington, "Melodrama."

85 Akhmatova, *SS6*, 4:158.

86 Akhmatova, *SS6*, 4:41.

87 Etkind, "Bessmertie," 354.

88 *Mishnayoth*, 4:263, emphasis mine.

89 Naiman, "Slova," 177.

90 Etkind asserts that subjective lyricism, which had grown throughout the cycle, is suddenly cut off in the tenth poem, with its third-person depiction of the crucifixion ("Bessmertie," 358). However, the last two lines again sound sharply personal. It is the speaker who turns our attention to the place no one can bear to look and to the fact of their averted gaze. It is "she" who *feels* the absence of those gazes.

91 Akhmatova, letter to Anatoly Naiman, spring 1964 (Naiman, *Rasskazy*, 161).

92 "The hidden existential leitmotif of Akhmatova's personality, in all of its different manifestations (early and late, poetic and day-to-day, public and private, calculated and spontaneous) was the consistently 'feminine' strategy of gaining power through weakness" ("K pereosmysleniiu"; trans.: https://dornsife.usc.edu/alexander-zholkovsky/rethi-sh/). Cf. "Strakh, tiazhest'"; "Obverse of Stalinism," 64.

93 See Zholkovskii, "Obverse of Stalinism," "Strakh, tiazhest'," and "Mezhdu." See also Panova, "'I vsiudu kleveta …'" and "'Kleopatra'"; Harrington, "'Golden-Mouthed Anna.'"

94 Zholkovskii, "Mezhdu," 115. The core of Zholkovsky's argument in this article is a wide-ranging demonstration of how Akhmatova "naturalizes" for the reader her deviations from the Horatian monument topos (which establishes expectations regarding the poet's relation to monuments) through grafting this topos onto the traditional topoi, in elegy and poetic

"testaments," of the poet's requests regarding his or her grave. In the latter contexts, a concrete enumeration of preferences is the norm.

95 Zholkovskii, "Mezhdu," 116.

96 Amert, *In a Shattered Mirror*, 59. On the co-opting and distortion of Pushkin's legacy in 1936–7, see Sandler, *Commemorating Pushkin*, 107–16.

97 Zholkovsky notes that other poets of prominence either expressed distaste for or at least demurred from fantasizing about the idea of their own physical monument; that Akhmatova selects for her monument real estate on the Neva implicitly elevating her; and that she more than exaggerates the contribution of the words of her "nevol'nye podrugi" (involuntary friends [f.]) to the texture of *Requiem* ("Mezhdu," 116–20, 131–2). On the latter, see also Basker, "Dislocation," 13. Basker's observations on the "implicit association of Akhmatova's "poetic 'veil' (*Pokrov*)" with the "Protecting Veil with which the Mother of God is entreated" only exacerbate the potential charge of hubris ("Dislocation," 22).

98 Zholkovskii, "Mezhdu," 115–16.

99 Bird, "Voices of Silence," 339–40. The passage significantly downplays Niobe's hubris, though it can be inferred.

100 Bird notes a kinship with Antigone, but outside of Antigone's affiliation with Niobe ("Voices of Silence," 337–9).

101 Ovid, *Metamorphoses* 1:298–309. Bird asserts that "the theme of petrification" through the mother's grief runs through *Requiem* (Bird, "Voices of Silence," 340ff.). In fact, this image is held at the edge of consciousness, tantalizingly unrealized: "kamennoe *slovo*" (stone *word*); the *modal* "Nado, chtob dusha okamenela" (the soul needs to become stone); the displacement of petrification imagery to son and disciple in poems 9 and 10; the *bronze* of Akhmatova's monument.

102 Sophocles [*Works*], 2:81; Ovid, *Metamorphoses* 1:298–309.

103 Iarkho, "Amfion," in Meletinskii, *Mifologicheskii slovar'*, 43. Ovid mentions the "magic of my husband's lyre" (*Metamorphoses*, 301).

104 Cf. his programmatic "Iambic Pentameter Verses" ("Piatistopnye iamby") in the original 1913 version.

105 Zholkovskii, "Strakh, tiazhest'," 535–8, 543–4.

106 Ovid, *Metamorphoses*, 1:301.

107 Ovid, *Metamorphoses*, 1:300. Cf. "mŏvĕo, mōvi, mōtum, ēre, privodit' v dvizhenie, dvigat', I) =dvigat' tuda i siuda, *potriakhivat'* […]" (Petruchenko, *Latinsko-russkii slovar'*, 399, my emphasis). Akhmatova studied Latin when she was enrolled in law courses as a young woman (*Sochineniia*, 1:18).

108 Compare Zholkovsky on Akhmatova's curating of her physical image ("Obverse," 49).

109 Ovid, *Metamorphoses*, 1:301, 303, 307, 309. Cf. Akhmatova's "I called doom upon those dear" ("Ia gibel' naklikala milym," 1921).
110 Ovid, *Metamorphoses*, 1:307.
111 For the text of the letter, see Golovnikova and Tarkhova, "'I vse-taki,'" 123.
112 Zholkovsky sees the "i" (here, even) in lines 27–28 ("Затем, что и в смерти блаженной боюсь / Забыть громыхание черных марусь" [Because even in blessed death I fear / To forget the rumbling of the black Marias (i.e., the automobiles in which the arrested were taken away)]), in combination with "boius'" (I fear), as illogical – "since oblivion is awaited only and specifically in death" ("Mezhdu," 129, see also 130). However, the entire phrase takes on a more natural, if still hyperbolic, aspect if we replace "boius'" (I fear to) with "ne vol'na/ne smeiu" (I am not free to/I dare not). The poetic "shift" is thus to be detected in the choice of the word "boius'." And this "boius'" provides a bridge to the immediate context of the poem's composition in March 1940. This was the second anniversary of Lev's arrest (hence, "pominal'nyi chas" [hour of remembrance]), but also the time of Akhmatova's unexpected, seemingly triumphant public revival. Her poems had been published in prominent journals, two books were in process at different publishing houses, Akhmatova had been inducted with pomp in January into the Writers Union, given a one-time financial relief payment and a higher pension (later cancelled) as well as encouragement regarding an apartment. Later that year, she would be nominated for the Stalin Prize in literature (see Koroleva, "Anna Akhmatova," 663–9; Golovnikova and Tarkhova, "'I vse-taki,'" 126). This sudden success could only drive an ersatz, or perhaps real, schizophrenia since, while her son continued to languish in the camps, Akhmatova certainly knew that her own continued ascent among the ranks of official Soviet writers represented his best, and possibly only, chance for a reprieve (cf. Golovnikova and Tarkhova, "'I vse-taki,'" 126–9). All would unravel as the print run of *From Six Books* (*Iz shesti knig*) was arrested (Koroleva, "Anna Akhmatova," 669–70; Golovnikova and Tarkhova, "'I vse-taki,'" 129; Chukovskaia, *Zapiski*, 191]). Returning to March 1940, however, it seems possible that personal success, accompanied by a major upsurge in writing (cf. Toporov, "Ob istorizme," 195–6), could spur a *fear* that long-desired acceptance and status as a prominent Soviet author, along with the hope this brings for a reversal of Lev's sentence, and perhaps, time itself, might blunt – even in this life – the memory of the horrors she has experienced.
113 Nor does it cancel the simultaneous requisition for pity which the image of Niobe represents. Cf. Panova's astute analysis of Akhmatova's

interpolation of the word "zhalost'" (pity) and its pragmatic function in her "Cleopatra" ("'Kleopatra,'" 234–5).

114 Trilling, *Sincerity and Authenticity*, 3.

115 Nedobrovo, "Anna Akhmatova," 63.

116 Bogomolov, "Zametki," 328–9.

117 Toporov, "Ob istorizme," 194.

118 See note 39 above.

119 While I realize that I am in danger of trivializing here the philosophical problem raised by Theodor Adorno, I would underscore that there are also non-trivial psychological and *artistic* dimensions to this "how."

120 Azadovskii, "Ob odnom," 9–11. The poem's sophisticated and resourceful off-rhymes anticipate Brodsky's later work.

121 The version in the posthumous 1988 volume *Priznanie* (5–6) is marked "1946, 1981." It includes two stanzas missing in a publication by Evgeny Yevtushenko dated "1946–1984" (*Ogonek* 32 [5–12 Aug. 1989], 27). In both cases, the new version removed some of the bolder language and images, wreaked havoc with the poem's composition and the meanings it conveyed, and tiptoed around the question of Stalin's leadership. Arguing in support of Levin's substantial initiative in revising (notwithstanding Yevtushenko's assertion that the new version was generated at his request) is Liudmila Sergeeva's testimony (see below) as well as a subtle shift in time frame within the poem to encompass a more recent perspective.

122 Brodsky wrote this version down for Azadovsky, who committed it to memory, but this copy was lost. See "Ob odnom," 12, 19. Sergeeva, who transcribed cassette tapes dictated by Levin late in life for publication in the posthumous volume *Priznanie* (1988), writes that many versions of the poem exist as "folklore" and calls the version in *Priznanie* the fruit of years of rewriting and editing and "Kostia's will and testament" (Sergeeva, "'Nas khoronila,'" 133–4). Answering Azadovsky, she "risks the presumption" that some lines he cites may have been "finished" for the author (Sergeeva, "'Nas khoronila,'" 133). Indeed, lines may have been tweaked or distorted on the way to Brodsky or even by Brodsky or, possibly, to a lesser extent, in Azadovsky's memory. (It is worth pointing out, for the Western reader, that the culture of memorization and recitation of poetry – including, often, quite long texts – is far more developed in Russia than here.) In any case, it seems hard to believe that the poem's unique sensibility and tonality as well as its precisely ordered composition (on which below) are not Levin's own. (Additionally, Kornilov's memoirs present evidence supporting the authenticity of key stanzas of Azadovsky's version [Kornilov, "Odin iz nikh"; Azadovsky, "Ob odnom," 13].)

123 Azadovsky, "Ob odnom," 15.

124 Azadovsky, "Ob odnom," 15–16.
125 According to Benedikt Sarnov, the main political accusation against the poem when it was read at the Literary Institute was "contrasting the front to the home front" ("'Protivopostavlenie fronta tylu'"), *Perestan'te*, 314. Kornilov asserts that Levin was kicked out of the Literary Institute on account of a different poem, the anti-judeophobic "We unforgivably age" (My neprostitel'no stareem) ("Odin").
126 Kornilov, "Odin iz nikh."
127 Shklovskii, *O teorii*, 13ff.
128 Cf. the "fairer" later version: "Vsemi obrublennymi nervami / V natruzhennykh rukakh medsluzhby" (With all [our] lopped off nerves / In the hard-worked hands of the medical ward).
129 Cf. Dal's first and third definitions of *muzhestvo*: "stoikost' v bede, bor'ba, dukhovnaia krepost', doblest' […] terpen'e i postoianstvo" (firmness in calamity, struggle, spiritual strength, the highest spiritual courage […] patience [in suffering] and constancy).
130 One is also struck by the past perfective "otlichil" (distinguished). If they are "unnamed," how has Stalin "distinguished" his "favourites?" In his mind? If so, what sort of "defence" would this present?
131 Cf. Azadovskii: "The Stalin theme was embodied in Soviet poetry not only in openly false sounding glorifications […] What can one do? The bewitching, hypnotic effect of Stalin on our countrymen […] is a historical fact […]" ("Ob odnom," 16).
132 See pp. 4–5 and 7–9.
133 This quality of vision is perhaps reinforced subliminally through the poem's freshness and crispness of language.

6 Case Studies in Turn-of-the-Millennium Sincerity

 1 "Тем не менее, я думаю, что, правда, Борис – тот поэт, который на рубеже веков как-то заговорил по-настоящему, в полную силу и с какой-то очень убедительной, иногда очень болезненной интонацией." Grigorii Danskoi, concert at "Gnezdo glukharia," 9 Sept. 2008. http://rutube.ru/tracks/1026041.html (0:40). Last accessed 2009. Internet trace at: https://vk.com/club4100792.
 2 See, for instance, Purin, "Pamiati," 235–6; Kazarin, "Poet," 708ff.; Lekmanov and Sverdlov, "Opredelenie"; Kushner, "Stikhi, perepiska," 86ff.
 3 Cf. Purin, "Pamiati," 236. Ryzhy's sophistication and virtuosity are well demonstrated in Zholkovskii, "Ob infinitivnykh."
 4 See Trilling, *Sincerity and Authenticity*, on this brand of authenticity, linked to a penetration beneath the 'crust' of civilization.
 5 Ryzhii, *Stikhi*, 313.

6 Ar'ev writes of Ryzhy's "shy, chaste, 'estranged [ostranennaia]' and still, yes, utmost confessionality" ("Blok, Ivanov, Ryzhii," 207); Zholkovskii calls him "a poet of traditional romantic-ironic bent" ("Ob infinitivnykh," 196).

7 Ryzhii, *Stikhi*, 332.

8 Ryzhii, *Opravdanie*, 492.

9 "Nadiktui mne stikhi o liubvi" ("Dictate me lines about love," 1999); Ryzhii, *Stikhi*, 295. Cf. the logic of the finale of Ryzhy's poem about "going native" while working on a geological expedition in the rough-and-tumble mining town of Kytlym, "I worked on a dredge in the outpost Kytlym" ("Ia rabotal na drage v poselke Kytlym," 1999): one can't completely deceive people, and therefore their love is evidence that my play at being one of them was not all masquerade. Ryzhy felt that, in his next selection of poems in *Znamia*, "Bugle boy" ("Gornist," 2000), he overcame to some extent the gravitational pull of his hero's milieu, a positive development (letter to Kushner, 14 July 2000, Ryzhii, *Opravdanie*, 512).

10 Letter of 11 November 1997 (Ryzhii, *Opravdanie*, 510).

11 Ryzhii, *Stikhi*, 358.

12 Cf. Trilling on the ancient origins of the term "authentic": "*Authentes*: not only a master and a doer, but also a perpetrator, a murderer, even a self-murderer, a suicide" (Trilling, *Sincerity and Authenticity*, 131).

13 Phaedra's suicide outweighs the audibly sincere reactions of Hippolytus, causing Theseus to reject his son's honesty as a ruse and to wish aloud that each person had two distinct and distinguishable *voices*, one for truth, one for everything else.

14 Dozmorov, "Kytlym," 66, 64.

15 Cf. Rosenbaum on the critic's quandary following the death of Sylvia Plath (*Professing*, 150). On the most basic plane, the simple, but potent constative which opens "Lady Lazarus" ("I have done it again"; *Ariel*, 14) simultaneously speaks, from beyond the grave, to the biographical, fomenting a misreading which makes this "it" the act of suicide and also instantiates the poem's key trope in which the poem *is* the resurrected subject, object of the reader's titillated and voyeuristic probing.

16 On this possibility of non-execution that circumscribes the imperative as "performative," see Zholkovskii, "Gamlet," 259.

17 This phenomenon is raised to the level of high, humorous, and tragic poetry in Venedikt Erofeev's novel *Moscow to the End of the Line* (*Moskva-Petushki*, 1969).

18 Cf. Gandlevskii: "Diadia v shliape, ispachkannoi golubem, / Otrazilsia […]" ("An older guy in hat soiled by a pigeon, / Was reflected […]"; *Prazdnik*, 79).

19 The topos has deep and diffuse roots. Cf. Odysseus's scar (Book 19) or those scars and birthmarks which in folk narratives allow for the recognition of lost children.

20 The roots of this motif can perhaps be sought in Dostoevksy's Ivan Karamazov, who wishes to return "his ticket" to God in the face of innocents' suffering (*PSS30*, 14: 223) and in Tsvetaeva's lyric, "O tears in the eyes" ("O slezy na glazakh," 1939), which concretizes Karamazov's anti-theodicy at the beginning of the Second World War, as it would turn out, two years before her actual suicide.

21 Performatives need not contain the word that vocalizes their illocutionary force (Austin, *How to Do Things*, 59, 61–2), and it is easy enough, here, to supply the implied "klianus'" (I swear).

22 Cf. Searle and Vanderwenken, *Foundations*, 193.

23 Culler, in discussing performatives in the lyric, suggests restricting this notion to "the poem's success in bringing about what it describes, as when Sappho's superb lyric craftsmanship creates the effect of making Aphrodite respond" (*Theory*, 131). However, this substitutes a collateral element (the illusion of embodiment in the poem of the imagined results of the illocutionary act) for what is essential – the performance of the illocutionary act itself.

24 Sofer, "How to Do Things."

25 Cf. Tsvetaeva's (uncustomarily direct) 1941 comment to Akhmatova, "How could you write [the 1915 "Prayer," where the lyric voice asks God to] 'take child and beloved and mysterious lyric gift …' [in exchange for an end to the war]? Don't you know that in poetry everything comes to be?" (Il'ina, "Anna Akhmatova," 588.)

26 On word and Word in Russian culture, see esp. Seifrid, *Word Made Self*.

27 Cf. Pasternak: "О, знал бы я, что так бывает, / Когда пускался на дебют, / Что строчки с кровью – убивают, / Нахлынут горлом и убьют! // От шуток с этой подоплекой / Я б отказался наотрез. […] Но старость – это Рим, который / Взамен турусов и колес / Не читки требует с актера, / А полной гибели всерьез. // Когда строку диктует чувство, / Оно на сцену шлет раба, / И тут кончается искусство, / И дышат почва и судьба." (O, if only I knew it could be thus / When I set out on my debut, / That lines drip blood – they kill; / They'll gush the throat and kill! // I would have flat out rejected / Jests with such a lining. […] But old age is a Rome which / In place of machines and wheels [=empty talk (from idiom), S.G.] / Demands not declamation from the actor, / But rather death for real. // When a line is dictated by feeling, / It sends a slave onto the stage, / And here is where art ends, / And respire soil and fate; *Stikhotvoreniia*, 1:366–7.) For a recent scholarly examination, see Clare Cavanagh, who, in *Lyric Poetry*

and Modern Politics, 109–19, considers this cultural paradigm against the foil of the metaphoricity of Western pronouncements on "the death of the book" in Derrida's *Of Grammatology* and the death of the author in Barthes and Foucault.

28 See John Milton, "The Verse," in *Paradise Lost*, 4; Robert Lowell, interview with Frederick Seidel, cited in Forbes, *Sincerity's Shadow*, 211n10. Forbes, however, cautions against applying this paradigm to Lowell's shift to less formalized verse (63).

29 See Lotman, speaking broadly about the verbal masterpiece, in *Struktura khudozhestvennogo teksta*, 41. Cf. Khagi, *Silence*, 17, on Schopenhauer's pessimistic view of the subliminal suasion of rhythm and rhyme. Cf. also Culler: "one effect [of rhyme] is to lend authority to lyric pronouncements" (*Theory*, 183); "musicality authenticates poetry" (Robert von Hallberg, cited in Culler, *Theory*, 134, 350).

The effect of the "right word in the right place" appears to be comparable, if less broadly appreciated, in masterful free verse. Dmitrii Manin has conducted a quite rigorous experiment demonstrating that, even after the impact of metrical constraints is calculated out, it is significantly harder to guess a missing word in traditional poetry than in prose but also significantly easier to predict the correct word from between the actual one and an incorrect guess produced by another study participant. Free verse is similar in this latter effect, implying an analogous overall structural cohesiveness perceptible to the reader (Manin, "Chopped-up Prose").

30 Line 4, more than any other, flouts this tendency, with an inversion, a participle, and an idiom that can be literary as well as oral.

31 Cf. Forbes on readers' initial reactions to "Lady Lazarus" (*Sincerity's Shadow*, 75).

32 Villon, *Complete Works/Uevres complettes*, 2. I thank Tatiana Kozhanova for her assistance with the French idioms. The translation is mine, but I have borrowed from the translator, Anthony Bonner, for the final line.

33 The reader will recall that Blok's living incarnation of the Eternal Feminine was *Liubov* Dmitrievna Mendeleeva.

34 Ryzhii, "Rubashka v kletochku," 53, author's emphasis.

35 One posthumous edition, published by U-Faktoriia in Ekaterinburg, goes so far as to "correct" this (Ryzhii, *Opravdanie*, 255.) The editor of *Stikhi*, Komarov, who worked with the poet's manuscripts, gives "12," strongly confirming that this is the correct representation of Ryzhy's text.

36 Cf. "Shestnadtsat' strochek. Ty dovol'na?" (Sixteen lines. You satisfied?), Ryzhii, *Stikhi*, 331.

37 Ryzhy enjoys playing on the colour of different variants of names. One poem hangs on the contrast between the "Lysov Evgeny" of the body, who, though a close acquaintance, figures as statistic and government

official and the "Zhenya" of the final line: "vprochem, chto zhe, zhili-byli … / V zatylok Zheniu zastrelili" (Anyway, what to say, once there lived … / They shot Zhenya in the back of the head; Ryzhii, "From Sverdlovsk," 151–2). Cf. also "– Prochti mne Odena, Boriska …" (– Read me Auden, Boriska); "nadmennyi i veselyi B.B.R." (cocky and fun-loving B.B.R.); "'[…] eto p'ianyi Ryzhii Bor'ka, / pervyi v gorode poet'" (that's drunken Borka Ryzhy / The city's top poet; Ryzhii, *Stikhi*, 299, 161, 131).

38 Particularly the brand of paper – KYM Lux, a European brand of Finnish provenance, which became popular in post-Soviet office supply stores – is telling in this regard. Ryzhy is of course not the first poet to concentrate attention on his typewriter, plume, etc.

39 These moves reinforce the more subtle kenotic gesture of writing himself out of the poem proper and resonate with poet's self-diminishing roles in "Give the beggar." On Ryzhy's deflation of values, his manner of break-ing off a nascent "credo" in an "inarticulate interjection," see Zholkovskii, "Ob infinitivnykh," 198; Ar'ev, "Blok, Ivanov, Ryzhii," 207.

40 On this "movement," or cluster of movements and trends, originating somewhat earlier in Russia than the West, see, for instance, Epshtein, *Postmodern*, 274ff.; Rutten, "Strategic Sentiments" and *Sincerity after Communism*; Magill, *Sincerity*, 194–213; Jameson, "What we talk about"; Kelly, "Dialectics." See also Davydov, who places the new sincerity in the context of naïve poetry and primitivism (cogently differentiated) in "Ot primitiva." On Prigov's highly specific "new sincerity" project, see i.a., Prigov and Epshtein, "Popytka"; Lipovetskii, "Prakticheskaia"; Iam-pol'skii, *Prigov*, 157–84; Rutten, *Sincerity after Communism*, 93–105.

41 See Ryzhii, "Otvety na voprosy ankety k 60-letiiu Iosifa Brodskogo," in Ryzhii, *Opravdanie*, 489; Zholkovskii, "Ob infinitivnykh," 196, 202; Lek-manov and Sverdlov, "Opredelenie."

42 Timur Kibirov, "Russian song" ("Russkaia pesnia," 1989); "To Igor Pomer-antsev. Summer Musings on the Fate of Belles Lettres" ("Igoriu Pomerant-sevu. Letnie razmyshleniia o sud'bakh iziashnoi slovensnosti," 1992).

43 For sophisticated readers' direct and indirect avowals of Kibirov's sin-cerity, see, for instance, Nemzer and Lipovetsky ("[…] he invariably achieves an effect of striking sincerity" ["Kibirov"]); Zorin (poetry "free of internal falsity [fal'shi]"; Kibirov "speaks through [the ready-made styles of the epoch] with his own voice" ["'Al'manakh,'" 262, 263]); Aizenberg: "the perception of Soviet realia here is not distanced-ludic [otstranen-no-igrovoe], like in Prigov, but very immediate […] And he truly *speaks* in verse, verse is his direct speech" (Aizenberg et al., "Zadushevnaia," 8, author's emphasis). Cf. also "naturalness," "lyrical-pathos-laden, inti-mate irony" [liriko-paticheskaia, zadushevnaia ironichnost'] (Bavil'skii, "Zazemlenie," 20).

44 See above, esp. introduction, pp. 7–9; chapter 2, part 1, pp. 50–1.
45 See Kibirov, *Kto kuda*, 172 ("Literaturnaia sektsiia" ["Literature Working Group"]); Gandlevskii, "Sochineniia," 6; Nemzer, "Timur," 6–7; Kulle, "'Ia ne veshchaiu,'" 16.
46 Historically, Sentimentalism was focused not on individuality, but on the development and expression of a set of normative, desirable emotions – *chuvstva dobrye* [meritorious/good feelings], as Kibirov has called them, using a Pushkinian turn of phrase (Nikolaeva and Nikolaev [interview], "'Uchat vse.'"). Despite a memoiristic streak and the relation of frequent, often uncomfortable or mildly indecorous, personal stories (as when, in *Latrines* ["Sortiry," 1991] he humorously narrates bolting from a sexual encounter due to the runs) as well as the prevalence, especially in the period from 1986 to 1998, of poetry pointedly addressed to family and cohort, these offerings to the reader mask, it seems, a notable personal reticence. (Try putting "biografiia Kibirova" into a search engine!) On his roots and early life, see Bogdanova, "Kibirov"; Sid and Brazhkina, "Skonchalsia terskii kazak" (interview with Kibirov's father). On the importance of "sincerity" within the "lyro-epic" metatext constructed of Kibirov's circle-based friendly epistles, see Glushakova ("Sbornik").
47 This sense of "humanity" diverges from traditional "humanism," encompassing a deep empathy for the human condition, its weaknesses and indignities.
48 Lekmanov, "Kibirov glazami."
49 See Toddes, "'Entropii vopreki,'" esp. 70; Aizenberg, Prigov, and Rubinshtein each touch upon this in various ways in "Zadushevnaia beseda," 8, 9. See also Zorin, "'Al'manakh,'" 261; Nemzer and Lipovetsky, "Kibirov"; Leibov, Lekmanov, and Stupakova, *Gospod'!*, 59–60.
50 "Poetry! – big fucking deal!" ("Poeziia! – big fucking deal!," 1998) is a programmatic, almost expository statement regarding the triangulation – through poetry's worn language ("Parcha, protertaia do dyr" [Brocade worn right through to holes]), tricks ("Poskol'ku glaz ustroen tak: / bez fokusov – kromeshnyi mrak" [Since the eye's constructed so: / with no parlour tricks it's black as coal]), tinsel and lies – which is the necessary and seemingly sole path, if any exists, to approach truth: "Gliadi zh, patsan, *skvoz'* etu vetosh', / Skvoz' etu mishuru i lozh' [...]" (So, fella, look out *through* these tatters / through this tinsel and these lies [...]; *Ulitsa Ostrovitianova*, 10, emphasis mine).
    In the 2000s, however, Kibirov seems at times tired with poetic expression per se, adopting as one of his postures the prosaic directness and bile of the culture warrior.
51 As concerns immediacy, cf. the eloquent "List of Consulted Works" at the end of *Intimate lyric* ("Intimnaia lirika," 1998), which include Zalizniak's

grammatical dictionary, very inclusive, alphabetized by last letter and thus a source for rhymes. On graphomania and the contrast with Soviet "poeticity," see Zorin, "'Al'manakh,'" 260; Kuznetsova, "Pravila," 222; Kulle, "'Ia ne veshchaiu,'" 12.

52 See Gandlevskii, "Sochineniia," 5.

53 Epshtein, *Postmodern*, 275. Cf. Toddes, "'Entropii vopreki,'" 69–70; Khagi, *Silence*, 184–9; Freidin, "Transfiguration of Kitsch." Kibirov in his interviews takes care to distinguish his art from Conceptualism (the movement with which he is most closely associated), while acknowledging the broader sense in which his poetry is unavoidably "postmodern." See Basinskii, "Kara-Baras"; "Kulle, "'Ia ne veshchaiu,'" 16; Kuznetsova, "Pravila," 214. See also Aizenberg et al., "Zadushevnaia beseda."

54 Epshtein, *Postmodern*, 282, 280. Cf. Levin, "O vliianii," 219.

55 In this mode, Kibirov has written some of his masterpieces like "Twenty Sonnets to Sasha Zapoeva" ("Dvadtsat' sonetov k Sashe Zapoevoi," 1995) and "To Igor Pomerantsev" (1992).

56 Cf. Kelly, "Dialectic."

57 Nikolaeva and Nikolaev, "Timur Kibirov. 'Uchat vse,'" emphasis mine.

58 "[…] [I am] a person with a playful streak [po skladu – chelovek dostatochno igrovoi]. But this, for me, is not enough" (ibid.). Cf. Kulle, "'Ia ne veshchiau,'" 14.

59 Kibirov: "My reader is not dumber than me and […] possesses approximately the same [readerly? S.G.] experience" (Kulle, "'Ia ne veshchiau,'" 12). One may recall such "straight" lyrical texts as "Epitaphs to my grandmother's yard" ("Eptitafii babushkinomu dvoru"; written mostly by 1985 according to the interview with Kuznetsova ["Pravila," 223]). However, this cycle is broken up, dispersed among other texts in different and more ironic modalities when published as part of *Sentimentalities*. Other, more recent texts also flirt with an unreconstructed, traditional lyricism, but Kibirov tends to undercut this in some way. Compare poems 14 (1995) and 16 (1994) of the "To the Memory of Derzhavin" cycle in *Periphrasis* (*Parafrazis*, 1997), the first a traditional elegiac (in the broad sense) lyric written from a perspective entirely during the sex act, the second a meditation on time, death, and immortality entitled "Romance" ("Romans"; a genre of performative art song).

60 Kibirov, *Kara-baras*, 48–60.

61 The closest analogy in Anglo-American children's poetry to Chukovsky's linguistic brilliance and capacity to engage is Dr. Seuss.

62 On relativism and Christianity in Kibirov with reference to his use of children's poetry, including in "Kara-baras!," see also Rutts, "Detskaia literatura," 228–34, 236–7.

63 For the text see Shapir, *Universum versus*, 2:253–6. On *stiob*, the late-Soviet
    mode of irony most relevant to this poem, see esp. Matizen, "Stiob"; Yur-
    chak, *Everything*, 249–54.

64 Cf. B.M. Gasparov on the poem's "infectious liveliness, dynamism and
    mirth" ("Moi do dyr," 318).

65 See "The tenant's latest song" "(Ocherednaia pesn' kvartiranta," in *Ka-
    ra-baras*); "Walking from gallery to gallery" ("Perekhodia iz zala v zal,"
    in *Na poliah "A Shropshire Lad"*, 2007). "Prodigal son" ("Bludnyi syn," in
    Greko- i rimsko-kafolicheskie pesenki i poteshki, 2009).

66 Kevin Platt's tying of Kibirov's ethos in the poem to traditional Russian
    values in opposition to destructive Western influences ("The Post-
    Soviet," [18]) seems misguided. The positive heroes in the collection
    (other than Pushkin, invoked ironically) are G.K. Chesterton, Hans
    Christian Anderson, and a cowardly knight.

67 Kibirov, *Kto kuda*, 285.

68 "Kara-baras!" is cited from Kibirov, *Kara-baras*, 48–56.

69 Cf. "Tam pod dukhovnost'iu pudovoi / zatikh navek vertliavyi Pushkin"
    (There beneath a ponderous spirituality / has gone forever silent squir-
    rely Pushkin; *Kto kuda*, 140).

70 A general subtle shift occurs towards the beginning of the poem from
    interpretation of Chukovsky's words within the idiosyncratic conceptual
    framework Kibirov has generated to outright rewriting of the narrative as
    an interpretation of "Kibirov's" cultural situation.

71 Cf. the tavern-like "home" with icons askew in a 1974 song by Vladimir
    Vysotsky: "Почему – во тьме, / Как барак чумной?" (Why in the dark
    / Like a pestilent barracks?" (*Sochineniia*, 1:463); Kibirov's own "Lev Se-
    menych, my v Rossii. / Mrak, bardak da peretak" (Lev Semenych, we're
    in Russia. / Gloom, grand mess and hell with this) from "To L. S. Rubin-
    stein" (*Santimenty*, 169).

72 See note 63 above.

73 Cf. particularly, the caricature of artist and author on pp. 22–3, repro-
    duced in B.M. Gasparov, "Moi do dyr," 310–11. A scan of the full first
    edition is available at imwerden.ru.

74 Platt emphasizes the importance of the *stiob* aesthetic in "Kara-baras!"
    ("The Post-Soviet"). We differ, however, on the bearings of Kibirov's
    irony.

75 An analogously broad, life-affirming vision can be seen in the interpreta-
    tion of Easter in "The aged cadet Shmidt" ("Prestarelyi iunker Shmidt,"
    pub. 1999).

76 The dissonance generated here is more radical than that in the run-up
    to the finale of "To L. S. Rubinstein" ("Leva, nekhrist' bestolkovyi, /
    sporim, vse my ozhivem!" [Lyova, you dunderheaded infidel, / Bet you

we all rise from the dead!]; *Santimenty*, 182), which does not imply the immediacy of personal longing inherent in "chaiu" and which, coming at the end of a more substantial fifty-four-line build-up, does not feel quite so glib.

77   Cf., for instance, the reading at the "literary salon 'Na samoteke'": https://youtu.be/9RUMHFwKDuw (last accessed 3 May 2020). Note how Kibirov also downplays the exclamation points attaching to "S nami Bog!" and "Kara-baras!"

78   The phrase "Kara-baras" itself evokes senselessness. Cf. the concordant *tarabarshchina* (gibberish); Derzhavin: "Provorchu tara-bara" (I'll grumble *tara-bara*; *Sochineniia*, 534); Dal': "karámara" – "tarabarshchina" [*Tolkovyi*, 2:90; with apparent adaptation to Turkic morphology, S.G.]. Cf. also Kibirov: "И видимо, мира основы / держались еще кое-как / на честном бессмысленном слове / и на простодушных соплях" (And apparently, the world's foundations / were holding still by a thread / on the honest, senseless word [cf. Mandelstam, "In Petersburg we will gather anew"] / and on simple-hearted snot" [i.e., sentimentality] ("Onward to deconstructionism! They did it" ["Daesh' dekonstruktsiiu! Dali," 1998; *Kto kuda*, 356]).

79   One of the more concrete biographical references is notably tongue-incheek. After the lyric persona's return, the Logos exclaims: "Nakonets-to ty, synulia, / Logopedu ugodil!" (Finally, sonny, you've satisfied the logopaedist). This seems like a bit of outright silliness, but a similar sentiment could in fact have been directed at the poet in early childhood to judge by his "A June bug flew in from preschool days" ("Maiskii zhuk priletel iz doshkol'nykh vremen," 1984).

80   Cf. Rutts on "Out-of-school Reading" ("Vneklassnoe chtenie"), "Detskaia literatura," 231–4; Kibirov, *Kara-baras*, e.g., 26–31, 36–7. Kibirov uses Mandelstam's phrase ("[tsennostei] nezyblemaia skála") in "To Igor Pomerantsev."

81   Cf. Nemzer, "Timur," 13–15; Sverdlov, "Poslednii epos," 440–1. This first high-profile publication was the 1990 partial printing of "To L. S. Rubinstein" (1987), which drew the ire of *Pravda*. See, i.a., Toddes, "'Entropii vopreki'"; Nemzer, "Timur," 10; Epshtein, *Postmodern*, 275–7.

82   Emphasis mine. "Epilogue" is cited from *Kara-baras*, 57–60.

83   While the relevant lines of Chukovsky's poem are not illustrated in the first edition, at least two well-respected illustrators, Vladimir Suteev and Grigory Eliseev, show the washtub overturned and raised up.

84   Evripid, *Tragedii*, 2:431, 433.

85   Ivanov, *SS*, 1:541.

86   Merezhkovskii, *Voskresshie*, 101.

87 Merezhkovsky's Dionysus is a transfigured satanic figure, Hyrcus Nocturnis, and in both these poems ("See what kind their God is!" ["Ikh-to Gospod' – von kakoi!"] and "Corporate Holiday" ["Korporativnyi prazdnik"]), the cry *evan-evoe* is associated with the Antichrist. Cf. also Kibirov's 1999 poem "We moan on the rivers of Babylon" ("Na rekakh vavilonskikh stonem"), where the beating of timbrels and cymbals is paired with images derived from the witches' sabbath. In the much earlier, "Regarding the Question of Romanticism" ("K voprosu o romantizme," 1989), "evan-evoe" is repeated four times in a text in which Romantic rebellion is equated with nihilism, egoism, atheism, and rejection of all ethical boundaries (Kibirov, *Santimenty*, 269–73). If, however, there, Kibirov separates himself through irony from such phenomena, in "See what kind …" he allows for his complicitness in anti-Christian relativism: "– Evan evoe! – pliashet rod liudskoi. / Byt' mozhet, i my s toboi" ("Evan evoe!" the human race wildly dances. / Perhaps, we two as well; *Greko- i rimsko-kafolicheskie*, 7). Cf. also the pointedly ironic: "S pafosom, s khaosom i s Dionisom / Logosu nado nastavit' roga […]" (One must run around with pathos, chaos and Dionysus, / Cuckolding the Logos […]; Kibirov, *Greko- i rimsko-kafolicheskie*, 36).

88 To best approximate the Russian Synodal translation, I have combined from *Holy Scriptures*, NIV and KJV.

89 For a definition of *iurodstvo* (holy foolishness), see above, p. 106.

90 Cf. Dante (in Lozinsky's translation): "А впереди священного ларя / Смиренный псалмопевец, пляс творящий, / И больше был и меньше был царя" (And before the sacred chest / The humble psalmist, dancing, / Was both more and less than king; Dante, *Novaia*, 266; *Purgatorio*, X, 64–6). Cf. Platt on the poem's tone: "there is a self-infantilizing humility to this poem, which reduces Kibirov to child or clown while allowing Chukovskii, Pushkin, and the Logos to remain, despite the poet's antics, as true authorities" ("The Post-Soviet," [17]).

91 This phrase is also subject to potential slippage, and Kibirov felt a need to conduct an explicit rescuing of the words "God is with us!" (imperial slogan of Byzantium, Germany and Russia) from potentially statist overtones in "Said the madman in his heart, 'There is no God!'" ["Rek bezumets v serdtse svoem: 'Nest' Bog!,'" pub. 2009).

92 For some readers, the poem remains fundamentally ironic. Thus, one of the reviewers of the manuscript asks: "Why is it that so many critics I know and often agree with find sincerity in Kibirov's poetic mix of a beloved children's poem about personal hygiene with an Orthodox liturgy and I don't? A generational difference?" (Perhaps.) "The fact that they know Kibirov as a good friend and a funny person?" (In my opinion,

less likely.) I personally heard the ending of "Kara-Baras!" for quite some time as consummately ironic (but forming, by contrast, a platform for a sincere voice in the following "Epilogue"). My perception shifted in light of Kibirov's following book and in response to more intensive reading of his earlier works.

93 At the same time, the "Epilogue" diverges productively in tone from the pointedly frontal a-lyricism of some of Kibirov's other texts of this period. Cf. *Kara-baras*, 13, 20–1, 36–7, 43–5.

94 This "personal" *ty* differs notably from the universal *vy* at the end of "Kara-baras!"

95 See Dood, *Idea*, 175ff.

96 If we look at the final six lines, we see yet another parameter intensifying the sense of verse organization – line length. The final six lines are rhymed ABc BDc but also form, in counterpoint, the pattern: short-short-long (but also the poem's only actual short line, palpable in relation to the underlying amphibrachic tetrameter) + long-short-short: 2-deficient 2–3 + 4–2–2.

97 Lekmanov, "Kibirov glazami."

98 Curiously, the "destructive" quality of irony implied within this archetypal narrative is at odds with Kibirov's own deployment, here at least, of an irony hardly corrosive.

99 Kibirov, *Greko- i rimsko-kafolicheskie*, 56.

100 Cf. the reaction of (Archpriest) Mikhail Ardov to this boldness ("Timur Kibirov. Greko- i rimsko-kafolicheskie"). The collection unites both new and much older poems.

101 Kulle, "'Ia ne veshchaiu,'" 14.

Conclusion

1 The two poles, as constituted here, would likely not map precisely to experience outside the realm of culture, though it seems they would to an extent – for instance, in terms of attitudes towards the verisimilitude of degree of emotion in a given context (intensity). Focusing on a different quality – immediacy, one might ask: does a given person tend to see someone thoughtful as sincere or someone impulsive? And what then are the prosodic, syntactic, stylistic, phonetic, and vocal elements (as well as facial mimicry, posture, etc.) that potentially help reinforce the impression of thoughtfulness or impulse? These would be akin to our markers. Then, we might ask what higher order discursive and interactional strategies the speaker has engaged (whether consciously or unconsciously) to position him or herself as a sincere person, understood as one thoughtful or impulsive? These might map to pragmatic framings in our theoretical

framework. Of course, these thoughts are only very preliminary, and it would take an extensive and careful enquiry with substantially differing methodology to transfer this study's insights to the realm of real-world communication. In any case, I believe we could be fairly certain that the personal cultural codes of listeners will have a demonstrable impact on reception, especially if we are talking about public speech and casual and work relationships.

2 Lipovetskii notes how Prigov manipulates the rhetorical codes of sincerity attaching to differing subjectivities ("Prakticheskaia," 29). Prigov himself states that "[…] if you precisely divine the discourse, let's say, of the sincerity of some utterance, then for a person [these models of behaviour] […] serve as instant triggers, on-switches for this same sincerity" (Prigov and Epshtein, "Popytka," 69). At the same time, one generator of Prigov's "shimmering aesthetics" are sudden transitions to "markedly incommensurate discursive frames" (Lipovetskii, "Prakticheskaia," 14). In other words, Prigov works with sincerity discourses (codes) – both intuitively ("vpadaiu v nego" [I fall into it]) and on the basis of mental preparation (meditative procedures with his linguistic and discursive axiological apparatus) (Prigov and Epshtein, "Popytka," 69–70) – but his poetic work relates not only to the inhabiting and reproduction of these codes but to a parallel, multidimensional undermining that never permits his poems to read as sincere in a traditional sense projecting a stable subject. Cf. also on the catalogue-like aspect of his lyric subject's "inner life," which has the effect of eviscerating individuality (Lipovetskii, "Prakticheskaia," 39).

3 Cf. Rutten on reception of Prigov, *Sincerity after Communism*, 102–4.

4 The inscription of such a sincerity often involves the supplanting of internally anchored discursive and biographical framings by higher order pragmatic framing, like that which posits the reduction to "vision" and abdication of an openly subjective and self-referential voice as an active authorial stance, a corrective to excesses and tendencies antagonistic to sincerity in expressive-Romantic statement.

At the same time, one can fruitfully juxtapose such an anti-Romantic stance to the hyper-Romantic "A whisper, guarded breathing" ("Shepot, robkoe dykhanie," 1850, 1889?) by Afanasy Fet, similarly bereft of deictic markers and with solely contextual ("lobzan'ia" [kisses]) indication of an intensely perceiving subject.

5 For this definition, see the Introduction, pp. 4–5.

6 See Introduction, note 70. By traditional, I mean lyric which is not avant-garde or post-structuralist, though not at all necessarily Romantic-expressive. Not all of these relationships are, of course, explicitly activated in any given text.

Appendix

1 Dmitriev, *PSS*, 365. On Dmitriev's translation in regard to "Pamiatnik," see Alekseev, *Stikhotvorenie*, 223, citing Wilhelm Busch.

2 While it has never been connected to "Monument," Zhukovsky's epistle has been compared with Pushkin's "Conversation of the Bookseller with the Poet" ("Razgovor knigoprodavtsa s poetom," 1824). See Zhukovskii, *PSSP*, 1:705. It was also noted by Yuri Tynianov as a source for the image of the crown of thorns in Lermontov's "The Poet's Death" ("Smert' poeta," 1837), the most prominent poetic statement on Pushkin's death (Eikhenbaum, *Lermontov*, 108, 164n25). Despite the line "Nor care if courts or crowds applaud or hiss," Byron's well-known "English Bards and Scotch Critics" (1807–8), even more than Pushkin's similarly youthful "To Zhukovsky" ("K Zhukovskomu," 1816), demonstrates an ethos antithetical to that which concludes "Monument" – a pugilistic enthusiasm to take the fight to poetic opponents and critics.

3 Pushkin, *PSS16*, 1:142.

4 Vasily Lvovich Pushkin, "To Prince P. A. Viazemsky" ("K Kniaziu P. A. Viazemskomu," 1814); Viazemsky, "Answer to an Epistle. To Vasily Lvovich Pushkin" ("Otvet na poslanie. Vasil'iu L'vovichu Pushkinu," 1814).

5 Zhukovskii, *PSSP*, 1:346, author's emphasis.

6 The third stanza of Zhukovsky's "Good Advice" ("Dobryi sovet. V al'bom V. A. A[zbukinu]," 1814), which again concerns Memnon, is a likely source for Pushkin's more consonant "Poet" (1827).

7 On the gift, see Kahn, *Pushkin's Lyric Intelligence*, 28n56. On the rich semantics of Pushkin's image, see esp. Proskurin, *Podvizhnyi palimpsest*, 278–88. Since it is mentioned only in Hesiod among more widely read authors, it seems doubtful Pushkin was aware that Memnon was Ethiopian (providing an echo for Pushkin's genealogy and self-presentations).

8 Pushkin, *Rabochie tetradi*, v. 5, PD 838, l. 86.

9 See Lotman, "Tekst i struktura auditorii," 1:164–5; Peschio and Pil'shchikov, "Proliferation," 85–8.

10 In one of the two brief references we have to the poem from 1836, Alexander Turgenev wrote in his diary: "His portrait in imitation of Derzhavin: 'Ves' ia ne umru!' ['Not all of me will die!']." See Alekseev, *Stikhotvorenie*, 19. This terse comment unfortunately does not convey what meaning or qualities Turgenev, one of the Arzamas brethren, imputed to this "portrait."

11 See Alekseev, *Stikhotvorenie*, 180ff. Note the palpable discomfort with Delvig's elevated tone evinced in Pushkin's answer, "To Delvig" ("K De'lvigu," 1815).

12 Pushkin questioned the relevance of the Ozerov episode for contemporary readers (*PSS16*, 12:215), but in evoking it here he is not so much

reliving the faded travails of Ozerov as positioning himself as today's bearer of the "thorny crown" (see Zhukovskii, *PSSM*, 1:347, 705). At the same time, Pushkin unobtrusively demonstrates his mastery over the topoi of a second father figure (besides Derzhavin) – Zhukovsky. On the latter as poetic mentor for the young Pushkin, see Korovin and Makarov, "Etapy razvitiia," 209–24.

13 See *PSS16*, 6:614; Alekseev, *Stikhotvoreniia*, 228.

14 *PSS16*, 13:100, 97; Dobritsyn, *Vechnyi*, 484.

15 Note Pushkin's light tone in the letter: "S drugoi storony den'gi, Onegin, sviataia zapoved' Korana – voobshche moi egoizm" (On the other hand, money, Onegin, the sacred commandment of the Koran – in general, my egotism), *PSS16*, 13:100.

References

Abrams, M.H. *The Mirror and the Lamp: Romantic Theory and the Critical Tradition.* Oxford: Oxford UP, 1971.

Adorno, Theodor W. "The Curves of the Needle." *October* 55 (1990): 49–55.

Aizenberg, Mikhail, Viktor Koval', Dmitrii Aleksandrovich Prigov, and Lev Rubinshtein. "Zadushevnaia beseda, ili Diuzhinu let spustia." *Literaturnoe obozrenie* 1 (1998): 8–9.

Akhmatova, Anna. *Desiatye gody.* Compiled by R D. Timenchik and K.M. Polivanov. M.: MPI, 1989.

– *Rekviem. 1935–1940.* New York: Tovarishchestvo Zarubezhnykh Pisatelei, 1969.

– *Requiem.* Compiled by R.D. Timenchik and K.M. Polivanov. M.: MPI, 1989.

– *Sobranie sochinenii.* 6 vols. M.: Ellis Lak, 1998–2005.

– *Sochineniia.* 2 vols. M.: Pravda, 1990.

Alekseev, M. P. *Stikhotvorenie Pushkina "Ia pamiatnik sebe vozdvig…" Problemy ego izucheniia.* L.: Nauka, 1967.

Alig'eri (Alighieri), Dante. *Novaia zhizn'. Bozhestvennaia komediia.* M.: Khud. lit., 1967.

Allen, Elizabeth Cherish. *A Fallen Idol Is Still a God: Lermontov and the Quandaries of Cultural Transition.* Stanford, CA: Stanford UP, 2007.

Allison, Alexander W., et al. *The Norton Anthology of Poetry.* 3rd ed. New York: W.W. Norton & Company, 1983.

Amert, Susan. "Akhmatova's 'Song of the Motherland': Rereading the Opening Texts of Rekviem." *Slavic Review* 49, no. 3 (1990): 374–89.

– *In a Shattered Mirror: The Later Poetry of Anna Akhmatova.* Stanford, CA: Stanford UP, 1992.

Andrews, Larry R. "D.V. Venevitinov: A Sketch of His Life and Work." *Russian Literary Triquarterly* 8 (1974): 373–84.

Annenkov, P.V. *Materialy dlia biografii Aleksandra Sergeevicha Pushkina.* SPb.: Voennaia tipografiia, 1855.

Annenskii, Innokentii. *Knigi otrazhenii*. M.: Nauka, 1979.

Ardov, Mikhail. "Russkaia poeziia obrela 'religioznuiu pochvu'. Timur Kibirov. Greko- i rimsko-kafolicheskie pesenki i poteshki." *Znamia* 10 (2009): 209–12.

Ar'ev, Andrei. "Blok, Ivanov, Ryzhii: O stikhach Borisa Ryzhego." *Zvezda* 9 (2009): 205–12.

Arkhangel'skii, Aleksandr. "Chas muzhestva." *Literaturnoe obozrenie* 1 (1988): 48–51.

Austin, J.L. *How to Do Things with Words* [1962]. Eastford, CT: Martino Fine Books, 2018.

Averintsev, Sergei. "Sud'ba i vest' Osipa Mandel'shtama." In Osip Mandel'shtam, *Sochineniia*, 1:5–64.

Azadovskii, Konstantin. "Ob odnom stikhotvorenii i ego avtore." *Voprosy Literatury* 4 (2014): 9–20.

Bailey, James. *Three Russian Lyric Folk Song Meters*. Columbus, OH: Slavica, 1993.

Bakhtin, M.M. *Iskusstvo i otvetstvennost'. K filosofii postupka. Avtor i geroi v esteticheskoi deiatel'nosti*. Kiev: Next, 1994.

Ball, Patricia M. "Sincerity: The Rise and Fall of a Critical Term." *Modern Language Review* 59, no. 1 (1964): 1–11.

Barsukov, Nikolai. *Zhizn' i trudy M. P. Pogodina*. 2 vols. SPb.: Tip. M.M. Stasiulevicha, 1888–9.

Barthes, Roland. "The Grain of the Voice." In Sterne, *Sound Studies Reader*, 504–10.

Basinskii, Pavel. "Kara-Baras nashego vremeni." *Rossiiskaia gazeta* 4665 (22 May 2008). https://rg.ru/2008/05/22/kibirov.html. Last accessed 18 June 2020.

Basker, Michael. "Dislocation and Relocation in Akhmatova's *Requiem*." In Rosslyn, *Speech of Unknown Eyes*, 1:5–25.

Batiushkov, K.N. *Opyty v stikhakh i proze*. M.: Nauka, 1978.

Bavil'skii, Dmitrii. "Zazemlenie." *Literaturnoe obozrenie* 1 (1998): 20–3.

Belinskii, V.G. "Stikhotvoreniia M. Lermontova. S.-Peterburg. 1840." In his *M. Iu. Lermontov. Stat'i i retsenzii*, 132–205. L.: OGIZ, 1941.

Benjamin, Walter. "The Work of Art in the Age of Mechanical Reproduction." In his *Illuminations: Essays and Reflections*, 217–51. New York: Schocken Books, 1985.

Berggol'ts, Ol'ga. *Sobranie sochinenii v trekh tomakh*. Vol. 2. L.: Khud. lit., 1989.

Besnier, Niko. "Language and Affect." *Annual Review of Anthropology* 19 (1990): 419–51.

Bethea, David M. *Khodasevich: His Life and Art*. Princeton, NJ: Princeton UP, 1983.

– *Realizing Metaphors: Alexander Pushkin and the Life of the Poet*. Madison: U of Wisconsin P, 1998.

Bird, Robert. "Voices of Silence: Antigone and Niobe in Akhmatova's Requiem." In *Poetics. Self. Place: Essays in Honor of Anna Lisa Crone*, edited by Catherine O'Neil, Nicole Boudreau, and Sarah Krive, 331–49. Bloomington, IN: Slavica, 2007.

– "Envoicing History: On the Narrative Poem in Russian Modernism." *SEEJ* 51.1 (2007): 53–73.

Blok, A.A. *Sobranie sochinenii*. 8 vols. M.: Gos. izd-vo khudozh. lit-ry, 1960–3.

– *Sobranie sochinenii*. 6 vols. M.: Khud. lit., 1982.

– *Stikhotvoreniia*. 3 vols. SPb.: Severo-zapad, 1994.

– *Zapisnye knizhki*. M.: Khud. lit., 1965.

Boileau. *Oeuvres complètes*. Bruges: Éditions Gallimard, 1966.

Bogdanova, O.V. "Kibirov." In *Russkaia literatura XX veka. Prozaiki, poety, dramaturgi. Biobibliograficheskii slovar'*, edited by N.N. Skatov, 179–82. M.: OLMA-Press Invest, 2005.

Bogdanovich, E.V. "Druzheskoe poslanie 1810-kh godov: obraztsy i istochniki." *Vestnik Permskogo universiteta* 2, no. 14 (2011): 131–8.

Bondi, S.M. *O Pushkine: Stat'i i issledovaniia*. M.: Khud. lit., 1978.

Booth, Wayne C. *A Rhetoric of Irony*. Chicago: U of Chicago P, 1974.

Borovkova-Maikova, M. "Mitskevich v pis'makh P. A. Viazemskogo k zhene," *Zven'ia* 3/4 (1934): 215–21.

Boym, Svetlana. *Death in Quotation Marks: Cultural Myths of the Modern Poet*. Cambridge, MA: Harvard UP, 1991.

– "Loving in Bad Taste: Eroticism and Literary Excess in Marina Tsvetaeva's 'The Tale of Sonechka.'" In *Sexuality and the Body in Russian Culture*, edited by Jane T. Costlow, Stephanie Sandler, and Judith Vowles, 156–76. Stanford, CA: Stanford UP, 1993.

Briusov, Valerii. *Sobranie sochinenii*. 7 vols. M.: Khud. lit., 1973.

– *Sredi stikhov, 1894–1924. Manifesty. Stat'i. Retsenzii*. M.: Sov. pis., 1990.

Broitman, S.N. *Poetika russkoi klassicheskoi i neklassicheskoi liriki*. M.: RGGU, 2008.

Brown, Clarence. *Mandelstam*. Cambridge: Cambridge UP, 1973.

Bukhshtab, B.Ia. "Blagodarnost'." *Literaturnoe nasledstvo*, 406–10. Vol. 58. M.: Izd-vo AN SSSR, 1952.

– "Poeziia Mandel'shtama." *Voprosy literatury* 1 (1989): 123–48.

Bulgakova, Oksana. *Golos kak kul'turnyi fenomen*. M.: NLO, 2015.

Burdina, S.V. *Poemy Anny Akhmatovoi: "vechnye obrazy" kul'tury i zhanr*. Perm: Izd-vo Permskogo universiteta, 2002.

Burlaka, D.K., ed. *Mikhail Lermontov: pro et contra. Lichnost' i tvorchestvo Mikhaila Lermontova v otsenke russkikh myslitelei i issledovatelei. Antologiia*. Compiled by V.M. Markovich and G.E. Potapova. SPb.: RKhGI, 2002.

Byron, Lord. *The Complete Poetical Works*. Vol. 4. Oxford: Clarendon Press, 1986.

Calinescu, Matei. *Five Faces of Modernity: Modernism, Avant-Garde, Decadence, Kitsch, Postmodernism.* Durham, NC: Duke UP, 1987.

Calvino, Italo. *Under the Jaguar Sun.* Translated by William Weaver. New York: Harcourt Brace, 1988.

Carlyle, Thomas. *On Heroes, Hero-Worship, & the Heroic in History.* Los Angeles: U of California P, 1993.

Catullus. *The Poems of Catullus: An Annotated Translation.* Translated by Jeannine Diddle Uzzi and Jeffrey Thomson. Cambridge: Cambridge UP, 2015.

Cavanagh, Clare. *Lyric Poetry and Modern Politics: Russia, Poland, and the West.* New Haven, CT: Yale UP, 2009.

– *Osip Mandelstam and the Modernist Creation of Tradition.* Princeton, NJ: Princeton UP, 1995.

– "Rereading the Poet's Ending: Mandelstam, Chaplin and Stalin." *PMLA* 109, no. 1 (1994): 71–86.

Cavarero, Adriana. "Multiple Voices." In Sterne, *Sound Studies Reader,* 520–32.

Chukovskaia, Lidiia. *Zapiski ob Anne Akhmatovoi.* Vol 1. M.: "Soglasie," 1997.

Chukovskii, Kornei. *Sobranie sochinenii.* 15 vols. M.: FTM, 2013.

Clark, Katerina, "'Wait for Me and I Shall Return': The Early Thaw as a Reprise of Late Thirties Culture?" In *The Thaw: Soviet Society and Culture during the 1950s and 1960s,* edited by Denis Kozlov and Eleonory Gilburd, 85–108. Toronto: U of Toronto P, 2013.

Clark, Katerina, and Galin Tihanov. "Soviet Literary Theory in the 1930s: Battles over Genre and the Boundaries of Modernity." In *A History of Russian Literary Theory and Criticism: The Soviet Age and Beyond,* edited by Galin Tihanov and E.A. Dobrenko, 90–108. Pittsburgh: U of Pittsburgh P, 2011.

Costello, Bonnie. *Marianne Moore: Imaginary Possessions.* Cambridge, MA: Harvard UP, 1981.

Crone, Anna Lisa. "Antimetabole in *Requiem*: The Structural Disposition of Themes and Motifs." In Rosslyn, *Speech of Unknown Eyes,* 1:27–41.

– *The Daring of Deržavin: The Moral and Aesthetic Independence of the Poet in Russia.* Bloomington, IN: Slavica, 2001.

– "Deržavin's 'Na Sčastie' as the Undoing of 'Felica': Reflections on Deržavin's Anti-Ode." *Russian Literature* 44 (1998): 17–40.

Culler, Jonathan. *Theory of the Lyric.* Cambridge, MA: Harvard UP, 2015.

Cummings, E.E. *is 5.* New York: Liveright Publishing Corporation, 1926.

Dal', V.I. *Tolkovyi slovar' zhivogo velikorusskogo iazyka.* 2nd ed. [1880]. M.: Rus. Iaz., 1989.

Dante. *See* Alig'eri.

Davie, Donald. "Sincerity and Poetry." *Michigan Quarterly Review* 5, no. 1 (1966): 3–8.

Davydov, Danila. "Ot primitiva k primitivizmu i naoborot (russkaia naivnaia poeziia XX v.)." *Arion* 4 (2000). https://magazines.gorky.media/arion/2000/4/ot-primitiva-k-primitivizmu-i-naoborot.html. Last accessed 26 October 2020.

de Man, Paul. "Anthropomorphism and Trope in the Lyric." In his *The Rhetoric of Romanticism*, 239–62. New York: Columbia UP, 1984.

– "Lyrical Voice in Contemporary Theory: Riffaterre and Jauss." In *Lyric Poetry: Beyond New Criticism*, edited by Chaviva Hošek and Patricia Parker, 55–72. Ithaca, NY: Cornell UP, 1985.

Derzhavin, G.R. "Primechaniia na sochineniia Derzhavina" (*see* Kononko).

– "Rukopis' 90-kh." Arkhiv Derzhavina. Institut Russkoi Literatury i Iskusstva, SPb. F. 96, op. V, no. 4, ll. 78 ob.-84. Manuscript.

– *Sochineniia*. SPb.: Akad. proekt, 2002.

– *Sochineniia. Chast' I* [1795]. Otdel rukopisei RNB. Arkhiv Petra Petrovicha Dubrovskogo. F.XVI.16. Manuscript.

– *Sochineniia Derzhavina. Chast' I*. M.: V Universitetskoi Tipografii u Ridigera i Klaudiia, 1798.

– *Sochineniia, s ob''iasnitel'nymi primiechaniiami Ia. Grota*. Edited by Ia. Grot. 9 vols. 1st ed. SPb.: Izd. Imperatorskoi Akademii Nauk, 1864–83.

– *Stikhotvoreniia*. L.: Sovetskii pisatel', 1957.

– *Zapiski G. R. Derzhavina. 1743–1812*. M.: v Tipografii Aleksandra Semena, 1860.

de Vries, Hent. "Must We (NOT) Mean What We Say? Seriousness and Sincerity in the Works of J. L. Austin and Stanley Cavell." In van Alphen, Bal, and Smith, *Rhetoric of Sincerity*, 90–118.

Dmitriev, Ivan. *Polnoe sobranie stikhotvorenii*. L.: Sov. pis., 1967.

Dmitrieva, N.L. "K istorii sozdaniia stikhotvoreniia A. S. Pushkina 'Est' roza divnaia: ona …'." *Russkaia literatura* 1 (1998): 54–7.

Doak, Connor. "The Emotion as Such: Un/Masking the Poet in Mayakovsky's Work." In *Behind the Masks of Modernism: Global and Transnational Perspectives*, edited by Andrew Reynolds and Bonnie Roos, 135–57. Gainesville: UP of Florida, 2016.

Dobrenko, E., I. Kukulina, M. Lipovetskii, and M. Maiofis. *Nekanonicheskii klassik: Dmitrii Aleksandrovich Prigov (1940–2007). Sbornik statei i materialov*. M.: NLO, 2010.

Dobritsyn, Andrei. *Vechnyi zhanr. Zapadnoevropeiskie istoki russkoi epigrammy XVIII–nachala XIX veka*. Bern: Peter Lang, 2008.

Dolar, Mladen. "The Linguistics of the Voice." In Sterne, *Sound Studies Reader*, 539–54.

Dood, Penelope Reed. *The Idea of the Labyrinth from Classical Antiquity through the Middle Ages*. Ithaca, NY: Cornell UP, 1990.

Dozmorov, Oleg. "Kytlym, Kyshlym i Kytlym: Istoriia sozdaniia neskol'kikh stikhotvorenii Borisa Ryzhego." *Russian Literature* 67, no. 1 (2010): 57–66.

Dostoevskii, F.M. *Polnoe sobranie sochinenii*. 30 vols. L.: Nauka, 1972–90.

Durilyn, S.N. "Na putiakh k realizmu." In *Zhizn' i tvorchestvo M. Iu. Lermontova. Sbornik*, edited by N.L. Brodsky, 163–250. M. Gos. izd-vo khudozh. lit-ry, 1941.

Egorov, B.F. *Apollon Grigor'ev*. M.: Molodaia gvardiia, 2000.

– "Apollon Grigor'ev – poet." In Grigor'ev, *Stikhotvoreniia. Poemy. Dramy*, 5–47.

Eikhenbaum, B.M. "Anna Akhmatova. Opyt analiza." In his *O poezii*, 75–147. L.: Sov. pis., 1969.

– *Lermontov. Opyt istoriko-literaturnoi otsenki*. L.: Gos. izd., 1924.

– "Sud'ba Bloka." In *Ob Aleksandre Bloke*, 39–63. SPb.: Kartonnyi domik, 1921.

Eliash, N. "K voprosu o vliianii Batiushkova na Pushkina." In *Pushkin i ego sovremenniki. Materialy i issledovaniia*, 1–39. Vyp. 19/20. Petrograd: Komis. dlia izd. soch. Pushkina pri Otd. russk. iaz. i slovesnosti Imp. akad. nauk, 1914.

Eliot, T.S. *The Sacred Wood: Essays on Poetry and Criticism*. London: Methuen, 1948.

Epshtein, Mikhail. *Postmodern v Rossii. Literatura i teoriia*. M.: Izd. R. Elinina, 2000.

Esterhammer, Angela. "The Scandal of Sincerity: Wordsworth, Byron, Landon." In Milnes and Sinanan, *Romanticism, Sincerity and Authenticity*, 101–19.

Etkind, E.G. "Bessmertie pamiati. Poema Anny Akhmatovoi 'Rekviem'" In his *Tam, vnutri*, 343–68.

– *Tam, vnutri. O russkoi poezii XX veka. Ocherki*. SPb.: Maksima, 1996.

Evripid. *Tragedii*. 2 vols. M.: Khud. lit., 1969.

Fauchereau, Serge. "Ou Pound et Eliot rencontrent Goumilev, Mandelstam et Akhmatova." *Europe* 601 (1979): 57–73.

Fedorov, A.V. *Lermontov i literatura ego vremeni*. L.: Khud. lit., 1967.

Feinberg, Il'ia. *Chitaia tetradi Pushkina*. M.: Sov. pis., 1985.

Fishzon, Anna. *Fandom, Authenticity, and Opera: Mad Acts and Letter Scenes in Fin-De-Siècle Russia*. Basingstoke: Palgrave Macmillan, 2013.

– "The Operatics of Everyday Life, or, How Authenticity Was Defined in Late Imperial Russia." *Slavic Review* 70, no. 4 (2011): 795–818.

Fitzpatrick, Sheila. *Tear off the Masks!: Identity and Imposture in Twentieth-Century Russia*. Princeton, NJ: Princeton UP, 2005.

Fleishman, Lazar'. "Iz istorii elegii v pushkinskuiu epokhu." *Pushkinskii sbornik* [*Uchen. zapiski Latviiskogo universiteta* 106] (1968): 24–53.

Forbes, Deborah. *Sincerity's Shadow: Self-Consciousness in British Romantic and Mid-Twentieth-Century American Poetry*. Cambridge, MA: Harvard UP, 2004.

Foucault, Michel, and Joseph Pearson. *Fearless Speech*. Los Angeles: Semiotext(e), 2001.

Freidin, Gregory. "Transfiguration of Kitsch – Timur Kibirov's *Sentiments*: A Farewell Elegy for Soviet Civilization." In *Endquote: Sots-Art Literature and Soviet Grand Style*, edited by Marina Balina, Nancy Condee, and Evgeny Dobrenko, 123–45. Evanston, IL: Northwestern UP, 2000.

Freidin, Iu. L. "'Prosvechivaiushchie slova' v stikhotvoreniiakh O. Mandel'shtama.'" In *Smert' i bessmertie poeta: Materialy mezhdunarodnoi nauchnoi konferentsii, posviashchennoi 60-letiiu so dnia gibeli O.E. Mandel'shtama (Moskva, 28-29 dekabria 1998 g.)*, compiled by M. Z. Vorob'eva et al., 236–41. M.: RGGU, 2001.

Frizman, L.G. *Zhizn' liricheskogo zhanra. Russkaia elegiia ot Sumarokova do Nekrasova*. M.: Nauka, 1973.

Gaidenko, P. "Soblazn 'sviatoi ploti' (Sergei Solov'ev i russkii serebrianyi vek)." *Voprosy literatury* 4 (2006): 72–127.

Gandlevskii, Sergei. *Prazdnik*. SPb.: Pushkinskii fond, 1995.

– "Sochineniia Timura Kibirova." In Kibirov. *Santimenty. Vosem' knig*, 5–10.

Gasparov, B.M. "Moi do dyr." *NLO* 1 (1992): 304–19.

– *Poeticheskii iazyk Pushkina kak fakt istorii russkogo literaturnogo iazyka.* [=Wiener Slawistischer Almanach 27]. Vienna, 1992.

– "Pushkin and Romanticism." In *The Pushkin Handbook*, edited by David Bethea, 537–67. Madison: U of Wisconsin P, 2005.

Gasparov, M.L. "Katull, ili Izobretatel' chuvstva," In his *Izbrannye stat'i*, 371–94. M.: NLO, 1995.

– *Metr i smysl. Ob odnom iz mekhanizmov kul'turnoi pamiati*. M.: RGGU, 1999.

– *O. Mandel'shtam: Grazhdanskaia lirika 1937 goda*. M.: RGGU, 1996.

– "'Solominka' Mandel'shtama (poetika chernovika)." In his *Izbrannye stat'i*, 185–97. M.: NLO, 1995.

– *Zapisi i vypiski*. M.: NLO, 2001.

– "'Za to, chto ia ruki tvoi …' – stikhotvorenie s otbroshennym kliuchom." In *Mandel'shtam i antichnost'. Sb. statei*, edited by O.A. Lekmanov, 107–111. M.: Mandel'shtamovskoe obshchestvo, 1995.

Geertz, Clifford. "Deep Play: Notes on the Balinese Cockfight." *Daedalus* 101 (Winter, 1972): 1–38.

Gershenzon, M.O. *Mudrost' Pushkina*. M.: Knigoizd. pisatelei v Moskve, 1919.

Gershtein, Emma. *Memuary*. SPb.: Inapress, 1998.

– "Pushkin i Batiushkov." In his *Stat'i o Pushkine*. 18–30. M.: Gos. Akad. Khud. Nauk, 1926.

Gilenko, Viktor. "Poeziia i sud'ba." *Znamia* 8 (1989): 225–6.

Ginzburg, Lidiia. *O lirike*. L.: Sovetskii pisatel', 1974.

– "Opyt filosofskoi liriki (Venevitinov)." *Poetika* 5 (1929): 72–104.

– "Pushkin i Benediktov." *Vremennik Pushkinskoi komissii* 2 (1936): 148–54.

– "Pushkin i liricheskii geroi russkogo romantizma." In *Pushkin: Issledovaniia i materialy*, 140–53. Vol. 4. M.-L.: Izd. AN SSSR, 1962.

– *Tvorcheskii put' Lermontova*. L.; Gos. izd. "Khud. lit.," 1940.

Gippius, Zinaida. "Literaturnye zametki. *Stikhi o Prekrasnoi Dame*." In Aleksandr Blok, *Sobranie sochinenii*, 12 vols, 1:332–9. 1904. M.: Litera, 1995.

Gluck, Michael. "'I Want to Be Honest': The Rhetoric of Sincerity in Soviet Russian Literature, 1953–1970." PhD diss., Columbia University, 2021. ProQuest.

Glushakova, T.S. "Sbornik Timura Kibirova 'Izbrannye poslaniia' v sotsiokul'turnom kontekste 1980-kh – 1990-kh godov." *Iaroslavskii pedagogicheskii vestnik* 2 (2002): 42–7.

Goethe, Johann Wolfgang. *Sämtliche Werke. Briefe, Tagebücher und Gespräche*. 40 vols. Frankfurt: Deutscher Klassiker Verlag, 1987–2013.

Gofman, M.L. "Neizdannye rukopisi Pushkina." *Okno: Trekhmesiachnik literatury* 3 (1924): 369–72.

Golburt, Luba. *The First Epoch: The Eighteenth Century and the Russian Cultural Imagination*. Madison: U of Wisconsin P, 2014.

Goldberg, Stuart. *Mandelstam, Blok and the Boundaries of Mythopoetic Symbolism*. Columbus: Ohio State UP, 2011.

Golovnikova, O.V., and N.S. Tarkhova. "'I vse-taki ia budu istorikom!'" *Zvezda* 8 (2002): 114–35.

Golstein, Vladimir. *Lermontov's Narratives of Heroism*. Evanston, IL: Northwestern UP, 1998.

Golynko-Vol'fson, Dmitrii. "Chitaia Prigova: Neodnoznachnoe i neochevidnoe." In Dobrenko et al., *Nekanonicheskii klassik*, 145–80.

Gornfel'd, A.G. *Muki slova*. SPb.: Tipo-Litografiia A.E. Vineke, 1906.

Greenleaf, Monika. *Pushkin and Romantic Fashion: Fragment, Elegy, Orient, Irony*. Stanford, CA: Stanford UP, 1994.

Grekhnev, Vsevolod. *Mir pushkinskoi liriki*. Nizhnii Novgorod: Nizhnii Novgorod, 1994.

Grigor'ev, Apollon. *Estetika i kritika*. Edited by A.I. Zhuravleva. M.: Iskusstvo, 1980.

– "Lermontov i ego napravlenie. Krainie grani razvitiia otritsatel'nogo vzgliada. <otryvki>." In Burlaka, *Mikhail Lermontov: pro et contra*, 200–19.

– "O pravde i iskrennosti v iskusstve. Po povodu odnogo esteticheskogo voprosa. Pis'mo k A. S. Kh-vu." In his *Estetika i kritika*. 51–116.

– *Pis'ma*. M.: Nauka, 1999.

– *Russkie narodnye pesni s ikh poeticheskoi i muzykal'noi storony*. Vol. 14 in *Sobranie sochinenii Apollona Grigor'eva*, 14 vols. M.: Tipo-lit. t-va I.N. Kushnerev i Ko., 1915.

– *Stikhotvoreniia. Poemy. Dramy*. SPb.: Akademicheskii proekt, 2001.

– *Vospominaniia*. M.: Nauka, 1988.

Groys, Boris. "Self-Design and Aesthetic Responsibility: Production of Sincerity." *E-flux* 7 (2009). https://www.e-flux.com/journal/07/61386/self-design-and -aesthetic-responsibility/. Last accessed 26 October 2020.

Guilhamet, Leon. *The Sincere Ideal: Studies on Sincerity in Eighteenth-Century English Literature.* Montreal: McGill-Queen's UP, 1974.

Gukovskii, G.A. *Russkaia literatura XVIII veka.* M.: Aspekt Press, 1999.

– *Russkaia poeziia XVIII veka.* L.: Academia, 1927.

Gumilev, Nikolai. *Sobranie sochinenii.* 4 vols. M.: Terra, 1991.

Habermas, Jürgen. *The Theory of Communicative Action.* Vol. 1. *Reason and the Rationalization of Society.* Boston: Beacon Press, 1984.

Halfin, Igal. *Terror in My Soul: Communist Autobiographies on Trial.* Cambridge, MA: Harvard University Press, 2003.

Handwerk, Gary J. *Irony and Ethics in Narrative: From Schlegel to Lacan.* New Haven, CT: Yale UP, 1985.

Harrington, Alexandra. "'Golden-Mouthed Anna of All the Russias': Canon, Canonisation, and Cult." In *Twentieth-Century Russian Poetry: Reinventing the Canon*, edited by Katharine Hodgson, Joanne Shelton, and Alexandra Smith, 63–94. Cambridge: Open Book Publishers, 2017.

– "Melodrama, Feeling and Emotion in the Early Poetry of Anna Akhmatova." *Modern Language Review* 108, no. 1 (2013): 241–73.

– *The Poetry of Anna Akhmatova: Living in Different Mirrors.* New York: Anthem Press, 2006.

Harris, Jane Gary. "The Creative Imagination in Evolution: A Stylistic Analysis of G. R. Derzhavin's Panegyric and Meditative Odes (1774–1794)." PhD diss., Columbia University, 1969.

Hartman, Geoffrey H. "Romanticism and 'Anti-Self-Consciousness.'" In *Romanticism and Consciousness: Essays in Criticism*, edited by Harold Bloom, 46–56. New York: Norton and Company, 1970.

Heaney, Seamus. "Dylan the Durable? On Dylan Thomas." *Salmagundi* 100 (1993): 66–85.

Holdsworth, Carole A. "Some Modernist 'Manías Verbales' and Their Connotations, in the 'Revista Moderna.'" *Hispania* 55, no. 1 (1972): 60–5.

The Holy Scriptures. According to the Masoretic Text. Philadelphia: Jewish Publication Society of America, 1955.

Horace. *Odes and Epodes.* Edited and translated by Niall Rudd. Cambridge, MA: Harvard UP, 2004.

Hulme, T.E. *The Collected Writings of T.E. Hulme.* Oxford: Clarendon Press, 1994.

– *Speculations: Essays on Humanism and the Philosophy of Art.* New York: Routledge and Kegan Paul, 1924.

Hutcheon, Linda. *Irony's Edge: The Theory and Politics of Irony.* London: Routledge, 1994.

Iampol'skii, Mikhail. *Prigov. Ocherki khudozhestvennogo nominalizma.* M.: NLO, 2016.

Ichin, Korneliia, and Milivoe Iovanovich. "K razboru elementov muzykal'noi struktury *Rekviema* A. Akhmatovoi." In their *Elegicheskie raskopki.* Belgrade: Filologicheskii fakul'tet, 2005.

Ihde, Don. *Listening and Voice: Phenomenologies of Sound*. 2nd ed. Albany: SUNY P, 2007.

Il'ina, Nataliia. "Anna Akhmatova. Kakoi ia ee videla." In *Vospominaniia ob Anne Akhmatovoi*, 569–94. M.: Sov. pis., 1991.

Iovanovich, Milivoe. "K razboru 'chuzhykh golosov' v *Rekvieme* Akhmatovoi." *Russian Literature* 15 (1984): 169–82.

Iufereva, E.V. "Eshche raz o probleme 'Iskrennosti' v poezii (K interpretatsii 'Dnevnika liubvi i molitvy' Ap. Grigor'eva." *Ural'skii filologicheskii vestnik* 1 (2014): 91–9.

Ivanov, Viacheslav. *Po zvezdam*. SPb.: Ory, 1909.

– *Sobranie sochinenii*. 4 vols. Brussels: Foyer Oriental Chrétien, 1971–86.

Ivanov, V.V. "K issledovaniiu arkhaizmov v 'Pamiatnike' Pushkina." In his *Izbrannye trudy po semiotike i istorii kul'tury*, 62–7. Vol. 2. M.: Iazyki russkoi kul'tury, 2000.

Jakobson, Roman. "Closing Statement: Linguistics and Poetics." In *Style in Language*, edited by Thomas A. Sebeok, 350–77. New York: John Wiley and Sons, 1960.

– *Language in Literature*. Cambridge, MA: Harvard UP, 1987.

Jameson, A.D. "What we talk about when we talk about the New Sincerity, part 1." Blog post. 4 June 2012. http://htmlgiant.com/haut-or-not/what-we-talk-about-when-we-talk-about-the-new-sincerity/. Last accessed 15 July 2020.

Jauss, Hans Robert. "Literary History as a Challenge to Literary Theory." *New Literary History* 2, no. 1 (1970): 7–37.

Kahn, Andrew. *Pushkin's Lyric Intelligence*. New York: Oxford UP, 2008.

Karabchievskii, Iu.A. *Voskresenie Maiakovskogo*. M.: Russkie slovari, 2000.

Karamzin, N.M. *Sochineniia*. 2 vols. L.: Khud. lit., 1984.

Katz, Boris. "To What Extent Is *Requiem* a Requiem? Unheard Female Voices in Anna Akhmatova's *Requiem*." *Russian Review* 57, no. 2 (1998): 253–63.

Kazarin, Iurii. "Poet Boris Ryzhii. Postizhenie uzhasa krasoty." In Ryzhii, *Opravdanie zhizni*, 521–814.

Keats, John. *The Letters of John Keats*. Vol 1. Cambridge, MA: Harvard UP, 1958.

Kelly, Adam. "Dialectic of Sincerity: Lionel Trilling and David Foster Wallace." *Post45* (post45.research.yale.edu, 10.17.14). https://post45.org/2014/10/dialectic-of-sincerity-lionel-trilling-and-david-foster-wallace/. Accessed 14 May 2020.

Khagi, Sofya. "Silence and the Rest: The Inexpressible from Batiushkov to Tiutchev." *SEEJ* 48.1 (2004): 41–61.

– *Silence and the Rest: Verbal Skepticism in Russian Poetry*. Chicago: Northwestern UP, 2013.

Khitrova, Daria. *Lyric Complicity: Poetry and Readers in the Golden Age of Russian Literature*. Madison: U of Wisconsin P, 2019.

Khlebnikov, Velemir. *Sobranie sochinenii.* 6 vols. M.: IMLI RAN, "Nasledie," 2000–6.

Khodasevich, V.F. *Derzhavin.* Paris: Sovermennyia zapiski, 1931.

– "Fragmenty o Lermontove." In Burlaka, *Mikhail Lermontov: pro et contra,* 434–43.

– *Nekropol': Vospominaniia. Literatura i vlast'. Pis'ma B. A. Sadovskomu.* M.: CC, 1996.

Kibirov, Timur. *Greko- i rimsko-kafolicheskie pesenki i poteshki. 1986–2009.* M.: Vremia, 2009.

– *Kara-baras. 2002–2005.* M.: Vremia, 2006.

– *Santimenty. Vosem' knig.* Belgorod: Risk, 1994.

– *"Kto kuda – a ia v Rossiiu …"* M.: Vremia, 2001.

– *Ulitsa Ostrovitianova.* M.: Proekt OGI, 1999.

Kiukhel'beker, V[il'gel'm]. *Polnoe sobranie stikhotvorenii.* M.: Biblioteki Dekabristov, 1908.

Klein, Ioakhim. "Istina i iskrennost' v panegiricheskoi poezii Derzhavina." *XVIII vek.* Vyp. 27 (2013): 187–219.

– *Pri Ekaterine. Trudy po russkoi literature XVIII veka.* M.: IaSK, 2021.

Kochetkova, I.D. "'Ispoved'' v russkoi literature xviii v." In *Na putiakh k romantizmu. Sbornik nauchnykh trudov.* L.: Nauka, 1984. 71–99.

Kononko, E.N. "Primechaniia na sochineniia Derzhavina (prodolzhenie)." *Voprosy russkoi literatury* 23, no. 1 (1974): 81–93.

Kornilov, Vladimir. "Odin iz nikh, sluchaino vyzhivshii … (Vospominaniia o sorok deviatom gode)." *Lekhaim* (June 2001). https://lechaim.ru/ARHIV /110/kornilov.htm. Accessed 17 May 2018.

Koroleva, N.V. "Anna Akhmatova. Zhizn' poeta." In Akhmatova, *Sobranie sochinenii,* 1:495–672.

Korovin, V.I., and A.A. Makarov. "Etapy razvitiia russkoi poezii: Zhukovskii i Pushkin." In *Zhukovskii i literatura kontsa XVIII–XIX veka,* edited by V.Iu. Troitskii, 206–37. M.: Nauka, 1988.

Kostrov, Ermil. *Sochineniia.* SPb.: Izd. A. Smirdina, 1849.

Kovalenko, S.A. "Kommentarii." In Akhmatova, *Sobranie sochinenii,* 3:463–763.

Kozlov, Denis. *The Readers of Novyi Mir: Coming to Terms with the Stalinist Past.* Cambridge, MA: Harvard UP, 2013.

Kropotkin, Prince [Petr]. *Ideals and Realities in Russian Literature.* 1905. New York: Knopf, 1915.

Kulagin, A.V. "Pushkinskii proteizm kak istoriko-literaturnaia problema." In *Boldinskie chteniia. Sbornik,* edited by N.M. Fortunatov, 5–12. Nizhnii Novgorod: Nizhegorodskii univ., 2000.

Kulakova, L.I. "O spornykh voprosakh v estetike Derzhavina." *XVIII vek.* Vyp. 8 (1969): 25–40.

Kulle, Viktor. "'Ia ne veshchaiu – ia boltaiu …' Beseda s Timurom Kibirovym 21 noiabria 1997 g." *Literaturnoe obozrenie* 1 (1998): 10–16.

Kushner, Aleksandr "Stikhi, perepiska, razgovory s Borisom Ryzhim." *Russian Literature* 67, no. 1 (2010): 85–96.

Kuznetsova, Inga. "Timur Kibirov. Pravila igry." *Voprosy literatury* 4 (1996): 214–25.

Lappo-Danilevskii, K.Iu. "K istorii druzheskoi polemiki vokrug ody Derzhavina 'Izobrazhenie Felitsy' (1789)." *XVIII vek.* Vyp. 26. (2011): 203–19.

Lapushin, Radislav. "'Lyric Poetry … under Suspicion': Vicissitudes of 'Self-Expression' in the 1950s." *Novyi filologicheskii vestnik* 4 (35) (2015): 84–94.

Layton, Susan. "Aleksandr Polezhaev and Remembrance of War in the Caucasus: Constructions of the Soldier as Victim." *Slavic Review* 58, no. 3 (1999): 559–83.

Leibov, Roman. *"Liricheskii fragment" Tiutcheva: Zhanr i kontekst.* Tartu: Tartu Ülikooli Kirjastus, 2000.

Leibov, Roman, Oleg Lekmanov, and Elena Stupakova. *"Gospod'! Prosti Sovetskomu Soiuzu!": poema Timura Kibirova "Skvoz' proshchal'nye slezy": opyt chteniia.* M.: Ob"edinennoe gumanitarnoe izdatel'stvo, 2020.

Leiderman, N.L. "Bremia i velichie skorbi." *Ural* 12 (1994): 207–27.

Leighton, Lauren G. "Denis Davydov's Hussar Style." *SEEJ* 7, no. 4 (1963): 349–60.

Lekmanov, O.A. *Kniga ob akmeizme i drugie raboty.* Tomsk: Vodolei, 2000.

– "Nikolai Gumilev v 'Rekvieme' Anny Akhmatovoi." *Russkaia Rech'* 3 (2000): 26–8.

– "O dvukhadresnoi ustanovke poezii Anny Akhmatovoi. Na primere chetyrekh fragmentov tsikla 'Rekviem.'" *Novyi mir* 6 (2021): 186–95.

– "Timur Kibirov glazami cheloveka moego pokoleniia. Timur Kibirov. Kara-baras. 2002–2005. M., 'Vremia', 2006, 64 str." *Novyi mir* 9 (2006): 174–7.

Lekmanov, Oleg, and Mikhail Sverdlov. "Opredelenie poezii. Variant Borisa Ryzhego." *Russian Literature* 67, no. 1 (2010): 113–21.

Lemon, Alaina. *Between Two Fires: Gypsy Performance and Romani Memory from Pushkin to Postsocialism.* Durham, NC: Duke UP, 2020.

Lermontov, M. Iu. *Polnoe sobranie stikhotvorenii.* 2 vols. L.: Sov. pis., 1989.

– *Sobranie sochinenii.* 4 vols. M.: Khud. lit., 1983–4.

– *Stikhotvoreniia M. Lermontova.* SPb.: V tip. Il'i Glazunova i ko., 1840. Google Books copy.

Lermontovskaia entsiklopediia. M.: Sov. entsiklopediia. 1981.

Levin, Aleksandr. "O vliianii solnechnoi aktivnosti na sovremennuiu russkuiu poeziiu." *Znamia* 10 (1995): 218–20.

Levin, Iu.I., D.M. Segal, R.D. Timenchik, V.N. Toporov, and T.V. Tsiv'ian. "Russkaia semanticheskaia poetika kak potentsial'naia kul'turnaia paradigma." *Russian Literature* 7/8 (1974): 47–82.

Levin, Konstantin. *Priznanie: Stikhi.* M.: Sov. pis., 1988.

Liapina, L.E. "O literaturno-khudozhestvennoi funktsional'nosti peonov ('Bor'ba' A. P. Grigor'eva)." In *Otechestvennoe stikhovedenie: 100-letnie itogi i perspektivy razvitiia*, 108–16. SPb.: Fil. fak. SPbGU, 2010.

Liszt, Franz. *Des bohémiens et de leur musique en Hongrie*. Paris: Librairie Nouvelle, 1859.

Lipovetskii, Mark. *Paralogii, transformatsii (post)modernistskogo diskursa v russkoi kul'ture 1920–2000-kh godov*. M.: NLO, 2008.

– "Prakticheskaia 'monadologiia' Prigova." In Prigov, *Monady. Kak-by-iskrennost'*, 10–45.

Livak, Leonid. *In Search of Russian Modernism*. Baltimore: Johns Hopkins UP, 2018.

Lomonosov, M.V. *Izbrannye proizvedeniia*. L.: Sov. pis., 1986.

Lotman, Iu.M. *Karamzin*. SPb.: Iskusstvo-SPB, 1997.

– *Pushkin. Biografiia pisatelia*. In his *Pushkin*, 23–184. SPb.: Iskusstvo-SPB, 1995.

– *The Structure of the Artistic Text* [=Michigan Slavic Contributions 7]. Ann Arbor: U of Michigan P, 1977.

– *Struktura khudozhestvennogo teksta*. In his *Ob iskusstve*, 14–285. SPb.: Iskusstvo-SPB, 1998.

– "Teatr i teatral'nost' v stroe kul'tury nachala XIX veka." In his *Ob iskusstve*, 617–36. SPb.: Iskusstvo-SPB, 1998.

– "Tekst i struktura auditorii." In his *Izbrannye stat'i*, 1:161–6. 3 vols. Tallinn: Aleksandra, 1992.

Lotman, Iu.M., and Z.G. Mints. "'Chelovek prirody' v russkoi literature XIX veka i 'tsyganskaia tema' u Bloka." In Lotman, *O poetakh i poezii*, 599–652. SPb.: Iskusstvo-SPB, 1996.

MacDowell, James. "The Metamodern, the Quirky and Film Criticism." In *Metamodernism: Historicity, Affect and Depth after Postmodernism*, edited by Robin van den Akker, Alison Gibbons, and Timotheus Vermeulen, 25–40. New York: Rowman and Littlefield, 2017.

Magill, R. Jay. *Sincerity: How a moral ideal born five hundred years ago inspired religious wars, modern art, hipster chic, and the curious notion that we ALL have something to say (no matter how dull)*. New York: Norton, 2012.

Magomedova, D.M. *Avtobiograficheskii mif v tvorchestve A. Bloka*. M.: Martin, 1997.

Maimin, E.A. "Dmitrii Venevitinov i ego nasledie." In Venevitinov, *Stikhotvoreniia. Proza*, 403–59.

Makogonenko, G.P. *Tvorchestvo A. S. Pushkina v 1830-e gody (1830–1833)*. L.: Khud. lit., 1974.

Maksimov, D.E. *Poeziia i proza Al. Bloka*. L.: Sovetskii pisatel', 1975.

– *Poeziia Lermontova*. L.: Nauka, 1964.

Mandel'shtam, Nadezhda. *Vospominaniia*. New York: Izd. im. Chekhova, 1970.

Mandel'shtam, Osip. *Polnoe sobranie sochinenii i pisem*. 3 vols. M.: Progress-Pleiada, 2009–11.

– *Polnoe sobranie stikhotvorenii.* SPb.: Akademicheskii proekt, 1995.
– *Sobranie sochinenii v chetyrekh tomakh.* 1967–81. M.: Terra, 1991.
– *Sochineniia.* 2 vols. M.: Khud. lit., 1990.
– *Stikhotvoreniia. Proza.* M.: AST, 2001.
Manin, Dmitrii Y. "Chopped-up Prose or Liberated Verse? An Experimental Study of Russian Vers Libre." *Modern Philology* 108, no. 4 (2011): 580–96.
Mann, Iu[rii]. *Russkaia filosofskaia estetika.* M.: MALP, 1998.
Manning, Nicholas. *Rhétorique de la sincérité: La poésie moderne en quête d'un langage vrai.* Paris: Honoré Champion, 2013.
Manukyan, Kathleen. "The Poet and His Readers: Three Lyrics and an Unfinished Story of Alexander Pushkin." *Pushkin Review* 12–13 (2009–10): 17–44.
Markovits, Elizabeth. *The Politics of Sincerity: Plato, Frank Speech, and Democratic Judgment.* University Park: Pennsylvania State UP, 2008.
Masing-Delic, Irene. "The Mask Motif in A. Blok's Poetry." *Russian Literature* 5 (1973): 79–101.
Matizen, Viktor. "Steb kak fenomen kul'tury." *Iskusstvo kino* 3 (1993): 59–62.
McGann, Jerome J. *Byron and Romanticism.* Cambridge: Cambridge UP, 2002.
– *Fiery Dust: Byron's Poetic Development.* Chicago: U of Chicago P, 1968.
– "Hero with a Thousand Faces: The Rhetoric of Byronism." *Studies in Romanticism* 31 (1992): 295–313.
Meletinskii, E.M., ed. *Mifologicheskii slovar'.* M.: Sovetskaia entsiklopediia, 1990.
Merezhkovskii, D.S. *Dve tainy russkoi poezii. Nekrasov i Tiutchev.* Petrograd: Izd. I.D. Sytina, 1915.
– *Voskresshie bogi (Leonardo da Vinchi).* M.: Panorama, 1993.
Mickiewicz, Adam. *Dzieła.* 4 vols. Warsaw: Czytelnik, 1993–5.
Milnes, Tim, and Kerry Sinanan, eds. *Romanticism, Sincerity and Authenticity.* New York: Palgrave Macmillan, 2010.
Milton, John. *Paradise Lost.* Indianapolis: Odyssey Press, 1980.
Mints, Z.G. "K genezisu komicheskogo u Bloka (Vl. Solov'ev i A. Blok)." In her *Aleksandr Blok i russkie pisateli*, 389–442. SPb.: Iskusstvo-SPB, 2000.
Mishnayoth. 7 vols. Gateshead: Judaica Press, 1983.
Mur'ianov, M. "Dva etiuda o slovoupotreblenii Pushkina." *Voprosy literatury* 4 (1989): 206–17.
Naidich, E. "'Iz plamia i sveta rozhdennoe slovo …'" In his *Etiudy o Lermontove*, 156–63. SPb.: Khud. lit., 1994.
Naiman, Anatolii. *Rasskazy o Anne Akhmatovoi: iz knigi "Konets pervoi poloviny XX veka."* M.: Khud. lit., 1989.
– "Slova poslednikh uteshenii." *Oktiabr'* 6 (1995): 173–7.
Narodnyia russkiia pesni iz sobraniia P. Iakushkina. SPb.: A.A. Kraevskii, 1865.
Nechaeva, V.S. "K istorii teksta stikhotvoreniia 'Valerik' (spisok iz arkhiva Iu. F. Samarina)." In *M. Iu. Lermontov. Stat'i i materialy*, ed. N.L. Meshcheriakov, 70–3. M.: SOTsEKGIZ, 1939.

Nedobrovo, Nikolai. "Anna Akhmatova." *Russkaia mysl'* 7 (1915): (2nd pagin.) 50–68.

Nekrasov, N.A. *Stikhotvoreniia. 1856*. M.: Nauka, 1988.

Nemzer, Andrei. *Dnevnik chitatelia. Russkaia literatura v 2007 godu*. M.: Vremia, 2008.

– *Pri svete Zhukovskogo. Ocherki istorii russkoi literatury*. M.: Vremia, 2013.

– "Timur iz pushkinskoi komandy." In Kibirov, *"Kto kuda – a ia v Rossiiu ..."*, 5–28.

Nemzer, Andrei, and Mark Lipovetsky. "Timur Iur'evich Kibirov (Timur Iur'evich Zapoev)." In *Russian Writers since 1980* (*Dictionary of Literary Biography*, 285), edited by Marina Balina and Mark Lipovetsky, 137–48. Detroit: Thomson Gale, 2004.

Nikolaeva, Ol'ga, and Aleksandr Nikolaev. "Timur Kibirov. 'Uchat vse. No odni – dobromu, a drugie – zlomu.'" *Vremia MN*, 8 February 2001.

Ovid. *Metamorphoses*. 2 vols. Translated by Frank Justus Miller. Cambridge, MA: Harvard UP, 1984.

Panova, Lada. "'I vsiudu kleveta ...': Akhmatova, po(chitateli), akhmatovedy." *Russian Literature* 3–4 (72) (2012): 425–502.

– "'Kleopatra' Akhmatovoi: Avtoportret-kriptogramma." *Letniaia shkola po russkoi literature* 11, no. 3 (2015): 209–40.

Pasternak, Boris. *Stikhotvoreniia i poemy*. 2 vols. L.: Sov. pis., 1990.

Pavlovich, Nadezhda. "Vospominaniia." In *Osip Mandel'shtam i ego vremia*, 63–4. M.: L'age d'Homme–nash dom, 1995.

Penhallurick, Robert. "Welsh English: Phonology." In *Varieties of English. 1. The British Isles*, edited by Bernd Kortmann and Clive Upton, 105–21. Berlin: Mouton de Gruyter, 2008.

Perkins, David. "The Challenge of Sincerity." In his *Wordsworth and the Poetry of Sincerity*, 1–32. Cambridge, MA: Harvard UP, 1964.

Petruchenko, O. *Latinsko-russkii slovar'*. 9th edition. 1914. Reprint. M.: Greko-latinskii kabinet Iu. A. Shichalina, 2001.

Peschio, Joe. *The Poetics of Impudence and Intimacy in the Age of Pushkin*. Madison: U of Wisconsin P, 2012.

Peschio, Joseph, and Igor' Pil'shchikov. "The Proliferation of Elite Readerships and Circle Poetics in Pushkin and Baratynskii (1820s-1830s)." In *The Space of the Book: Print Culture in the Russian Social Imagination*, edited by Miranda Remnek, 82–107. Toronto: U of Toronto P, 2011.

Piatkovskii, A.P. "Biograficheskii ocherk." In *Polnoe sobranie sochinenii* by D.V. Venevitinov, 1–60. SPb.: V tip. O. I. Baksta, 1862.

Picket, Howard. *Rethinking Sincerity and Authenticity: The Ethics of Theatricality in Kant, Kierkegaard, and Levinas*. Charlottesville: U of Virginia P, 2017.

Pil'shchikov, I.A. "Simvolika Eliziia v poezii Batiushkova." In *Antropologiia kul'tury* 2, 86–123. M.: Novoe izd-vo, 2004.

Pinsky, Anatoly. "The Origins of Post-Stalin Individuality: Aleksandr Tvardovskii and the Evolution of 1930s Soviet Romanticism." *The Russian Review* 76, no. 3 (2017): 458–83.

"Pis'ma k A. S. Khomiakovu." *Russkii arkhiv* 5 (1884): 221–9.

Plamper, Jan. "Fear: Soldiers and Emotion in Early Twentieth-Century Russian Military Psychology." *Slavic Review* 68, no. 2 (2009): 259–83.

– "Introduction." *Slavic Review* 68, no. 2 (2009): 229–37.

Plath, Sylvia. *Ariel: The Restored Edition*. New York: Harper Collins, 2004.

Platt, Kevin. "The Post-Soviet is Over: On Reading the Ruins." *Republics of Letters: A Journal for the Study of Knowledge, Politics, and the Art*s 1, no. 1 (2009): [1–26]. https://arcade.stanford.edu/rofl/post-soviet-over-reading -ruins. Last accessed 13 November 2022.

Pogosian, Elena. "Uroki imperatritsy: Ekaterina II i Derzhavin v 1783 g." In *"Na mezhe mezh Golosom i Ekhom". Sbornik statei v chest' Tat'iany Vladimirovny Tsiv'ian*, compiled by L.O. Zaionts, 241–68. M.: Novoe izdatel'stvo, 2007.

– *Vostorg russkoi ody i reshenie temy poeta v russkom panegirike 1730–1762 gg.* Tartu: Tartu Ulikooli Kirjastus, 1997.

Polevoi, N.A. *Literaturnaia kritika. Stat'i i retsenzii. 1825–1842*. L.: Khud. lit., 1990.

Polezhaev, A.I. *Stikhotvoreniia i poemy*. L.: Sov. pis., 1987.

Pollak, Nancy. *Mandelstam the Reader*. Baltimore: Johns Hopkins UP, 1995.

Pomerantsev, V.M. "Ob iskrennosti v literature." *Novyi mir* 12 (1953): 218–45.

Pound, Ezra. *Literary Essays of Ezra Pound*. New York: New Directions, 1968.

Powelstock, David. *Becoming Mikhail Lermontov: The Ironies of Romantic Individualism in Nicholas I's Russia*. Evanston: Northwestern UP, 2005.

– "Burying the Elegiac Corpse: Selfhood in Pushkin's Late Lyrics." *Pushkin Review* 3 (2000): 81–132.

Pratt, Sarah. *Russian Metaphysical Romanticism: The Poetry of Tiutchev and Boratynskii*. Stanford, CA: Stanford UP, 1984.

Prigov, Dmitrii Aleksandrovich. *Monady. Kak-by-iskrennost'*. M: NLO, 2013.

– *Sovetskie teksty: 1979–84*. SPb.: Izd-vo Ivana Limbakha, 1997.

Prigov, Dmitrii Aleksandrovich, and Mikhail Epshtein. "Popytka ne byt' identifitsirovannym." Interview. In Dobrenko et al., *Nekanonicheskii klassik*, 52–71.

Proskurin, Oleg. *Poeziia Pushkina, ili Podvizhnyi palimpsest*. M.: NLO, 1999.

Proskurina, Vera. *Creating the Empress: Politics and Poetry in the Age of Catherine II*. Boston: Academic Studies P, 2011.

– *Imperiia pera Ekateriny II. Literatura kak politika*. M.: NLO, 2017.

– "Mezhdu Felitsei i Fortunoi: Derzhavin i Barkoviana." In *Permiakovskii sbornik*, edited by Nataliia Mazur, 128–43. M.: Novoe izdatel'stvo, 2010.

– *Mify imperii. Literatura i vlast' v epokhu Ekateriny II*. M.: NLO, 2006.

– "Oda G. R. Derzhavina 'Na Schastie': politika i poetika." *NLO* 3 (97) (2009): 114–39.

Psoi Korolenko (Pavel Lion) and Alena Alenkova. *Russkoe bogatstvo. Vol. I.* Sound recording. M.: Otdelenie VYKhOD, 2007.

Pumpianskii, L.V. "Lomonosov i nemetskaia shkola razuma." *XVIII vek.* Vyp. 14. (1983): 3–44.

– "Ob ode A. Pushkina 'Pamiatnik.'" 1923. Publ. N. Nikolaev. *Voprosy literatury* 8 (1977): 135–51.

– "Ocherki po literature pervoi poloviny XVIII veka." *XVIII vek.* 1 (1935): 83–132.

– "Stikhovaia rech' Lermontova." *Literaturnoe nasledstvo 43/44. M. Iu. Lermontov.* M.: Izd. AN SSSR, 1941. 1:389–424.

Purin, Aleksei. "Pamiati Borisa Ryzhego." *Zvezda* 7 (2001): 233–7.

Pushkin, A.S. *Polnoe sobranie sochinenii.* 16 vols. L.: Akademiia nauk SSSR, 1937–59.

– *Polnoe sobranie sochinenii.* 10 vols. 2nd ed. M.: Izd. Akademii nauk SSSR, 1956–8.

– *Rabochie tetradi.* 8 vols. SPb., London: Pushkinskii dom; Saint Petersburg Partnership Consortium, 1995–7.

Pyman, Avril. *The Life of Aleksandr Blok.* 2 vols. Oxford: Oxford UP, 1979–80.

Radishchev, A.N. *Polnoe sobranie sochinenii.* 3 vols. M.: Izd-vo Akademii nauk SSSR, 1938–52.

Ram, Harsha. *The Imperial Sublime: A Russian Poetics of Empire.* Madison: U of Wisconsin P, 2003.

Reddy, William M. *The Navigation of Feeling: A Framework for the History of Emotions.* Cambridge: Cambridge UP, 2001.

Romains, Jules. *Les Copains.* Paris: Le rayon d'or, 1952.

Ronen, Omry. *An Approach to Mandel'štam.* Jerusalem: Magnes Press, 1983.

– [Ronen, Omri]. *Poetika Osipa Mandel'shtama.* SPb.: Giperion, 2002.

Rosenbaum, Susan B. *Professing Sincerity: Modern Lyric Poetry, Commercial Culture, and the Crisis in Reading.* Charlottesville: U of Virginia P, 2007.

Rosslyn, Wendy, ed. *The Speech of Unknown Eyes: Akhmatova's Readers on Her Poetry,* 2 vols. Nottingham: Astra Press, 1990.

Rozen, E.F. "Stikhotvoreniia M. Lermontova, tri chasti, s portretom avtora. S.-Peterburg, v tip. Il'i Glazunova i komp., 1842." In Burlaka, *Mikhail Lermontov: pro et contra,* 145–58.

Rusinko, Elaine. "Acmeism, Post-Symbolism, and Henri Bergson." *Slavic Review* 41, no. 3 (1982): 494–510.

"Russian Acmeism and Anglo-American Imagism." *Ulbandus* 1, no. 2 (1978): 37–49.

Russkaia literatura. Vek XVIII. Lirika. M.: Khud. lit., 1990.

Rutten, Ellen. "No Truer Truth: Sincerity Rhetoric in Soviet Russia." In *Uslyshat' os' zemnuiu: Festschrift for Thomas Langerak on the Occasion of His Retirement,* edited by Ben Dhooge and Michel De Dobbeleer, 491–503. Amsterdam: Pegasus, 2016.

– "Russian Literature: Reviving Sincerity in the Post-Soviet World." In *Reconsidering the Postmodern: European Literature beyond Relativism*, edited by Thomas Vaessens and Yra van Dijk, 27–40. Amsterdam: Amsterdam UP, 2011.
– *Sincerity after Communism: A Cultural History*. New Haven, CT: Yale UP, 2017.
– "Sovetskaia ritorika iskrennosti." *Neprikosnovennyi zapas* 3 (2017): 172–92.
– "Strategic Sentiments: Pleas for a New Sincerity in Post-Soviet Literature." In *Dutch Contributions to the 14th International Congress of Slavists*, edited by Peter Houtzagers, Janneke Kalsbeek, and Jos Schaeken, 201–15. Amsterdam: Rodopi, 2008.
Rutts, M. "Detskaia literatura v tvorchestve Timura Kibirova: Mnogoplanovye argumenty postmodernistskoi diskussii o tsennostiakh." *Detskie chteniia* 11, no. 1 (2017): 214–43.
Ryzhii, Boris. "From Sverdlovsk with love." *Znamia* 4 (1999): 150–3.
– *Opravdanie zhizni. Lirika. Proza. Kritika. Interv'iu. Pis'ma*. Ekaterinburg: U-Faktoriia, 2004.
– "Rubashka v kletochku." *Znamia* 6 (2001): 52–5.
– *Stikhi. 1993–2001*. SPb.: Pushkinskii fond, 2003.
Sandler, Stephanie. *Commemorating Pushkin: Russia's Myth of a National Poet*. Stanford, CA: Stanford UP, 2004.
Savchenko, S. "Elegiia Lenskogo i frantsuzskaia elegiia." In *Pushkin v mirovoi literature. Sbornik statei*, 64–98. L.: Gos. Izd., 1926.
Schelling, F.W.J. *System of Transcendental Idealism (1800)*. Charlottesville: UP of Virginia, 1978.
Schiller, Friedrich. *Werke. Nationalausgabe*. Weimar: Hermann Böhlaus Nachfolger, 1983.
Schönle, Andreas. *Authenticity and Fiction in the Russian Literary Journey, 1790–1840*. Cambridge, MA: Harvard UP, 2000.
– "The Scare of the Self: Sentimentalism, Privacy, and Private Life in Russian Culture, 1780–1820." *Slavic Review* 57, no. 4 (1998): 723–46.
Searle, John R. "How Performatives Work." *Linguistics and Philosophy* 12, no. 5 (1989): 535–58.
Searle, John R., and Daniel Vanderveken. *Foundations of Illocutionary Logic*. Cambridge: Cambridge UP, 1985.
Seifrid, Thomas. *The Word Made Self: Russian Writings on Language, 1860–1930*. Ithaca, NY: Cornell UP, 2005.
Semenov, L.P. *Lermontov i Lev Tolstoi. K stolietiiu so dnia rozhdeniia Lermontova*. M.: Tip. V.M. Sablina, 1914.
Sergeeva, Liudmila. "'Nas khoronila artilleriia'. Lichnost' i stikhi Konstantina Levina." *Znamia* 9 (2020): 131–53.
Serman, I.Z. "Sud'ba poeticheskogo 'ia' v tvorchestve Lermontova." In Burlaka, *Mikhail Lermontov: pro et contra*, 928–42.
Severnye tsvety na 1832 g. M.: Nauka, 1980.

Shapir, M.I. *Universum Versus. Iazyk – stikh – smysl v russkoi poezii XVIII–XX vekov*. Vol. 2. M.: Iazyki slavianskoi kul'tury, 2015.

Sharp, Tom. "Sincerity and Objectification." *Sagetrieb* 1, no. 2 (1982): 255–66.

Shcheglov, Iu. K. "Igrovaia ritorika 'Felitsy.'" In his *Izbrannye trudy*, 168–88. M.: RGGU, 2013.

Shchegolev, P.E. *Iz zhizni i tvorchestva Pushkina*. M.: Gos. izd. khud. lit., 1931.

Shelley's Poetry and Prose. Authoritative Texts. Criticism. New York: Norton, 1977.

Shevyrev, S.P. "Stikhotvoreniia M. Lermontova. S.-Peterburg. 1840. V 12-iu d. 168 stran." In Burlaka, *Mikhail Lermontov: pro et contra*, 131–42.

Shklovskii, Viktor. *O teorii prozy*. M.: Federatsiia, 1929.

Sid, Igor', and Anna Brazhkina. "Skonchalsia terskii kazak, veteran VOV Iurii Zapoev." https://terskiykazak.livejournal.com/474303.html. Last accessed 8 June 2020.

Slovar' Akademii Rossiiskoi. 6 vols. SPb.: Tip. pri Imper. Akademii Nauk, 1789–94.

Slovar' iazyka Pushkina. M.: RAN Institut Russkogo Iazyka/Azbukovnik, 2000.

Sofer, Andrew. "How to Do Things with Demons: Conjuring Performatives in 'Doctor Faustus.'" *Theatre Journal* 61, no. 1 (2009): 1–21.

Sologub, A.I. "Formy povelitel'nogo nakloneniia v russkikh govorakh." *Trudy Instituta iazykoznaniia* 7 (1957): 367–465.

Solov'ev, Vladimir. "Znachenie poezii v stikhotvoreniiakh Pushkina." *Vestnik Evropy* 12 (1899): 709–11.

Sophocles. [*Works*]. 3 vols. Translated by Hugh Lloyd-Jones. Cambridge, MA: Harvard UP, 1994–6.

Staël, Madame. *De l'Allemagne*. Paris, Firmin Didot, 1856.

– [Madame the Baroness de Staël-Holstein]. *Germany*. 2 vols. New York: Derby and Jackson, 1860.

Sterne, Jonathan, ed. *The Sound Studies Reader*. New York: Routledge, 2012.

Stevens, Wallace. *Harmonium*. London: Faber and Faber, 2001.

Struve, Nikita. *Osip Mandel'shtam*. London: Overseas Publications Interchange Ltd., 1988.

S[umarokov], A[leksandr]. "O stikhotvorstve kamchadalov." In *Trudoliubivaia pchela*, 63–4. January 1759. 2nd ed. SPb.: pri Imperatorskoi Akademii nauk, 1780.

Sverdlov, Mikhail. "Poslednii epos." In Leibov et al., *"Gospod'! Prosti Sovetskomu Soiuzu!"*, 436–41.

Taranovskii, Kirill. *Russkie dvuslozhnye razmery: stat'i o stikhe*. M.: Iazyki slavianskoi kul'tury, 2010.

Taylor, Charles. *Sources of the Self*. Cambridge, MA: Harvard UP, 1989.

Taylor, Jane. "'Why Do You Tear Me from Myself?' Torture, Truth, and the Arts of Counter-Reformation." In van Alphen, Bal, and Smith, *Rhetoric of Sincerity*, 19–43.

Thomas, Dylan. *The Collected Letters of Dylan Thomas*. London: J.M. Dent, 1985.
– *Collected Poems. 1934–1952*. London: J.M. Dent & Sons, 1967.
Tiutchev, Fedor. *Polnoe sobranie sochinenii i pisem*. 6 vols. M.: Klassika, 2002–4.
T[iutchev], F. [F.] "Feodor Ivanovich Tiutchev. (Materialy k ego biografii)."
    Istoricheskii vestnik. Istoriko-literaturnyi zhurnal 93 (1903): 189–203.
Timenchik, R.D. *Anna Akhmatova v 1960-e gody*. M.: Vodolei, 2005.
– "K genezisu akhmatovskogo 'Rekviema.'" *NLO* 8 (1994): 215–16.
– "Zametki ob akmeizme. II." *Russian Literature* 5, no. 3 (1977): 281–300.
Todd, William Mills. *The Familiar Letter as a Literary Genre in the Age of Pushkin*.
    Princeton, NJ: Princeton UP, 1976.
Toddes, Evgenii. "'Entropii vopreki': vokrug stikhov Timura Kibirova." *Rodnik*
    4 (1990): 67–71.
Toporov, V.N. *Akhmatova i Blok (k probleme postroeniia poeticheskogo dialoga:*
    "blokovskii" tekst Akhmatovoi. Berkeley, CA: Berkeley Slavic Specialties, 1981.
– "Ob istorizme Akhmatovoi: Dve glavy iz knigi." In *Anna Akhmatova:*
    1889–1989, edited by Sonia Ketchian, 194–237. Berkeley, CA: Berkeley Slavic
    Specialties, 1993.
Trilling, Lionel. *Sincerity and Authenticity*. Cambridge, MA: Harvard UP 1972.
Tsvetaeva, Marina. *Sobranie sochinenii*. 7 vols. M.: Ellis Lak, 1994–5.
Tynianov, Iurii. *Arkhaisty i novatory*. 1929. Munich: W. Fink Verlag, 1967.
– "Blok i Geine." In *Ob Aleksandre Bloke*, 235–64. SPb.: Kartonnyi domik, 1921.
– "Promezhutok." 1924. In his *Arkhaisty i novatory*, 541–80.
Urban, Adol'f. "'I upalo kamennoe slovo …'" *Literaturnaia gazeta* 17 (5135), 22
    April 1987.
Usievich, E. "K sporam o politicheskoi poezii." In *Literaturnyi kritik* 5 (1937):
    62–102.
Uspenskii, B.A. "Iazyk Derzhavina (k 250-letiiu so dnia rozhdeniia)." In *Iz*
    istorii russkoi kul'tury, 4:781–806. 5 vols. M.: Shkola "Iazyki russkoi kul'tury,"
    1996–2002.
van Alphen, Ernst, and Mieke Bal. "Introduction." In van Alphen, Bal, and
    Smith, *Rhetoric of Sincerity*, 1–16.
van Alphen, Ernst, Mieke Bal, and Carel Smith, eds. *The Rhetoric of Sincerity*.
    Stanford, CA: Stanford UP, 2009.
Vatsuro, V.E. "Chuzhoe 'ia' v lermontovskom tvorchestve." In his *O*
    Lermontove, 312–25. M.: Novoe izdatel'stvo, 2008.
– "'K Vel'mozhe'" In *Stikhotvoreniia Pushkina 1820–1830-kh godov. Istoriia*
    sozdaniia i ideino-khudozhestvennaia problematika, 177–212. L.: Nauka, 1974.
– *Lirika pushkinskoi pory. "Elegicheskaia shkola"*. SPb.: Nauka, 1994.
Venevitinov, D.V. *Polnoe sobranie sochinenii*. 1934. Mouton: The Hague, 1967.
– *Polnoe sobranie stikhotvorenii*. L.: Sov. pis., 1960.
– *Sochineniia D. Venevitinova. Chast' pervaia. Stikhotvoreniia*. M.: V tip. Semena
    Selivanovskogo, 1829.

– *Stikhotvoreniia. Proza.* M.: Nauka, 1980.

Venevitinov, M.A. "K biografii poeta D. V. Venevitinova." *Russkii arkhiv* 1 (1885): 113–31.

Veresaev, V. *V dvukh planakh. Stat'i o Pushkine.* M.: Nedra, 1929.

Verheul, Kees. "Public Themes in the Poetry of Anna Achmatova." *Russian Literature* 1 (1971): 73–112.

Viazemskii, Kn[iaz' Petr]. "Po povodu predydushchei stat'i." *Russkii arkhiv* 12 (1869). Cols. 2032–45.

Villon, François. *The Complete Works of François Villon / Uevres complettes de François Villon.* Translated with biography and notes by Anthony Bonner. New York: Bantam, 1964.

Vinogradov, V.V. *Stil' Pushkina.* M.: Gos. izd. khud. lit., 1941.

Viskovatov, P.A. *Mikhail Iur'evich Lermontov. Zhizn' i tvorchestvo.* 1891. M.: Sovremennik, 1987.

Vittaker [Whittaker], R[obert], and B.F. Egorov. "Zhizn' Grigor'eva v pis'makh." In Grigor'ev, *Pis'ma*, 293–319.

Volkov, Solomon. *Dialogi c Iosifom Brodskim.* M.: Nezavisimaia gazeta, 1998.

Voogd-Stojanova, T. "Tsezura i slovorazdely v poeme A. Akhmatovoi *Rekviem*: K probleme izucheniia vzaimootnoshenii ritma i tematiki." In *Dutch Contributions to the Seventh International Congress of Slavists: Warsaw, August 21–27, 1973.*, edited by A.G.F. Holk, 317–33. The Hague: Mouton, 1973.

Vysotskii, Vladimir. *Sochineniia.* 2 vols. M.: Khud. lit., 1991.

Wachtel, Michael. *A Commentary to Pushkin's Lyric Poetry, 1826–1836.* Madison: U of Wisconsin P, 2011.

– *Russian Symbolism and Literary Tradition: Goethe, Novalis, and the Poetics of Vyacheslav Ivanov.* Madison: U of Wisconsin P, 1994.

Weintraub, Wiktor. "The Problem of Improvisation in Romantic Literature." *Comparative Literature* 16, no. 2 (1964): 119–37.

Wierzbicka, Anna. *Emotions across Languages and Cultures: Diversity and Universals.* Cambridge: Cambridge UP, 1999.

Williams, William Carlos. "The Ideal Quarrel." *The Little Review* 12 (1918): 39–40.

Wordsworth, William. *Literary Criticism of William Wordsworth.* Lincoln: U of Nebraska P, 1966.

– *The Thirteen-Book Prelude.* Vol. 1. Ithaca, NY: Cornell UP, 1991.

Wordsworth, [William], and [Samuel Taylor] Coleridge. *Lyrical Ballads. 1798.* London: Oxford UP, 1967.

Wright, Jane. "Sincerity's Repetition: Carlyle, Tennyson and Other Repetitive Victorians." In Milnes and Sinanan, *Romanticism, Sincerity and Authenticity*. 162–81.

Yurchak, Alexei. *Everything Was Forever, Until It Was No More: The Last Soviet Generation.* Princeton, NJ: Princeton UP, 2006.

– "Post-Post-Communist Sincerity: Pioneers, Cosmonauts, and Other Soviet Heroes Born Today." In *What Is Soviet Now? Identities, Legacies, Memories*, edited by Thomas Lahusen and Peter H. Solomon, 257–76. Berlin: Lit, 2008.

Zapadov, V.A. "Neizvestnyi Derzhavin." *Izvestiia Akademii nauk SSSR. Otdelenie literatury i iuzyka* 17, no. 1 (1958): 45–54.

– "Problema literaturnogo servilizma i diletantizma i poeticheskaia pozitsiia G. R. Derzhavina." *XVIII vek*. Vyp. 16 (1989): 56–75.

Zeeman, Peter. *The Later Poetry of Osip Mandelstam: Text and Context*. Amsterdam: Rodopi, 1988.

Zhirmunskii, V.M. "Anna Akhmatova i Aleksandr Blok." In his *Teoriia literatury. Poetika. Stilistika*, 323–54. L.: Nauka, 1977.

– [Zhirmunskij]. *Introduction to Metrics: The Theory of Verse*. The Hague: Mouton, 1966.

– "Preodolevshie simvolizm." *Russkaia mysl'* 12 (1916): 25–56.

Zhitenev, A. "'Oskorblennyi i oskorbitel': estetika vyzova v proze O. Mandel'shtama." *Miry Osipa Mandel'shtama. IV Mandel'shtamovskie chteniia: materialy mezhdunarodnogo nauchnogo seminara*, 258–70. Perm: PGPU, 2009.

Zholkovskii, Aleksandr. "Gamlet s pistoletom, ili Poetika povelitel'nosti." *NLO* 5 (159) (2019): 256–64.

– "How to Show Things with Words: On the Iconic Representation of Themes by Expression-Plane Means" In his *Themes and Texts: Toward a Poetics of Expressiveness*, 217–36. Ithaca, NY: Cornell UP: 1984.

– "Invarianty i struktura teksta 'Ia vas liubil …' Pushkina." *Russian Literature* 7, no. 1 (1979): 1–25.

– "K pereosmysleniiu kanona: sovetskie klassiki-nonkonformisty v postsovetskoi perspektive." *NLO* 1, no. 29 (1998): 55–68. Translation available at https://dornsife.usc.edu/alexander-zholkovsky/rethi-sh/. Last accessed 9 December 2022.

– "Mezhdu mogiloi i pamiatnikom: Zametki o finale akhmatovskogo 'Rekviema' (1940)." In *Ot Kibirova do Pushkina. Sbornik v chest' 60-letiia N. A. Bogomolova*, 114–42. M.: NLO, 2011.

– "Ob infinitivnykh 'Stikhakh uklonista B. Ryzhego.'" *Zvezda* 12 (2005): 196–205.

– "The Obverse of Stalinism: Akhmatova's Self-Serving Charisma of Selflessness." In *Self and Story in Russian History*, edited by Laura Engelstein and Stephanie Sandler, 46–68. Ithaca, NY: Cornell University Press, 2000.

– "Prevoskhoditel'nyi pokoi: Ob odnom invariantnom motive Pushkina." In *Raboty po poetike vyrazitel'nosti. Invarianty–Tema–Priemy–Tekst. Sbornik statei*, by A.K. Zholkovskii and Iu.K. Shcheglov, 240–60. M.: Progress, 1996.

– "Strakh, tiazhest', mramor (iz materialov k zhiznetvorcheskoi biografii Akhmatovoi)." In his *Poetika za chainym stolom i drugie razbory*, 527–62. M.: NLO, 2014.

Zhukovskii, V.A. *Polnoe sobranie sochinenii i pisem*. 20 vols. M.: Iazyki russkoi
kul'tury, 1999–.
Zorin, A.L. "Al'manakh – vzgliad iz zala." In *Lichnoe delo No. – : literaturno-
khudozhestvennyii al'manakh*, 259–63. M.: V/O "Soiuzteatr," 1991.
– "Chtoby zhizn' vnizu tekla (Dmitrii Aleksandrovich Prigov i sovetskaia
deistvitel'nost')." In *Sovetskie teksty – 1979–84*, 10–17. SPb.: Izd. Ivana
Limbakha, 1997.
– *Poiavlenie geroia, iz istorii russkoii emotsional'noi kul'tury kontsa XVIII – nachala
XIX veka*. M.: NLO, 2016.
Zukofsky, Louis. "Sincerity and Objectification: With Special Reference to the
Work of Charles Reznikoff." *Poetry* 37, no. 5 (1931): 272–85.

Index